D0329069

THE CENTURY PSYCHOLOGY SERIES

Richard M. Elliott, *Editor*
Kenneth MacCorquodale, *Assistant Editor*

Toward Understanding Human Personalities

Robert Ward Leeper
University of Oregon

Peter Madison
Swarthmore College

Toward Understanding Human Personalities

NEW YORK

APPLETON-CENTURY-CROFTS, INC.

692-3

Library of Congress Card Number: 59-14151

PRINTED IN THE UNITED STATES OF AMERICA

E-54862

To
Wolfgang Köhler
and
Edward Chace Tolman

PREFACE

In our work on this book, what we have sought to do is to serve two purposes that may not seem to belong within the same volume. On the one hand, we have tried to write a book that would be understandable and valuable to persons who are not professional psychologists and who may have had little or even no previous technical background in psychology. On the other hand, we have sought also to offer a serious discussion of the basic concepts of personality and even to make, if possible, some significant contributions to them.

There are good reasons for trying to write so simply and clearly that the ordinary intelligent adult, even with no previous formal training in psychology, can understand the book if he is willing to invest some real effort. Day in and day out, the ordinary person—whether as a student or in the years beyond the period of college or university work—has to deal with significant problems of personality. He has to deal with them in very responsible ways. Such problems cannot be solved for him by experts. In the guidance of his own life, in dealings with friends, in his work, in relationships with his wife and children, and in his attempts to understand the broader social problems of his day, the average person has to try to understand and deal with many problems that are essentially matters of personality. A book such as this does not deal with questions that are interesting merely as challenging theoretical questions. It deals with problems and processes that are the heart of actual human life and that primarily decide whether that life goes well or ill. So it seems to us highly appropriate that this book should seek to throw as much light as possible on the significant practical problems of everyday human life.

This first objective may seem inconsistent with our hope that the book may make some significant theoretical contributions. But we think not. Human life is exceedingly complex and is manifested in an infinite series of concrete forms. It hardly seems, therefore, that there would be any great use in a book on personality phrased in terms of a multitude of little rules-of-thumb about how to handle human problems. Or perhaps we should say that although there probably are some values served by that other sort of book, it is not the sort of book we intended to write. Our conviction is that for a great many practical purposes, the concepts that a student or other person needs to master and carry with him are highly generalized or basic concepts—ones that have exceedingly wide applications—rather than specific rules for this or that particular situation.

However, if ordinary persons are to be provided with such significant basic concepts, a large amount of work still needs to be done. Our scientific knowledge about personality has not advanced to the stage where the necessary basic concepts have all been developed and tested and where all that remains to be done is to explore some relatively advanced elaborations of these. Instead, the psychology of personality is still at a stage where we are shaping many of our fundamental conceptual tools.

In this sort of situation, our own faith is that there are great advantages in trying to state all of the theoretical issues as clearly and simply as possible and in trying to relate them to the clearest possible illustrative material. It seems to us that this is essential, not merely for the sake of better communication with other persons, but also for the perhaps more fundamental purpose of arriving at a clear and effective means of thinking by professional workers who are seeking to develop and evaluate such basic concepts. The need for this seemed particularly apparent to the senior author when he was working on Kurt Lewin's concepts for his 1943 monograph on them and when he was evaluating Clark Hull's writings for reviews published in 1944, 1952, and 1954. So, if we have put things simply, this has partly been in an attempt to make our own thinking as effective as possible.

It might be helpful if, in this Preface, we were to indicate the main differences between the over-all approach of the present book and the over-all approaches of several other main interpretations of personality. Thus, first, let us indicate the relationship of the present book to the regular Freudian or psychoanalytic system. The latter has aroused a great deal of interest as a basic framework for thinking about personality. It has appealed not only to laymen, who still give Freudian books a huge market because of their belief that Freud's is the one viewpoint that really recognizes the most profound truths about personality, but also to a large portion of psychiatrists and psychologists. The present book, in contrast, is frankly very skeptical about many of the basic psychoanalytic principles. It is not that we are unappreciative of the tremendous accomplishments of Freud, nor do we believe that subsequent technical workers can afford not to return to Freud's writings for insights not mined by previous adherents to his views. We grant the tremendous historical significance of Freud's work as a contribution to our present understanding of personality. But neither as a conceptual background for everyday living nor as a technical framework for professional workers does the psychoanalytic system seem to us a basically satisfactory approach.

Perhaps we should speak more specifically. It is not that we doubt that human life contains very powerful motives of sex, hostility or destructive feeling, and anxiety. Nor do we doubt that human beings engage in a good deal of the bizarre phantasy (or perceptual and interpretive activity) that the Freudians have stressed. We agree also that psychotherapy must sometimes be mainly concerned with such motives and such phantasy processes. Our doubts are not on those scores. They lie on such matters as the following. First, the psychoanalytic theory seems to us too negative an approach, with far too much emphasis merely on what to avoid or restrict and too little conception of what constructive processes need to be built up. Second, psychoanalytic theory seems too limited in its conception of human motives, partly because it is not sufficiently a "field approach," partly in turn because it has been so unappreciative of cultural factors in human life. Third, it is inadequate biologically and psychologically in being so negligent, in general, of learning processes in man. Fourth, it has had too narrow a concept of what processes are unconscious. Fifth, it has been too unappreciative of the interpersonal influences in individual lives and has greatly overrated, instead, the degree to which some narrowly biological factors are decisive. Or in general, it seems to us, the regular psychoanalytic approach has been too insensitive to relatively subtle factors in human life. Current psychology will still have to do a lot of hard work to take advantage of all that is valid and even indispensable in Freud's picture of life, but the valid and important contributions need to be given a place in some different over-all conceptual system. At least, that is our view.

Next, let us compare the present book with an approach to personality developed by writers who have worked primarily from the background of "general psychology" (experimental psychology, animal psychology, and the like) and who, still more narrowly, have worked primarily from the standpoint of what most psychologists speak of as the "stimulus-response" or "S-R" theory, a view developed particularly by such workers as Ivan Pavlov, Edward Lee Thorndike, John B. Watson, and Clark Hull. A considerable series of books on personality have explored various implications of this approach. Mention might be made especially of Floyd Allport's *Social Psychology*, William Burnham's *The Normal Mind*, E. Bagby's *Psychology of Personality*, Ross Stagner's *Psychology of Personality*, E. R. Guthrie's *Psychology of Human Conflict*, John Dollard and Neal Miller's *Personality and Psychotherapy*, and Joseph Wolpe's *Psychotherapy by Reciprocal Inhibition*.

These books have made important contributions. They have called attention to some important factors not emphasized by psychoanalytic writers. They have made progress in showing that the field of experimental psychology and the field of personality ought to be related to each other.

In some respects, the present book is in the tradition of these books we have just mentioned. It differs from them, however, in a great many fundamental points of interpretation. It is not, for instance, that we doubt the importance of learning, or of different arrangements of reward and punishment and nonreinforcement, or of such variables as the time relations between responses and rewards. The S-R workers have advanced our knowledge on many scores, and their best contributions need to be used as fully as possible. But still, in the case of this approach, as with the psychoanalytic one, we feel that the basic approach falls seriously short. We doubt that verbalizations are as important as S-R theorists tend to say; instead, we believe that the complexities of psychological processes lie in their basic nature, rather than just in the cultural invention of language, important though this is. We doubt that the main fact about a psychological process is that it is a link between particular situations and particular overt responses; we feel, instead, that the full nature of psychological mechanisms can be inferred only by seeing what responses are produced under some great diversity of situations. We believe that psychological explanations must be sought in terms of mediating processes whose full nature can hardly be revealed by the behavior of any brief moment. Still further, though we do not doubt that there are "acquired drives," we feel that these have much greater diversity and specificity of character than the S-R theory has hypothesized. Similarly, it is not that we doubt that there are crucial influences from rewards and punishments and nonreinforcements, but that we believe the mode of operation of these must be understood in different terms.

In the S-R approach, therefore, as in the psychoanalytic theory, it seems to us that the relatively tangible aspects of human life have been overemphasized and that the theory provides no adequate abstract conceptualization of human life. We are not questioning the appropriateness of the ancient precept known as Occam's razor, that "Entities should not be multiplied without necessity." Our view is simply that the available data of psychology and psychiatry call for a recognition of a much richer collection of "entities" (of abstractly conceived independent and dependent variables, processes, relationships) than the S-R approach envisages.

The basic conceptual approach that seems most promising to us and that we have sought to develop is one which, in many different respects, has been explored separately by two main professional groups. On the one hand, it is an approach that has been developed by a number of psychiatrists and psychologists who have been interested mainly in problems of psychotherapy—especially Alfred Adler, Otto Rank, Frederick Allen, Karen Horney, Harry Stack Sullivan, Frieda Fromm-Reichmann, Carl Rogers, and George Kelly. On the other hand, it is an approach that has been developed too by a great many workers dealing in psychological laboratories with processes much simpler than those of personality—psychologists such as Wolfgang Köhler, Kurt Lewin (and other Gestalt psychologists), E. C. Tolman, K. S. Lashley, N. R. F. Maier, Frederic Bartlett, Heinz Werner, R. S. Woodworth, Konrad Lorenz, and David Krech.

Both of these groups of workers have conceived of human life in terms of complex, dynamically organized processes and in terms of goal-directed activities. They have explored markedly different phenomena and have used markedly different methods of research in the two cases, and yet there are fundamental similarities of interpretation between these two groups. One of the most important things that currently needs to be done in the psychology of personality is to unify these two streams of thought and research and to see what fresher conceptions of personality might come from this union. Several books have already attempted this to some extent—particularly Prescott Lecky's little book, *Self-Consistency*, Arthur Combs and Donald Snygg's *Individual Behavior*, Gardner Murphy's massive and masterly volume, *Personality*, and the very readable and well-documented book, *Personality and Temperament*, by Solomon Diamond. We are deeply indebted to these men. Our present work primarily carries on the undertaking they have pursued.

If there are such parallels between a good deal of thought about personality and a good deal of work in experimental psychology, it becomes a puzzle as to why the interrelationships have received so little consideration. A lack of interest and background and time on the part of personality theorists has certainly been part of the difficulty. However, it seems to us that difficulties have also come from some conceptions too commonly held by experimental psychologists regarding the perceptual and conceptual processes they have been studying. It seems to us that experimental psychologists need more thoroughly to shake themselves loose from certain traditional modes of thought about their own subject matter. Thus, it has been unfortunate that experimental psychologists generally have treated perceptual processes merely in terms of the introspective approach, rather than conceiving of perceptual responses as processes that might be either conscious or unconscious. Second, it is unfortunate that we have neglected the possibility that perceptual processes might be motivational processes (or motivating processes) rather than exclusively such motivationally neutral and hence transitory processes as are usually the focus of perceptual research—merely for considerations of expediency. Third, we have generally failed to stress the continuity between what ordinarily are called perceptual processes and what ordinarily would be called processes of set or direction and have failed to include the latter as parts of the total territory of perceptual processes. Rather frequently we have failed to realize how profoundly learning may change perceptual processes and how complex, in consequence, our perceptual activities may become. Fifth, we sometimes have not stressed sufficiently how genuinely biological are perceptual processes, even when highly complex, and how little they are to be understood in intellectualistic terms such as we inherit from everyday thought. But these shadings in the thought of experimental psychologists are not basic. Even from the standpoint of getting good theory in experimental psychology, they ought to be changed in ways that would also help us see the fundamental relationships between what the experimental psychologists have worked with and what has been studied in the field of personality.

Since the main interpretation of the present book is in line with the two main groups mentioned above, both of which have basically the same emphasis on complex organizing processes within the organism, the approach we have used might conceivably be called a perceptual theory of personality. But we have made so many alterations in the common interpretation of perceptual processes that this expression generally would be misunderstood. We would prefer therefore to speak of it as an *organizational theory* of personality.

In addition to the writers we have mentioned above as ones to whom we have such great indebtedness, it is a pleasure to list some others who have been important for us through personal contacts and discussions as well as through their writings. As such, we would like to mention especially (in the case of R. L.) W. S. Hunter, David Krech, R. Dreikurs, Carl Rogers, and Leona Tyler; and (in the case of P. M.) Gordon Allport, Robert White, Solomon Asch, and Wolfgang Köhler. Both of us are particularly indebted to the spirit and ideas of Wolfgang Köhler and Edward C. Tolman and are delighted to dedicate the volume to them. The approach of this book almost certainly is also partly influenced by certain older writers—essayists and poets—who unfortunately are relatively unknown now, but whom we regard as having had some particularly significant understandings of human life. We refer especially to Hamilton Wright Mabie's *Works and Days*, the books by John Woolman, Rufus Jones, and William F. Quayle, Edward Carpenter's *Towards Democracy*, Olive Schreiner's *Dreams*, and Don Marquis's *The Awakening and Other Poems*.

For their critical reading of the manuscript and suggestions regarding it, we are greatly indebted to Gordon Allport, Leona Tyler, Solomon Asch, and Robert White. Mr. Curtis Avery, director of the E. C. Brown Trust, gave great help on many questions of organization and style. Probably only those who are directly familiar with Richard M. Elliott's work can imagine what painstaking and helpful editing he gave to the final manuscript. For all this help, we express the thanks of our readers and of ourselves.

It is a pleasure also to acknowledge support from several sources which helped provide the considerable amounts of time invested in this writing. Such is the case with the award to R. L. of a Guggenheim Memorial Fellowship in 1948-1949 and a Fulbright lectureship at the Univerity of Aberdeen, Scotland, in 1955-1956. We are indebted also to Swarthmore College and to financial assistance from the E. C. Brown Trust of Portland, Oregon, for freeing considerable periods of time for the second author. A great portion of the work was done at the University of Oregon, and a real debt of gratitude is due people of that state who developed an institution so favorable for scholarly work.

For the drawings that are scattered through the book, we thank one of the younger members of our households, Arthur Leeper. Our only regret is that we were not able to provide him with more leads as to how to translate key ideas into visual form.

The developments of thought that have come to fruition in this volume started a long time ago for both authors. Perhaps one of us (R. L.) owes some debt even to the introductory course he took in college in 1922, which so disappointed him with psychology as a source of a better understanding of human life that he shifted from his intended major in psychology and had no further contact with the subject until, after college, he chanced on some books by Carleton Parker, Floyd Allport, and Wolfgang Köhler and, from them, learned about some possibilities of psychology he had not glimpsed before. In his regular graduate courses at Clark in 1927-1930, there was little chance to pursue his interests in personality, but he is grateful to that work for starting his second main line of interest, in basic learning theory, which he sees as strongly related to personality. Furthermore, the contacts at Clark with R. R. Willoughby, then assistant editor of the *Psychological Abstracts,* and Lewis B. Hill, then assistant superintendent of the Worcester State Hospital, did give him an early introduction to psychoanalytic thought. His first efforts at stating a theory of personality appeared in a privately printed pamphlet, "Psychology of Personality and Social Adjustment," issued in 1937 primarily for his classes at Cornell College. Starting from that, under Dr. Elliott's encouragement, he began work on a regular volume on personality. Notes, ideas, and partial drafts have been accumulating ever since, although this work periodically was interrupted for other projects that often proved more time-consuming than anticipated. In 1941 a lithoprinted "Psychology of Personality" was published by Edwards Brothers, assembling what ideas had been developed thus far. Over this whole period, much of his work was in the more general phases of psychology, rather than in personality, but he hopes that this will have helped him to relate personality to a broader base of psychological thinking than frequently is used.

The other author (P. M.) began in 1939 the interests that led to our joint work on this volume. It was then that he became interested in psychoanalytic writing and found, in it and in clinical case studies generally, a new orientation to human nature. This led to psychological study at the University of Oregon and a student acquaintance with the senior author and his ideas on personality, an acquaintance that has remained an enduring personal and intellectual companionship. Four years of practical work in clinical psychology in World War II deepened this interest in personality and led to graduate study at the Social Relations Department at Harvard, where Robert White introduced him to the ways and thought of the Harvard Clinic. At Harvard, through Talcott Parsons and Clyde Kluckhohn, he had his second major intellectual experience in the discovery of sociology and anthropology, truly "mirrors for man," and found in Gordon Allport a cognitive psychology of personality foreshadowing the present work. Swarthmore and Gestalt psychology provided the third major intellectual impact for him. The interest both of us share in this group has been a main basis for our present reformulation of personality theory.

The major work of writing and developing the basic ideas of this book has come, however, in the last five years, starting in 1954-1955 when we were able to work intensively together for fourteen months. That first period was used particularly to re-examine our previous concepts and to work out a lot of implications of what we had glimpsed previously. It proved to be only the beginning of a very strenuous five years of developing of ideas, writing and rewriting, condensing and clarifying. Each of us has reworked the other person's material so thoroughly that it would be well-nigh impossible to say what each wrote originally. It has become a truly joint work and, we believe, definitely better than either of us could have done separately.

There is certainly an enormous amount of empirical research and of theoretical analysis that needs to be done on personality if we are to get as deep and sound an understanding of this aspect of human life as we need —or, even, must have—in this modern age. Hence our choice of the title for this book, "*Toward* Understanding Human Personalities," is no chance matter. It reflects our realization that at best, this book can have taken only some very small steps toward the sort of knowledge and understanding that need to be achieved. But, we hope this book will have gone *some* distance toward the goal it names. There has been a lot of magnificent, daring, and painstaking work in the field of the psychology of personality. It is our hope that we have made some important parts of this work available to a wider group of readers and that we have suggested some means whereby this work can be integrated into a more penetrating and helpful conception of human life.

R. L.
P. M.

CONTENTS

Part I

PERSONALITY IN EVERYDAY LIFE

CHAPTER 1

What Is Personality, and What Role Does It Play in Our Everyday Life?

A YOUNG MOTHER—let us call her Mrs. A—is putting her small boys to bed. She has had a strenuous, tiring day. The boys are dirty from romping, and she has put them in the bathtub together to bathe. The boys begin to splash each other. Soon the tired three-year-old starts to cry. "Ow, he's splashing soap in my eyes. I hate him. I'm going to shoot him."

"You were splashing too," retorts the five-year-old. "Anyway, you ought to keep your eyes shut."

"I did keep them shut. You meant to splash soap in my eyes. I asked you to stop. Ow! . . ."

When this happens, Mrs. A's reaction is one of feeling more tired than ever and of feeling some very strong resentment and impatience. "Must you boys always be fighting and squabbling like this when I'm tired?" she asks. "Jimmy, you're older than your brother. Why do you always have to pick on him? Why can't you help mother by being nice to him instead of acting like a bully? And Philip, stop screaming and yelling like a baby!"

Afterwards, she moans to herself, "Why did I ever get into this business of being married and having a family? Dirty faces, dirty overalls, squabbles about who has the biggest piece of cake. Always fighting and crying when I'm tired out myself. It never fails!"

It seems easy to understand why she reacts in this way. She is tired and had been hoping to get the boys off to sleep quickly so she could lie down and rest. But what has happened is that the boys have been making more trouble than usual. It might seem, in fact, as if any young mother would react in the same way under the same circumstances.

But down the street, Mrs. B is putting her boys to bed. When she is bathing them they begin to splash in exactly the same way, and soon the three-year-old is saying: "Ow, he's splashing soap in my eyes. I hate him. I'm . . ." And so on, just as in the case of Mrs. A's boys. She tries to quiet the crying of the three-year-old; but mostly it appears as if she is trying to extricate herself from an unpleasant situation as quickly as possible. As soon as the boys are in bed, she almost flees to her own room, where she throws herself face down across the bed. The encounter leaves her with some strong feelings, too, but they are not feelings of impatience and irritation as in the case of Mrs. A. What Mrs. B experiences is a deep feeling of failure as a mother. She is glad no one was around to hear the children fighting. Her feeling is something like this: "I simply don't understand children, I guess. They shouldn't be unhappy and quarreling like this, but I can't cope with them. I remember that I was afraid to have children. I guess I was right; I guess I just don't know how to be a mother."

This reaction differs from Mrs. A's reaction, but it still reflects an unhappy state of mind and leads to some general thoughts about the burdensome character of family life. So it is not altogether different from Mrs. A's belligerent reaction. But let us suppose that exactly the same situation occurs also in a third home.

Mrs. C says: "All right, you boys. You're both tired, and I'm tired, so let's get you in bed real quick." She pulls the younger boy out of the tub and rubs him down with a rough towel, howls and all. When he eases up somewhat in his yelling, she tells him: "Now you run along, and get into your pajamas as fast as you can. Before you go to sleep, we'll have some time for a few pages of that book we were reading. And now, Jimmy, it's your turn. Out you come!"

We ask her afterwards: "Doesn't it bother you when the boys get to quarreling like that?"

"Oh," she says, "I don't take that too seriously. I feel that way too, when I'm tired. And, besides, I like to see a child who can assert himself when he should. They're fine boys, even though they do have their little ups and downs."

We persist with our questioning. We ask her: "Don't you wish you hadn't married and didn't have troubles like this?"

She just laughs at us. "Oh, it is tiring sometimes. And there are things I can't have, now that I'm a mother. But it would be missing too much not to have a family like mine. No, I wouldn't trade this for anything."

We have been imagining that in each of these three families this little incident between the two boys occurred in exactly the same fashion. And, indeed, we might find other common factors in the three households. It is quite possible, for instance, that the three mothers are of the same economic and social level, same educational background, and same intelligence. The husbands in all the families might have exactly the same sort of jobs. The three young women might belong to the same church, or all of them might belong to none. In physical appearance, the three homes might look much alike. And yet, despite these factors in common, the three young women respond in three fundamentally different ways. Apparently there is something about the women themselves which accounts for the difference in response.

We see this again when we examine some much larger aspects of people's lives. Suppose we talk with two surgeons, each of whom has been highly respected for his work. We ask the first: "Isn't your work tiresome and confining, and even somewhat depressing at times? Here you are, hour after hour, day after day, dealing with people who are injured or suffering. Doesn't it get you down! Isn't it basically rather distasteful work?"

"It's true that it is exacting," he answers, "but I don't mind that. I doubt if I could find any work more interesting or varied. I'm constantly running into new problems. And when you say that the people I work with are suffering—of course they are—and that's why I feel that my work is significant. Personally, I don't think there's anything else I could do that would be more useful, or would be more appreciated by other people."

"Yes," we insist, "but don't you sometimes have the experience of making mistakes and even of failing to save the life of some person who might have been saved by someone more skillful than yourself?"

His face sobers. "That's true," he replies. "I'm no genius, and there are cases so tough that I lose the race because I'm not quite skillful enough or don't understand the problem well enough. That's why I seize every chance I can to watch other surgeons and why I like to have some of them watch me at times and criticize what I do. But you make mistakes, of course, just as people do in any field. You've just got to try to minimize those and make sure the good you do will vastly outweigh the mistakes. There's no use imagining what a perfect surgeon could do in my place, however, because if I weren't here, there wouldn't be any 'perfect' surgeon to replace me. Right now, in fact, there wouldn't be anyone here to do this work if I didn't do it. So, it's a privilege, all right."

We talk, then, to the other man and ask him how he likes his work as a surgeon.

"Oh," he replies, "I had to give it up. Too much strain. Too much responsibility. I liked the technical problems involved, and I was quick and accurate enough so that some of my colleagues couldn't understand why I dropped that type of work. But I just couldn't stand it emotionally. I had one gastric ulcer after another as long as I stayed in it. There's too much that can go wrong, and too fast. And often you know you can't succeed. I was sorry to stop it, but I had to."

It is perhaps puzzling to us that a man could be doing work which clearly had great social value, which was so well respected by his colleagues, and yet feel so unhappy in it. We might try to reason with him about it. "Don't you think," we might ask, "you ought to have a different feeling about surgical work? Suppose it is true that you couldn't save the life of every patient on whom you operated. People have always known that. They didn't ask the impossible of you. But they knew that you saved the lives of a lot of people who would have died otherwise; and they knew that, even though you could not prevent some of your patients from being crippled to some extent from injuries they had received, you saved a lot of them from much worse crippling. Couldn't you take pride in this? Couldn't you feel happy about your work because you knew that you were doing a skilled job that meant a tremendous lot to many families?"

We might say all that; we might elaborate the logic of it; and the physician might be quite capable, intellectually, of granting that everything we said was right. "But still," he might say, "the fact remains that I tried to change my feeling about my work by stressing all of those things. I know that my friends have been right when they've said that I act as if only my failures were realities, and not my successes too. I tried to change my thinking about it all. But I couldn't. I'm just not the kind of person who is suited to that work. That must be it."

The difficulty of recognizing one's own personal patterns

When this second physician speaks in this way, recognizing that he properly should have had a different sort of emotional reaction to his work, he is probably expressing an outlook which is different from that of Mrs. A. We might ask her a similar question: "Don't you think it is somewhat unfortunate that little situations like this in your home cause you to become irritated and impatient? Wouldn't it be happier for you if you realized that the boys tend to act this way when they're tired, and that you merely increase the likelihood of later fighting between them when you scold them? You remember you told Jimmy that he was acting like a bully, and told Philip that he ought to stop crying like a baby. Wouldn't it be better if you were somewhat more patient with them?"

We might speak to Mrs. A in this way. But there is not very much likelihood that she would change her behavior. She might well reply: "So! I should spread sweetness and light, eh? But the fact is that Jimmy *does* act like a bully. What am I supposed to do—not see the facts that are before me? Not speak to him about it—just let things go? Well, I'll tell you. Maybe when I get old I'll write papers about the sweet innocence of children. Right now I know too much about what children are really like."

For various reasons people tend to keep on responding in much the same way year after year. Sometimes they cannot change their ways of responding even when they make valiant efforts to do so. Sometimes they do not even attempt to change. They are perhaps suffering from some of the ways in which they deal with life, but—not realizing that those responses come from within themselves—they believe they are dealing with life in the only way an intelligent and realistic person can deal with it.

This raises some difficult questions for us. It seems that, even in the same objective situation, different people interpret situations in distinctive ways as a result of different tendencies or characteristics within themselves—tendencies and characteristics which, in everyday thought, we would be likely to think of as differences of personality. We can see that these individual interpretations greatly affect the happiness of the person, his impact on others, and the whole character or nature of his life. And yet, although some persons appreciate this fact about themselves, others do not see it as an individual matter at all. They believe that they are responding in the only ways that intelligent and sensible people can respond in the objective situations in which they find themselves. This puzzles us because it seems that the same people who generally are able to act with insight on certain other matters that are of major importance to them are often unusually hampered in recognizing their own personality processes. Why should this be?

It is true that each person's life is very complex and shifting and that no situation ever recurs in exactly the same way. And it is true, consequently, that later responses are never exactly the same as earlier ones. One never finds the exact duplications which would make it easy to say, "Oh, yes, I guess that's what I must characteristically do!" Consider the following account, which might be paralleled from the observation of almost anyone:

I had hired four or five students to pick cherries for me on a lot which we had recently purchased, and which we were intending to use as a site for our house. One of the fellows did not come on the first day, but showed up on the second. When he arrived on the scene, one of the first things he did was to ask how many pounds of cherries each person picked on the day before. When he was given the figures, he sniffed, "Well, it is easy to see that no one has been working around here." Later in the day, he inquired as to where we planned to build a house on the lot. I pointed to a sloping part of the lot where we felt that we could get the best view. "People sure will build in some funny places nowadays," he opined. A girl who was picking tried to move one of the ladders. It was too heavy for her and fell to the ground. He sprang to the rescue and put it against the tree, but she pointed out that it was not placed where she could reach many cherries and asked if he would change it. His immediate reply was, "You *are* fussy, aren't you?" At that, with the tact of a born diplomat, she told him just to put it wherever he thought that she could reach the most cherries. The other workers all stopped at noon to eat lunch. He also had brought a lunch with him; but, instead of stopping, he worked right through till the end of the day and had, at the end, as apparently meant a good deal to him, the heaviest load of cherries of all.

This was a young fellow of good intelligence. In the years since then he has gone through medical school. But it certainly didn't seem to me that he showed his intelligence then. It is almost as though he went out of his way to say things or do things which would antagonize the rest of us, rather than make us like him. And yet I suppose, in all this, he was trying to get some worthwhile effect out of his social relations. But what a way to do it!

In a case such as this we see a life organized somewhat like a piece of music called "Theme with Variations." The young man doesn't do exactly the same thing in each situation throughout the day. But the pattern is so consistent—so much a recurrent theme—that one is puzzled again, and is led to ask once more, "What is there that keeps us from seeing such consistent tendencies in ourselves? Do we do this sort of thing much more often than we realize? Are the themes so subtle, sometimes, that they are hard to identify? Might it possibly be that we live most of our lives this way, merely repeating over and over, with but minor variations, some mode of life which may be no more adapted to our needs than were the responses of this young cherry-picker?"

Persistent themes of response in small children

A five-year-old boy came pedaling down the sidewalk on his tricycle. He slowed down as he approached the front lawn of a house where two little girls, age six and four, were playing with their dolls.

Susan, the elder, eyed the cyclist with obvious interest. She and Barbara had brought out their toys and purposely seated themselves in front of the house in the hope of attracting playmates.

The boy pedaled slowly by, watching the girls intently. At the end of the block he turned and pedaled back vigorously, again slowing down as he approached. It was clear that he wanted to play but was either too shy to stop or hesitant about the doll-play as a "girl's" game.

Susan suddenly dashed to the garage, pulled out her tricycle, and without looking at the visitor directly or overtly inviting him to join her, pedaled furiously down the walk making a fire-siren noise.

In a moment the visitor had joined her. The younger sister, who had been watching both, ran for her tricycle and the three were soon yelling and laughing together.

After a few minutes of such "boy's" play, the two girls led their visitor off to the backyard, where he was persuaded to play "Daddy" in a doll and housekeeping game for the rest of the morning.

This is merely one incident. But long observation of these two girls showed the same pattern occurring over and over, with each of the sisters consistently playing roles similar to those in this example. The younger one was always very happy to join in group play, but she tended not to take the lead in forming new groups or in initiating new activities. The older one, on the other hand, acted in a way which was characteristic of her, very actively seeking to include new children in the play group and perhaps playing an unduly active role in deciding the nature of the play; but nevertheless doing so in a way that was fairly sensitive to the interests and wants of the other children. She seemed to see such group situations as ones where the rule that applied was "the more the merrier."

Some other children of the same age do not seem to feel at ease in such group play. They are comfortable when they are playing alone or perhaps with one other child; but a larger group seems to make them shy, and they prefer to retire to some quieter setting. For still other children, the group appears to pose some sort of threat. They respond by efforts to break up the group and to create divisions within it, rather than by allowing themselves to become integrated into it.

Mary, a rather stocky but nice-looking six-year-old girl, was such a child. Repeated observations of her play showed a consistent pattern, of which the following incident is typical:

Mary came upon three younger neighborhood children happily engaged in "playing house." They were in the midst of a very imaginative and co-operative game that had been going on busily and peacefully for an hour or more. She surveyed the happy scene for a moment and went down to the playhouse. The other children were well known to her and, as far as *their* feelings were concerned, she could easily have entered into the play and had a splendid time.

Instead, Mary began pointing out what "baby" things they were doing. She said: "I'm older than you are" (she was a year older) and "I'm bigger than you are." Finally she mentioned a particularly interesting activity that she knew one of the other girls dearly loved and suggested that they two go off and play.

"We don't like them, do we?" she said, pointing disparagingly to the other two younger ones, now standing in tearful bewilderment at finding their game broken up.

Mary and the selected child went off yelling: "We don't like them, we don't like them," with Mary alternately interjecting, "I'm bigger than you are, Ha! Ha! Ha!"

Teachers in nursery schools, dealing with children of three and four years of age, report that children already have very marked differences in emotional and social reactions at the start of this age period.

This appearance of definite personality characteristics at an early age raises a whole series of questions. How much of personality is a product of very early childhood? Is it almost entirely determined there? Or is personality determined, to some great degree, at each age of a person's life? Are the factors which influence personality similar at different ages? Are personality traits learned more easily than many other things we learn? When personality traits are learned in early childhood, is the learning quite different in character from the later learning activities of human beings? Is early learning less a matter of forming concepts and of thinking about things and more a matter of acquiring habits in some relatively primitive way? Or, perhaps, is personality not modified much by learning? Suppose, for example, that we hear a mother say of her child, "He's stubborn, all right, but it's no great wonder. He gets that from his father's side of the family." Is she correct?

These questions raise many complex issues, and we shall want to consider a great many different facts before we attempt to frame our answers. But such questions do suggest that we ought to look at personality in the process of development, rather than merely at the end products of this development. We turn, therefore, to two longer sketches that have this value.

The stories of Ann and Beatrice as portrayals of personality development

The students in a course in the psychology of personality had been invited to write summaries of their life experiences, trying particularly to identify some of their own personality characteristics and trying to see where these had originated. Each of the following accounts was written by a girl of more-than-average college ability. Each of the girls was living in much the same immediate surroundings; each was away from home and living in a college dormitory.

The one girl, whom we will call Ann, wrote as follows:

When I was about ten years old, my mother bought me a playsuit of which I was very proud. My uncle made fun of it and laughed at me. He started a nickname of "Johnny." My mother tried to console me, but the hurt has never been entirely erased. People seem to take great delight in teasing me, probably because I become confused so easily.

One summer it was my task to carry water and run errands for the men in the hayfield. I thought it great fun. I wasn't afraid to take things to the haymow if I could go up the inside way. I had heretofore never been afraid to climb and would go anywhere in the barn. This particular day, a tall ladder was propped against the side of the barn. I was told to take a pail of water up to the men. I was afraid and didn't want to go. My stepfather and uncle urged me on, and I was afraid not to go, but was panicky about going, for with the water I had only one hand with which to hang on. I cried every step of the way up, but they kept laughing at me and my mother told me to go on, that I shouldn't fall. When I got to the ground I was so shaky I could scarcely stand. To this day I am desperately afraid of high places, and it is all I can do to climb a ladder, as my hands seem to go limp and just won't hold. I often think of this incident today and hate those men for laughing at me.

When I started to school in town, I was very conscious of my clothes. I often didn't do my studies justice because I was worrying and terribly self-conscious because I wasn't dressed like the other girls.

Also, about this time, I was preached to about being "boy crazy"; and for fear of being scolded I was afraid to speak to any boys. The idea had never occurred to me until then, as I had always been friendly to members of both sexes. I had been told several times when I was younger that I would never marry, but this had never particularly bothered me until then. I began to draw more and more within myself and concluded that maybe I was different. How I longed to be with the other young people and to do as they did!

I think I never shall forget the first basketball game I went to. I was so excited. My folks had company that evening when I arrived home. After the company had departed I was told I had been too excited and that I should not have behaved that way. I remember I was rather brimming over with excitement, but I had been thrilled and happy because it was an entirely new experience for me. From that time on, I gradually learned to try to keep my true feelings to myself with no outward display of how I felt.

I also didn't dare do anything for the neighbors for fear I'd be asked reproachfully, "Now, you won't do that at home, why do you do it for others?" I gradually came to be afraid to do anything for fear of not doing it correctly. I've even had others call me queer for not doing certain things, when in reality I was lying and wanted to do them terribly, but was afraid to. I didn't even enjoy going to parties and could find most any excuse, even to feigning illness, to get out of going. I can look back now and see that I was (and still am) so stiff and reserved it is no wonder people shied away from me.

There seemed to be everlasting quarreling and bickering among my relatives and in my immediate family. I longed for peace and tried desperately to think of ways to bring it about. But I've given up all hope now. I often let myself be run over rather than stand up for my rights, as I do hate to quarrel.

When I was smaller I used to pretend I had a father to whom I could take my troubles, and I find myself now often going back to this world. Even my college studies are sometimes hampered by my worrying about conditions at home.

I've grown into a person who is afraid to do anything for fear of being laughed at or of not doing it correctly. I am very self-conscious and find it hard to make friends of either sex. I constantly find myself distrusting people, thinking they don't like me. I never can seem to make a decision; even for some trifle it becomes a great problem for me to decide what to do. I think this is probably due to the fact that I was afraid to make decisions for fear they wouldn't be approved at home; so I let the home folks make them for me, which they did quite readily.

It seems every year, as I grow older, that my mind comes to be more in a state of such confusion that I don't know which way to turn.

This was Ann's account of her life experiences. Beatrice, on the other hand, described her life in the following terms:

Mother and Dad did not consciously follow any set pattern in bringing me up. They wanted me to enjoy a pleasant, happy childhood and to develop into a person who was ladylike, efficient, understanding, morally good, and happy. This was their plan, but they did not put it into words, it was just in the back of their minds. They had no hard-fast rules to adhere to; they were just average parents who wanted their children to develop into average Americans.

My parents were of the old school that believed in "spare the rod and spoil the child." However, only in extreme cases can I remember this rule being applied. One time when I was about seven, I vaguely remember the lesson taught to me by this method. I told a lie. It wasn't a very serious one, but it was a lie; so my Dad spanked me. At first I was resentful towards him, but later I developed a sense of guilt when I told a lie. After that, when I did tell a fib, I would go to him, tell him about it and tell him to punish me. My fibs became fewer and fewer, and finally, because I hated so to have the feeling of guilt that I always experienced when I told a lie, I quit telling them. Spankings weren't habitual punishment in my family; if punishment was needed it was usually given in the form of a talk. These talks taught me something I shall never forget. I learned that better results can be got by talking over the situation than by physical combat.

I vaguely remember the lesson taught me by this method, one time when I was about five years old. We had a young couple working for us who had a little girl just about my age. We attended the same school, and I remember how I looked down upon her because her family worked for us and because the children in the school regarded her as socially inferior, too.

I wouldn't play with her unless some older people, particularly my parents, were watching. One day I was playing in my sandbox, and she came and wanted to play too. I said that if she did I'd throw sand in her eyes. She disregarded my threat and proceeded to get into the box. I threw the sand, and it did get into her eyes. Fortunately (or unfortunately, as it seemed to me at the time) my Mother had been watching me from the porch without my knowing it. She overheard our conversation and observed my childish prank. She immediately came to the little girl's rescue, not saying a word to me. I was by nature a generous and sweet-tempered child, and after they had gone, I sat in the box no longer wishing to play. A few moments later my Dad came, and we sat down and talked. He heard my side of the story and then proceeded to talk to me, not as if he were talking to a child, but as he might to an adult. This, together with what he said, had a considerable effect upon me. He told me about how God had created us equal and because He had, we should all treat each other the same. He said no grownup judged a person by the size of her house or by the pretty dresses she wore; he made me to understand that we judge people by what is inside them and that, if we don't like what we find there, then we should feel sorry for them and still treat them nicely because God had created them. For a young child this was pretty serious, but he made it so understandable that to this day I still try to apply it.

The biggest disappointment of my life occurred when I was just about six years old. Of all the things I remember from my earliest childhood, this stands out most clearly. There was nothing I liked better than to go into town with my Dad on business trips. Invariably, I would be left in the car with an ice cream cone and my dog, to watch the people go by. I loved to do this and, on the particular day I am speaking about, such an outing was in store for me. Mother told me if I would change by dress and brush my hair myself by two o'clock she would have a surprise for me. I don't remember now why I didn't do as she said, but when she came to see if I had obeyed her, she found me as she left me. Then she told me that if I had changed my dress I could have gone into town with Dad. Because he was in a hurry and because Mother wouldn't let me go as I was, I couldn't go. That was the most heartbreaking thing I ever experienced even to this day. It made me understand the importance of obeying orders. It made me realize how much the little things in life count.

There is a great deal of love in our family. Not an outward expression of it, so much, but a deep understanding of each other. This was developed in me too as a result of the actions of my parents. They were kind, understanding, and considerate people. Love in our family isn't so much based on physical factors. That is, it isn't developed by having someone touch you or by words, only. Mother and Dad aren't what most people would call sentimental people. When I was little, they protected me with their love in an understanding way. That is, they expressed true feelings of love and did not just cuddle and pet me for the sake of it. Real feelings can mean so much more than mere actions, and even a child can sense it when the wrong kind of love is shown to her. It is the true understanding of a person (sympathy and regard for their wishes) that constitutes love.

My parents realized the importance of keeping me occupied during my childhood. I had specific tasks to do each day. Usually they were of such nature that if I didn't do them, it would result in my discomfort and affect no one but myself. For instance, if I didn't put away my toys each day, no one else would do it for me. Consequently, the next time I wanted them, I would first have to find them. Crying or begging were of no avail. Mother would tell me that she hadn't seen them. She didn't tell me that, if I had put them back where they belonged, I wouldn't always have to look for them. A sense of responsibility and independence was developed from this that has helped me all through life. I know that if I want something, people will not just hand it to me; I have to work for it.

Mother made a game of doing things with me. That is, we would decide to complete a task in a certain period of time. I learned as a result of this to work rapidly and to concentrate on what I was doing. It also helped to develop a sense of responsibility. I had a job to do, and Mother saw to it that my share was such that it was possible for me to do it. I experienced a feeling of accomplishment when I finished the task.

At an early age, I experienced the satisfaction of being clean. Mother taught me this by insisting that we keep my dolls clean, as they didn't like to be dirty. I enjoyed dressing and undressing them and soon began to feel that I, too, did not like to be dirty. We would give my dolls a complete bath and then put talcum powder on them to make them smell nice. I liked the smell of the powder, so when I wanted it I had to have a bath before I could use it. Toys that I liked were put in my bathtub, and baths were real fun for me.

My father is a conservative person who spends his money carefully and does not spend money for things when he can't pay for them all. So, when my parents began to give me spending money for the week, I always kept a very detailed record of how I spent it. I liked the feeling of having money if ever I really needed it (an idea I got from my father, because he always sets aside money each month for the future when "we might need it"). However, the allowance was sufficient, and I didn't have to become a miser in order to save some of it; but I did learn to spend it carefully.

From the age of thirteen I have been bothered by an inferiority complex that has retarded the whole development of my personality in positive ways. At the age of twelve or thirteen, I became what everyone called "pleasingly plump." More than I had ever hated anything before in my life, I hated being chubby. I didn't attack the problem as I should have. Instead of trying to find some solution to the problem, I pretended that it didn't bother me. But I was conscious of it whenever I said or did anything. I worried a great deal about it.

My parents did everything they could for me. They took me to our physician. They thought it might be something in my diet. However, my problem was not caused by what I ate; my pituitary gland was not functioning correctly. They didn't tell me this, but put me on a sort of diet. They thought the psychological effect upon me might help. Few things were taken off my eating list, but I thought I was doing something about it and imagined myself to be thinner.

As for the general effect it had on my personality, much can be said. At first, I developed a defensive attitude. When my schoolmates chided me about it, I became furious, but I showed no outward signs. I sincerely believed no one liked me. My self-esteem and my self-confidence were greatly reduced during this time. I felt insecure and unhappy. However, because I tried so hard to get rid of my extra fat, I developed something that has been of great help to me. I learned patience; I knew it would take time, and by constantly telling myself this I began to believe it. I learned another thing, too, and this one means more to me now than any other positive trait I may possess. It is in the form of a little sentence that I say to myself, and it developed, I know, directly from my chubbiness: "If you want to do a thing badly enough, you can do it." At times in my life there have been things I wanted badly, and I would say this and then go to work. I sincerely believe it is true; if you exert enough effort you can have anything you want.

When I was a child, my parents were able to give me nearly all the things that I wanted. However, they were wise enough to make me realize the value of money in relation to what it could buy. From the age of nine, I received an allowance. Dad and I would sit down and figure out a budget for the week and then when the week was over we'd check it again. He didn't order me to do this, but he made me want to do it. He made a game of everything we did. A few extra nickels were put into my bank only if I deserved them. I had to purchase such things as shoelaces, my dolls' clothes, and pay for what I put into the Sunday School collection box. Dad used to make out his reports and budget sheets at the same time that I did. He would patiently explain different costs to me, and as I grew older I could comprehend what a job he had.

People in my family rarely brag. Good work is done by a person, and the others are quick to notice it and to give their thanks or compliments. We were made to realize the value of doing things right. Mother and Dad were very conscientious hard workers. They did or attempted to do a job well. Somewhere way back in the past I learned that it is best to do a job thoroughly or not to do it at all. I had to learn to do things by myself. When I had studying to do, I had to do it or it would not get done.

At the present time I am putting myself through school. I do receive some help from home, however. I do not have to put myself through school, but I feel that I owe it to my family. I realize they have worked hard for what they have, and I know that I can do it, so why shouldn't I? My brothers are the same type. We like to be self-sufficient and independent. We still depend upon our family for affection and inspiration. At the time my older brother was ready for college, my father wasn't financially able to do it all for him. He came to school anyway, and during the time he was in college he put himself through completely by himself. A year after he had entered, my father was able to do more for him, but he said "no." This had a great effect on me. I decided that if he could do something for the family so could I. I went downtown one weekday and with no selling experience whatsoever, talked the owner of one of the best women's apparel shops into permitting me to work in his store on Saturdays during school. My self-confidence and self-esteem were greatly improved. My parents were proud of me, and this had a good psychological effect upon me, too.

Mother and Father taught me never to be afraid of work. It would hurt no one and would only raise me in the eyes of others.

I am able to converse freely with members of both sexes. During early childhood we held family conferences each week. We were allowed to say anything we wanted, permitted to ask any questions. As a result of the close contact I have had with my family, I can "get along" with everyone.

I believe my personality is positively developed; I have high morals, ideals, can get along with all people, and all in all, I am a happy, contented person.

Most of us are not accustomed to having anyone speak as favorably of himself as this girl does at the end of her account. But other people would have agreed with her evaluation. She was an exceedingly pleasant and genuine person. And it was no namby-pamby niceness. A few days before the final exam in one of her courses, she came to the instructor to ask if she might take the exam later. She had just received word, she said, that her brother had been killed at Pearl Harbor, and she felt she ought to go home to help her mother. The instructor said, of course, that this would be all right. But when the exam came, a few days later, she was there. She said that her mother had wired her to take her exams as usual, if she could, and then come home when they were done. So there she was—rather pale, but with no word of complaint that she couldn't have prepared for the exams or that she couldn't concentrate on it—even though a brother's death, especially in that closely knit family, had been a profound shock.

These accounts suggest, at least, that Ann and Beatrice mostly *learned* their different personalities. It may be, of course, that Ann's parents transmitted to her some hereditary factors which predisposed her to feelings of insecurity and isolation, and that Beatrice's parents transmitted heredity which was more favorable to a vigorous and happy reaction to life. But it seems doubtful whether heredity can have been the major causal factor. If Beatrice had been adopted into Ann's family when she was a very small child, and if she had been treated as Ann was treated, it seems likely that she would have developed in much the same way that Ann developed. In some ways, after all, she is like Ann. She has a strong need for a feeling of acceptance by others; she is strongly socially oriented, just as Ann is. Probably each of them had some learning experiences that made other people important to them. But Ann had the sort of learning experience which tended to teach her that others were unsympathetic and overly critical; Beatrice had the sort of learning experience which taught her that she could win affection and respect from other people.

These two accounts, furthermore, suggest that personality development does not occur only in early childhood, but is a continuing process. Ann was exploring a new pattern of response when she went to her first basketball game. She was able to lose herself in the group, apparently, and had some real experience of happy, lively social participation. But her parents, instead of nourishing this new trend so deeply needed in her personality, discouraged and obstructed it. Ann learned that spontaneous and hearty reactions, even though they might be safe enough for other children, were not something she could afford in her particular family setting. Or again, even though Ann was learning a very inhibited way of behaving at her own home, it seems that she still felt free to act more spontaneously at the homes of neighbors. She might have developed and used two different patterns of response, as if following the rule that "it is safe to be natural and helpful in most social situations, but it isn't possible to act that way at home." But the criticisms from home ("Now, you won't do that at home; why do you do it for others?") tended to prevent this solution.

Beatrice, too, was learning as the years went along. It is probably correct to say, as she does, that she was a friendly child even when she was quite small. Nevertheless, she did tend to look down on the daughter of the couple who worked for her parents. Some other children at school were treating this child as inferior because of her poorer clothes and social position, and Beatrice was not independent enough to accept the child on her merits. But her parents were able to help her escape from this snobbishness into a more unprejudiced reaction to others.

Beatrice did not learn all at once, at some early age, the vigorous and self-confident approach that she had to life. Both of her parents helped her to learn how to handle many situations and to be confident in them. They probably helped her, too, by what they refrained from doing and saying as well as by what they did do and say. Often, in fact, different children in the same family will follow different lines of development, much as though each child concludes that he cannot compete in some area of excellence which an older brother or sister has explored. Sometimes, therefore, when the oldest child in the family has made a name for himself as a student, the next child may turn to athletics or to practical skills. But Beatrice was able to develop an ideal for herself partly by seeing what her older brother had done. She tended to say: "If he earned his way through college, so can I." Her personality characteristics were being molded as they were perhaps partly because the parents did *not* point to the older brother and say, "There's a good example for you; do you think you could live up to that?" Her personality development may have come from many relatively subtle influences, therefore, rather than merely from direct training. If this is true, perhaps it will be unusually difficult to understand some of the processes of learning that are involved in personality.

What definition of personality is suggested by all of the above examples?

Every once in a while, in the preceding discussion, we have spoken of *personality* or *personality characteristics* but we have not paused to define these terms. One reason is that it is so hard to arrive at a good, explicitly-stated definition of a broad term like *personality*. Another reason is that, to some extent, we may not need an explicit, abstractly-stated definition. In most of our thinking and communication we learn implicit definitions long before we can set forth a clear and adequate abstract statement. For example, you wouldn't get any very good definition from a 10-year-old boy if you asked him what he meant by a *board*. He might reply: "It's a piece of wood." You point to an object and ask: "Is that, then, a board?" 'No," he says, "that's a stick." We might have trouble in getting him to see that the object in question still reasonably comes under his definition of a board as "a piece of wood." But he could, nevertheless, show us by his choices from a series of objects that he does have a good *implicit* definition of board, even though he cannot state it.

When we try to define the word *personality* we are in a similar situation. It is so hard to find an adequate abstract definition that we might well be excused if we declined the task and said merely: "Personality is what is illustrated especially by such examples as we have been talking about, above. Personality is the respect in which Mrs. A and Mrs. B and Mrs. C differ; it is the respect in which the two surgeons differ; it is the respect in which Susan and Mary differ; it is the difference between Ann and Beatrice." Actually, we might get along fairly well with such an unverbalized, implicit definition. Even if we succeeded in arriving at a good abstract definition of personality, most of the understanding of the abstract terms in the definition would have to come from our acquaintance with such concrete examples as these.

There is, nevertheless, some clarity that comes from explicit definitions, and we therefore ought to try to state what is meant by personality.

Should we say, for one thing, that personality seems to be something within the person that makes him represent or perceive life situations as he does? Mrs. A, for instance, saw the little incident with the boys as more evidence that the care of children is an irritating, exasperating business that one can reasonably complain about. Mrs. B, on the other hand, saw the same situation as one which testified that she was unsuited for her responsibilities. The one surgeon saw his work as a fascinating opportunity to handle important problems and be helpful to others; the other surgeon saw the same work as a precarious task where all sorts of dangerous possibilities lurked. The external realities can be exactly the same in some given situation, and yet, because of personality differences, one person will attribute one meaning or significance to the situation, while another person will seize upon a totally different meaning.

Are we going to say, however, that all representational or perceptual processes are matters of personality? Suppose that two physicians examine a child and that they both agree, "He's coming down with the mumps." Does this mean that because the physicians represent the same external reality in the same way they have similar personalities, at least to some degree? Or, on the contrary, are we going to say that there is a great host of representational and perceptual processes in a person which we hardly would speak of as matters of personality? Thus, should we make a distinction between personality on the one hand and technical knowledge and skills on the other?

At least in the foregoing examples, we were not emphasizing similarities and differences of factual knowledge. We were pointing, instead, to differences of representation or perception that were *emotionally significant* to the individual. The first surgeon represented his work in a way that gave him a warm feeling of pride and usefulness. When Beatrice thought of her family, she thought of them with affection and gratitude; when she thought of her age-mates, she thought of them as persons who almost certainly would be cordial and friendly to deal with. When Ann thought of her age-mates, however, she could not keep from distrusting them, as she put it, or from feeling that they disliked her. Perhaps, therefore, personality is more limited than the *entire* stock of habits or knowledge that we use in interpreting or grasping the meaning of situations we meet. Perhaps personality must be considered to be, for the most part, confined to those habits or ways of thought which are directly related to certain emotionally significant aspects in our experience.

In the examples we used, however, there was another prominent element. These examples involved emotionally significant representations. But they involved more than that. In each case, the person in question tended to *deal* with the situation in some way more or less characteristic of him. The process he had within him which represented the situation in certain terms was also a process that pressed for action. Mrs. A did not merely perceive her boys as causing trouble for her by their fighting; she was impelled toward scolding them and warning them not to do such things again. The little six-year-old, Mary, who tended to be such a disruptive factor in play groups, did not merely see other children as potential enemies; she also tended to single out some one child from such a group as an ally and then to taunt and ridicule the other children. Ought we to say, therefore, that personality is related to action as well as to representational and emotional processes?

Of course, we all know that a person may not at a given moment show in his behavior some of the tendencies that he possesses. Ann, for instance, remarked at one point in her life history that, whenever she recalled the incident involving her having to climb the tall ladder, she *hated* the men for making her do it. In most of her life, Ann has become so timid that she certainly doesn't seem to act like one who, to some extent, *hates* other persons. But the chances are that she was speaking honestly here; furthermore, the likelihood is that she experienced some hate toward a good many other people—the children who teased her for her poor clothes, the parents who scolded her for acting spontaneously, and so on. She has, however, learned some stronger controlling processes of fear and hence has not tended to show any proneness toward retaliation. But personality processes can *press* toward action or can *tend* to translate themselves into overt behavior without getting any clear expression. At least we assume this in everyday life, as when we say, "I was so mad that I could hardly keep from telling him off; but of course I didn't dare do it." Does this give us a clue for part of our picture of personality? Is personality merely what is shown directly and clearly in behavior? Or is personality something instead that *tends* to get translated into behavior, but which may or may not be thus expressed, depending upon circumstances?

We have a puzzle, too, in the relation of personality to conceptual processes within the person. Ordinarily we think of concepts as intellectual in nature, and tend to make a contrast between them and personality characteristics. We regard concepts as more susceptible to change, or more responsive to logical argument and to factual demonstrations, than is personality. But some other considerations suggest that maybe personality is partly, at least, a matter of concepts. You may remember how Beatrice remarked, after her description of her early-adolescence problem of chubbiness and of her effort to control it, that she came to have this conviction about life: "If you want to do a thing badly enough, you can do it." We don't need to ask whether this was an entirely reasonable concept, or whether Beatrice meant it in fully literal terms. But it does seem that she probably had learned something here which proved helpful when she applied for her first job or, in the still later years, when she was earning a good share of her college expenses. By *concept* we mean that a person has taken a series of concrete events and has made a generalization from them that he then can apply to new instances. This is what Beatrice had done. This is what Ann had done in a whole series of problems.

We might even say that when personality processes press for overt action, they tend to follow channels that open up because of the concepts the individual has formed. In other words, each person acts on the basis of his individually-developed concepts that "in such and such an objective situation, such and such emotional values may be achieved by such and such actions." Maybe there is really a high degree of unity to personality processes in some respects. It may be that each of our personality processes is actually a single but complex process—thus each process might be simultaneously emotional, representational or interpretive, and pressing-for-action. And yet each single process, with these different qualities in it, may also be a conceptual process.

One thing that makes us hesitate on this last thought is the fact that personality apparently develops largely in early childhood. This makes us hesitant about suggesting that personality characteristics often—perhaps even typically—are matters of the concepts the individual has formed, because it hardly seems likely that a two- or three-year-old would be doing what we think of as an intellectual feat—that is, forming concepts.

But we need to be careful before we become too skeptical about this possibility. When we watch small children of these ages, we notice some odd things about their use of language. They tend to enrich it by using words in unusual but perfectly logical ways, and they tend to smooth out the barbarous irregularities of the mother tongue. For example, they say: "Look, it's winding and raining outside." "Let me unkey the door." "I drinked all my milk." "That's the goodest stuff I ever eated." One small child in a nursery school, after trying unsuccessfully to force a large carrot into a small food-grinder, turned to the nursery school teacher and said, "Please unfatten this for me, will you?" Another child, watching his father build a platform and hearing him remark that it was not adjusted properly yet, said to him, "You'll have to higher it over here." Another child once asked: "Who moke this house?" Then, seeing that he was not communicating, he corrected himself by asking, "Who maked this house?"

In most of these illustrations, we can be reasonably sure that the child had never heard other people use these expressions. In fact, whenever a child does hear his parents speak, he hears them use such terms as *ate, drank, held, best,* and the rest of the irregular forms. But these concrete things the child has heard are not what appear in his own speech. He could not possibly explain that you indicate past time by adding an "ed" sound, or that you indicate the opposite of something by putting "un" before a word. But, from his behavior, we know that he must have formed these concepts. He has taken a series of particular examples, derived a generalized rule from them, and applied this rule easily and resourcefully to new cases. In fact, as we were saying, he applies his abstract rule, his concept, even in those particular cases where he has heard something else and where he understands what the parents mean by their particular irregular expressions!

Of course, if we define *concepts* in such a way as to limit the term to those instances where the person can explain in some adequate way what he is doing, these small children have not yet learned concepts. But we may well wonder whether we ought to define concepts in that more limited sense. Ought we to define concepts in that way? Or should we say that concepts have been formed when other things in the person's behavior plainly indicate a use of concepts that he cannot state?

If we do define concepts in the latter way, then it may be true that personality development, even at an age of two or three years, may be a matter of concept-formation to some considerable degree. At least in this more behavioral sense, small children apparently can form concepts. This idea still seems at odds with many of our notions about personality.

It seems to suggest a process which is too intellectual. But is this the real difficulty? Is it possible that our definition of concept has been too limited?

These are some questions that naturally come up when we try to frame a satisfactory definition of personality. They are complex questions, and many of them we ought not to try to settle at this stage in our whole discussion. Therefore, even though we have not reduced the matter to something stated within a dozen words or so, the authors of this book are not inclined to try to be more specific at this point. A reader has some rights too! Accordingly, if the material tends to lead you to a different definition from the one we would suggest, well and good! We can come back to this matter again when we have explored a lot of questions in more detail. Definitions cannot rest on a priori decisions, after all. They are supposed to group together those things that have important characteristics in common, and they are supposed to exclude some other things that have some other important characteristics not shared by examples included under the definition. Consequently, definitions need to reflect all of the empirical knowledge we can get regarding the thing defined. We need, therefore, to examine many different factual questions before we can do more than hazard some tentative definitions.

Ought we to think of personality as merely a matter of responses to other people?

You may have noticed that almost all the examples we have considered have centered on the interpersonal relations of people. When Ann and Beatrice were trying to describe their personalities, for instance, they spoke almost entirely, or perhaps entirely, about their relationships with other persons. It certainly seems that experiences with other persons are at least a major means by which personality is developed and a major mode of expression of personality.

Some writers in the field of personality have in fact gone so far as to define personality as solely a matter of the interpersonal relations of the individual. But one wonders whether such a definition may not be incomplete. One wonders whether personality may not also be shaped by the rest of the world in which the person lives and not merely by the social part of that world.

Some years ago, at a small conference of foreign students in the United States, the students were asked to describe in writing some of the earliest things they could remember. Most of them described interpersonal experiences. For instance, one of the students from India wrote:

> I recollect when I started learning the English language at a very young age. It was fascinating to find that I could use different sounds to communicate

the things that I knew in my own language. When I had only a very limited vocabulary, I felt I had a special quality that many others did not possess, and it was very interesting to try this power in times when a few could understand and others could not. Almost like a class superiority.

The other students were invited to guess who wrote the account. Almost with one shout they named the student in question—a very talkative and extroverted participant who generally played an important part in the whole group.

In a small minority of cases, however, the earliest recollection described was of a different sort. For example, the following was written by a German girl who was in the United States to study art history:

I was standing at the window of my room one morning. I was looking at the raindrops which were slowly running down on the glass. I think the sun came out then; for suddenly the colors of the rainbow started playing in the water. I had a toy that I liked best of all the things I knew; it was a little glass ball that shimmered and shone in many different colors. And now there was a connection between this wonder of my small world, which belonged only to me, and the big things which were happening in the outside. The sheltered feeling of staying in a room on a rainy day was suddenly mixed with a strange kind of curiosity that wanted to reach the life of the outside. It was fear and a feeling of a happy discovery at the same time.

Possibly an example like this is not an instance of the influence on personality of nonsocial factors. Perhaps we might argue: "The German child would have been sensitive to such things and would have experienced this effect only if she previously had known one kind of interpersonal experience rather than another; some tiny factor like this would not have had an influence if it had not been for some predisposing social influences."

Suppose we agree, however, that this girl's experience was related to earlier social experiences. Did this response to the physical world add nothing to her personality? Was she the same afterwards as she would have been if she had not had this contact with the physical world?

One wonders about many other examples. When one lives on an isolated western ranch, is his personality uninfluenced by the hills and rocks and broad stretches of sagebrush country all around him? These may establish such powerful emotional values in one's life that later there may be no setting that seems quite so satisfying. Is this merely because one had pleasant interpersonal relations in that setting? Or does the physical world appeal to us and influence us partly because we are influenced *directly* by the play of colors that can change such hills from season to season, and even within swift moments at sundown or sunrise? What are we to say about a workman's love of good tools, about a young person's love of skiing, or about a farmer's or gardener's joy in watching things grow?

In city life, and especially in the upper socioeconomic levels of city life, we tend to be out of contact with such things. We have made our surroundings relatively static and changeless. Rainstorms are something to flee from. Snow is a nuisance—something that soon will be black with soot and churned into slush by thousands of feet. We tend to occupy ourselves chiefly with our relationships to other persons, as though we see them as the sole natural content and preoccupation of human life.

But we might well stop and ask whether this is the full nature of man. Or are our personalities instead the natural means of relating ourselves, not merely to other persons, but also to the rest of the real world we occupy? We can wonder whether we have tended to have too much of a "big city" view of personality. We can wonder whether some of the problems of modern man perhaps come about because he lacks contact with the subtly changing physical world that lies beyond static, lifeless, man-made things. One wonders, when we are inclined to see personality as merely a matter of interpersonal relations, whether we may be missing the fact that man has been molded more than we can imagine by the physical environment around him; perhaps we need to give thought to making a nonsocial world that is better adapted to our needs.

This is again a question which we cannot possibly settle on a priori ground. The primary issue is factual. If the principles that describe how the nonsocial environment affects us are, to some large degree, like the principles that describe how the social environment molds the emotional, representational, action-tendency parts of us that we regard as our personality, then we must say that personality is more than merely a matter of interpersonal relations. But this is a question of fact; it is not a question to be settled arbitrarily.

Is personality merely a matter of the conscious part of our lives?

Particularly in the longer examples cited above, we have described different personalities in terms of the descriptions that different students had given of themselves. This fact suggests that we are thinking of personality as composed of characteristics that the individual can consciously recognize about himself. To some extent, indeed, this is true. To some extent, and in some persons more than in others, personality is something we can recognize within ourselves.

Some of our other examples, however, have suggested that the individual may reveal some consistent, recurrent tendencies in his behavior that he cannot recognize in himself. These may be important in his social relationships, of course, and may be indirectly influential in their effects on his own conscious experience, even though the person in question does not detect what it is he is doing. Apparently self-descriptions are merely one means of getting light on personality processes. We may need to conceive of personality as frequently including much more than the individual himself can recognize about himself.

Consider, for example, the following account by Leon Saul, in his book *Emotional Maturity*.[1] Saul was describing a 30-year-old woman who had been born into a family of high social standing and rather rigid social standards:

The life of a young woman who had been born with a silver spoon illustrates what can result when anger and rebellion are stimulated but meet with the restraints of high social standards of training. . . . She was subjected to insistent pressure by her family. Instead of educating her in the . . . sense of "leading out" and facilitating the development of the personality, . . . her parents taught her only to submit to the plan of life which was given to her. She rebelled against these constraints and became very angry at her parents. Her rebellion and anger, aroused by this sociologic factor, were greatly intensified by a personal emotional factor. This was the parents' relative rejection of the girl emotionally in favor of her older brother. . . . But, in spite of her rebellion, the training took considerable effect and she internalized it as a strict but unaccepted conscience. Her anger at her parents . . . took the . . . form of . . . depreciating herself socially. In this way she both took revenge upon them and satisfied her own conscience by punishing herself. She associated only with people who had no social or economic standing and with many who were on the fringe. She would have nothing to do with the wealthy, accomplished, attractive and socially prominent young man selected for her by her parents, but went chiefly with inadequate, ineffectual, unstable persons on the fringe of society, and unconsciously she managed matters so that she was repeatedly in situations which shocked and distressed her parents. Here was a girl who was born to every advantage of person and background. She was beautiful, intelligent, sensitive and cultured. She had offered to her the best of education and of social contacts. She had no need for financial worry. She had her choice of the most eligible young men. Nothing in the external situation or in her personal endowment and capacities was lacking. Yet I happened to see her because she came to the clinic for help. She was dressed in the poorest clothes; her shoes were worn. She had left her home town and was tired out from struggling to make both ends meet. She lived alone in a slum area. She always became interested in men who could not decide whether or not to

[1]Leon Saul, *Emotional Maturity* (Philadelphia, J. B. Lippincott Co., 1947), pp. 102-103.

marry her and who, in the end, after months or years of indecision, frustration and heartache, finally broke off. Except for a few girl friends, she dragged along alone, down at the heel and miserable.

In trying to help this young woman work out her personality problems, Saul reports that he got some unexpected help from a traffic policeman. Here she was, Saul says,[2]—a girl

> . . . who was not aware of her hostility and took it out subtly but devastatingly upon herself, discarding every advantage of birth and endowment for a life of useless misery. She could not realize in what a rage she usually was, although this was obvious in her expression, manner and behavior as well as in her psychologic outlook. One day while she was waiting to cross the street, the policeman genially remarked, "What is the matter—why are you so angry?" She looked up in surprise. "You look as though you want to murder someone," said the policeman good-naturedly. She was deeply impressed by this and began to understand what I had been trying to help her see.

In a case like this, the girl would probably have known, clearly enough, that she had certain sorts of emotional reaction, such as resentment against her parents. And probably, in each instance in which she accepted or rejected a young man, she could have pointed to something specific which struck her as justifying the choice she had made: "True, he's intelligent and dependable, but so stuffy!" or "True, maybe he has been disowned by most of his friends, but he has very good taste in music." Consequently, in each case, she would have felt that what she did or said was an intelligent reflection of actualities. She would not have seen that, over and over again, she was picking out and stressing the defective aspects in those persons and situations that would mainly have been favorable for herself and picking out and stressing only the favorable features of the situations which were calculated to lead to costly disappointments for herself. Her behavior was consistently in line with one pattern of action. It was disastrously self-punishing. And yet she could not see that she had formed a rule comparable in principle to the notion of the little child we referred to above: "You always indicate past action by adding the 'ed' sound."

When we try to understanding personality, therefore, we are interested in more than the individual's *conscious* knowledge and *conscious* understanding of himself and his personality processes. This does not mean that we lack interest in such conscious awareness in ourselves and others. But it seems as though, if we are to understand and explain the conscious experiences we have, we will have to go beyond our conscious processes into broader areas of our lives.

[2]*Ibid.*, p. 111.

This exploration may lead us into difficulties of terminology because we will want to use technical terms which a great many psychologists have been inclined to define as identifying conscious processes—for example, *emotion*, *perception*, *concepts*, *meanings*, *goals*, *representations*, and *motives*. The question is whether we can really recognize, both in ourselves and in others, that personality may come in considerable part from sources outside of those we are consciously aware of.

How significant is the influence of personality on our lives?

The people whose problems we have reviewed in this chapter have perhaps spoken well enough for themselves. Ann ended her account, for example, with such statements as these: "I've grown into a person who is afraid to do anything for fear of being laughed at. . . . I constantly find myself distrusting people, thinking they don't like me. . . . It seems every year, as I grow older, that my mind comes to be more in such a state of confusion that I don't know which way to turn." Beatrice, on the other hand, had a feeling about herself which she summed up in these words: "I believe my personality is positively developed; I have high morals, ideals, can get along with all people, and, all in all, I am a happy, contented person." The people who knew her, furthermore, had the same impression of her. It is obvious that the contrast between her and Ann is a vital one.

The other persons we described illustrated other marked contrasts that come from personality differences. It is undeniably clear that life can become a profoundly dissimilar thing for different persons because of their differences in personality. And yet it will be noted that we have not spoken of the real extremes of personality. We have purposefully confined ourselves to only a small portion of the total population—persons fairly well educated and having a social and economic status usually referred to as middle class. Even within this group, we have not spoken about the more divergent personalities. There are such, of course. Here is a student, for instance, who is bothered because it does not seem to her that she herself is doing and saying things, but rather as if another person were acting in her place while she is observing from a corner near the ceiling. Here is another student who is so distraught he can hardly sleep more than a few hours a night, even though he takes sleeping pills, and who vomits several times each day, even though physicians have checked him very carefully and are confident that there is nothing wrong with him physically. Here is a man who began a life history of overt homosexuality when he was about 12 or 13, who was dishonorably discharged from the Navy for this behavior, who later married and for some years seemed to others to have a splendid marriage, but who broke it off after some years and returned to a frank homosexual relationship. Here is a student who seems cold-bloodedly to lie, engage in stealing, break rules flagrantly, and "sponge" off others, and who seems to suffer no remorse as long as he can "get away with it."

There are such relatively unusual cases of students with really marked difficulties, as anyone who is familiar with counseling work in colleges or universities knows. But we have chosen not to speak of these relatively extreme cases, although we could have illustrated them from some of our own counseling experience. What seems more important to stress, however, is that there are really profound personality differences even among the more ordinary members of an ordinary group of persons within our culture.

Among all the forms of life existing on the earth, human beings appear to be the creatures outstandingly equipped with rich emotional potentialities and tremendous capacities for learning. They have developed complex tools, complex technical skills, complex civilizations. In human societies, remarkably diverse personalities develop. Some of the personal qualities that appear are valuable assets in the life of a person, making possible a dignity, a fineness, and a deep satisfaction in living which we wish might become a good deal more common. But, on the other hand, the complications of emotional potentiality and learning ability often produce a life that is merely passably satisfactory to the person himself and to those around him. Far too frequently the outcome is worse, and bitterness, defeat, wasteful rebellion, or some other pattern of personality maladjustment results. It seems, therefore, that personality is something important for us to understand, not merely because it determines so much of our lives, but because it does not work with any uniformity to produce successful living. The forms of behavior that result from personality are unlike such behavior as breathing, salivary reflexes, perspiring, and heartbeat. Though these are important because they are processes indispensable to life, ordinarily we need not give much thought to them. Most of the time they operate satisfactorily whether we understand them or not. But personality is not so predictable; it operates with profoundly different degrees of success in different persons. In good part, these differences come from environmental influences that conceivably are or might be brought under our control, provided we could learn to act intelligently and effectively. But only occasionally, at present, does personality flower into the sort of thing we would like to see more generally in human life. There are profound differences of adjustment even among persons who are contributing in fairly important ways to the workaday activities of the world.

We wish to point out that the cases we have used in this chapter may have been misleading in one respect. Differences between different personalities are not merely differences of degree of adjustment or maladjustment. Our examples may not have illustrated this fact, perhaps, because too often we were seeking to contrast maladjusted and adjusted reactions in the same sort of circumstances. But now, if you should return to the examples we used, you might see that this is not at all the only sort of difference. Ann, for instance, was not the same sort of person as Mrs. A, and neither of them was the same sort of person as the girl described by Leon Saul. The belligerent cherry-picker had a partial resemblance to the little six-year-old Mary who acted so disruptively in groups that she joined; still there were differences between these two. All of these persons might be described as "maladjusted," but that is only part of the story. People differ from one another in the *kinds* of maladjusted personalities they have, and not merely in the degrees of maladjustment. In this first chapter, too, we have not had much opportunity to describe unusually successful personalities, or to illustrate at all clearly how many diverse possibilities there are among such well-adjusted individuals. But diversity is the rule with the well-adjusted too. The material which challenges our interest in the field of personality, therefore, is not merely material that concerns some abstract continuum of adjustment-maladjustment. It is much more complex material.

Of course, you may have recognized before now many of the problems sketched in this chapter and felt discouraged about trying to deal with personality or even about trying to understand it. You may have been tempted to say, "I agree—personality does seem to make an enormous difference in human life. But it is too complicated to deal with. You can rejoice in the fine things that come from personality when it develops as it should, and you suffer when something goes wrong with it. But there is almost nothing that you can do about it. Furthermore, when our personalities seem more calculated to produce pain and frustration than joy, what can we do about that? Apparently we simply will have to accept the fact that the basic raw materials of human nature are poor."

In many other aspects of life the people of earlier centuries felt that they were confronted with insoluble problems, and yet the difficulty finally turned out to be due only to the failure of human beings to study and to try to understand their world. The terrible plagues of the Middle Ages, for instance, were not inevitable and inescapable. Perhaps our present difficulties in the field of personality may be overcome by attempts to study personality carefully, patiently, and resourcefully.

If we set out to study and understand personality, we might first ask what kinds of ideas about human personality we now tend to use in our everyday life. Next we might look briefly at the findings of several different kinds of technical work that might provide us with some better understanding. Then, more in detail, we might attempt to identify various relatively new ideas which might come from those several technical fields and determine how, in the light of these ideas, we can reorganize our everyday understanding of personality. This will be the general plan of this book. In the next chapter, therefore, we turn to a discussion of the problem of how we ordinarily understand personality and how we try to deal with it with the aid of our everyday conceptions.

Summary

In this chapter, we have aimed to provide concrete examples to show what personality is and what profound differences exist in human life by virtue of differences in personality. We have avoided the use of extreme cases and have sought to show that there are significant differences in personality even among those who are commonly regarded as being representative of decently provided for and educated segments of modern society. That the range of personality differences might prove to be much greater than we have illustrated has not concerned us for the moment. We have been trying to see whether, even in a fairly homogeneous part of society, personality differences are really profoundly important.

In the discussion of these cases, we have attempted in this chapter to raise many questions and we have avoided suggesting dogmatic answers to them. However, it is quite true that the discussion above has favored the suggestions that (1) personality is only a part of the whole life of the individual, rather than the "sum total of his psychological characteristics"; (2) personality is particularly a matter of how the person represents and deals with things of emotional significance to him; (3) personality is in some considerable degree a matter of the development and operation of the emotional potentialities of a person; (4) personality is rather heavily social but is not limited merely to the interpersonal relations of the individual; and (5) personality is not restricted solely to the parts of a person's life which he can include within his self-descriptions. We have raised the question as to whether personality might to a considerable extent be dependent on rather broad concepts which the person has formed about living. We have noted that this seems, at least at first thought, an overintellectualized hypothesis and one ill-adapted to observations of how personality develops significantly in early childhood. But we also reviewed some material suggesting that even very small children are good at forming concepts, if we will use a behavioral criterion of concept-formation and concept-use. We have, therefore, at least suggested that an understanding of personality may lead us into a study of certain rather broad and comprehensive processes within the life of the person.

Some of our examples have suggested, too, that personality is a difficult and obstinate sort of material to try to mold or understand, and we might have said that is it easy to sympathize with those who take the view that personality is like the weather, which everybody talks about but nobody does much about. Consequently, we might well have ended the chapter with the suggestion that even though personality may be as resistant to efforts at deliberate control as is the weather, we still might find it helpful to learn to understand and predict the phenomena of personality. Even when we cannot alter some effects, we can adapt more effectively when we know how to predict them beforehand.

But it would be an exaggeration to say personality is not subject to our control at all. Even though there are great difficulties in using any penetrating understanding of personality when we deal with concrete cases, there is still a very real possibility that a better understanding of personality can be highly useful and rewarding as an aid in creating in human life the results that are worth striving for. There is a very real possibility that some of our difficulties in dealing with personality in our lives arise because we base our everyday life on ideas about personality that are not actually justified. In the next chapter, therefore, we turn to the question of what conceptions about personality are rather commonly held in our everyday thinking. Then, in the still later chapters, we will turn to a description of the technical sources from which a more adequate understanding of personality has been emerging.

CHAPTER 2

Our Everyday Concepts about Personality

One valuable result of scientific work is that scientific concepts become absorbed into everyday thought. It took a lot of difficult reasoning and observation to develop our knowledge that the alternation of day and night is produced by the rotation of the earth, rather than by any movement of the sun. It took a lot of work to develop the idea that many diseases are produced by bacteria or viruses and that some other diseases result from vitamin deficiencies. It took a lot of work in genetics to arrive at the idea of dominant and recessive genes and to discover the fact that children of the same parents usually differ considerably in the chromosomes and genes they receive from their parents. But, even though these and many other scientific ideas were difficult to develop and to prove, they have been incorporated more or less widely into our general knowledge. "Everybody," we tend to say, "knows that the earth is round. Everybody knows that you get certain diseases because you get germs from other persons. Everybody knows that sedimentary rocks often contain traces of clam shells because such rocks were formed in the bottoms of oceans long ages ago."

Some of the scientific ideas that have been developed about personality already have been absorbed into everyday thought in this same way. It would be hard to untangle the parts of our everyday thought coming thus from scientific studies from those that have come from other origins.

In the present chapter, however, we want to ask what everyday notions about personality we have which come from sources other than scientific studies. Perhaps we can answer this question only in a rough way, but the inquiry may give us some valuable perspective.

Except as he gets them from scientific sources, does the man in the street have many concepts about personality?

We have suggested that personality is a very complex thing and that it is relatively subtle in many aspects. Because of these properties of personality, it might seem that the ordinary person, before he began to read books and articles dealing with personality, and before he saw Hollywood versions of psychoanalytic work, would not have developed much in the way of concepts about personality.

This impression is further borne out when we ask ordinary people what concepts they have about personality. They are likely to exclaim, "Why, that's something I don't know anything about. I'm not a psychologist. I don't see any point in fussing around with such things, anyway."

This is much the view that was expressed to one of the authors when he visited some friends who had a somewhat out-of-the-way ranch in Oregon. They asked him what he was doing in Oregon for the year. He explained that he was helping to write a book on the psychology of personality. "You mean," they said, "that you're spending a whole year on that? But what is there that you could say?" Obviously they regarded this activity as unreal and unnecessary. The young man who owned the ranch was much more interested in showing the visitors his ranch, in talking with them about horses of different types, and in discussing irrigation problems.

As the talk continued, however, the young rancher and his wife finally got to other matters that concerned them. For instance, they mentioned that their small boy had been born with a clubfoot. They had made arrangements for surgery to try to remedy this abnormality, but they were disturbed about the effects this abnormality might have had on him and about the possible aftermath of the operation and his stay in the hospital. They were troubled also about their small daughter. Their home was so isolated from others that there was little chance for her to play with children of her age. There was an opportunity for her to meet with other children at a Sunday school not too far away; but her parents could not sympathize with the fundamentalist beliefs taught there, and they were wondering whether her attendance would create more problems than it would solve. They spoke of other similar problems too.

They simply did not see these perplexities as *personality* problems. In no way did they think of themselves as attempting to work out some concepts for dealing with personality problems. Nevertheless, this young man and his wife were finding themselves in the same situation that all of the rest of us are in, regardless of whether or not we think of ourselves as psychologists. The fact is that personality problems are important to us, and we have to deal with them as best we can. They are concerned with the basic problems and processes of living. A person cannot wash his hands of them and say, "Far be it from me to deal in any responsible way with matters of personality. I have no technical background for understanding such matters; so I refuse to deal with them." We may try to dodge things in this way, just as the young rancher and his wife might have said that they could not possibly know how to help their children meet whatever emotional and social difficulties they had. But we cannot avoid dealing somehow with such problems; hence our question becomes not "*Shall* we deal with personality problems?" but "*How?*"

Sometimes it dawns on us, in a way, that we do have some ideas about personality, and we formulate our concepts in more or less definite terms. For example, one young couple was perplexed as to what they should do with their eleven-month-old baby in the matter of putting him to bed at night. They believed that it probably was best for the boy to go to bed at a regular time. But sometimes, when they put him to bed, it seemed that he was not at all sleepy, and instead of dropping off to sleep, he would stand at the side of the crib and scream for an hour or more before he would lie down and drop off to sleep. The mother was inclined to delay his bedtime if she knew that the baby had had some extra sleep in the afternoon. The father, however, was a person with a pretty firm and indomitable spirit. Throughout his life he had shown that he could overcome obstacles and battle difficulties effectively. There is no denying that he would be rated as having an unusually well-adjusted personality, and his activity in Boy Scout work and the like has testified to his keen interest in his children. But, you might say, his good adjustment was of the sort that does not believe in bending before the wind. Consequently, when this problem arose with the baby, his advice to his wife was: "You'll probably have to fight it out with him some time as to who is boss; you may as well do it now." His view was expressed further in terms like these: "A child has to learn to accept some things without questioning. He has to learn that when you say something you mean it. He'll cry less in the long run if he learns that lesson now."

We are not interested now in the question of whether or not he was expressing a sound and adequate concept, though perhaps he was not, if we may judge from part of the child's later behavior. People who knew the child when he was about six years old characterized him by saying: "It doesn't do much good to tell Andrew what to do or what not to do. He doesn't say anything; he simply listens with a grim expression on his face, and then he goes off and does what he meant to do anyway." This example is interesting merely as illustrating the point that, in our everyday life, we, like this father, do tend sometimes to formulate explicitly, even though roughly, *some* concepts regarding personality.

For the most part, though, people don't even do much rough formulating. This was true, almost certainly, with the parents of Beatrice, whose life history was summarized in the preceding chapter. Those parents helped Beatrice to grow into a remarkably fine person. But the chances are that if you had asked them what rules they followed or what concepts they had used, they could not have told you more than a few unimportant things, as Beatrice herself said at the start of her account.

Maybe we are confronted here with something like the child's use of speech. As we said in the last chapter, the small child shows clearly *in his behavior* that he has learned how to alter words to indicate past time, negation, action, and intensification. But he cannot tell you why he makes up such words as *holded, unfatten, pianoing,* and *goodest.* In their experiments on concept-formation, as we shall see in later chapters, psychologists have found it profitable to say that concepts have been formed wherever behavioral evidence of a concept exists, regardless of whether or not the person can formulate an explanation of what he is doing. Therefore, if we follow this usage of research workers dealing with concept formation, we shall say also that the small child has such and such concepts about speech, regardless of whether he can express them, and we shall say that the everyday person perhaps has important concepts about personality, even though he cannot formulate them. Here is a question, therefore, which we shall have to decide by watching what people *do* and not merely by asking them what they *think* they do.

Everyday concepts about personality are difficult to determine

We have said that one difficulty exists because people cannot explain what concepts they have. The trouble comes also from other sources. The first of these might be illustrated by this example: Suppose you ask a person how he makes a turn to the left when he is riding a bicycle. He is likely to have an answer. He thinks he knows what he does—he probably believes that he makes the turn by leaning to the left and by turning the handlebars so that the front wheel will point toward the left. Actually, however, this is not what he does. He would fall off the bicycle if he did. As you can demonstrate by following the tracks made by his tires, he turns to the left by making an initial turn to the right. From some of his background of experience he has learned this particular reaction or skill. But from some other sources he has learned to think that he makes the turn in what he thinks is the direct and simpler way he describes. Thus, even when a person thinks that he knows how he handles some given kind of problem, to the point that he will argue at length about the matter, this still may not be the case.

Even when the concepts a person has learned about personality have come to him from his broader cultural background, he may not know what concepts he has absorbed. Many different sources have contributed to our present "everyday" concepts about personality. The great literary figures of the past—Shakespeare, Victor Hugo, Dickens, Tolstoi and Mark Twain, for example, not to mention a huge number of others—have made innumerable contributions to our deeper understanding of human nature. Such philosophers and political thinkers as Voltaire, Locke, Rousseau, Thomas Jefferson, Marx, Emerson, Thoreau, and Spengler have developed our ideas greatly. The same could be said for many great religious thinkers and for many educational reformers such as Comenius, Froebel, and Madame Montessori. Our "everyday" thought, therefore, is an exceedingly complex pattern, with many different things woven into it. No one of us has had a chance to make all of this his own. But we have been exposed to many different bits of thought that trace back to different parts of our cultural heritage, and we think about personality in complex ways partly because of all of this rich development of human thought.

The complexity of this cultural heritage accounts partially for the fact that different persons in everyday life certainly have different concepts about personality and certainly deal with personality in different ways. Consequently, when we ask, "What are our everyday concepts about personality?" the question to be asked in return is, "Whose everyday concepts are you asking about?" There is such a diversity among people of different cultural and religious backgrounds, and among different individuals in the same society, that it is very difficult to get a representative picture of everyday concepts about personality.

The difficulty is not only that individuals differ from one another; they differ within themselves—any given person is apt to have more or less different concepts about personality in different relationships in his life. A mother may act a great deal more sympathetically and tolerantly toward her sons than toward her daughters. She may have grown up with a feeling that other girls were generally able to surpass her in good looks and general appeal. And, even though she does not know that she is doing this, she may still tend to see her daughters as competitors and not in the way she sees her sons. Or the mother may be able to identify with her daughters in a way that is impossible for her with reference to her sons and be much more sympathetic and patient with them. There is a great deal of special coloring in the way we deal with personality. At best, therefore, this chapter can give only a very rough characterization of some of our tendencies in interpreting personality in everyday life.

We, the authors of this book, freely admit that, having an ax to grind, we are likely to emphasize some of the *deficient* aspects of everyday thought concerning personality. After all, the authors of a book like this are naturally interested in those considerations which argue that everyday thought needs to be overhauled rather drastically in the light of relatively technical concepts. You are warned, therefore, that you ought to watch out for this bias and keep your fingers crossed when you read the rest of the chapter. You may conclude that we are not giving sufficient credit to the sort of understanding of personality that we tend to use in everyday life. But, on the other hand, even if we are painting the picture blacker than we should, you may find that we are pointing to some very important deficiencies in our everyday thinking about personality.

Some examples of "everyday concepts" at work

One of the best ways of discovering what concepts a person has is to put him face-to-face with some especially difficult problems while you watch to see what guiding ideas he tends to use in his efforts to solve them. The two following quotations describe persons whose life circumstances had put them up against real difficulties. As you read what they did, ask yourself what their guiding ideas were.

The first example comes from the life of the well-known American painter and maker of woodcuts, Rockwell Kent. During the depression of the 1930's, he and his wife had bought a farm, but they had no adequate income from it. Some of what happened during this period is told in the following portion from Rockwell Kent's autobiography, *This Is My Own:*[1]

And so it was that when our friend, Dr. Merrill Moore, who, as psychologist and poet, knows profoundly much about the human mind, told us that we could do a lot for his recuperating patients, we, knowing how very much he knew, became so enormously pleased with ourselves that we said, of course, at so much per, we'd take 'em. And one by one up to the sum of five they came. We liked them. Some were kindred souls. They felt at home.

I don't think that either Frances or I incline to meddle with the lives of others. She with her placid brow and wide-spaced open eyes looks out at people and the world with such unquestioning, warm, and friendly acceptance of the much that pleases her—the *good,* a moralist might say—that, as one well pleased with life, she'd have no wish or thought to pry behind the scenes. And I? I guess I just don't care enough. Let people—what they were, do, have done, want to do, what inhibits them, what doesn't, their psyche, ego, libido—let people be. We two, I think, agreed on that. At any rate, now 1936 is past, we do.

We lived that summer as it were between an upper millstone which was the external world—the mountains and beyond—and a nether one which was the vortex of unbalanced minds turned in upon themselves. The outer world was ours: we felt, and shared to some extent, its troubles. The inner one with which we would normally have been to no degree involved drew us, sucked us in, as whirlpools suck into their vacuums all floating things that come their way. Its troubles, which were not our own, we had to share. And through them recognize—we had to and we did—how near the sanest of us are to being batty. From this recognition, or perhaps from its corollary—our failure to perceive that much was wrong with them—came all the good, if any, that we did our patients. The midnight hours we spent discussing "problems" were

[1]Rockwell Kent, *This Is My Own* (New York, Duell, Sloan & Pearce, Inc., 1940), pp. 265-267.

a waste, and failed completely, always, to effect a cure. Problems, to normal minds, crave a solution. And minds not normal crave the problem. It often seemed to us that patients would exert their minds, good minds, *against* the trend of common sense and reason, lest these destroy for them their normal tortured status quo. Think and *decide;* stop thinking; *act;* there lay the cure. Whether the motive was to stay uncured or just from sloth or fear to keep from acting, the patient would resort to the most specious argument to leave things undecided. . . .

If the issues involved had been to any small degree impersonal we might not, as the months advanced, have felt so fed up with practitioning. They weren't. And, let me tell you, when you've sat up night after night, discussing a man's woman problem, which of two women—equally grand, of course, or one very noble and the other very seductive, or neither very much but equal—which of two equal quantities to choose, and, with your wife wilting before your eyes from sheer exhaustion of the mind and heart, have at last won your patient to a choice by lot, and have drawn lots, and have shaken his hand in congratulations on the choice, and have wished him a happy life and pleasant dreams tonight and evermore, and have seen him, beaming with a newfound happiness, to bed—when, after all this happy ending, you see him come in haggard from a sleepless night to breakfast and hear him say to you: "Now on the other hand"—you mentally throw up the sponge. You're through.

This suggests a number of points immediately. Before we attempt to analyze them, we shall add a second example written by a young woman in training for work with children in nursery schools. It tells of the problems that she and the other workers had with a young child who unquestionably was more severely maladjusted than were most of the children with whom they were working. What she reported is quoted by Dorothy Baruch, as follows:[2]

John was four years and three months old on entrance to nursery school. No health problems were evident. His mother, however, reported extreme constipation. His appearance was attractive. He had dark hair, blue eyes, and a round button nose. He was of sturdy build with some evidence of fatigue posture.

John had various problem manifestations. He refused food, disturbed the nap room, and objected to all routine. He kicked, spit, and slapped smaller children without provocation. At the same time, however, he was unable to defend himself or his rights when children of his own size approached him. He would become hysterical when his rights to a toy were challenged but

[2]Dorothy W. Baruch, "Procedures in Training Teachers to Prevent and Reduce Mental Hygiene Problems," *Journal of Genetic Psychology,* Vol. 67 (1945), pp. 143-178.

would make no attempt to regain the article. In the yard, he urinated and defecated. He was curious yet furtive about sex. Use of abusive terms was a favorite device to annoy the teachers and children. . . .

Since no parent contacts were made, it was assumed that he was an indulged, "spoiled" child and that all he needed was to learn to accept authority. Accordingly when he refused food and created a disturbance at meal time he was denied dessert and was moved to a "baby table" where he was punished by being made to wear a bib. Only when he would promise "to be good" and "to eat all his dinner" was he allowed to return.

At nap time when he shouted and annoyed the other children, the teacher would place her hand over his mouth and would say, "If you can't keep your mouth quiet, I'll have to hold it for you." If he thrashed around on the bed, he was turned on his stomach and a blanket was wrapped tightly around him so as to pinion his arms to his sides. The teacher would then forcibly hold him down until he lay still.

He was shaken for hitting children, was told he was "naughty to them" and was "benched" in isolation in order "to think about behaving nicely instead."

His interest in exploring his own body was ignored and avoided. The general policy was to see that he was kept busy so that he would "forget" such activities. When he urinated or defecated in the yard, he was made to clean up, was told that what he had done was "not nice" and was seriously advised to use the toilet.

When he used abusive terms, he was told to stop such "horrid" language. Several times, in addition, his mouth was washed out with soap.

Fairly strong methods were used with this child. But they did not solve the child's problems. If anything, they made the problems more intense. Later, when the teachers working with the child were led to make a different approach, it was possible to help the child clear up his difficulties. But, before that, when they failed to get good results, they did not change their methods or their basic theory about how to proceed; they merely intensified their efforts.

These are merely two examples, of course, and, as we have said earlier, they certainly do not reflect the full range of concepts about personality we tend to use in our everyday life. However, these examples and many other observations of our everyday behavior indicate certain major beliefs that seem to show up as our everyday concepts about personality. These major concepts seem to be the following:

1. *We tend to take personality problems as they look on the surface instead of realizing that we may have to look for indirect origins of the effects we see.* The teachers who were responsible for Johnny, for example, did not ask whether something else, something really different from what his behavior seemed to indicate, lay back of the obnoxious,

troublesome behavior they were out to change. They took each of his troublesome tendencies as a specific, directly expressed habit—something to be worked on as such. They did not ask whether perhaps he had some underlying problem of craving for affection or of being confused and afraid about some aspects of life. If they had, they might have thought about exploring some techniques of dealing with him quite different from those they used. But such questions simply did not occur to them. It was simpler for them to take each symptom at face value and to try to work with it as though it had a direct origin uncomplicated by anything else.

You probably have seen this same thing many times. How often, for example, have you heard people say something like this? "He boasts so much that he's unbearable; what he needs is for someone to take him down a few pegs!" But the usual fact is that a lot of people *have* tried, over and over, to take him down a few pegs—the real difficulty is that he has met discouragement and rejection too frequently in his life; he is acting on the notion that he cannot win the respect and affection of others except by boasting.

In the same way, people tend to take their own personality problems too much at face value, too. The following case is a good example of this. It was written by Jean, a girl who had been asked to give the same sort of account of her own personality that Ann and Beatrice had given.

When I was two years old, Mother wrote down a prayer I prayed one night when I didn't want to say the usual "Now I lay me . . ." At the end of the prayer, I said, "And please, God, let me grow up to be a beautiful lady." . . .

My relatively happy babyhood came to an end about the time I was nine years old. It was then that I became conscious of my freckles. They loomed as large in my eyes as moles, and I might as well have had a severe case of pimples. I cried myself to sleep many nights, and often cried during the day as well. Schoolmates were characteristically unkind; and, even in college, boys tease me about my freckles.

Then I began to get fat! The climax came the day when I sought Mother in a Ladies' Aid meeting, and one of the pillars of the church patted my stomach and said cheerfully (how could she!), "My, Jean, you *are* getting fat!" . . .

Thus all my hope of being a "beautiful lady" crashed . . . My freckles were bad, but I wasn't really fat in high school. I became accustomed to think of myself as fat, though, and I could not get it out of my head. I saw myself as fat.

In high school I began to realize that I did have beautiful hair, and I didn't feel so horrid-looking because I always had at least one boy who seemed to like me especially and for whom I felt affection. But now that I'm a junior in college, I'm old stuff, and the fellows I'd like to go with prefer the freshman girls. The carefully nurtured feeling of the last four years that I was really attractive has been completely blasted. Even my hair is no comfort now because I saw a play in which a homely girl remarks, "They always tell a homely girl she has beautiful hair."

. . . I try to make believe I'm attractive. When I am not in front of a mirror, I can pretend very well. Not many people know, however, that after an evening of pretending to be beautiful I look into the mirror and have to fight back the tears. I have quit crying except inside, but it hurts just the same and I don't get the relief I used to get . . . I find myself looking down on everyone who acts as though he likes me. I feel that any fellow who takes me out must have first been turned down by some girl who matters. Often I have liked a boy until he began to date me, and then I disliked him distinctly. I know that I have my good points, but I have gotten fatter since I've been in college, and that has become the dominant fact in my consciousness. My mother is very large, and I don't want to be.

This year I have been able to keep myself out of the terrible moods I suffered last year. The only way I can do this is by looking in the mirror as little as possible and, and when I do, to look at my eyes—and pretend the rest of the time.

I think that if I can get some passionate interest in some work or cause I can become less egocentric and think less of myself. I used to have the hope that I would be beautiful when I grew up. Now that I am grown up I have lost that hope. My only hope now is in becoming absorbed in something worthwhile outside of myself, so that I will forget that I ever longed to be beautiful, and never can be.

This girl felt that she had some sufficient causes for her rather strong emotional reactions. She felt she knew what these causes were, and that her reaction could be traced to them. Actually, however, there must have been some other origins for her reactions. For one thing, Jean had no idea as to why it meant so much to her to be a "beautiful lady," and why she had been unable to shift to some other goal when she became convinced that this first objective could not be reached. For another thing, the truth of the matter was that, actually, Jean was counted a rather unusually attractive girl. It was true that she had a few freckles; but her hair was, in truth, a beautiful chestnut brown, and her few freckles were not unbecoming. She was not heavier than she should have been. Most college girls would probably have been quite willing to exchange their appearance for hers or their chances for boy friends with hers. Not only is it true, therefore, that not many people knew how often she wept over this matter of her appearance, as Jean said, but also most people would not have believed it possible that she would do this.

Many of us have had an experience something like this. We have had reactions which we thought we understood. We felt sure that our reaction to the situation was justified by the realities we experienced. But other persons, with a better perspective or more objective viewpoint, could easily see—once they knew the facts about our reactions—that we must be reacting on the basis of some problems other than those we were conscious of. With our own problems, therefore, as well as with the problems of others, we tend too much to take them directly at face value.

2. *In our everyday thinking we have too much faith that the main processes of personality are conscious processes.* The idea that the main processes in a person's life are conscious processes is a rather understandable hypothesis for us to have. We all know, as truly as we know anything, that we do a great many things consciously. We realize that we may perform some minor actions in an absent-minded way, unconscious of what we are doing. But it seems to our everyday thought that when things really are deeply important to us we always work with clear consciousness of what is going on.

This is part of the reason why we tend to take personality problems at face value. It is part of the reason, for example, why Rockwell Kent and his wife spent hours and hours trying to help their boarder "patients" analyze their ostensible problems. Thus, the Kents might have said, "Well, if these people have some tough problems, wouldn't they be conscious of them? Since they have confidence in us, as they seem to have, won't they come straight out and discuss them with us? Maybe they are naturally hesitant until they get to know us well, but surely these people know what questions they would like to solve in some better way!" Rockwell Kent was baffled because his heroic efforts did not seem to do any good, but it hardly occurred to him that the problems these patients thought were real problems were not the main problems with which they were wrestling.

Another expression of this emphasis on consciousness was given by a physician who was asked about the methods used in lancing the eardrums of children with middle ear infections or earaches. He was asked whether lancing the tympanic membrane was painful to the child and, if so, whether anesthetics were used to guard against the pain. The physician answered that care was used to give a good local anesthesia with adults, because it was a fairly painful incision. But with babies, he said, this was not stressed so much "because, after all, it is only a momentary thing and the baby can't remember it afterwards."

He was assuming, of course, that the experience would have no later effects on the baby because there would be no ability in later years to remember *consciously* the ear operation. Of course, when we stop to think about it, we realize that an ability consciously to remember the incident whereby something was learned is not a necessary condition for the formation and later use of some habit. You cannot now tell anything, for instance, about the particular experiences by which you learned to spell most of the words you know; but those past learning experiences left you with fairly permanent memories of how to spell. We can realize that the same logic probably applies to the effect on a baby of having its ear lanced. But we tend not to stop and think of such things; in our everyday thought it seems fairly reasonable to say that experiences which are not consciously remembered probably have not left any important effects.

3. *We have a great deal of faith in the rationalistic tradition—that is, a great confidence in reasoning when trying to change ourselves or others.* We feel that people—especially if they are intelligent—should be able to listen effectively to clear-cut arguments, should be able to utilize clear-cut evidence, and should be able to adapt their feelings and behavior accordingly. Or, if all of the evidence we have gives no method of deciding that one alternative is better than another, we say that people should be able to grant this and not continue to debate the merits of such alternatives, but should settle the issue by drawing straws or tossing a coin or letting any little minor factor decide. Rockwell Kent proceeded on this assumption. It is as if he reasoned: "Here are persons of high intellectual ability. They can think clearly enough on many things. If we reason with them, we can help them solve these problems too." But, the Kents finally concluded, "The midnight hours we spent discussing 'problems' were a waste and failed completely to effect a cure."

We can see that certain things would be *reasonable* for people to do, but they don't always behave in accordance with what seems to us to be eminently sensible. Consider the young man of whom a college faculty member complains as follows:

I can't understand Harold—he seems unable to complete the writing of his Ph.D. thesis. He was well recommended by the staff of the graduate school from which he came. He has a very high level of ability. Why does he keep on postponing the completion of his thesis? He has all of the data gathered and could easily work on it. He is willing to take almost any amount of time to help others with their problems. But he can't seem to get to work to complete his own project.

This is Harold's first teaching job, and it is important for him to make a good record here. We have told him that we feel it is important for him to finish that last portion of his graduate work because we want to develop a doctoral program of our own. But several years have passed now. He works hard on other things, but he won't work on what we tell him is his most important responsibility.

A person like this tends to baffle us. Rationality dictates a course of action that is as plain as day. We feel sure that when the person sees the facts, he will act accordingly, proceeding in the way that obviously would serve his interests and is clearly within his intellectual capacity. When he doesn't act this way, we try to reason with him all over again, just as the nursery school teachers tended to reason with Johnny. "Man is basically a rational creature" is our motto, so how else should we proceed except by pointing out the various rational considerations involved!

4. *We have an unwarranted amount of faith in verbal means of changing personality.* The two following examples illustrate our very general assumption that verbal exhortations can change emotional habits.

Betty looked solemnly up out of her five-year-old eyes at her father. "Look, Honey," the father pleaded, "you have just got to stop scratching that place on your cheek. It's making another scar that you will have all of your life. Do you want to grow up with scars all over your face? Well, that's just what will happen unless you quit this habit."

Betty promised that she would stop right away, just as she had promised to do on countless similar occasions. The father's next inspection of Betty's face showed exactly the same discouraging results that he had come by now to expect, but this little scene was repeated many times during some three years without in any way affecting the habit.

"Children," warned the father, "remember what happened on Mother's Day when we opened presents. This is Mother's birthday and things have got to be different. Before she comes downstairs we're going to have a little conference. Remember how excited all of you got when Mother opened her presents? All of you yelled and jumped around and insisted on 'helping' her open things and just generally raised such a rumpus it nearly spoiled everything.

"Ellen, you're nearly seven, and Jean, you're five. You two at least ought to be able to behave. Johnny is too little to understand, but you two, you *must* remember this is Mom's birthday and not yours. Promise you won't spoil things!"

The net effect of this verbal conference was not noticeable to this man's wife. At the end of the birthday celebrations, she was limp and frazzled. The children behaved in exactly the same way they had on the earlier occasion.

We certainly have many experiences that encourage us to attempt to deal with personality problems by such verbal exhortations. We have many experiences that demonstrate, beyond any doubt, that we can change the behavior of people in some situations by verbal means. Thus, if a stranger asks you how to get to the post office, you don't need to take him by the arm and lead him there. It is sufficient to use verbal symbols to indicate the route that he should follow. If a student does not understand some problem in economics or history or physics, a careful verbal presentation will usually be sufficient to help him understand and accept some concepts and ways of acting that he did not possess previously. We have abundant evidence, therefore, that verbal communications are powerful means of influencing other persons. It is not surprising that, in everyday life, we tend to place a great deal of reliance on verbal appeals as a means of influencing the personalities of other persons.

Actually, however, we could realize, even just on the basis of everyday experience, that there are many things that verbal communications cannot accomplish. All of us know that you cannot teach another person to swim merely by telling him how to swim—we know there is no substitute for his getting into the water and learning through concrete experience with different strokes. We know there is no way for a person to learn to like some new food except by eating it. We know that there is no way for a person to become a skillful writer except by practicing writing. Consequently, even on the basis of our everyday knowledge alone, we ought to be skeptical about the hypothesis that we can do very much for another person in matters of personality just by telling him how he ought to respond. Our everyday thought, however, gives us little reason for distinguishing between those situations where verbal communications are effective and those other situations where they are relatively ineffective. And because most of our life gives testimony to the efficacy of talking, we assume that this same technique will be sufficiently useful for dealing with problems of personality.

5. *In everyday thinking, we put too much faith in punishment and threats of punishment as means of bringing improvements in behavior.* When we see some conduct we regard as objectionable, we assume that it can be corrected by inflicting or threatening some form of punishment. We figure that the person needs to be shown what unpleasant consequence will follow if he keeps on with his habits. Once he understands this, we feel sure, he will take it into account and change his behavior

accordingly. These are the reasons Johnny was scolded for some of his actions, made to sit with a bib when he was careless with his food, made to clean up the mess when he urinated or defecated in the yard, and had his mouth washed with soap when he used naughty language.

There are some powerful psychological forces behind our proneness to rely on punishment, and it would be good if we could understand them better. This tendency proves destructive when applied ruthlessly in cases of severe personality problems. It has often been ruinous in our handling of social and international affairs.

Today it is recognized that this punishment psychology has not worked in some areas. We no longer lock up, beat, or torture the insane to improve them. But in many, many aspects of life we still tend to rely on punishment and do not attempt the longer-range thinking that would be required for constructive positive approaches to human problems.

6. *We have considerable confidence in the value of putting the individual through the actual motions of what we wish he would do.* This is a policy based on a kind of "externalistic" psychology that we use a lot. Somehow, we think, we can drill the necessary changes in behavior into the person if we make sure that he goes through the proper external motions. This is seen in the case of Johnny. When his teachers wanted him to learn new habits, he was put through the outward motions that a person having such habits would show. Thus, when he tossed around too much at nap time, he was held tightly restrained until he would be quiet; when he shouted too much the teacher held her hand over his mouth and told him that, if he could not keep quiet himself, she would have to help him do so. In the same way, we often insist that a small child must say "please" before he is given something and that he must say "thank you" or suffer the penalty of having the thing taken away from him.

As parents, we tend to use this bit of psychology particularly with feeding problems. We want the child to eat heartily so he will grow strong and healthy. If he doesn't eat readily, we make him finish his plate. It is as if we were saying to ourselves: "He needs to learn to eat. The way to help him do this is to put him through the right external motions. Make him get the food in his mouth, swallow it, make him do this until his plate is clean. If he goes through the outward motions of doing what we want him to do, he will experience inwardly what it means to eat heartily and thus learn to be a good eater."

We are astonished when we often produce, by such methods, children who become and remain major feeding problems. We are mystified, too, when our neighbor who has invited our child for lunch exclaims about how much and how well he ate.

An extension of this external-motion psychology is the idea that the person must not only be put through the right motions but be made to *repeat* these over and over. As a familiar example, most of us as school children have been victims of this external-motions-plus-repetition belief, or have seen other children made to write a persistently misspelled word fifty times on the blackboard. The fact that the offending word is typically still spelled in the same old way after this treatment does not seem to lessen our confidence in the technique. We are likely to conclude that some evil impulse in the heart of the child is behind it all and that the way to stamp it out is to make him write the word a hundred times!

7. *We tend to explain behavior by emphasizing the free will of the individual—except when we are acting on our faith in such simple external factors as punishment and repetition of desired overt behavior.* Somehow we do not hold with free will in every respect. Admittedly, our everyday thought is somewhat confused on these matters. Thus, we justify the punishment of criminals on the grounds that this will tend to discourage criminal actions. We recognize a causal influence of punishment. But, at the same time, we tend not to think about crowded slum areas as breeding places for delinquency and crime. In other words, we believe in cause and effect relations in some degree. But we tend to limit very greatly our conception of what causal roles operate in human life.

Part of the reason why we do not search more diligently for possible causes of human conduct is that we insist that a great deal can be accomplished by the spontaneous, uncaused choices of the person. Over and over, what we believe is virtually this: "This person, of course, could act in a different fashion if he would just *choose* to do so! It's will power that he lacks. He doesn't *need* to act that way. He's just making things hard for himself, and he ought to be able to see this and change his behavior accordingly." We might find, for example, that a problem child like Johnny has brothers and sisters who are much more stable and well behaved. In this situation, we tend to say, "That shows, doesn't it, that these things are under the free choice of the person. These children all had the same environment, didn't they? So it doesn't seem to be a matter of what 'causes' have been operating on them. It must be something within the child himself that makes the difference."

8. *We tend to see emotional responses as unfortunate and disrupting influences, as something to be minimized in human life.* To contrast human beings with other creatures, we have adopted for ourselves the species name *homo sapiens*—"wise man." A whole series of influences have inclined our thinking in this direction. In political life we are accustomed to thinking of the demagogue, like Hitler, as one who appeals to the "emotions" of people, and who could not possibly come to power unless the people allowed their "emotions" to interfere with their "reason." In the religious tradition, a contrast is drawn between a person's responsible, ethical conduct and the failures that result from his "emotions." Sometimes, of course, we qualify this and speak of the trouble

coming from the "base" emotions of the person. But generally we do not bother with such a qualification. We see the ordinary, well-controlled life of the person as governed chiefly by his "intelligence" or "reason," and we see his mistakes and misdeeds as coming from his "emotions." Our complex technology encourages this view; in a complex civilization we have to dovetail our efforts very neatly with one another, and this seems to presuppose a control of life by rational factors rather than by emotional factors. "Emotions" are things which produce wildcat strikes, race riots, panics, and "unnecessary" wars. So, we think, even though it is natural enough that small children often act emotionally, normally this is something that they should outgrow.

Everyday concepts cannot be all wrong—often, it appears, they really do work

In the cases with which we began this chapter—the one from Rockwell Kent and the case of Johnny—the concepts and techniques of everyday life failed dismally. This does not prove that they are altogether useless. It is worthwhile to think back to several of the cases mentioned in Chapter I, for example, that of Beatrice. You will remember that her parents believed in helping her go through the actual activities they wished to have her learn. Her mother helped her to bathe her doll and keep it clean and neat; the father took time to explain the family accounts to her and to help her make a budget of her own. We can see also that they depended on punishment somewhat, as in the incident where Beatrice was told that she could take the trip to town with her father if she got ready by a certain time, but then was left behind when she neglected to make the preparations they asked for. To cite still another point, they depended on rational appeals to their daughter when she had thrown sand in the eyes of the little girl whose mother worked for their family. The father talked to her in terms of the basic worth of all persons, regardless of the cost of their clothes, and of the way he hoped she would learn to value people for what was inside them, rather than for surface qualities.

We could multiply examples which would show some truth in the everyday notions we have examined above. To some extent we *are* conscious of our personality processes. To some extent we *can* affect our personality processes by rational thought. To some extent our key problems *are* revealed directly, and what appears on the surface *can*, indeed, be taken at face value. We *are* affected by rewards and punishments. We *do* acquire values sometimes by actually doing things, rather than by just deciding that we should do those things. When we make a strong effort of will, to some extent we *do* accomplish things that we would not accomplish with less effort. And, at least in some respects, there *are* emotional processes that can keep us from dealing with life situations as soundly as we might have done if we had been free from those particular emotional processes.

And yet, one difference seems to stand out between the story of Beatrice and the stories of Rockwell Kent and Johnny. Beatrice had a happy and secure personality. She already had a deep self-respect and a deep confidence in the affection of her parents. For example, when she was punished by being left at home after failing to prepare for the trip to town with her father, she seems to have used "discipline by natural consequences" in a constructive way although it involved a real disappointment. She already had strong identifications with both her mother and her father. When they suggested that she do things with them, such as working on budgets, she did not see this as something to rebel against in order to secure some independence from too much coercion, but as something that was delightful to do, partly because it meant doing the same things as the father whom she admired and liked so much.

It seems, therefore, that the different concepts marking our everyday thought are true at least within certain limits.

The need to replace partial truths with more adequate understandings

People used to say, for instance, that "the sun rises in the east." Now we know that they were "wrong." That is, we know that we may express the relation between the sun and the earth in this way, but that it is more economical and efficient for most purposes of astronomy to think of the apparent movement of the sun as due to a rotation of the earth. It is worth noting, however, that even though we adopt this more adequate conception, we still find it useful to keep the older mode of statement for certain purposes. We still find it convenient, for example, to say that the sun rises at different points on the horizon at different seasons. And, as a matter of fact, it is probably true that most people still think basically of the sun as moving, rather than the earth. When they see a "sunrise" or a "sunset," they see what those words naturally suggest. They have a "feel" that the sun moves—not a feel that a point on the surface of the earth moves toward the sun or away from the sun. They use the latter concept for certain purposes, but they do not have it thoroughly assimilated into their thinking.

Most people learned part of their astronomy before they could be told about Copernicus' discovery. They learned from their own direct observation, and they still continue that mode of thought, even though, logically speaking, they ought to replace it with one consistent mode of thinking. But the reason they tend not to do this is partly the fact that truths are rarely, if ever, whole truths, and that inadequate ideas rarely are entirely wrong. Usually a proposition is true within some limits of accuracy or within some limits of application. It is perhaps a 55 per cent truth. We cannot hope to replace it with any whole truth, but we can replace it with a 63 per cent truth or a 70 per cent truth.

Thus, it is not entirely wrong to say that the earth is flat. If you measure any fairly small part of the earth's surface, such as a small lake, you will find that, for all practical purposes, it is flat. Within the limits of rather accurate measurement, its flatness can be demonstrated. But, in a broader sense, it is important to see that it is not flat. Columbus never would have sailed out into the Atlantic if he had kept on believing this particular partial truth. It is more satisfactory for us to have a comprehensive concept to help us understand why the limited area will *seem* to be flat even though it really is not. In the same way, even though many of the everyday concepts about personality are true *within certain limits*, or under certain unstated conditions, it perhaps is important for us to replace them with more adequate and comprehensive ideas. At the same time we can expect that we surely will find later that these, too, are less complete than we had thought they were and that they will need to be replaced by still better concepts.

The inadequacy of everyday concepts

In our everyday way of thinking, there is a great tendency to stress merely the factors that are relatively tangible, relatively invariable in their effects, and relatively immediate in their influences. Perhaps all of this would be clearer if we used our knowledge of nutrition as an example. It did not take any modern research for mankind to learn that potatoes tasted like potatoes and not like turnips. These tastes were directly perceptible, relatively invariable, and relatively immediate. Nor did it take any scientific research to discover that a person felt more satisfied and would maintain his weight if he had a sufficient amount to eat, rather than inadequate amounts.

Not until recently, however, was it apparent that diet must include a lot of fairly specific materials. Take the matter of our body's need for slight supplies of iodine. Gordon Seagrave, in his autobiographical *Burma Surgeon,* has told that when he visited mountainous areas between Burma and China, he found large numbers of the Chinese peasants with greatly overdeveloped thyroid glands—masses of tissue the size of small hams hanging from their necks. This was no mystery to him because he knew that where the iodine has been almost entirely washed out of the soil and is inadequately provided by the food of the region, the thyroid gland overdevelops in an attempt to provide sufficient thyroid secretion. Though the abnormality was quite tangible and quite burdensome to the natives, they could not see wherein their ideas about nutrition were merely partial truths. The underlying factors responsible for the goiters were too intangible.

In the same way, our everyday thought perhaps fails to recognize many of the less readily perceptible influences that affect our personalities. It is difficult for parents to realize, for instance, how much their children can be influenced by the tendency children have to *identify* with their parents—to imitate them merely through the desire to be like them. This may have been the chief factor in Beatrice's favorable personality development, rather than the specific things her parents did in trying to handle particular problems that arose. It is difficult for parents to realize how much influence is exerted by the little signs that let the child know the parents have a deep respect and affection for him or, contrariwise, an underlying hostility and rejection. Perhaps it doesn't matter so much whether the parents typically make sacrifices for children and treat them generously—perhaps it is a matter of the background realities of parental attitude that a child can sense and respond to.

These subtle influences are hard to see, however, just as the curvature of the surface of a lake is hard to demonstrate, or just as the presence or absence of iodine in the diet is hard to detect. We have to appeal to much broader areas of observation or resort to much finer techniques of study before we can learn about such things and take advantage of them. But to achieve many important goals we have to learn about such things. Subtle, intangible factors can often produce more important tangible results than most of the more tangible influences can produce.

The need for resourceful techniques

To some extent, dealing with any set of problems is not merely a task of *understanding* them. At least, it is not a task of understanding them merely in terms of factors already operating with reference to them. It is also a task of invention—a task of developing new tools and new techniques by means of which more satisfactory results can be achieved.

Farmers, for instance, had long worried about the excessive erosion that occurred in some regions and about the inadequate rainfall in other areas (not to mention the existence of both problems in some places where the rains, when they did come, tended to come in torrents of short duration). The farmers were deeply concerned over these problems, but still it seemed to them that the one proper way to plow their fields and plant their crops was in good straight lines. It might have occurred to them that this was almost a cordial invitation for a too-rapid runoff of the water. Expensive machinery was not needed in order to plow along the contours of the hills, or to introduce slight terracing at intervals along the hillsides, or to provide occasional strips of sod. But a lot of good topsoil of the United States had to be lost before these procedures were invented and added to the common-sense know-how of farmers.

In our everyday thought about personality, it may be that we have a knowledge of tools and techniques that work rather well when they are used under favorable conditions, just as plowing with straight furrows introduces no problems under some conditions. But we may be hampered by the lack of inventions which are suited for less favorable conditions. We have reason to be curious about technical workers, therefore, not merely as ones from whom we might get a better understanding of cause-and-effect relationships, but also as toolmakers. It is worth asking whether they have some devices and techniques which are useful for ordinary persons too.

As we saw in the previous chapter, it makes a lot of difference to us whether we handle personality problems successfully or not. We have been given material with fine potentialities. But there is nothing to guarantee, in any given case, that these fine potentialities will be realized. Our everyday thought does not seem to provide us with a sufficient understanding, even though it contains some partial insights. It becomes very important for us, therefore, to ask whether the people who have devoted themselves professionally to the study of personality have any additional insights. Do they recommend any drastic modifications of our everyday views that we ought to investigate? In the three following chapters we turn to an introductory survey of three such scientific areas of work.

First of all we shall turn to the psychotherapists. They are the oldest of the professional groups who have necessarily attempted to deal with personality in all of its complexity. They are the ones who had to keep dealing with such men and women as Rockwell Kent and his wife were trying to help. The psychotherapists did not decide that "henceforth we'll have nothing to do with people who crave problems rather than solutions." Instead they had to try to find wherein our everyday concepts were inadequate; they sought ways of supplementing and correcting those everyday notions. What they say may definitely be worth our attention.

Summary

All of us have to be psychologists, at least in one sense of the word, because all of us are deeply interested in matters of personality in ourselves and others. All of us have to deal in highly responsible ways with questions of personality even if we protest that we know nothing about such matters and try not to accept any such responsibility. This does not mean that we usually have explicitly formulated concepts. Our routine concepts about personality are usually like the small child's concepts of language—something that must be inferred from the way we act. Sometimes, in fact, when we have explicitly-stated concepts, these are just window trimming. They are not the concepts that we use in real life. Sometimes we use different concepts in different parts of our daily social relationships.

Our common thinking about personality, as we find it today, has been enormously enriched by contributions from many different sources—literature, philosophy, education, and religion, as well as various areas of practical experience. Our everyday thought contains many different strands, therefore, and takes many different forms in different persons.

As can be seen in a number of concrete cases, however, there are certain deficiencies that tend to occur over and over in popular thought about personality. For example, we tend to take personality problems too much at face value. We have too much faith that the main processes of personality are always *conscious* processes. We have too much confidence in reasoning and in verbal appeals as methods of changing personality. We have undue faith in punishment as a means of control and change. We have too much faith in the value of "putting the individual through the right motions," rather than thinking in terms of the processes that are going on within the person. We have too much confidence in free will. And we tend too much, perhaps, to see emotional processes as disruptive and hampering, rather than seeing them as indispensable constructive influences as well.

We have to realize, however, that people who act without scientific concepts are nevertheless sometimes remarkably successful at dealing with personality. For example, some parents with no technical knowledge of personality concepts have helped their children to develop personalities that are perhaps just as fine as the world will ever see. Such people, however, are producing these results partly through the influence of the example of their own personalities. These people also may be effective because they have formed and used some concepts about personality which are inadequately represented in our *common* thought about personality. And they may be effective also because of the fact that even the common everyday concepts are not all wrong, but are partial truths that have valuable applications under limited conditions such as may be found, for instance, in homes where most of the development is proceeding happily and successfully.

Everyday concepts, however, tend to be unnecessarily inadequate because of their failure to recognize anything except relatively tangible factors and because of their lack of tools and techniques for handling a wide range of problems of personality. It becomes fairly important for us, therefore, to try to learn what the various groups of scientific workers have been learning and to see whether some of their concepts may not be helpfully absorbed in our everyday way of looking at personality. Our next chapter turns to the work of psychotherapists as perhaps a natural place to begin the study of the various kinds of relatively technical work in personality.

Part II

MAIN SOURCES FOR A BETTER UNDERSTANDING OF PERSONALITY

CHAPTER 3

Psychotherapy as a Source of Understanding of Personality

IN OUR EVERYDAY LIFE we do not ordinarily speak very frankly or openly to one another about ourselves. For example, there were students who knew Ann (Chapter 1) as a rather quiet and reserved person, perhaps a little bit on the self-conscious side. But she had never felt free to talk to any of them about the things she wrote in her autobiographical sketch, things she knew full well about herself. The same is true of the much happier life experience of Beatrice.

Much of our lives is covered by conventional veneer. We usually talk of relatively impersonal and external things—what we think about this or that other person, what we have seen in this or that book or movie, what the chances are that such and such a team will win. But what is really close to our hearts, and what we would perhaps like to discuss with some others, we rarely feel we can bring into the open. Even persons who have "known each other for years and years" usually do not know each other very deeply. Parents as a rule do not know a great deal about what goes on in the minds of their children, and children usually do not know a great deal about what goes on in the minds of their brothers and sisters and parents. As a result, on the basis of our daily contacts, what we know about personality is not likely to penetrate very deeply. We see only the outer portion of the personality of another person—only the part that the person probably exhibits with effort in order to resemble as much as possible the outsides of the lives of the people he sees most.

Sometimes, of course, we know a few persons in a really close and intimate way. But we rarely know more than a few persons in that fashion. We could not possibly know many persons closely. Furthermore, we tend to spend a lot of time only with those persons with whom we already have a lot in common.

The psychotherapist, however, is in a different and very special situation. He is trying to help people who have problems that are far too tangled, usually, to be solved in any simple and easy way. If he is to help such persons, he has to spend a lot of time with them. He has to listen patiently and at length to what they have to say. He has to get to know them with a thoroughness that goes far beyond the kind of knowledge we ever ordinarily possess about other persons. In some types of therapy, for example, the therapist would not regard it as unusual to spend an hour a day with each patient, three or four days a week, for a year or more. Perhaps never in any previous period of history have any professional workers shown such patience listening to one person talk about himself!

The therapeutic situation encourages the maladjusted person to talk honestly and frankly about himself. He has powerful reasons to get away from the superficial expressions of himself that mark his other social relationships. He has powerful reasons for wanting to be as accurate and complete in his self-revelations as he can be.

The psychotherapist has another advantage. He does not get to know merely a few persons in this intensive way; he comes to know many of them. Furthermore, he often gets to know people who have family backgrounds and social backgrounds drastically different from his own. He gets to know people whose basic outlooks on life are markedly different from those that he might have taken for granted. He has access to material, therefore, which is highly instructive to a student of personality.

Consequently, one of the contributions that has come from psychotherapists is a wealth of concrete descriptive material regarding personality. Their case histories provide the rest of us with a kind of material that we hardly can get from our own experience. The therapists are like geologists who go into all sorts of out-of-the-way places to study volcanoes, lava fields, sand-blown deserts, and oil-well drillings. Most of us cannot make such field studies. But we can get a much more adequate knowledge through the opportunity to examine the photographs and charts and specimens of rock that the geologists assemble out of their wide concrete observation. In selecting the case studies presented in this chapter, one of the purposes the authors have had in mind is to provide such rich descriptive material regarding personality. Even if on no other count, therapeutic records would be valuable on this score.

Psychotherapy as a field of developing and testing theories about personality

The therapist is more than merely a gatherer of concrete descriptive data. He tries to help people make changes in their personalities. Consequently he has to proceed in what is roughly, at least, an experimental way. He has to construct hypotheses as to what methods and what influences will produce favorable results in his patients or clients. He has to try out these methods, rather than merely theorize about them, because only by actually trying them out can he have any hope of accomplishing his purpose as a therapist. He has to see whether the methods that seemed helpful with one individual, with one sort of personality difficulty, also seem helpful with other persons who have somewhat different difficulties.

When the therapist thus tests different hypotheses, he does so under extremely complex circumstances. His work in no way resembles neat laboratory experiments. In a laboratory, situations are artificially controlled so that the influence of special factors may be more clearly demonstrated. In the work of the psychotherapist there is no such simplicity, of course. He has to take the powerful, dramatic material provided by people who are immersed in painful personality troubles and disturbances and try to work with that. It is difficult for him to judge whether this particular person, with whom he tries one thing, is essentially like another person, with whom he tries something else. And yet, there is something of the character of laboratory experimentation in the therapist's work because he does not have to wait for outside influences to operate in order to observe their effects; he can deliberately try out different influences to see what effects they seem to create. To facilitate his work, it is inevitable, too, that the therapist try to generalize his observations into adequate theoretical principles regarding personality difficulties and processes of therapy.

Compared with most other workers, psychotherapists have had much more contact with personality; hence it is they who have formulated most of our present scientific principles regarding personality. This situation will probably not continue indefinitely. In much the same way, practicing physicians first developed most of our concepts and hypotheses about the structure and functions of the body. But, as such work developed, much of the research came to be the responsibility of other specialized workers, including embryologists, histologists, neurologists, geneticists, and endocrinologists. The field in which the explorations started and in which the pioneer hypotheses were framed was not the field in which the main development of physiological knowledge continued to occur. In the same way, the work of the psychotherapists increasingly is being supplemented by work in other areas, and such other areas may come, in time, to be the main sources of our understanding of personality. Up to the present, however, it is doubtful whether such a shift has yet occurred, and consequently it is exceedingly important, in trying to get a better scientific understanding of personality, to ask how the psychotherapists work and what some of their resulting concepts are.

It must not be rashly assumed that psychotherapy is the situation in which most changes in personality are brought about. Furthermore, psychotherapists have come to be cautious about claiming that fundamental changes are often made by psychotherapy. We all know, on the other hand, that a young person may change a good deal between the freshman and senior years in college, or as a result of being placed in a new environment, or of undertaking new responsibilities, or of getting married, or of finding a new kind of work that proves exceedingly challenging.

Accordingly, when we use material from psychotherapy in the present chapter, we do not want to imply that psychotherapy is the only means or necessarily the most important means whereby changes in personality are brought about. But, even though there are significant changes of personality in ordinary life, psychologists and psychiatrists and sociologists have only begun to study them and to trace them to their causes. On the other hand, very good records are available on psychotherapeutic patients, because these patients pay good money to have experts work with them, listen to them, and keep records of their problems. We therefore have a valuable professional literature about psychotherapeutic observations and changes, but a serious shortage of observations of personality change in less formal situations. Hence the material we can draw upon comes mainly from psychotherapy, but this must not be interpreted to mean that personality never changes except when professional observation and treatment are provided. The world would be a very different place if the rule of no change without professional therapy prevailed.

How this chapter is organized

In this chapter we want to describe for you the methods of four main types of psychotherapy. The method that we shall discuss first is the simplest of the four. It is a rather straightforward counseling method—really much like the one that Rockwell Kent was trying to use, as summarized in the previous chapter. It depends a great deal more upon listening, however, and tries to make suggestions and give encouragement only after it has gone beyond the surface problems of the individual. The three other methods of psychotherapy that will be described are the psychoanalytic method, the nondirective method, and another method that might well be called that of complex interpretation, though at present it has no single accepted designation. Of these three last methods, it would be hard to say which is the most complex or the least complex. Probably the advocates of each of these last three methods would argue that their particular method is the most sophisticated and adequate of them all.

In describing these methods, it will not be wise for us to proceed in simple one-two-three order. We are interested also in getting some preliminary understanding of the kinds of phenomena that are revealed when these therapeutic methods are employed. Our discussion of methods will therefore be interwoven with a discussion of some of the main lessons that have come from psychotherapy.

We hardly need to emphasize that this discussion obviously cannot be more than a very simple introduction to this topic of methods and implications of psychotherapy. The whole area is highly complex, and there is a large and rapidly-growing technical literature devoted exclusively to it. But because the work in psychotherapy has been the source of so many of our scientific ideas about personality, an introduction to the material is important at this point.

Whose work are we describing when we speak of psychotherapy?

Perhaps, before proceeding to describe psychotherapy, we ought to say a word about the people who have been particularly important in this work, because their different backgrounds have helped to determine what concepts they developed.

The first scientific workers who occupied themselves with psychotherapy were physicians. They had some background for psychotherapy because their profession had been occupied to some extent with trying to understand and treat the various sorts of insanity or psychosis. This work had at first taken the form largely of efforts to find physiological causes and physiological methods of treatment for such disorders. But, nevertheless, familiarity with such cases had given physicians some background knowledge of personality.

Psychotherapy developed in medicine because some patients who were suffering only from personality problems went to doctors for treatment in the belief that their symptoms were physical in origin. These were generally people whom we now recognize as cases of *hysteria.* They were people who seemed to be suffering from genuine blindness or deafness, or who seemed to have lost the sense of feeling in some part of their bodies, or who were crippled by the loss of ability to move arms or legs. They were people, however, where the difficulties actually were only *psychological* in character, even though the symptoms were analogous to some real physical ills. Such patients went to physicians and neurologists because they felt sure that they were suffering from physical ills and that what they needed was regular medical treatment.

Another reason that psychotherapy originated in the medical field was that physicians were men whom people trusted as being wise, sincere, and skillful. People respected doctors for their professional attitudes toward their work. They trusted them to deal confidentially with matters of personal importance to patients. Furthermore, the physicians had had plenty of experience in other situations where they needed to try to give help even though they could not guarantee success. They were habituated to the task of trying to make sense out of difficult and baffling disorders. They were not experimentalists who would say: "This is much too complicated—we won't understand things like this for some decades, if then. Come back in fifty years!"

Social workers were in a somewhat similar situation. They were occupied, in the early days of their profession, with problems of financial and legal aid—helping families who needed what we now call relief, helping to arrange for medical care when this was required, and assisting immigrant families to understand their legal rights in a new world. They were occupied with relatively external matters, rather than with personality. But, as they dealt with such problems, social workers were driven more and more to thinking about personality problems, too. They might be working, for instance, with a family that was continually on relief. But didn't it seem more desirable to find, if possible, why the father of the family was a persistent alcoholic and hence unable to keep a job? Here was a boy convicted over and over again of delinquent acts. Wouldn't it be appropriate to try to learn why, and to try to help him change, rather than just to deal with him as a delinquent? Social workers had in many ways the same professional background and professional attitudes that physicians had.

For a long time, meanwhile, the psychologists looked upon themselves merely as experimentalists or research workers. They were trying to understand psychological processes in a careful, scientific way. Hence they tended to start with relatively simple phenomena which could be readily subjected to laboratory control. They read, sometimes with interest, about the work of the psychotherapists. Thus William James took an interest in the work of Pierre Janet in France. G. Stanley Hall took an interest in the work of Sigmund Freud and eventually arranged for him to come to the United States in 1909 and give a short series of lectures before a conference of American psychologists at Clark University in Massachusetts. But for the most part the psychologists proceeded on the conviction that they ought first to deal with simpler phenomena and leave the relatively complex material of personality to the efforts of applied workers in medicine and social work.

Ever since the appearance of psychology as a distinct profession in about 1880, however, the field of interest of psychologists has constantly expanded. The development of methods of research on relatively simple phenomena helped in the development of hypotheses regarding much more complex issues as well. It was inevitable, therefore, that psychologists sooner or later should come to include personality processes in their field of interest. It was inevitable that personality should become an important area of research.

What is more, psychologists were virtually forced to undertake some responsibilities in the field of psychotherapy. The psychologists constituted a group of professionally-trained men, familiar with personality processes, who could be drawn on to fill a growing need for psychotherapeutic help. The number of psychiatrists has always been severely limited because of practical reasons. A psychiatrist is a physician and must first obtain a regular medical degree before going through specialized training in psychiatry. This preparation is so expensive and so time-consuming that the number of psychiatrists was insufficient to meet the need as greater numbers of persons began to seek psychotherapeutic help as a consequence of their growing familiarity with such work. Many people therefore began to seek out psychologists with some such request as: "I suppose I ought to go to a psychiatrist, but there is no psychiatrist here. You're supposed to know something about psychological processes, and my doctors tell me that there's nothing wrong with me except something 'emotional' or 'psychological.' So, won't you try to help me?"

Sometimes these requests came from physicians. They knew that the children they were trying to treat, for example, had no organic or physiological difficulties, but they could see that personality difficulties were arising because of certain factors in the family situation. Or they knew that some of their adult patients were ill—even sometimes physically ill—because of emotional strains and complications. They therefore often said to psychologists: "This is a situation where you ought to be able to help."

In mental hospitals the requests for psychologists to enter psychotherapeutic work sometimes came from psychiatrists. "You know something about learning and about social influences on behavior," they said. "You ought to be able to contribute some new ways of thinking to this work. We need you." Sometimes they spoke in these words: "Our training in psychiatry was training from a long time back. It was training in diagnosis and classification. It was training in some of the physical methods of treatment. But we had our training before psychiatrists were being given much background in psychotherapy. We need your help, therefore."

The professional personnel of the therapeutic scene, therefore, has been enlarging as time has passed. It is likely to enlarge still further. Particularly it is likely that a large number of ministers will come to deal with people, not in the traditional ways of religious counseling, but with methods that borrow heavily from the insights and methods of psychotherapists, or that even directly duplicate such methods.

The fact that psychotherapy has been practiced by representatives of different professional fields has been definitely fruitful. The medical training of physicians gave them familiarity with physiological considerations. But physicians had little acquaintance with social or cultural factors and tended to miss seeing them. Social workers were trained to emphasize the very factors, however, that the medical people overlooked. Psychologists possessed still another background of knowledge, one more concerned with the ordinary processes of learning and thinking and perception within the individual. Because of this, they tended to emphasize certain things that neither of the other groups knew much about.

Today there is no one field, therefore, that alone is responsible for work in psychotherapy, and this is likely to be even more true as time goes on. This is fortunate, both practically and theoretically. The problems of personality and psychotherapy are complex. It is fortunate that a variety of backgrounds have been drawn upon to contribute to their solution.

Over and above differences in professional backgrounds, different psychotherapists also have different personalities themselves, and these affect their thinking and methods. This fact, too, is fortunate, because it has led to an exploration of many more different avenues of approach than would otherwise have been thought of.

It is the work of a very diverse group, therefore, that we will try to depict in this chapter.

The method of direct counseling

A psychotherapeutic method that is perhaps more simple and more closely related to common-sense modes of thought than the others is the method of direct counseling that is illustrated in the following case, taken from Caroline Zachry's book, *Personality Adjustments of School Children.*[1] This is a rather long case, but it is well worth the space that it requires. Not only is it a good example of the severe difficulties under which some children live and of the effects that can come from these, but it also is a good example of what can be accomplished, under favorable circumstances, by a relatively simple procedure—that is, by providing the maladjusted person with a sympathetic listener, by giving him correct information on various crucial matters, by pointing out to him how he might envisage his life in more serviceable terms, and by helping him to change his objective environment. Zachry presented this case as follows:

Jim is a member of the eleventh grade of a high school. He is a boy of unusual mental ability, and his school work has been successful throughout the grades. He has decided ability in several school subjects and is captain of his football team. In spite of this fact, he is literally terrified of people, is afraid to speak in class, and refuses to mingle with the students socially. He states that he is capable of bossing the boys on the football field but is afraid to stay with them as an equal when they change their clothes afterwards. The thought that he may receive recognition for his successes is painful to him. He was considered the best actor in the class and yet refused to take the prominent

[1]Caroline Zachry, *Personality Adjustments of School Children* (New York, Charles Scribner's Sons, 1929), pp. 214-227.

part that was offered him on a school program. He and another boy were nominated for a class office, and while they were out of the room during the election, he prayed that he might not get it because he felt so different from other people and wondered what they would think if they knew the truth about him. He is a fine-looking boy with good manners, who would draw people to him if it were not for his desire to keep them away. For two or three months before any help was given him he was convinced that he was losing his mind, and constantly asked the other boys on his team if they noticed anything queer in his behavior. He had been spending restless nights and crying out in his sleep.

The appointment for the first interview was made a day in advance, and Jim explained that he was not at all sure that he would be able to keep it. During the first talk he said that his family were very poor and that he had never had the home, clothes, etc., that his classmates had had. He continued to talk at some length about the tenement he lived in, the poverty of his childhood, and the fact that his father drank. In the middle of this story he broke down and said, "This is not what I came to tell you, but I am afraid that I am not going to be able to tell you what I really came for." He finally explained that his mother had died and that he had not heard from his father for many years and that the first news he had of him was the formal notification that he was in prison. This was followed almost immediately by a statement from a state hospital explaining that his father was insane and had been moved from prison to the hospital. He was certain that insanity was hereditary and that, try as he might, he could never be very different from his father. When questioned further about his ideas on heredity, he said that he was not only afraid of inheriting his father's mental condition but was afraid of inheriting his criminal tendencies as well. He said that from the age of nine the uncle with whom he lived had taunted him whenever he misbehaved with the statement that he was just like his father.

Jim was told that his father's mental illness was probably something that had been acquired—the outcome of faulty habits of thought and action—and that such acquired characteristics could not be transmitted through heredity. Jim accepted this idea without any great difficulty. But the discussion led on to a related matter. During the period when Jim had been greatly troubled about the problem of whether he might inherit the mental disease of his father,

. . . a school athletic director asked what the trouble was. Jim told none of his story except to make the statement that he was worried because his father was insane. The athletic director vouchsafed the information that insanity was not hereditary but that his father probably had syphilis which could have been passed on to him.

The question of syphilis was the next thing to be taken up with Jim, but before discussing this it might be well to mention that all during this period his fatalistic conception of heredity made suicide seem the only escape. Even in relation to suicide he felt inferior, stating that he had devised means for committing suicide, but that he did not have enough courage to go through with it. He also stated that suicide would have called too much attention to him and so he wished that the bus would turn over and he could be killed without any attention being given to his problem.

His complete identification with his father is difficult to describe. He seemed at first never to have thought of himself as a personality apart from the father. Much of the work in his case consisted of trying to make him see himself as an individuality and realize that the only taint that his father might have given him was the possible one of syphilis and that this could be determined through a physical examination. A Wasserman was arranged for at once. Jim was very much excited and impressed the doctor as being in a seriously nervous state. From the fact that the doctor decided to have a second test made, he concluded that the first one must have been positive, and he was faint and ill for a morning after this second blood test.

A letter was written to the father's physician stating Jim's anxiety and asking for information on the father's case. The reply to this letter stated that the father was disturbed to such a degree that little had been determined about the diagnosis. In this letter the doctor stated that he did not feel that the boy had any cause for anxiety for himself. This reply and the report that the Wasserman was negative were discussed with Jim at the same time. He showed some relief, but in the meantime he had disclosed other things that indicated that some of his anxiety was due to conduct that he had already shown.

At the close of an interview in which the emphasis had been placed on Jim as an individual able to stand and act apart from his father, he said, half laughing, "What would you do if you found out that I was a criminal?" Three days elapsed between this and his next interview. When Jim entered he showed great excitement. He said, "You needn't close the door. I'm likely to run out on you." Then he started to cry and gave as his reason that he had been told in a previous interview that the school principal had said that a boy who had put up the fight that Jim had put up deserved all the consideration that the school could give him. Up to this time Jim had seemed convinced that if the school authorities knew his home life they would ask him not to return. He now said that the only reason the principal could make such a statement was that he had not known what he really was afraid to tell for fear he would never be allowed to come back again. He said that when he first heard that his father was insane, and life seemed entirely hopeless, he stayed in school one night until after all the other pupils had left. Just before leaving the building, he went into the washroom and saw a watch lying on a washstand. He said he had no use for the watch and did not want it for himself, but could not help taking it. This compulsion was tied up with the idea that he inherited thieving from his father. He gave the watch to his uncle, who suggested that they pawn it. He urged his uncle not to do this and then never referred to the matter again. After his treatment began and he realized that there was a possibility of re-establishing himself with other people he was relieved to find that it had not been pawned, and the day before his appointment with the . . . [counselor] he placed the watch in the lost and found box.

This story was immediately followed by accounts of experiences connected with sex. He told the story of a long struggle with auto-eroticism. It seems hardly necessary here to go into the details of this conflict. One incident, however, is particularly interesting. He said that he had always heard in his church that when we sin, the soul turns black. After each masturbatory experience, he could picture his soul getting black. He says he threw himself into the playing of football with the idea that each time he made a goal a part of the black was being washed away from his soul. When for some reason the football field had to be given up, he conceived the idea that this was God's vengeance against him for losing this fight.

Let us turn back for a minute and put together the fragments of the childhood story Jim told us. He says that his earliest recollection is of the extreme poverty of a tenement district in New York. His memory of his father is that he was always drunk and that he beat him with a strap. He is inclined to idealize the memory of his mother, stating that she was beautiful and gentle. He says that whenever his father beat him, he ran to his mother for comfort and that sometimes his mother succeeded in hiding him from the father. One early recollection is of the mother climbing on a chair to hide money in a cupboard so that the father could not get it. Most of this early recollection is tied up with his mother's being ill. During this period he stayed at home and managed things as best he could. At this time he told a little boy upstairs that his mother was dead. He says he wanted sympathy and hoped to get it this way, but the little boy's mother would not let them play together any more because she considered Jim a liar.

The incident which has made the greatest impression on his mind is the following. One day while he was taking care of his mother he saw some children through the window. They were playing marbles. He suddenly decided to run away and play, too. He took twenty-five cents that his father had left for the gas meter and bought the marbles with this. He stayed out for the rest of the day without considering the consequences until he started home. He became very terrified at the thought of what his father would do. The father lived up to Jim's expectations and thrashed him with the strap. As on other occasions he turned to his mother to be comforted and hidden from the father. When he reached the bed, the mother had become delirious and did not know him. Seeing his mother in this condition was very terrifying, and he asked the . . . [counselor] over and over again to explain how his mother could look at him and not know him. The next day two Roman Catholic Sisters came to get the mother ready to take her to the hospital. They found a bottle in the room and implied that the mother had been drinking. The thought of this accusation still puts Jim on the defensive, and he feels that it was quite unfounded. At this time the child was taken to his uncle's. He never saw his mother again except after her death. The period of the funeral and the days that followed were handled by the uncle in a most destructive way. The child was scolded for crying for his mother and told that God had taken her and that He would be angry if Jim objected to the working of His will. The uncle threatened in very vulgar language that if the child cried he would not be able to urinate. This was tied up with threats and punishments for crying. Consequently Jim cried only at night. Sometimes he lay awake crying, sometimes he cried, talked, and walked in his sleep.

The uncle is an ignorant person and a spendthrift. He is diabetic, high-strung, and quarrelsome. He did not want Jim's friends in the house and begrudged Jim any good times. The child learned to say that he had not enjoyed himself when he came in from playing with his friends because the fact that he could have a good time seemed to make his uncle furious. Jim's mother had been very careful about the boy's appearance. The uncle, on the contrary, made him wear worn-out suits that were conspicuously different from those of other boys. This seems to have made a great impression on the child and, with the other shortcomings of his new home, added to his feeling of insecurity. Jim's attitude toward his uncle is often one of pity. He says that the uncle gave him every material thing that he could, but never loved him. The child seemed to have more kindly feeling toward his aunt-in-law, but this feeling is more pity than love. He says that the uncle makes her life unbearable and that it makes him sick to see his uncle go through his aunt's things for money and letters. As far back as the child can remember, his uncle used to get him to steal money from his aunt and give it to his uncle. Jim says that on one occasion he stole from his aunt's coin bank for himself. . . .

During the period of his treatment, Jim was very much confused in his classes. On one occasion he became so mixed up that he went to the wrong class. The fact that he could do such a thing added to his anxiety. At this time he went to see the . . . [counselor] and made the statement that he had come because he did not know what else to do. Several times he said that he thought he was deaf. At other times he said that he had gone for so long without ever discussing his affairs with anyone else that they sounded like a fairy story to him and he wondered if they sounded like a fairy story to the . . . [counselor].

His home is undoubtedly of the poorest in every sense. There are constant quarrels, bad table manners, and lack of modesty and of finer sensibilities along all lines. In spite of this fact the boy himself is essentially sensitive and refined. He has a fine, gentle manner, and is thoughtful of the feelings of others. He explained that he tried to improve the situation at home. He explained with great pride that, in going off on trips with the football team, he had watched the athletic director's manners very carefully and soon felt that he did as well as any of the other boys.

Experience with sex seems to be coincident with Jim's earliest experiences. While the family were living in the tenement district above mentioned, a neighboring building caught fire. During the confusion of this fire an adolescent boy took Jim, who was then no more than eight years old, into a near-by factory, where he taught him mutual masturbation. He is vague as to the number of times he met this boy, but he has remembrances of sex practices in a cellar with another little boy. He cannot understand why, at this time, he tried to protect a third little boy, of whom he seems to have been very fond, from finding out what was happening in the cellar. After Jim moved to his uncle's, his sex practices were entirely auto-erotic and were the cause of the struggle described above.

He believes that he was in the room when his mother had a miscarriage. He says he can only remember peering over the edge of the bed to see what had happened but that his father and the doctor kept getting in the way. During the period of his own struggle over auto-eroticism he was disturbed at night by hearing his aunt and uncle quarrel over their own sex relationships. However, during this time, he was forming very high ideals on questions of sex. His struggle to be worthy of a girl of whom he was fond added to his conflict over masturbation.

. . . Jim knew, from as early a period as he could remember, that his father was dissolute with women. One of the things for which he hates his father most is the fact that the father, after his wife's death, married a dissipated woman. However much his opinion of this woman was colored by his uncle's remarks about her and her lack of respectability, the fact remains that the child's only clear recollection of his step-mother is that she threw a pail of beer at him.

Let us examine the changes that have taken place in Jim since he has learned to think of himself as a person with independent potentialities.

He now has a partial scholarship in a boarding school and has accepted a part-time position to defray the rest of his expenses. In work he is reliable and efficient. His employer said of him, "Jim does not just work to get through, but to do the best job he can." With the other boys the change is very marked. He does not hesitate to talk in class and is distinctly "one of them" in sports and all social activities. He is very popular with the boys and takes a keen interest in some of them who are not getting on very well. He has taken one of these boys to a mental hygiene clinic for help.

One of his greatest difficulties connected with going away to school was his fear lest he was not fair to his aunt and uncle. When the time came to leave them, he was still troubled with the idea that perhaps he belonged in a slum district and with the people of his uncle's type, rather than with people like those he had met at school. He kept saying that, even though his uncle had given him no affection, he had provided for him materially, and he did not want to be ungrateful. The night he received his scholarship he heard his aunt crying and realized that she was upset over giving him up. He said that he had never known that his aunt cared for him, but that he now realized that she cared because his uncle was so difficult and Jim made this easier for the aunt. He realized, however, that his aunt was a very childish person who made him promises that she could never fulfill, in the hope of keeping him with her. He compromised with her by promising to spend his holidays with her, and he explained to the . . . [counselor] that he meant to send her part of his money as soon as he was able.

One of the most gratifying results of this case, and one that was expected, is the fact that, since the dread and fear that he is like his father has been removed, the compulsion to act like his father has disappeared. In short, he has had no temptation to steal, does not think of himself as that sort of person, and is not afraid to be trusted. He is extremely interested in people and in helping them, and during vacations he directs a playground.

He is taking a very hopeful attitude toward girls. He has asked whether it would be wrong for him to marry some day. He wanted to know if he should talk this matter over with a doctor, and, if he should become interested in a particular girl, whether he should tell about his father at once. This attitude is more typical of the beginning of the change in Jim. Now, when he talks about his girls, it is in a lighter spirit and more typical of the average young boy just beginning to be interested in girls. It is not unusual to find adolescents who have been as deprived as this boy thinking seriously about the opposite sex at an early age. It seems to some of them their chance for the security of home which they have never had. Here is another instance of Jim's freeing himself from his family and his past. All that he knew of marriage from his own parents and his uncle and aunt was very sordid, and yet he has already begun to talk of girls and home in the terms of an idealist.

Perhaps the most striking comment that will make the reader understand the change in Jim's personality was made by a person who had no knowledge of his problem. He said, "I like to look at that boy. He always looks so happy."

We might say, in Jim's case, that, somehow or other, he had developed quite a few excellent personal qualities. He clearly was respected by his classmates, as witness his choice as captain of a high school football team and his being considered for one of the class offices. Back of everything else, too, we might say that Jim had somehow learned to define the issues of life in rather useful terms. He was not sure that he could live up to the ideal of being an honest, dependable, considerate, industrious person. He was not sure that he would be able to live up to his ideal of being a good husband if he married. But he had had some clear evidence on a number of scores of the unhappiness that had been produced by failures in these matters in the lives of his father and uncle and aunt. Consequently, the task of therapy was not the exceedingly difficult one of changing his ideals and his conception of possible objectives in life; it was the rather simpler problem of giving him encouragement and helping him work out in greater detail the very pattern of dependable, thoughtful, friendly living that he already had incorporated to a great degree into his personality.

This record from Zachry, however, shows that a person may suffer very painful and disabling emotional disturbances even when these come, not from some devious indirect origin, but from fairly simple and understandable sources of faulty information and from environmental difficulties that almost any individual would find trouble in enduring.

Free association as a method developed by psychoanalysts

In a large proportion of the cases dealt with by psychotherapists, the problems are not as basically simple and direct as in the case described above, and it is not possible to handle the problem with the method that was so helpful with Jim. In dealing with these more difficult cases, one method of psychotherapy that has been developed is the method of so-called free association. The following example[2] is a much simpler one than is usually involved in this method. But it is different from Zachry's case and illustrates the reason why psychotherapists had to develop some method in addition to that of direct counseling. The patient in this case was a man in his forties, and the difficulty that brought him to the psychotherapist had been a bothersome problem with him for a number of years.

At twenty-four, while sitting in one of the front pews of a church, he happened to glance over his shoulder and observe that the aisle was blocked by ushers and incoming members. He suddenly felt dizzy and ill and fell into a terrible panic. He felt that if he could not at once escape from the church he would go mad with fear and rave like a madman. After that, whenever he found himself in any situation where quick, unimpeded exit from an enclosure was not apparent, he would have one of these attacks. He could enter a moving picture theater while the lights were dimmed and leave it before they were turned up, but if he miscalculated the movements of the crowd and saw the aisles blocked by incoming and outgoing people, he would have an attack. Taking communion at church was a great hardship because it involved blocking of all easy exits from the place where this rite is performed. Matters were brought to a climax when he was called upon to preside at a labor convention, where his duties required him to face an audience which seemed to block his exit. He was compelled to seek an excuse for leaving the auditorium, fearing complete loss of self-control. . . .

[2]From Hamilton, G. V.: *Introduction to Objective Psychopathology* (1925, The C. V. Mosby Company), pp. 125-127.

The patient had no explanation to offer for his claustrophobia, and none appeared in a minutely detailed account of his life. He seemed to be on good terms with his wife, who verified his account of their sexual and other relations to one another. He was instructed to spend a half hour lying on a couch in a dimly lighted room on any evening when no guests were expected and after the children were settled for the night. His wife, whose presence was always reassuring to him, was to hold his hand while he was to practice nonresistance to any flow of reminiscences which might be initiated by a contemplation of his claustrophobic panics. He was instructed to avoid all efforts to explain his panics, and all conscious direction of his successive awareness.

On my return to my office a few days later, after an absence, the patient called me on the telephone and asked for an immediate appointment, and soon appeared in a state of enthusiastic excitement, announcing that he was cured. He told the following story:

At the first session on the couch there came into his mind the memory of an event which occurred when he was about eight years old. He made his first visit to the country, where he spent several days with an uncle, who was a farmer. One evening, while his aunt and uncle were visiting a neighbor, the farm hand in whose care the patient was left was visited by another farm hand from a nearby place. The two men disappeared with their guns, a lantern, and a 'coon hound. After an hour or so they returned, carrying a live animal (probably a raccoon or an opossum) and were greatly amused to find that the little boy from town was afraid of it. They chased him into an upstairs bedroom and threw the animal in after him. Then they locked him in the room with the live wild animal. The patient was utterly terrified and made frantic but ineffectual efforts to escape from the room. His shrieks of terror finally alarmed the farm hands, and they released him. He was ill for several days afterward, and the uncle's employee was discharged for his cruelty.

The patient stated that as the memory of this episode came into his consciousness he experienced a lively emotion of fear. He was convinced that it had conditioned him to react to blocked-exit enclosures as to the locked-in-the-room situation which he had so fortunately recalled. The circumstance that the conditioned fear reactions (claustrophobia in this case) first appeared sixteen years after the experience at his uncle's farm, remained unexplained, but he was too sure of his recovery and too uninterested in this phase of the problem to accede to my request that he return for further examination.

In this case, Hamilton suggested a very rough and ready use of one of the main methods of the psychoanalytic approach which Sigmund Freud originated back in the 1890's. This method of *free association*, as Hamilton explained to the man, asks the person to do the opposite of what we usually attempt to do when we are bothered by some serious problem. Usually we try to think about the problem in a connected, rational fashion. But Freud found that apparently people often could not recollect significant experiences from their past, or could not recognize significant aspects of their present responses, if they sought for self-understanding in this direct, logical fashion. Freud suggested that apparently the important associations or connections in such matters are not reasonable and logical ones. The thinking of the person will move toward significant material if it is given some freedom. But it will have to approach this significant material by being allowed to follow its own path, even if this leads into all sorts of detours and side paths that seem not to be in the right direction.

This method of free association seems rather surprising to us, and it is hard to believe that it would often be needed. We would hardly expect that any experience of such impact would be forgotten or lost, particularly when the later situation that was disturbing (that of "finding exits blocked") was so close in form to the original experience that had given rise to the problem. But in this instance the memory had been lost, as far as this man consciously had been able to tell. Some memory- or habit-traces still were there, and as a result the same sort of emotional reaction came out in these similar adult situations. When the man did recollect his childhood experience again by this free-association method, a terrific sense of fear came with the memory. This fear quieted in a short while. With this memory recaptured and assimilated, the man got over his fear of closed-in places.

Some of the books on the psychology of personality have cited this sort of case as though it were typical of neurotic disorders. Actually, it is a relatively rare type—much less common than the cases we shall describe later in this chapter. But it is theoretically important. It shows that a person can have a strong emotional effect from processes within himself that he cannot discern.

The free-association method in its more usual setting in psychoanalysis

When the psychoanalytic therapists ask their patients to use the free-association procedure, it is usually in an attempt to do something about much deeper difficulties or conflicts than occurred in the foregoing example. That is, it more typically is employed with cases where the person finds it much harder to recapture crucial, significant memories or to become aware of processes that are assuredly going on within himself. Such persons apparently have powerful emotional *resistances* against allowing their free associations to uncover some of the processes in their lives, and part of what has to be accomplished by therapy is a building up of a more adequate emotional attitude that will permit them to face certain feelings within themselves.

The two following cases illustrate this much more common situation in psychotherapy. The first is a case reported by Franz Alexander, director of the Chicago Institute for Psychoanalysis and a leader in the development of briefer forms of psychoanalytic therapy.[3]

The patient was a fifty-year-old physician who was suffering from a severe compulsion neurosis and phobia. He was an excellent physician, very able, and only his neurosis was responsible for the mediocrity of his medical career. He had an extensive practice in a poor district of the city. In an early interview we discussed his relationship to his older brother. He spoke about him in a tone of great respect and admiration, emphasizing the fact that his brother had always been very good to him. He was a businessman who had made much money and had helped my patient generously and tactfully. He had, for example, invited my patient to invest money in his business and paid him a very high rate of interest. In point of fact the business did not need any more capital, but in this way he could help his brother while giving the appearance of receiving instead of doing a favor. My patient had conscientious scruples in accepting this masked financial aid and had often considered whether he should not put an end to it. In other respects also he had guilt toward his brother, which he displayed in many ways during his analysis.

I tried to make him conscious of the repressed motives which lay behind his bad conscience about his brother. I pointed out that he envied his successful brother and that even in childhood he had regarded him as a competitor. He denied this and would not admit any hostile feeling. He emphasized again and again his positive feelings of gratitude toward his brother. Nevertheless my interpretation aroused guilt, and in the next hour [next session] he responded to it with the following dream:

"I meet my colleague N. on the street, and he asks me to substitute for him and see a very prominent patient of his, who is a senator." I asked him to associate to substituting for a colleague in his practice and he answered: "Oh, that is a thankless job; it is a favor which you have to do if a friend asks you, but for my part I don't like it at all." Then I asked him to talk about his colleague and learned from his associations that N. was a very prominent physician, an old friend and schoolmate of my patient, and had had much greater success than he. He lived in a fashionable district, and as time went on they had seen less and less of each other.

I then explained to him that the dream was an expression of a repressed envy felt toward his colleague. In the dream this colleague asks him to see one of his patients, but in reality he would like to have his colleague's practice. He disguises this wish in the dream by making his colleague ask him a favor and so represents his real wish to take away his colleague's practice by a favor. At first my patient would not accept this interpretation and defended

[3]Reprinted from *Fundamentals of Psychoanalysis* by Franz Alexander, M.D. (By permission of W. W. Norton & Company, Inc. Copyright 1948 by W. W. Norton & Company, Inc.), pp. 293-295.

himself by the same arguments which he had used in the dream, namely, that substituting for his colleague was a very disagreeable task. But on further discussion he gradually admitted that he felt it to be an injustice that his colleague with his inferior knowledge had a fine practice, and that he often compared himself with him and thought that he deserved the greater success. After he had become conscious of his repressed envy toward his friend N., I was able to return to a topic discussed in a previous analytic session, the relation of my patient to his older brother. I showed him that he had displaced the whole conflict from his older brother to his colleague because his feelings toward the latter were similar but less objectionable. The advantage of this displacement was evident. The emotional conflict with his colleague was identical in quality but much less intense. It was less objectionable to envy a colleague than to envy his own brother, who had always helped him and been so good to him. His colleague N. behaved in the dream in the same way as his brother had in reality. He referred to him a very desirable patient but arranged it so as to appear that he was asking a favor. By the interpretation of this dream I gained much ground in exposing his envy of both his colleague and his brother. I could thus convince him at least intellectually that the guilt toward his brother was based on repressed hostility and envy. In the next hours he produced confirmatory material from childhood concerning his competition with his older brother.

A similar case is described in a very brief but telling fashion by George Humphrey:[4]

I knew a young man who was deadly afraid when he had to go to the barber. As many of these abnormal fears originate in the family situation, he was questioned about his relations with his mother and father and two brothers. He replied that he was on good terms with them all and had a particular admiration for his older brother who had founded the business in which he worked.

It was only after months of questioning that the true state of affairs was uncovered. Actually, he had intensely aggressive wishes against his brother. At the final scene, when asked what he would do to the brother if he had the chance, without fear of retribution, he jumped up, ground his heels on the floor with an indescribably vicious expression on his face, and cried, "Such a man ought to be ground into the earth. His face should be smashed into a pulp." Yet for fifteen years or so he had been genuinely and completely unconscious of the shatteringly powerful motive.

Motives such as this, Humphrey continues,

. . . are uncovered only with difficulty. The young man had an urge to kill his brother which the conditions of society prevented him from satisfy-

[4]Reprinted by permission of Dodd, Mead & Company from *Directed Thinking* by George Humphrey (Copyright 1948 by George Humphrey), pp. 34-35.

ing. He had seen his brother shave with an old-fashioned razor and was afraid, without realizing this, that one day he might kill his brother with it. This disguised itself as a whole host of fears, fears that girls might notice that his beard was not very heavy (he had a very light beard), fears that he could not do his college work, fears that he might not make good in life, as well as the primary fear of entering a barber shop. All these endless fears were motivated by the unrealized wish to kill his brother [or, as it may be better to say, by his intensely hostile feelings toward the brother] with the correlative fear that he might do so. He recovered when his true motives were explained to him, which involved much patient work and severe mental anguish on his part.

In both of these cases the patients at first went out of their way to express great admiration and respect for their brothers and strongly insisted that this was their real attitude. But this conscious attitude, far from being their full response, seemed primarily to be a sort of smoke screen or camouflage that they maintained in order to hide from themselves some opposite sort of emotional reaction.

Psychoanalysts do not expect that people can use the method of free association easily and smoothly. They expect it to run into difficulties. They expect it to require a good deal of active intervention by the therapist, over a long period, to explain to the person why the free associations are not proceeding smoothly. As they express it, the therapist has to make a considerable contribution through "analysis of resistances."

The task of self-discovery as sometimes a task of revealing processes that would be socially approved, but that nevertheless have been repressed

Contrasting with the two previous cases is one of a rather surprising sort described in an article by Austin A. Wood.[5] In this case, a man who was undergoing psychoanalytic treatment had been clearly aware of a good deal of hostility toward his father, whom he regarded as an unduly strict and rigid person. The following was the patient's account of his relationship to his father before the therapy and his account of certain developments in the therapy:

My father was a very undemonstrative New Englander. His regime in the home was strict, he was always right, and he was unable as a rule to show more than the mildest manifestations of love or affection. And it was he, rather than my mother, who was usually the one who said "No." My mother, on the other hand, was more or less the opposite. All these and other things

[5]Austin B. Wood, "Another Psychologist Analyzed," *Journal of Abnormal and Social Psychology,* Vol. 36 (1941), pp. 89-90.

produced in me a picture (conscious) of Mother as all good and Father as all bad, as far as I was concerned. One aspect of our family life was an almost continuous conflict between Father and myself, punctuated by hot and bitter arguments in which we both got very angry.

Analytical explorations had turned up many recollections of events which I now saw, not from the point of view of the child that I had been when the event occurred, and with a child's fears and uncertainties, but from that of the young adult that I was at the time of analysis. I had seen, moreover, that many of these things pointed to the two-sided proposition that my Father was not entirely the villain of the piece but had loved me and I him.

At this point I began to recall a rather striking event which had transpired when I was eleven. I was run over by a street car and one hand was badly crushed. My father was called, came immediately, took me in his arms, and carried me the two blocks from the scene of the accident to our home. As he was carrying me home, I was crying loudly. He told me, "Be a big man, and stop crying," and I stopped.

Now, this series of events was such a dramatic and intense experience that I might have been expected to remember it very vividly, and so I did. I had probably recounted it, just about as given above, on the average of once a year since it occurred; thus it belonged to that class of memories available to consciousness. But, in the analysis, when I reached the point in recalling the experience where I stopped crying in response to my father's "Be a big man, and stop crying," the analyst asked, "Why did you stop?"

This was a question I had never asked myself. All previous accounts I had given had gone right on from there to recount subsequent events. So I . . . recalled the experience as vividly as possible and tried to see what there was in the whole situation that made me stop crying. What came was an "aha" [that is, an "insight"] experience, but emotional rather than intellectual. The situation was that of my father, holding me tenderly in his arms, and very much concerned over me. The barriers to showing his love for me were down. And the very tone of voice in which he spoke said far more than his words. It said, "I love you very dearly, and I know that you are a big man (and this too was very important to me), and that you will be man enough to stop crying if I ask you to." These two experiences—his deep love for me, and his confidence in my manliness—struck with such force that I lay for several minutes weeping.

When the emotion had passed, I felt that I had had a deep and intimate experience of the warmth and devotion between my father and myself, an experience which has affected my relations with him (and with other people and institutions for which he had become the prototype) ever since. It seems to me that the effect of this emotional experience on my subsequent personality was not less for its having been delayed some twenty-five years.

In this case we can hardly attempt to explain the repression in terms of the cultural tradition in which the person had been trained. Our culture teaches us that we ought not to feel hatred toward other members of our family or toward others who have helped us. It is not so surprising, therefore, to find a repression of hostility. But our culture encourages the experiencing and recognition of affection and respect, especially for parents. And yet what this man had done was to block off the strong feelings of love and affection that he felt for his father.

In interpreting clinical cases, Freud's own tendency was to seek explanations in relatively biological aspects of the person's life. Thus it is probable that, in this case, he would have suspected that the man had certain homosexual feelings tied up with this affection for his father and had repressed the whole assemblage of feelings because of this one element. Psychotherapists who are less strictly Freudian would tend to say that something like that might be a possibility, but that other reasons for the repression are more likely. Thus, they might conjecture that the child, having recognized his father as very demanding and strict, had felt that his feelings of fondness for the father were too likely to lay him open to unreasonable demands and, in consequence, had blocked off all recognition of them. A nation, it seems, does the same thing in time of war. It is hard, for example, to continue to recognize the fine traits of another people when your nation is at war with them. It is too hard to rain death on those whom you admire in some respects. Something like this may have happened in the case described by Wood.

The basic assumptions about personality and psychotherapy derived by psychoanalysts

On the basis of such case material, the psychoanalysts have developed certain major concepts as a means of understanding personality maladjustments. Let us pause to state briefly these main psychoanalytic concepts before we turn to a consideration of several other methods of therapy.

According to psychoanalytic theory, personality difficulties generally occur because something is pressing up in the personality from within, as one might say. Some powerful process or memory has been rejected by the person as too threatening, for one reason or another, to assimilate into the processes of his ordinary life. But such rejected or repressed processes continue to struggle for expression and produce a wearing conflict, partly because an important portion of the person's energy is tied up with the process that is repressed, and partly because it takes still more energy to keep the repressed process safely bottled up. Reduction in the amount of energy available to the person is not the sole outcome of repression, however. Instead, it is hypothesized, when repressed materials press for expression, they are likely to find some degree of expression in indirect ways. These might perhaps be socially valuable ways but are more likely to be bizarre symptoms, hampering to the person and puzzling both to him and to others.

This interpretation has been viewed by the psychoanalysts as setting both their task and their opportunity as therapists. According to their notion, when the person is offered the encouragement and freedom of free association, the repressed materials ought to exert a pressure (even though all of this is unconscious) toward some expression in the conscious experience of the individual. Consequently, even though the person may not be able to make contact with these repressed materials by deliberate thought, he becomes able to release them and get them out where he can examine them and deal with them more successfully. He can accomplish this release if he relaxes his ordinary, rational control over the course of his thinking and allows the unconscious pressures somewhat freer scope in which to operate.

As a part of this theory, it is held by the psychoanalysts that the individual will often have resorted to this process of repression, not because it was entirely necessary that he should do so, but because the ordinary, rational part of the personality (the ego, as the Freudians call it) was not strong enough. They therefore say that part of the task of therapy may be a task of strengthening the ego.

As may be seen, this theory emphasizes the relative strength of different portions of the personality. But it does not ask much about the ego except how strong it is. The theory does not ask much about the origins of processes that are subject to repression. It tends to assume that such threatening materials inevitably will be present in the individual's life and that the crucial question is merely what will be done about such things.

The Freudian theory, therefore, was based upon certain common findings of psychotherapy. One of its key features is its reliance in psychotherapy on the use of free association and on a use of interpretive suggestions that are intended to make contact with, and to release for conscious assimilation, some submerged and rejected portions of the individual's inner life.

The nondirective or client-centered method of therapy

Another method of therapy has developed as a deviation from psychoanalysis. It began first with Otto Rank, who was one of Sigmund Freud's closest associates for many years. From Otto Rank, the ideas were next picked up by Jessie Taft, Frederick Allen, and some other workers in the school of social work of the University of Pennsylvania in Philadelphia. Their development of Rank's ideas was carried still farther by the psychologist Carl Rogers who worked at first as a clinical psychologist in a child guidance clinic in Rochester, New York, in the 1930's. All of these psychotherapists have written about this general approach to psychotherapy, but the most extensive exploration and description of the method have been given by Rogers and his co-workers and students, and the method has come to be known as *nondirective therapy* or *client-centered therapy*, both of which are terms Rogers has used.

This method is in agreement with the psychoanalytic idea that in therapy a free-association process is likely to be needed. This is because the origins of personality difficulties are thought to be traceable, at least partly, to portions of the self that the individual has tried to disown and repress. But this method does not sanction *telling* a person to engage in a free-association process. Nor does it believe that the therapist should intervene to try to help in the disclosure of any rejected materials from within the person's life. These are *negative* specifications. Since it is difficult to state the basic *positive* assumptions concerning personality upon which this method rests, it will be a good plan for us to illustrate how the method works first, and then come back to some further exposition.

We will take, first, a relatively simple case, just as we introduced the free-association method by describing its operation in an unusually straightforward case. In this instance, the patient (or client, as the nondirective workers prefer to say) was a man forty-eight years old who came to Arthur Shedlin, formerly one of Rogers' students, for treatment.[6]

In the first interview, the man said that he had been having some serious digestive disturbances over a long period of time, but that all the physicians whom he had consulted had told him that there was nothing physically wrong with him. They said that the root of his trouble must be emotional or psychological, and that he ought to consult a psychotherapist. He had already been to a psychiatrist and had not been helped; but the physicians still insisted it was a "psychosomatic" disorder that he had, and that he should try therapy again.

The man spent part of the first interview explaining this reason for his coming. Most of the rest of the interview he spent in saying how useless he thought it would be to follow their advice. "Suppose it is true," he said, "that something is wrong with my personality. You can't teach an old dog new tricks. Here I am, forty-eight years old. You don't change your ways of thinking and feeling when you are that old. It's utterly useless."

From the standpoint of everyday thinking, the rather natural thing for the therapist to have said to him would be something like this: "Yes, I can sym-

[6]We are grateful to Dr. Arthur J. Shedlin, Todd School, Woodstock, Illinois, for this account of a case from his practice. Our version is not a verbatim reproduction but a paraphrasing of the main points of the case related in such a way as to bring out the points of interest for this chapter.

pathize with what you say. It probably is hard for a person to change when he gets along farther in years. But it's your only hope, isn't it, since you do believe your physicians when they tell you that this trouble does not come from some physical cause? It would at least be worthwhile to try out this matter of psychotherapy. After all, most of us have some troubles that bother us. Are there any that you have?"

That would have been a common-sense comment. But it is not the procedure of nondirective therapy. That method forswears any attempts to persuade the client. It avoids any attempt to encourage him or reassure him, any attempt to advise him or steer him, and any attempt to suggest to him where the roots of his difficulties might lie. So, when the client said that he thought the whole procedure was useless, Shedlin merely showed that he was thoughtfully attentive. His comments were not simple repetitions of sentences already used by the client, but they were almost as limited as that.

In the second and third sessions, the whole content was much the same. Thus, client: "I know there are some people who think that psychotherapy can do anything, but I think you have to recognize it has its limitations." Therapist: "There are some things that are so serious or deep-seated that therapy cannot touch them."

In the fourth session, speaking with great difficulty, the client brought up a new topic. His words were somewhat to this effect: "I don't see how this could have any bearing at all on what I came here about. There is one thing, however, that maybe I ought to bring up. I've never mentioned this to anybody—not even my wife, and I've tried mostly to keep from thinking about it myself. I don't see that it makes any difference anyway. But the fact is that I was brought up in a Jewish family in the South. I moved up here when I was just a young man. I just kept quiet about the fact that I was Jewish. If anybody pressed me as to what my religion was, I replied that I was an atheist, but that my general background was of the Protestant sort. I've built up a good business; I have a very fine wife and am generally respected. I wish now that I had told my wife, because I don't think she is prejudiced and I don't think it would have mattered to her. But I can't tell her now. I can't admit that, for twenty-six years, I've been deceiving her. It would hurt her too much. I just can't do it. It wouldn't be fair."

On these things, too, the therapist spoke merely in such ways as to show that he was listening carefully and attentively and following what the client was saying. But not going beyond that. Not saying, "Yes, but might it not be that this conflict is costing you more, emotionally, than it is worth?" Instead, when the client said that he thought it was too late to remedy the matter now, the reply of the therapist was something like his: "You have the feeling you could have dealt with this without too much trouble a long time ago, but that your chance is gone, now." To which the client would have answered, "Yes, that's it. It's too late, now."

When he arrived for his fifth session, however, he announced that he had decided, after going home, that he ought to tell his wife even if it would mean that she would reject him entirely because of his lying to her. And she had said she was hurt—not because of his being Jewish, but because of his not having had enough confidence in her and enough frankness to have told her originally. Though it had been a very difficult experience for both of them, he said, it had seemed to take a great weight off him, and he felt sure that he and his wife could work out their life on a surer basis now. Furthermore, he had gone ahead and had spoken to a number of the other persons that he knew. It had not been easy to do. But he had decided it was the best course to follow.

In reply, the therapist did not evaluate. No praising of the client for having made a difficult decision. No opinion that this ought to work out better. Merely an "accepting" and "reflecting" of the emotional attitudes underlying what the client himself was saying.

There were six sessions in all, each about a half hour in length, but the psychosomatic difficulties cleared up in a rather dramatic way. On the other hand, in his earlier therapeutic attempt, when the psychiatrist had used more nearly a common-sense approach of inquiring and advising, the man had kept all this to himself as something that he felt sure was not related to his difficulties.

In this man, there was no lack of awareness of the two things that fairly surely were related to each other as cause and effect. He was quite conscious of his deception, on the one hand, and of his digestive difficulties, on the other. But he did not see the two things as having any relationship to each other. The fact that the digestive problems disappeared when the deceptive marital behavior was changed is fairly clear evidence that there was a cause-and-effect relationship. But his knowledge of his own personality was not able to reveal this causal relationship.

In some respects, we might say that this case corresponds rather closely to the sort of cases that the Freudians have emphasized. True, the man had not repressed his dissatisfaction and uneasiness about having failed to be honest with his wife. But, nevertheless, he did have a process he had inhibited or held back, since he often had wished he could talk with her about it, and this rejected tendency was one that naturally had been pressing for expression.

Accordingly, one might well ask whether this case could not have been easily and efficiently handled if he had been asked to use the free-association method. Wouldn't he naturally have started to talk about this problem, and wouldn't he quickly and naturally have reached the same decision, if his therapist had told him, as a psychoanalyst would have done, that the requisite procedure would be for him to let his thinking proceed, as freely and unhampered as possible, and that he should speak freely about whatever came into his mind?

The view of the nondirective workers is that such a procedure would have neglected some very important motivational factors in the man's life. As it was, he actually did follow a free-association process to some extent. He allowed his thinking, and certainly his speaking, to proceed with a freedom that it had not had for 25 years or more. But the decision to follow such a mode of thought was his—not something prescribed by the therapist. When he spoke to the therapist about his background, the decision to speak out was entirely his decision—not something done because the therapist had told him that complete honesty within the therapeutic hour would be essential for successful progress in their discussion. It was a hard thing for him to bring himself to speak of this matter; but *he* was the one who wrestled with himself and decided that he should do it. Consequently, the nondirective therapists would say that, when he faced the question by himself as to whether he should speak honestly to his wife, one thing that helped to make a decision possible was that he already had had, in the therapeutic interview, the difficult and painful experience of asking whether he should discuss this with another person and of deciding, on his own responsibility, that he would go ahead with it. To put it in simple terms, he already had practiced frankness with the therapist.

The nondirectivist, therefore, wants to make every part of the therapeutic interview more like a real-life experience. He wants the client eventually to follow a free-association process, but he does not demand this, lest it might appear to the client as an attack on his privacy. Even if the client understood well enough, on rational grounds, that a free and open communication would be essential, it still might be true that part of the personality of the client would be responding as though it were saying: "Who is this fellow who demands that I be completely open with him? How do I know I can trust him? What right does he have to ask for things like this? I'm not sure yet that he's the kind of a person I want to talk to in such intimate terms; but here he is, laying down the law to me—'This is the Fundamental Rule,' he says, 'follow this procedure or I'll back out on you and refuse to try to help you.' "

The client-centered therapist, therefore, tends to see the responses of the client in some such terms as these: What needs to be done is to help the client to grow. But growth is a very special process; it is like the opening of leaves on a tree or the unfolding of blossoms. You, the gardener, may help to provide some of the conditions under which such growth can occur. But there is no way by which you can force growth. You will only hamper the growth if you take hold of the unfolding leaves and try to open them out. So, in psychotherapeutic work, similarly, we must try to understand the processes within the client and try to permit these to operate according to their own inner nature; we cannot risk rather artificial efforts to control them from without.

There is a further assumption that is basic to nondirective therapy. This is the assumption that personality difficulties generally do not come fundamentally from conflicts between repressed and repressing portions of the personality, but come from faulty patterns of response in the person. The basic way in which the person is trying to handle life situations is defective. This leads to the arousal of processes that he needs to try to repress. But the repression is incidental to something more fundamental. His trouble is not that his ego is not strong enough. His trouble is that his ego (if we wanted to put it that way) sees life in wrong terms and tries to deal with it with a wrong strategy. His trouble is that he needs to get some experience of a new sort of relationship to other persons and to his world generally, and needs to test this relationship out and see whether he can shift over to it. The therapeutic sessions therefore need to be an experimenting, on the part of the client, with some new types of response to life situations. They need to be real-life situations, but of a new sort for him.

The nondirective method in play therapy with children

Some of the implications and nature of nondirective techniques show up with special clearness in the manner in which play therapy is conducted with children. With children, the procedure used is not primarily verbal, as it typically would be with adults. The interview room is arranged with many different play materials in it, such as paints, clay, building blocks, dolls, trucks, guns, doll furniture, and a sink with running water—things that can be adapted to a variety of uses. In this situation, if the child chooses not to discuss things with the therapist at all but merely to direct all of his attention to the play materials, the therapist allows him to do just this.

In the first moment when he is left with the therapist, the child may be so frightened that he breaks into crying. It would seem that the helpful thing for the therapist to do, in response to this, would be to tell the child that he doesn't have any reason to be afraid, that the therapist sees a lot of other little boys and girls in this same room, that the other children know that it is a nice place to be, and that the therapist is there to help him. Such reassurances might quiet the child's fears to some extent. But they might accomplish this through an influence that the child already has learned to count on too heavily. These reassurances might merely strengthen the tendency of the child to seek protection by showing how fearful he is. They would not help the child to find out that there are situations in which he can be afraid, receive no outside reassurance, and yet go ahead anyway!

Accordingly, when a nondirective therapist is confronted with such a terror-stricken child, he will speak to him only to let the child know that he realizes how frightened the child is. Or, it might seem as though he is doing no more than this. But actually he is. By his manner, his tone, his words he is showing a certain sort of fundamental respect for the child by remaining quiet and unruffled. It is as though he were saying to the child, "Yes, I know that you are afraid; but I also have a deep confidence that you can handle this fear."

Does this get across to the child? It is hard to say. But it would be quite typical for such a child to do the following: The child quiets after a while, but remains very timid, as though ready to jump at the slightest noise. He may spend a lot of time rooted in one spot, but looking at one thing after another that he sees on the shelves. Then, timidly, he may say to the therapist, "I wish I could play with some of those things." Here again it would seem natural for the therapist to say to the child, "Sure, these are here for you to use. You can play with them any way that you want. This room is yours for this hour. You can do anything that you want to do with these things." Not only would this be the common-sense tendency for a therapist, but actually it was the procedure that was used in early play therapy with children, as in the exploratory study by C. H. Rogerson in 1935-37. In some degree, in the extensive experience of Frederick Allen, this same "structuring of the situation for the child" was used, too.

The more consistent and thoroughgoing application of nondirective methods, however, avoids giving the child any such support or external security. The child has almost certainly had too much practice, anyway, in having people reassure him. He needs to get an experience of a new sort of interpersonal relationship—one where, even though he is a child, he will take a greater amount of responsibility himself. Rather than rob the child of a chance to use the situation in a significant way, the nondirective therapist believes that it is better to let the child wait—if need be for quite a time—to make his own decision that the playthings can be used by him.

Children come to the therapist with personality problems of many kinds. Let us confine ourselves for the time being, however, to one type of case where it seems that the young client is overtimid and overfearful. The child returns for one session after another, but he does not continue doing the same sorts of things. After a while, he not only begins playing with the toys, but he starts to use them in new ways. He takes the soldiers, say, and lines them up in two lines. They are not fighting, he hastily says; they are just watching one another.

The next time he lines them up again. He says that some of them have been bad and that the others don't like it. But he doesn't go beyond that. In later sessions, however, the play becomes more and more violent and openly cruel. One of the figures may be designated as the therapist. This figure particularly does awful things, and the soldiers build a house, shut him in, closing the windows so that he can't breathe. They yell at him to ask whether now he will be good. The child pretends that the therapist-figure answers with a defiant "no." Then the other figures treat him in even more cruel ways, chopping him up, burning him, and so on. One wonders what has become of the timid little boy who was so plainly frightened when the therapeutic work started. And one wonders also, particularly if he is new in such work, whether the boy won't indeed be changed by the therapeutic experience—and not necessarily into something that will make him any more acceptable to the parents or teachers or playmates!

The play may reach a form so openly and vehemently cruel that an ordinary person, without emotional training for such work, cannot watch it without being disturbed. The child's actions set up stronger echoing processes within him than he is prepared to handle. But the play does not continue indefinitely in this form, even though the therapist does not indicate any disapproval of it. He merely attempts to give the child the same careful attention as before and to show the child that he has a quiet, deep respect for him even though the child is revealing these intensely aggressive feelings that originally had been entirely hidden. The therapist does not seek to show this respect by saying to the child any such thing as: "Of course, Tim, you know that I still think you are a fine boy even though you wish to play sometimes in this wild way." The respect is shown by the quiet manner that a person would naturally use if he were thinking to himself: "This child is doing something important. He is doing something courageous. He is exploring tendencies within himself that he never dared face before. He is exploring a sort of interpersonal behavior different from any he has ever dared to try. He'll set his own pace at this. I won't need to try to hurry him; I won't need to try to slow him up. He'll take these things as fast as he's emotionally ready for them."

What seems to be a fairly typical outcome is that the child, having tried such excessively violent conduct, finally acts as if such play no longer interests him. He settles down into a new kind of play where he is more healthily self-assertive, like any normal child, but intrigued, also, with the diverse possibilities that play materials can have and more interested in his developing contacts with other children than in returning for further visits with the therapist.

Consequently, even where the therapist does not proceed by actively interfering and guiding, as psychoanalysts do with their interpretations, it seems that the child's own processes will work back to influences that have been strongly repressed within him, and there will be the same sort of re-exploration and reorganization that occurs in the most effective of psychoanalytic work. Apparently, when we speak of the individual as having very powerful motivational forces within himself—greater in power than we ordinarily realize—we should not limit this idea to the forces of hostility, sex, and fear that the psychoanalytic theory has emphasized. It also seems true that the individual contains within himself something else that workers such as Otto Rank, Frederick Allen, and Carl Rogers have emphasized. It seems that there is another sort of motivational factor which is powerful, too. This is spoken of as *an urge to grow*. Other related terms are *constructive tendencies* and *courage*. All of these may at first seem to suggest something vague. But when you see a child, or it may be an adult, who is immersed in a nondirective therapeutic experience, going ahead and exploring things that he is afraid of, going ahead in spite of the fact that he is given no reassurance that he is dealing with a problem that he ultimately can handle—when you see this, you wonder whether the nondirectivists have not put their fingers on a real and important human tendency, despite its apparent indefiniteness.

Play therapy as an attempt to modify fairly fundamental patterns of personality

In play therapy such as we have described, it might well seem that the personality problem involved fits the traditional psychoanalytic theory of the nature of personality difficulties: the child is timid and ineffective in his play and in other areas of his life because he has repressed a lot of hostility within himself; the task of therapy is to bring this hostility into the open; the child then will be able to use this energy more effectively, as in reasonably self-assertive activity, and he can cease the wasteful conflicts within himself.

The outcome includes such things. But perhaps more than this is happening. Maybe the important fact is not merely that the child can use his aggressive feelings when he has them, but also that, whether consciously or unconsciously, he does not have as much hostile feeling as he had previously. He has learned new ways of relating himself to other persons; consequently his life does not involve as many frustrations and fears as previously. And in consequence of this, the motivational basis of his life is changed. To some extent he has worked out a new pattern of life.

It might be worthwhile to describe another case that illustrates even more clearly this sort of change as an outcome of such nondirective play therapy. This is a case from the work of Frederick Allen, a leading child therapist and for many years the director of the famous Philadelphia Child Guidance Clinic.[7]

Grace, an eight-year-old girl, was as selfless a person as ever came to the clinic. Everything about her was wrong, and her nickname of "stink pants"

[7] Reprinted from *Psychotherapy with Children* by Frederick H. Allen, M.D. (By permission of W. W. Norton & Company, Inc. Copyright 1942 by W. W. Norton & Company, Inc.), pp. 274-277.

called attention to the ever-present odor from constant enuresis. Grace's school work led her teachers to believe she was a defective child. The family was large and economically dependent. Yet in the family there existed a primitive type of unity. In their own crude way these parents were concerned with this girl who seemed to have so little. She received little attention, however, beyond nagging efforts to correct her diurnal and nocturnal enuresis.

In the first interviews that the therapist had with Grace, the child was able to do almost nothing. She did not seem to be particularly frightened, nor was she antagonistic in any way. She had a selfless quality as if she had so little awareness of being anyone. Grace was unable to respond with any feeling until the end of the first hour, when she said, in a barely audible tone of voice, that she wanted to return. The quiet and unobtrusive friendliness of the therapist, who could accept her as she was, helped Grace to smile a little as she left.

Her solemn, distant quality continued through her second hour, but at the end Grace expressed a desire to save a crude drawing she had made which portrayed, in form and description, a mixture of a boy and girl. . . .

In the third hour, the awakening process was accelerated. Grace drew her chair closer and talked about her activity that had more purpose. She thought the tea set on the therapist's shelf was very dirty, and she washed all the pieces saying reprovingly, "You ought to be ashamed to have such dirty dishes." . . .

The quiet and forceful determination in this child was revealed in a remark she made about being left-handed. "The teacher told me to put the pencil in my right hand. I does it but I say no to myself." Her first movement toward a positive relationship was in finding a person who was not trying to make her over and who was helping her to give some outward expression to her negative feelings.

By the end of her fifth hour, Grace was an alive and alert little girl, rather impish in her manner, but with a gaiety totally new for her. About this time she stopped her persistent soiling. She introduced two dolls into her play. She dressed the big one, handed it to the therapist, and said, "This big one is yours, the small one is mine." She stood very close as she spoke of herself as the mother and the therapist as the father of these two girls. . . .

The play activity in her seventh hour gave further evidence of her growth through this experience. She made a crude clay figure, saying, "This is you." An identical figure was made and described as, "This is me." Then she put them together and said, "They are both you, they wear the same pants, you and me sleep, we will be together." Then she said, "Half is me." A communal head was made for the two figures and then she was not in the figures at all. . . .

In the hour that followed, the clay figures were there but she announced: "I am not going to play with that today." She modeled clay into a baby, gave it to the therapist saying, "This is your baby, it's a little girl." Then she drew a house with a bedroom and had the therapist in bed. "You are lazy," she said, and in the drawing she had him falling out of bed, "Just as I did." . . .

In the hours that followed, Grace's play was easy and natural. The laughter and excitement were a part of the release she was finding in living.

Once she commented: "You look like an old man sitting in that chair." Grace talked of her home and casually spoke of the time "when I used to wet myself." In her play and games the emphasis was on being the stronger and she tried to be a little tyrant in her bossiness. All this was a part of Grace's need to live and to test her new-found strength in which she found the first creative use of herself. More and more her interest shifted to home and school affairs, and events outside the room interested her more than things inside. . . .

In her final hour, Grace brought two cents, asking "Would you give these back if I gave them to you?" "What do you think I should do?" the therapist asked. Promptly Grace settled the question and said, "If I give them to you, I wouldn't have anything left—I'll keep them." This was the point at which she had arrived about herself, and shortly after this Grace made her own decision about ending, which she carried through. [A footnote by Allen adds: "About once a year, this mother appears with Grace to show her off. She has become an interesting, normal child."]

Although this case involved only 19 interviews, it illustrates the most profound of all effects of therapy and involves a point about personality little appreciated in the earlier parts of psychoanalytic work. It is that the origins of personality difficulties commonly are not specific and limited. Difficulties are not always caused by a single traumatic experience that needs to be recaptured and assimilated, as in the case of the boy and the raccoon. Nor is it just that the person has repressed some major motive which he needs to become conscious of and be able to accept within himself, as with hostility in several of the illustrations above.

Instead, the basic cause of personality difficulty is often some faulty over-all approach to life that the individual has adopted, partly through feeling it is the only possible way to live. Grace, for instance, with all the failure and nagging and disgrace she experienced, had concluded that the only possible way to live was to fight back—and, furthermore, to fight back, not openly and violently, but by refusing to correct the things she was nagged about. In fighting back, she was working in a sort of vicious circle, eliciting from her mother the constant worry and nagging that caused the continued trouble, rather than the pride which the mother, when things cleared up, showed herself quite able to take in the child.

The basic assumptions of nondirective therapists regarding personality and psychotherapy

Although the therapeutic method we have been describing is called the *nondirective method*, it might properly be construed as the *nonco-operative method*. For, while the client takes one step after another to get the therapist to play the role that the client expects all other persons typically will play, the therapist will not go along with him. Thus, perhaps usually the client has been able to provoke other people into arguing with him. But the nondirective (nonco-operative) therapist won't argue. The client has been able to irritate his parents and get a lot of criticism and punishment and admonition from them, but not here. Or, usually the client has been able to appeal to the sympathy and helpful tendencies of other persons and has been able to make them take the responsibility for making decisions. But the nondirective therapist won't make decisions for him and won't give him reassurance or protection.

There are several basic assumptions the nondirectivists make that are their reasons for trying such a method of therapy. These are as follows:

1. The client does not need to be prodded or pushed from without to make him work on his problems and struggle vigorously with them. The individual is a growing thing. His motivation includes powerful forces that favor such growth.

2. Personality is not primarily a matter of how one part of the personality deals with another part of the personality within the individual. This may be one aspect of the whole matter, but only a secondary aspect. The primary feature of personality is the way the individual understands life situations and the way he tries to deal with the surrounding world.

3. In our dealings with the surrounding world, each of us tends to force every life situation into the form he expects. Even when the situation objectively would be more suitably dealt with in some other way, we go to work to coerce it into the usual form. Only in this way do we feel that we can gain the feelings of security, acceptance, or significance that we crave.

4. In ordinary life situations, it is hard for us to see that we do this. We are able to create some of the effects we anticipate, and we are able to point to these and to say: "You see, it is just as I anticipated—people *are* ready to criticize (or attack, or assume a somewhat stifling but nevertheless reassuring protective role toward me, or whatever). It isn't that I read such things into life. It is, rather, that this is the real nature of things."

5. For a client to come to realize these tendencies in himself, he needs a situation where other persons will refuse to play ball with him on his usual terms, and yet will at the same time preserve steady, assured respect for him. The person needs to have a chance to see clearly that he himself is forcing things to take a certain form even where they do not need to do this.

6. The client needs to have experience in making his own decisions, doing his own thinking, mobilizing his own courage for significant actions.

7. The client can sense, in various ways, the underlying attitude of the therapist. The therapist does not need to say, in so many words, "I feel sure that you have some reserves of strength within you." Or "I feel that there is some underlying fineness in your life, and that you are trying to work it out, even though you are doing many things that people bitterly disapprove." He does not need to express such underlying attitudes by definite statements. In fact, he would communicate these underlying attitudes less effectively, usually, if he did try to put it in that way. Even though the therapist's actions are embodied in a rather subtle language, those actions can speak louder than words.

8. The processes within the client are so complex that they cannot be adequately appreciated and recognized even by very wise and experienced therapists. It is better for the *client*, therefore, to decide whether or not he should tackle a certain problem at a given time, or retreat from it for a while, rather than that the therapist should try to decide such a thing for him. It is better that the client should formulate some possible alternative pattern of experience for himself; there is too little likelihood that any outsider can formulate a plan that will take sufficiently into account both the resources and the limitations and inner difficulties of the individual.

Another basic method (or group of methods) of psychotherapy: complex interpretation

Now we turn to an account of still another approach to the problems of psychotherapy, one that is neither psychoanalysis nor nondirective psychotherapy, and yet one that, like these, is more complex than the relatively simple and direct counseling we illustrated with the first case in this chapter.

The workers who favor this method agree with many of the concepts of the nondirective therapists, and up to a point they incorporate these into their own work. But they take a different view of one crucial matter. They hold that the outlook on life that lies at the heart of the individual's personality is usually too complex and elusive a thing for him to recognize by his own unaided thinking, even though he may, metaphorically speaking, have before him the "blank screen" the nondirective situation provides. Furthermore, they believe it is too difficult for the person, usually, to see what alternative pattern of experience he might use instead of the one he uses habitually, the one that has gotten him into difficulty. He needs the help of some other person before he can see alternatives he cannot think of by himself. He needs the help of some other person in developing a better construction to put on the facts of life. He needs some help in his complex problem-solving task, rather than to be left in the position where he must do it all for himself. Perhaps this helping figure will fail to perceive some shadings of thought and feeling within the client—that is to be expected. If this happens it is unfortunate, perhaps, but it is less serious than if the client, because he lacks outside suggestions, fails to see some of the major factors in his life situation.

Because of their view of these matters, the advocates of this method of therapy assume that, after they have acquired sufficient knowledge of the client, it is up to them to do a good deal of thinking for him and to communicate to him the results of their thinking in some rather clear and explicit way. He may not accept the results of this thinking, of course, even when it is sound. If such a rejection occurs, it may be because the counselor did a poor job in figuring out when to present the new ideas and how to do it. But maybe there just is no feasible way of getting the client to make the necessary changes. In that event, failure has to be accepted. No method of therapy can be expected to work all the time.

The psychotherapist with whose name this method of therapy has been associated for the longest time is Alfred Adler. His conception was that personality is basically a matter of a "life plan" or "life style" that the individual has adopted but can very seldom recognize in himself. His conception was, furthermore, that the therapist needs to be a person of keen perception so that he can see the delicate shadings of such life plans, clarify them for the person he is counseling, and help him to see alternative possibilities.

A number of other therapists whose ideas we will mention later in the book also have held the same kind of view. Karen Horney is one of the best known of these. Erich Fromm and Prescott Lecky are two others. Most recently this view has been urged in books by E. Lakin Phillips and by George Kelly. Kelly, in particular, has tried to develop this view in a careful and systematic way and to give it clear expression.

It is important to realize that the Freudian or psychoanalytic workers also have been moving in this direction. We said earlier that two features of their method were their use of free association and of interpretation of specific materials; but we mentioned that there was also a third main feature of psychoanalytic method which we had not described yet. The third feature is related to our present discussion. As their work progressed, the psychoanalysts came more and more to emphasize the fact that the personal interaction between the analyst and his patient was a very important part of psychoanalytic work. They saw the patient as tending to view the analyst in the role of the patient's father or mother or some other significant figure. This they called the "transference" phenomenon. They saw the patient as tending to live out, in his relations to the therapist, the pattern of personal relations he had experienced at various earlier periods in his life. And many of the psychoanalysts have come to say it perhaps does not matter whether the free associations ever succeed in recovering many of the early memories of the individual—the important thing is to use the "here-and-now" material to help the person see how he approaches life situations and how he might do better if he could learn some new ways of handling some of them.

The unresolved issues among different systems of psychotherapy

There are a great many ways in which all of the various schools of psychotherapy have challenged the everyday modes of thought we sketched in the preceding chapter. No psychotherapists take the symptoms of their clients at face value. Certainly none of them expects that all of the important processes of personality will be conscious processes. They know that putting a person through the proper motions will seldom mold his behavior in a corresponding way. They know that a good many other ideas about personality which come from everyday thought are far from satisfactory as starting points from which to set out to remold personality.

Some methods of psychotherapy involve more drastic shifts away from everyday assumptions than do other methods. You will remember that psychoanalytic therapy does not depend solely on the play of forces within the person, but permits the analyst to exert an appreciable steering influence. For example, when the patient who had failed to recognize his love for his father was telling how he stopped crying after his father's request, the analyst asked, "Why did you stop?" Not only that, but, as the example from Alexander illustrates, psychoanalysts feel that it is often necessary to point out some idea that apparently has almost risen to the level of the person's clear awareness, but that he seems to be shying away from. You will remember such expressions as these in Alexander's account: "I tried to make him conscious of the repressed motive which lay behind. . . . I pointed out. . . . He denied this and would not admit any hostile feeling. . . . I then explained to him. . . . At first my patient would not accept this interpretation and defended himself. . . ."

In the nondirective method, on the other hand, this appeal to rational intellectual processes is regarded as unnecessary. Open doubt is entertained about the effectiveness of verbal appeals. There is more dependence on some motivational processes seldom recognized in everyday thought. In some respects, therefore, this approach represents a more drastic departure from the concepts of everyday life than is true even of psychoanalytic method.

There remain great puzzles, however, as to whether such drastic departures from everyday conceptions are justified. It remains to be seen, for instance, whether many people *can* work out new patterns of personality under the sort of situation provided by nondirective workers, or whether there is more justification for the view, taken by other workers, that relatively fundamental changes can be made only when the person's own thinking is aided by the thinking and recommendations of other persons.

There certainly is a great stir in the field of psychotherapy, with much work and research into methods currently going on. This has given rise to new thinking about personality. We have indicated some parts of that thought in this chapter—perhaps more, even, than the reader feels ready for so early in this book. But we have touched upon only a small portion, at that, of all the range of new concepts emerging from therapeutic work. Our later chapters will take up more of these. For the present, however, our aim has merely been to indicate a few main types of psychotherapy and to indicate some of the theoretical concepts that characterize each of them.

Possible limitations of psychotherapy as a source of enlightenment in seeking to understand personality

Psychotherapeutic work is undeniably stimulating to the production of new ideas. It has produced some dramatic alternatives to everyday thought about personality. Even though most of us are not psychotherapists, it is very worthwhile for us to consider the new ideas that have come from psychotherapy.

The question may well be raised, however, as to whether psychotherapy will be able to supply all of the new concepts about personality we need. Psychotherapeutic interviews are a limited type of situation, after all, even though they are undeniably vivid real-life experiences as far as they go. One wonders whether even the theorizing about psychotherapy itself may not be suffering because it has been based on such a limited area of observation. One wonders whether there may be other kinds of situations, less limited in scope, which would reveal some very important truths that do not come to light within the therapeutic situation. After all, extremely careful measurements in a limited area could hardly prove that the earth is round, but Columbus and Magellan were able to provide very clear evidence on this point even though their factual data were very rough in a quantitative sense. Such considerations suggest that some fairly fundamental reorganizations of psychotherapeutic theories might be made if psychotherapists were to make use of a wider range of knowledge.

There is good reason for inquiring, for example, whether there may not be important new ideas coming from experimental studies of psychological processes. After all, psychotherapy is working with exceedingly complex materials. Perhaps certain factors and relationships cannot be seen in such a situation, but might show up in the more simple and artificially constructed situation of the psychological laboratory. Perhaps not. But the experience of medicine suggests that this should be the case. It is true that medical workers proposed most of the early hypotheses concerning how the body functions. But the practical situation where physicians were seeking to alleviate bodily ills was not favorable for settling many of these questions or for developing new and more complex hypotheses. The work of physicians had to be supplemented by laboratory work in all of the specialized branches of physiology. Perhaps the same thing will be true of psychotherapy. We will turn to this possibility in Chapter 5.

Maybe psychotherapeutic observations should be supplemented in many other areas of observation. Perhaps there are some very important differences between therapeutic situations and some other sorts of life situations. Perhaps the age range covered by psychotherapeutic observations is too narrow. Thus the first few years of infancy may contain some very important phenomena that ought to be studied, but that psychotherapists have no good opportunity to observe. Perhaps there are different cultural groups where different potentialities of personality would be revealed which would not be apparent within our limited culture of the West where psychotherapists have worked.

We need not try to answer such questions at the moment. Grateful and appreciative though we should be, however, for psychotherapy as a technical source of new understandings of personality, it is nevertheless quite clear that we ought not to limit our search for new ideas about personality to this one source.

Summary

Psychotherapy has been a rich source of new understandings of personality. Part of this contribution has been a broadening of our concrete descriptive knowledge about personality. Because of the nature and purposes of the therapeutic situation, patients speak much more openly and frankly in it than they ordinarily would, and therapists spend more time listening to each person talk about himself than would be possible in everyday life. Experienced therapists, from knowing a diversity of persons in this way, have learned more about what to look for.

To some extent, also, therapists have a chance to experiment with personality. Their task is not merely to observe, but also to try out different influences and see what influences produce what results. This, together with the varied nature of their subject matter, inevitably forces them to develop theories about the nature of what they are working with. A great portion of our current stock of principles about personality has come, therefore, from psychotherapists. We stressed the fact that personality change is by no means limited to what happens under psychotherapy. However, this is the only situation where changes have been intensively and sometimes systematically observed and recorded.

Work in psychotherapy started in the field of medicine. This was because physicians already had professional responsibilities and attitudes somewhat like those required in psychotherapists, and also because the first personality difficulties that psychotherapists studied were cases of hysteria, in which persons mistakenly believe that their difficulties are really organic problems. Social workers also naturally were led into the field of psychotherapy in an effort to find more fundamental solutions for the problems that harassed many of the individuals whom they sought to help. Psychologists confined their efforts for a long time to experimental research, but increasingly they too have been brought into the field of psychotherapy, partly because the areas of interest in their field have broadened greatly with the passage of time, and partly because pressures from outside of psychology were in the direction of getting them to participate. Each of these groups concerned with psychotherapy has tended to bring its own valuable special background not shared by the other groups.

Four methods of psychotherapy were sketched in this chapter: the method of direct counseling, the psychoanalytic method (with its three submethods of free association, interpretation, and utilization of the transference phenomenon), the nondirective method, and the method of complex interpretation.

The first of these methods can produce improvements in cases of persons whose difficulties seem fairly serious; but it seems probable that, as in the long example quoted, the method of direct counseling can be successful only when a good many favorable factors are involved. More difficult cases call for one of the other more complex methods.

Both the psychoanalytic and the nondirective methods often treat persons in whom, it seems, some rather powerful tendency or process has been disavowed and rejected or repressed by one means or another, but still is pressing for expression. This work indicates that such unconscious processes can have highly important influences in personality. Psychoanalytic theory has tended to consider such cases as providing the model for all sorts of personality difficulties. The nondirective theory has tended more to say that the basic personality difficulties are the outcome of the faulty ways in which the person understands his surrounding world and tries to deal with it. The nondirective method seeks primarily, therefore, to establish a therapeutic situation in which the person can get a better realization of how he tends to deal with life situations and in which he can explore some alternative and possibly better patterns of life.

Each of the different methods of therapy makes certain assumptions regarding personality that it has developed from its observations. Thus, the nondirective theorists stress the "urge to grow" that they believe is present in all persons. They stress the individual's need to experience making his own decisions. They stress the resourcefulness in thinking that people can show when they are freed from external praise and blame and are provided with a situation, instead, where the therapist communicates the fundamental respect that he feels for the person as he is. On the other hand, both the psychoanalysts and the advocates of the various forms of complex interpretation believe that the nondirective workers have overrated the capacity of people to develop new patterns of reaction without the aid of expert advice. Both of these groups make more use of verbal means of influencing the person—or more use of rational appeals, perhaps we might say—than are considered either necessary or desirable in nondirective work.

A great deal of experience with different methods of psychotherapy has now been acquired. An increasing portion of such work is being done with children, as by the play-therapy methods of nondirective workers. This work has been especially instructive. With the passing of time, the different methods of therapy have become a good deal more alike in many respects. All of them are at considerable variance with the concepts about personality that were reviewed in the previous chapter as too commonly marking our everyday thinking.

There are some serious limitations to psychotherapy, however, as a means of acquiring a basic understanding of personality. One of the most serious limitations is that the work of psychotherapists has all been concerned with persons living within the broad limits of modern Western culture. Psychotherapists have not had an opportunity to see what would happen to personality under the influence of some drastically different cultural influences. There are certain respects, therefore, in which the ideas from psychotherapy need to be supplemented by concepts, such as we will consider in the next chapter, that come from the wide-ranging work of anthropologists.

CHAPTER 4

Anthropological Data as a Source of Understanding of Personality

We are becoming more and more interested, nowadays, in discovering as far as possible what are the basic tendencies and the range of potentialities of human nature. With the growth of the physical and biological sciences, we know we can handle many of the problems which troubled previous generations. We have the means to produce an adequate food supply; we have achieved a large degree of mastery over the problems of disease; we have become sufficiently skillful in technology so that we know much of the drudgery of human life can be removed. But we are concerned and alarmed because it seems, sometimes, as if there are such deep hostilities and such self-centeredness in man that there is no possibility of solving the problems of international and other intergroup relations.

Furthermore, even if our desire to eliminate social conflict could be achieved, it might still seem as if we face insoluble problems in just living. Modern society often appears to create a basic restlessness or dissatisfaction that makes us question the value of civilization. It is not merely that we have high rates of delinquency, alcoholism, and divorce, with all the personal tragedy those often involve. Sometimes it seems that there is a more serious problem of wide discontent that seldom comes to such clear-cut expressions, but still is very important. It is as if many people in the modern world were tempted to say: "It isn't a question whether I can meet my personal and social responsibilities—I can and I will. But, there's too much of a treadmill character to my life. What's the point of it all?"

What creates the greatest concern is that, to many people, it seems that such effects are not transitory, dependent perhaps on the special conditions of our times, but are expressions of basic and perhaps ineradicable human characteristics. Part of what creates this impression of despair is the fact that the countries which got involved in the two world wars were not the "backward" countries of the world, but among the most "advanced." The barbarous prejudices and brutalities of the Nazi regime did not occur in some impoverished, handicapped area; they broke out in the center of European culture. It seems as if perhaps civilization is doomed to work under impossible encumbrances because of some inevitable limits upon man's altruism, his social-mindedness, and even his capacity for simple happiness. It seems as if perhaps human nature is forged from an inferior, bungling, and unimprovable kind of material that cannot be adapted to the demands of a complex modern society.

It is not merely laymen who have despaired. The same view, essentially, was expressed by Sigmund Freud, who perhaps made greater contributions than any other person to our modern scientific ideas about personality. In 1930, summing up the implications of his thinking for modern social problems, Freud published a book, *Civilization and Its Discontents.* In it, he noted the restlessness and hostility we have just mentioned. But, with reference to these, he did not support the idea that a deeper understanding of personality would help society to do much to allay those problems. On the contrary, he said, the technical insights of psychoanalytic theory indicate that hostilities and greed are features of human nature that are ineradicable to a degree never previously appreciated. Furthermore, he said, the necessary work of civilization can be accomplished only by accepting serious limits to simpler kinds of human satisfactions. Some of the unreasonable burdens of culture might be eased, he said, but it is inevitable that civilization will have a large measure of personal discontent and restlessness—this is one of the inevitable costs of modern life.

In reaching these conclusions, Freud was taking into account the broad social happenings of his day. He also had in mind the intensive and detailed studies of individual personalities made in the course of psychoanalytic therapy. Both types of evidence, he felt, indicated that human personality, in its fundamental characteristics, is strongly hedged in by the inborn nature of man.

We have a problem in finding methods and data applicable in answering the question as to the potentialities of human nature

It is important for us, in thinking both about broad social problems and about the lives of individual persons, to raise questions about the range of human potentialities. Much of our approach to human life will be determined by our conclusions about the basic kind of nature we possess and the range of our potentialities.

When we seek an answer to this question, however, it is first of all necessary to make sure that we use a method qualified to provide correct answers. We need to realize that almost all the observations of personality by psychotherapists and by experimental psychologists have been made under rather limited sets of conditions. The persons who have been scrutinized in each of these instances are almost solely persons who have grown up under the conditions of modern Western culture. For the most part the conditions have been even more restricted; they are the conditions that have molded the personalities of relatively well-educated, economically well-off, and socially favored individuals of this modern Western culture.

As a general scientific procedure, this is seriously open to question. Any limitation of the conditions under which observations are made imposes restrictions on the generality of whatever conclusions are drawn from the data. Since characteristics of human beings and of all natural phenomena can vary enormously, observations made under special and restricted conditions may give a very faulty picture of what might be discovered under a wider range of situations. No naturalist would describe a Douglas fir merely in terms of what he sees at the tree line of a mountain. If he did, he would portray this ordinarily magnificent tree—which frequently grows to more than two hundred feet tall, often with a diameter of six feet and more—as a stunted, scraggly, twisted dwarf. No chemist would describe any chemical after he had studied its reactions merely with a few other chemicals and under a narrow range of temperatures. The chemist knows that out of the approximately one hundred elements that are the building blocks, literally hundreds of thousands of compounds have been developed, each with its different and characteristic properties. And yet the chemist believes that his work of exploration has only begun, because he knows that the potentialities of the hundred-some elements can be learned only by studying them in different contexts.

Of course, even when conditions are varied there is a surprising stability to some of the characteristics of objects. A fir tree in a thick stand of trees will grow into a different shape from that which it will take when it grows alone. Still, its shape in the forest is not the shape an oak would take there, and the oak does not take the shape an elm or a sycamore would take. And, whether the tree grows in one climate or another, in one soil or another, it still has the same sort of needles, the same characteristic cone and seeds, and the same pattern of bark.

There are some qualities, then, that are more truly intrinsic than others. In living things there are some qualities that are more strongly genetically determined, or biologically determined, than others.

Mankind has always tended to think of personality characteristics as thus genetically determined. "You can't change human nature!" people say.

Is this true? Is human nature something that cannot be changed in important ways?

Of course we could settle this question in the affirmative by defining human nature as the inherent and unalterable characteristics of man. But if we engaged in such circular argument (either quite consciously or without realizing what we are doing), we really would not be settling anything. The question would still remain: "What are the qualities that are thus essential and invariable, and what are the qualities analogous to the different forms that the same fir tree would take if it grew in different places?"

When we try to deal with this question, however, it is well for us to realize that we are asking a kind of question that has appeared, in a generalized form, only late in the development of science. In all sorts of instances, it is natural, it seems, for people to believe that the properties they see "in an object" are properties of the object as such. It is difficult to realize that the properties of anything depend both on it and on its surroundings—that the properties seen are properties of "the object in such and such a setting." But science has had to come to this view. Even such a seemingly simple quality as the weight of stone is not a property of stone as such. If a sizable stone were transported to the moon, it could be lifted by a force only about one-sixth as great as would be required to lift on the earth; if the stone were transported, unchanged in all other respects, to something as massive as the sun, it would seem to change its properties in the other dircetion. As scientific workers often now express this matter, the properties that will be exhibited by anything depend on the total "field conditions," or on the total "field," and not merely on the object itself.

For many purposes we don't need to bother with this field concept. We haven't started transporting rocks to the moon yet. All of the things we want to weigh in ordinary life have almost exactly the same constant field conditions. Accordingly, we do not fall into significant error through our common-sense tendency to think of the weight of things as being in objects themselves. The earth provides the same setting for all of them.

But when we are thinking of personality characteristics, this may not be true. It may be that quite different cultural settings are possible, and it may be that these different cultural settings will bring out quite different properties—properties we will tend to attribute to "human nature as such," but that we ought to see as "properties of human nature in such and such a setting."

In other words, the "field approach" is often merely a luxury when we are thinking about physical objects, but it may be an indispensable part of our thinking when we want to understand human beings. And some of our present theories of personality, far from being thoroughly "deep" understandings of human nature, may be penetrating only on certain points. On other points, they may be seriously and dramatically in error through having failed to ask whether human nature reveals drastically different characteristics under other conditions. We can learn whether this is true or not only by turning to empirical observations. There is no means of answering this question in any a priori way.

Anthropological observations as a possible means of studying personality

To answer the question about the range of potentialities of human nature, it is particularly instructive to turn to the findings of anthropologists, who have studied primitive tribes with cultures very different from our own. Here are experimental situations, as it were, in which human nature is seen under an amazing diversity of conditions such as we could not possibly create by deliberate choice in experimental psychology. Here is a means, perhaps, of learning what is basic and unalterable in human nature and what depends on circumstances.

It is only rather recently that good anthropological information regarding personality has been available. In the past there were some people, such as fur traders and missionaries, who were familiar with primitive tribes. But few of them were interested in making careful and sympathetic observations of the cultures among which they were thrown—the characteristic aim was either to exploit the primitive peoples or to propagandize them, replacing their culture with what we regarded as the best features of our own.

Until recent decades, even anthropologists took little interest in the phenomena of personality. They concerned themselves principally with studying tools, pottery, art designs, kinds of social organization, and physical types. Matters pertaining to personality were too formless, as it were, to appeal to them. For example, in one of anthropologist Ralph Linton's books, in which he urges more attention to the phenomena of personality, he mentions that he remembers vaguely from some earlier field work in Africa a small child who had been punished and was crying bitterly. But who punished the child and for what, who comforted the child, if anyone, and what notice was taken of the whole affair by others? On all these things his notebooks were silent. This was the sort of thing which, at that point, he did not consider important material for himself as an anthropologist.

The older popular view, of course, was that primitive peoples all had quite simple cultures in which there was a minimum of the restraints and controls which govern people in modern society. There were many speculations about these "uninhibited savages," "children of nature," "unspoiled human beings." It was expected, of course, that they would be different from Western peoples in that they lacked most modern knowledge, modern books, and technology. But otherwise, according to the prevailing view, they would be just like us.

Actually, of course, primitive peoples have as long an ancestry as the rest of us. These people did not come into existence a few hundred or a few thousand years ago. From some of the remains dug up by the physical anthropologists, it is evident that a creature with manlike form existed as long as about 500,000 years ago. The primitive people who exist now are just as certainly descended from those very early origins as we are. Consequently, their customs and social institutions have developed over a tremendous period of time. Theirs are *old* cultures. There has been plenty of opportunity for their customs and traditions to become complex and intricate, and the geographical isolation of each group of such peoples from the others permitted vast differences to develop between peoples living in different regions. As a result, there are many different sorts of primitive culture.

A contributing factor in the development of modern anthropological work was a growing appreciation of the fact that primitive people are people with complex cultures. And this development was further stimulated by the growth of a more respectful or sympathetic or discerning attitude toward these primitive cultures. Human beings have always had difficulty in understanding and respecting those who are different from themselves. Other people, outside a given culture, have always been regarded as barbarians—their customs and mode of life have been merely something to laugh at or disparage. This view is still incorporated in one of the fossil items in our language—the term *outlandish*—which now means what is peculiar and unnatural, whereas originally it referred merely to what was from outside the country.

Before the full significance of cultural diversity was seen, men could easily take anthropological reports in their stride. It was not upsetting to hear that, in some societies, parents were killed by their children (the parents submitting gladly) while they were still well and strong, that others always killed one child of any pair of twins that was born, or that men in some societies were regarded as abnormal unless they had homosexual relations before marriage. Anthropological findings could be received with complete equanimity because Western man was profoundly convinced that his was the one right way of life. He saw himself as standing on a single lofty peak, towering above all forms of life and all cultures. If primitive people hunted with spears, used digging sticks instead of plows, wore no clothes, had several wives or husbands, these were merely very old stages in our own past—evolutionary stages that we had left behind many centuries ago.

In the early history of their science, anthropologists themselves shared this view. They sought to trace the steps by which the western European form of marriage ascended the evolutionary scale to its present state of perfection, to see how our institutions had evolved, after the Darwinian model for the evolution of animals, to today's eminence. This view, in more moderate, usually unrecognized ways, still is Western man's main view of other races and cultures.

As the work in anthropology developed, however, a new mode of thinking came into existence. It is a mode of thought that has begun gradually to spread even into our everyday ways of thinking. But it is still very incompletely shared by the majority of people. Primarily it is a view that sees human life in a much larger perspective than we ever ordinarily possess. It suggests that there is probably nothing more final or stable about our own present civilization than there was in any earlier civilization or culture. It suggests that perhaps man, at the present time, has only very imperfectly worked out customs and attitudes and traditions to adapt him to the changed material conditions of modern life. It suggests that social conditions are almost certainly continually changing, and that we need to seek a greater understanding of the factors involved in such change and of the means whereby it governs human living.

This does not mean that anthropologists believe we could turn to any primitive culture and find in it, directly, any good solutions for our own problems. We might find some particular customs and attitudes that are worth adapting to ourselves, much as we might copy some of their artistic designs in textiles or use some of their folk music as a basis for our compositions. But the anthropologist is not looking specifically for things to admire, any more than he is looking for things to disparage. He is looking for a means of understanding, in deeper and more penetrating terms, all of human life, whether primitive or modern. We might designate as the "culture concept" his mode of conceiving both so-called primitive and so-called advanced ways of living as subject matter to be studied in order to learn how human nature assumes its diversity of forms and methods of operating. It is this new attitude, quite alien to the thinkers of previous times, that needs to become our mode of thought if we are to use, in fullest measure, the lessons that can come from the diversity of human life to be found on the face of the earth.

In this chapter we shall utilize some of the anthropologists' material on personality differences. For the most part, we will not attempt to formulate abstract principles—the concrete material speaks effectively for itself. We will stress personality as we find it among groups of human beings that have been discussed in commonly available books, to which lay readers who wish to further their knowledge of this kind of material may turn. Particularly we will take up an Indian group that used to live on the Island of Vancouver, near the present city of Seattle, another group living in New Mexico, and several primitive groups in the South Pacific.

In doing this, we will focus on two main things. With a first set of cultures, we will give special attention to a number of different culturally-determined conceptions of the main nature and purpose of human life. In particular, we will discuss their ceremonials, and the traditions and interpretations related to these. Our interest, it must be remembered, is not primarily in the ceremonials as such, however—these are merely the expressions of more generalized attitudes and values among certain peoples—but in getting a clearer appreciation of the range of differences in human personality. In the second set of cultures we are to describe, we illustrate some specific views as to the proper roles and modes of life for men and women respectively.

How primitive societies differ in their conception of the main nature and purpose of life

The Kwakiutl Indians.[1] We look first at the Kwakiutl, as the Indians who lived on Vancouver Island, on the Pacific coast, were called. This group was fortunate as far as the conditions for a comfortable living were concerned. They obtained an abundance of food from the salmon entering the streams to spawn. Techniques had been developed for making large houses out of planks split from the huge cedar trees of the region, and for making large ocean-going canoes. Fairly definite agreement had been reached on which territories belonged to different groups for hunting and fishing purposes—and even on areas assigned for deep-sea fishing, these being marked off by double landmarks they could sight along while at sea. A good part of the activity of the people consisted of fishing, house-building, canoe-making, and the like. It was a country in which, accordingly, one might have expected a relatively co-operative and friendly society.

Routine activities such as fishing and hunting, however, were not the primary interest of the people, but merely humdrum means of providing

[1]This account of the Kwakiutl and the account of the Zuñi in the next section are drawn from Ruth Benedict, *Patterns of Culture* (Baltimore, Penguin Books, Inc., 1934), Chapters 6 and 4, respectively.

for what they felt was "really important." Main interest centered on intense and unrelenting attempts to get various "possessions" and to use them to humiliate rivals and to glorify themselves individually. The greater portion of the interest taken in these possessions was not because they provided comfort or convenience, but because they could be used for competitive purposes. Thus, crude pieces of native copper were among the most prized possessions, even though these were used for nothing except to enhance the status of their owners.

At a whole series of points in the life of a Kwakiutl male, he would engage in certain ceremonies called "potlatches." As a baby, each boy had been given a name that referred merely to his place of birth. But when he became of sufficient age to assume his first real name, the elders of his group were duty-bound to give him a supply of capital, as it were, to start with (most probably in the form of blankets made from the bark of the cedar trees). He in turn would make presents of these blankets to other boys in the region, distributing his whole wealth in this way. The other boys could not afford to refuse such offers. Such a refusal would be equivalent to admitting they had been shamed by the boy in question. But if they accepted the gift, they were bound to return it with about 100 per cent interest within a year, or be shamed for their failure. Thus the game was started—a game that might have had some of the outward appearance of generosity, but whose purpose was the exact opposite.

If a young man planned well, he gradually increased his reserves by means of such shrewd gifts and got the means of giving more and more impressive parties where he would distribute more and more lavish gifts (all of which always carried the obligation of repayment with outrageous interest). Yet, in the giving of these parties, there was not even the pretense of courtesy and kindliness. On the contrary, since the guests came in full realization that they would be taunted and ridiculed, they came with every intention of outdoing their host in such taunting and ridicule if they could.

In intertribe potlatches, sometimes each side attempted to outdo the other in showing how recklessly they could dispose of their own wealth. The chief who was offering the potlatch might command that several of his best canoes be brought to the lodge and smashed to bits and placed on the fire in the middle of the group. The fire might become so hot that it would scorch the guests, but the rule for them to observe was to show complete indifference, as if to say, "Such a puny fire, such a flop—is this supposed to be something impressive! Not to us!" To demonstrate their greater wealth, they might call for a number of their blankets to be brought, greater in trading value than the canoes that had been destroyed, and put them on the fire, showing that they were able to destroy so much property that they could put out the fire of their rival. To this he might reply by taking some expensive candlefish oil and pouring it over the blankets to make the fire blaze high anew.

Yes, but what does he mean?—"Really getting the feel of Kwakiutl culture, but cannot send manuscript. Had potlatch last week and burned most of it."

As they engaged in ceremonies like this, the chief or his followers would sing songs such as the following:[2]

> I am the first of the tribes,
> I am the only one of the tribes.
> The chiefs of the tribes are only local chiefs.
> I am the only one among the tribes.
> I search among all the invited chiefs for greatness like mine.
> I cannot find one chief among the guests.
> They never return feasts,
> The orphans, poor people, chiefs of the tribes!
> They disgrace themselves,
> I am he who gives these sea otters to the chiefs, the guests,
> the chiefs of the tribes.
> I am he who gives canoes . . .

The chief was not allowed to proceed in utter recklessness in these contests. His followers gloried in his boasting and display, and much of their working life went into the task of preparing what was required for these potlatches. Still, there was a general understanding that a person could not make "unreasonable" demands on his relatives or followers. If he could not win by using what could be spared without bringing economic disaster to the group, there was nothing he could do but to admit the humiliating defeat. In that event he had little reserve, because the whole society was centered in this arrogant, bombastic rivalry. He might, if the situation were humiliating enough, go to the village of the person who had worsted him and murder his competitor, in which case he

[2] *Ibid.*, pp. 176-177.

redeemed his honor and acquired all of the titles of honor that his competitor had won to date. Or he might—and this was by no means an uncommon outlet—escape through suicide if the circumstances were intolerable.

There were innumerable ramifications of this theme in the life of the Kwakiutl. Thus, what a man strove for was not merely these possessions, but a whole series of honorary titles or names which he could earn by such displays and by undergoing arduous initiation into various religious societies. He valued these titles because he then could boast of them and of the exploits of those who had carried these titles previously. Even such events as accidents or the death of a son or a wife were interpreted as humiliations in the eyes of other persons, to be balanced off only by humiliating others. There was only a limited belief in gods, but insofar as there was such a belief, it was brought into the consistent system. The gods were seen as hostile and threatening, and were to be scolded, shamed, and conquered if it seemed that they were working ill against the tribe.

All in all, life among the Kwakiutl called for a great deal of planning, working, sacrificing. Its greatest rewards were the rewards of surpassing and humiliating others, and sometimes of experiencing frenzy and vision in their religious initiation ceremonies.

Most of the other Indian tribes in North America shared many features of this culture. Many of them prized bravery and hardihood in battle, rather than possessions as with the Kwakiutl. But the same insistence on arrogant, boastful behavior, the same seeing of mankind as surrounded by malevolent spirits, and the same stressing of abnormal mental experiences of vision and supernatural "seizure" ran through most of them.

The Pueblo Indians. An extreme contrast with the other North American tribes—and even with neighboring tribes with whom they had appreciable contacts—is found in the Pueblo Indians of what is now Arizona and New Mexico. They have the same biological heritage as the other Indians. But what was made of it was dramatically different.

For example, the Zuñi of New Mexico, like the Kwakiutl, were relatively rich.[3] Their architecture was of stone; they had developed a skillful agriculture; they had produced beautiful weaving, metalwork, and pottery. Although they experienced the recurrent threat of inadequate rainfall, their life was relatively secure for a primitive people.

Among them, as among the Kwakiutl, there was a tremendous emphasis

[3]We have given the description of these Zuñi Indians in the past tense, just as we described the Kwakiutl Indians whose culture is now a thing of the past. There is some justification for this in the fact that the studies which produced this descriptive material were conducted some time ago and may not apply entirely to the present situation. However, the culture of the Zuñi Indians has been a remarkably stable culture, and most of the present description still holds good. The other cultures which will be described later in the chapter also are still in existence in more or less the form here described, but these we have also described in the past tense.

on ritual and ceremony and titles. But the whole purpose and emotional significance of these were different. They were, in no sense, the means by which an individual would seek to enhance his prestige and status in comparison with others. Rather, they were seen by the Zuñi as the means by which their group life could be brought to fulfillment—particularly by achieving the purposes of bringing rain to the crops, fertility to the animals, and fertility to the tribe itself. They were activities in which individuals had to co-operate, but in ways that always subordinated the individual to the requirements of the group.

Many of the dances and rituals of this group can still be seen, and much of the ancient culture of this people has survived. It has therefore been extensively studied and the old beliefs and customs accurately reconstructed.

In the ceremonies of the Zuñi, it was believed that, for the ritual to be efficacious, everything must be letter-perfect—costumes, masks, dance routines, and songs. The ceremonies required a reciting from memory of an amount of material that is staggering for us to contemplate. All of this was watched very attentively by the rest of the group. If the prayed-for rain failed to come, the whole community would spend its time for days or weeks discussing how the dance was performed, trying to find a mistake or imperfection, because only thus could they conceive that the ritual would not have had its intended effect. The gods were not believed to be unfriendly to the people; it was thought that they also liked dances and would be glad to co-operate with such efforts; but they would not be pleased if the ceremonies were not done just right.

In most other Indian groups there has been a serious problem with the alcohol that the white men brought. In many of them, trouble arose from use of the trance-inducing peyote obtained from certain forms of cactus. Among the Pueblo Indians, these have never been problems. They were alien to what the group valued. They were alien to what the group saw as essential for their life, whereas, to so many other Indian groups, alcohol and peyote had a fatal fascination because of the bizarre psychological states they could induce. The Zuñi would not have tolerated anyone who, because he drank, was clumsy in the dance, or forgetful of his lines, or neglectful of the sexual taboos that had to be observed by the main participants both before and throughout the duration of such ceremonies.

Rather than exalting arrogance and boasting, the Zuñi mainly sought moderation, sobriety, and dependability. They did not even compete for high status in the rituals. Instead, they expected that a man would modestly try to avoid distinguishing himself or raising himself above others, and the group had to select and encourage participants.

This does not say that the life of the Zuñi people was empty of positive emotional values or free from anxieties and fears. There must have been profound emotional satisfactions in all the elaborate ritual of the Zuñi people, with its bright masks and costumes, its colorful dances, its deep experience of group participation. But these were not types of emotional values tending to set one person off against another. Instead, they were values tending to prohibit rather than encourage or even tolerate anger and bitterness. Thus, when the priests were participating in the main ceremonies, it was not sufficient that they should engage in the proper external behavior; it was important also that they should feel no anger against any other person during that time. If the rain failed to come, possibly one of the participants had failed, not necessarily because he betrayed anger in a detectable way, but just because he might have *felt* angry.

Ruth Benedict cites an example of this from her experience:[4]

> One summer a family I knew well had given me a house to live in, and because of some complicated circumstances another family claimed the right to dispose of the dwelling. When feeling was at its height, Quatsia, the owner of the house, and her husband were with me in the living room when a man I did not know began cutting down the flowering weeds that had not yet been hoed out of the yard. Keeping the yard free of growth is a chief prerogative of a house-owner, and therefore the man who claimed the right to dispose of the house was taking this occasion to put his claim publicly upon record. He did not enter the house or challenge Quatsia and Leo, who were inside, but he hacked slowly at the weeds. Inside, Leo sat immobile on his heels against the wall, peaceably chewing a leaf. Quatsia, however, allowed herself to flush. "It is an insult," she said to me. "The man out there knows that Leo is serving as priest this year and he can't be angry. He shames us before the whole village by taking care of our yard." The interloper finally raked up his wilted weeds, looked proudly at the neat yard, and went home. No words were even spoken between them. For Zuñi it was an insult of sorts, and by his morning's work on the yard the rival claimant sufficiently expressed his protest. He pressed the matter no further.

Marriages were arranged and conducted with a minimum of excitement or intense feeling, and certainly with a minimizing of jealousy. As Benedict says:[5]

> Domestic affairs like marriage and divorce are casually and individually arranged. Zuñi is a strongly socialized culture and not much interested in those things that are matters for the individual to attend to. Marriage is arranged almost without courtship. Traditionally girls had few opportunities for speaking to a boy alone, but in the evening when all the girls carried the

[4] *Op. cit.*, pp. 97-98.
[5] *Ibid.*, p. 67.

water-jars on their heads to the spring for water, a boy might waylay one and ask for a drink. If she liked him she gave it to him. He might ask her also to make him a throwing stick for the rabbit hunt, and give her afterwards the rabbits he had killed. Boys and girls were supposed to have no other meetings, and certainly there are many Zuñi women today who were married with no more preliminary sex experience than this.

When the boy decides to ask her father for the girl, he goes to her house. As in every Zuñi visit, he first tastes the food that is set before him, and the father says to him as he must say to every visitor, "Perhaps you came for something." The boy answers, "Yes, I came thinking of your daughter." The father calls his daughter, saying, "I cannot speak for her. Let her say." If she is willing, the mother goes into the next room and makes up the pallet and they retire together. Next day she washes his hair. After four days she dresses in her best clothes and carries a large basket of fine corn flour to his mother's house as a present. There are no further formalities and little social interest is aroused in the affair.

Any disappointments or unhappiness in marriage could be handled by divorce proceedings that were even more simple. The wife, if dissatisfied, would put herself out to serve at ceremonial feasts and in this way make contact with a prospective husband. Then, when she was sure she would not be left husbandless, she would gather together the few possessions that were regarded as her husband's and leave them on the doorstep for him to find when he returned. Seeing them, he would be expected to pause and weep, as would also his mother's family when he then returned to the maternal home. But it would be no occasion for violent recriminations or revenge, even though the loss of his wife might be a genuine disappointment to him.

In spite of easy divorce, though, Benedict states that[6] "a very large proportion of Zuñi marriages endure through the greater part of a lifetime. Bickering is not liked, and most marriages are peaceful."

Another expression of their difference from the Kwakiutl is that whereas suicide was not infrequent with the Kwakiutl as the only way to escape an impossible situation, it was hardly known among the Zuñi. Benedict states:[7] "The more particularly you illustrate the practice of suicide to a Zuñi audience, the more politely and smilingly incredulous they become. It is very strange, the things that white people do [or, she might have said, that other Indian groups used to do]. But this is the most laughable of all."

For the Zuñi, what was psychologically disruptive was avoided, whether it was individualistic action that sought to improve traditional procedures, or whether it was a matter of intense emotion, use of alcohol,

[6]*Ibid.*, p. 68.
[7]*Ibid.*, p. 108.

or drugs. A number of things, such as the spreading of folklore about witches after the introduction of this notion from white culture, indicate that there must have been an appreciable undercurrent of anxiety in their culture. But the way that this was handled, along with the way that positive values were secured, was primarily through the stress on carefully-patterned and group-centered activities.

The Tikopians. The Tikopians live on an isolated volcanic island, scarcely three miles wide, in the South Pacific. When they were studied in 1928-29 by Raymond Firth,[8] from whose writings our account is drawn, they were a group of some 1200 people living virtually untouched by the outside world. They lived primitively in the sense that their technological level and their material achievement were low. They wore simple bark-cloth clothing, lived in sago-leaf thatched huts, and worshipped their ancient gods. Food was plentiful.

The ceremonial side of the life of the Tikopians was very highly developed. Marriage, death, and initiations were observed with elaborate ceremonies that were similar to those of the Kwakiutl, but that also stood in striking contrast to the potlatches. They were similar in being ceremonies at which huge quantities of food and goods were gathered and dispensed. Firth reports that an initiation ceremony was talked about and planned for as long as ten months ahead. Taro, the main food for the occasion, was planted in January in order to be ready for the ceremony in August. Great quantities of taro, coconut, fish, pandamus mats, bark cloth, and coils of sinnet rope were prepared co-operatively by large groups of the boy's kinsfolk.

Up to this point, the scene, except for its setting, could easily have presented a group of Kwakiutl preparing for a potlatch. But the Tikopians did not throw the mountain of mats, bark cloth, sinnet, and fishing gear into a fire. These were presented as gifts to all the relatives of the boy—and particularly to more distant relatives, both genealogically and geographically speaking. The whole purpose and tone of the ceremony was in striking contrast to a potlatch. Its purpose was to start the boy off in the adult world with as wide a circle of interested, friendly, and supportive relatives as possible. He was treated as a person of importance. For several days before, he went around the village conspicuously smeared with a red pigment and was the object of interested attention and deferent admiration. He was invited to the dwellings of nearby relatives and given food and a new bark cloth garment—for *arofa* (affection), the natives say.

Songs were practiced for the ceremony, mats plaited, food dug. The neighbors lent their ovens for the occasion, all in a spirit of co-operation. At the beginning of the three- to four-day ceremony, people began as-

[8]Raymond Firth, *We, the Tikopia* (New York, American Book Co., 1936), especially Chapter 13.

sembling from all over the island, bearing food and goods. As each item was added to the heap, the name of the donor was announced with a complimentary flourish. Some brought goods along for the deliberate purpose of seeing that people who wanted to contribute, but for some reason had not collected what they needed, could have something to put on the heap. The mats and other property were regarded as being in honor of the boy.

The difference between this ceremony and the potlatch in emotional tone and significance is already evident in the above. There were many complimentary references to how well the food was cooked. Some relatives whose standing entitled them to gifts declined them on grounds that the ceremonial obligations had already been too heavy an imposition on the father. The least known relatives got, not less, but more gifts than others. "It is good to give to another family," the Tikopians said. The gifts were announced and discussed in such a way as to honor the donors. The personal elevation of others, rather than their downfall, was the objective.

At the end of the ceremonial period the visitors went home bearing gifts, and the boy started on a round, several months in length, of visiting and living with the more remote of these relatives. The whole effect of the ceremony was to knit together a wide-ranging group of kinsfolk who were brought into a friendly, favorable acquaintance with the boy now treated as an adult. He was given a sense of importance and a feeling of support. One of the phrases used in the ceremony in referring to him meant *object of value.*

The everyday personal lives of the Tikopian people showed the same sort of view of the nature and purpose of living. It was not merely in their group ceremonials, but also in their customs in small personal matters that the sense of oneness with the group was fostered. A further expression of interest in children, for example, was the custom of one family's "borrowing" a child from another family. The borrowed child would live with them for some weeks, and then maybe with still another family, depending on what the child wished. Living conditions were simple. There was no question of whether there were beds enough for all, or whether the living space was getting too crowded for comfort. People preferred to sleep with others close beside them, so that there was a feeling of comfort and coziness rather than of aloneness. The thing that the Tikopians could least understand about our culture is our tendency to want to be by ourselves in many of our living and working arrangements so that, as we put it, we can work efficiently. To them, to have a small modern kitchen where there would be room only for the mother would seem cruel both to the mother and to others. And, equally, it would have seemed incredible to them that a man who was well respected in a business concern would be given a private office of his own, walled off from the rest of the group.

There was a minimum of formal social organization among these people, and yet they undertook and carried out a lot of rather large-scale and complex tasks, such as building large ceremonial houses. The anthropologists who worked with them were amazed at how effortlessly the work was done and at the apparently complete absence of any pressure or special rewards employed to get the men to contribute their labors. It was as though the Tikopian people felt: "Life is a secure, happy affair, and part of what is enjoyable about it is the chance to work with others and share activities with them. So, of course, if something like this is to be done, why would anyone need to be urged? Do you have to urge a child to eat!"

This did not adapt the Tikopian people for *some* situations. For example, when Western people moved in on nearby islands and recruited young Tikopian men to work for a period on their plantations, the results were disastrous. Even when special efforts were made to favor the young men, giving them extra time off and other special privileges, most of the young Tikopians would die within several months of transplantation to the new islands, away from their familiar group. It seemed that they literally died of homesickness, and regulations had to be adopted forbidding the recruitment of any Tikopian men for work on other islands. When they were cut off from the usual setting in which their lives had been lived, something was gone that was indispensable for life itself.

Here then were three primitive groups—Kwakiutl, Zuñis, Tikopians—who saw life in quite different terms. All of them might be described as living in a Stone Age culture. But this rough similarity of technological development is a minor matter in some respects, and the differences of personality in the three groups seem much more important. The fact that three peoples are all on the same technological level does not exclude their developing vastly different human characteristics. Surely here is light on the *origins* of personality.

How primitive societies differ in the roles they develop for men, women, and children

Some of the most fundamental facets of personality are the products of a person's conception of himself as a man, woman, boy, girl, child, or adult. These distinctions, so much a part of the ordinary family life of all peoples, might seem to be something that is primarily biologically determined. We tend to think of them in this way. We tend to feel that certain personality characteristics are essentially and naturally masculine, certain others essentially and naturally feminine. We see that small children, even at an age of two or three years, are beginning to act in characteristically boyish or girlish manners. This is one respect, we tend to believe, where human nature is fundamentally an expression of biological factors.

But anthropologists who have studied different societies are very doubtful. In these matters of family relationships and family role, their observations convince them that, once again, we need to see human nature as having a far greater range of potentialities than we would have expected from our knowledge of our own culture, even if we go back to the historical roots of our culture among the Romans, Greeks, and Hebrews.

To throw light on these matters, we shall describe three main groups, all of whom live in New Guinea, an island some distance below southeastern Asia. All three of the groups are closely related biologically, but their cultures are drastically different.

The Mountain Arapesh.[9] These New Guinea people lived in a steep, unfavorable region where it was difficult for them to get sufficient food and where many circumstances of life were hard. Both Arapesh men and Arapesh women were mild, inoffensive, gentle people. Their chief interest centered in their children and in the care of them or, even more broadly, in "helping things to grow," whether these were their children or their gardens. When the parents went from their houses up or down the steep mountain trails to their scattered plots of arable ground, their small children were carried patiently by either the father or mother. When work was done and they sat around for a rest, it was likely to be the father as much as the mother who was inclined to take a small child in his arms and play with him for the satisfaction it brought to him as truly as it did to the infant.

Garden plots were regarded as individually owned, but a family did not work merely on its own plot. The work and the products of the garden were shared. That people should work alone and guard jealously what they had grown was something they would have found hard to understand.

Marriage was arranged in keeping with this pattern of life. Even before a boy had reached adolescence, a wife was picked out for him from among the girls still younger than himself, and it was understood that the girl would then live in his house and that he would care for her and feed her, virtually as a parent would care for a small child. We hear the joking comment sometimes in our own society that the best way to get a good wife is to "get her young and raise her from a pup." With the Arapesh

[9]The accounts of the Arapesh, Mundugumor, and Tchambuli peoples in the following sections were drawn from Margaret Mead, *Male and Female: A Study of the Sexes in a Changing World* (New York, William Morrow & Co., 1949).

this would have been no joke—it would have been understood as the most natural way for a good marriage to be accomplished.

There were problems in this society—problems that their culture hardly knew how to meet. They could not always get a sufficient supply of food. Even though the parents wanted to keep their children happy and supplied with the means for growth, they sometimes could not do this. And when a child would throw himself on the ground in a temper tantrum and cry because the parents could not satisfy his hunger, the Arapesh parents had no defense for such a situation, and tended to become extremely baffled and angry with themselves.

But, for the most part, this was a happy and peaceful group, partly because of the fact that men as well as women had learned to accept what we would tend to call a maternal or nourishing and protective attitude and because most activities were co-operatively shared. When an Arapesh man was asked whether his group had any customs that would prevent the marriage of brothers and sisters, he could hardly see why such a question should be asked. After all, he would say, when you marry, you get a number of brothers-in-law who then will share with you the work of gardening and hunting; but if you married your sister you naturally would not be acquiring any brothers-in-law. So why would anyone ever even think of such a thing?

Arapesh children did get a picture of the roles of men and women as being different in some respects. In carrying loads, the women used a net or bag that hung from their foreheads; the men carried similar things on poles over their shoulders. The men hunted; women did not. Women had the special function, of course, of bearing and nursing children. So there were differences. But the view of temperament and general pattern of life for the two sexes was much the same. Even, it is said, one would hear comments like this: "Yes, he is a fine-looking man. But you should have seen him before he had so many children!"

The Mundugumor. Among the members of this New Guinea tribe, the attitude toward children was exactly opposite to that of the Arapesh, and also, we remember, of the Tikopians. Neither the Mundugumor men nor the women had a protective and nurturing attitude toward children. Women disliked being pregnant and tried to avoid it whenever possible. After the birth of the child, the same attitude prevailed. The baby was nursed only when it cried violently and was nursed no longer than the mother judged absolutely necessary to shut it up for a while. There was no fondling or playing with infants. Even the mode of carrying them was made impersonal by putting them in a basket of rather rough, harsh bark ropes.

The traditional occupations of men among the Mundugumor were formerly head-hunting and the securing of captives for cannibalistic ceremonies. Wood-carving and decorating wooden figures also were masculine occupations. Most of the fishing and farming, as well as other work, was done by the women and young boys. A great deal of time was spent in quarreling and plotting. Even within a family the arrangements were such as to tend to set one member of a family against another. Daughters were welcomed into the family by the father chiefly because the daughter could be traded for another wife; but his sons also could secure wives only by trading a sister or a valuable flute for a wife. Taboos prohibited two brothers from eating from the same dish or even speaking to each other except in anger.

The Tchambuli. Distinctive roles were assigned to men and women in this tribe, but their roles were different from those seen in many other cultures. Margaret Mead summarizes her observations of the Tchambuli people in these terms:[10]

> Adult males in Tchambuli are skittish, wary of each other, interested in art, in the theatre, in a thousand petty bits of insult and gossip. Hurt feelings are rampant . . . the pettishness of those who feel themselves weak and isolated. The men wear lovely ornaments, they do the shopping, they carve and paint and dance. Before the coming of British control, head-hunting had been reduced to the ritual killing of bought captives, and they put up no effective resistance against the depredations of the neighbouring Iatmuls, but fled inland instead. . . . Men whose hair was long enough wore curls, and the others made false curls out of rattan rings.
>
> This is the only society in which I have worked where little girls of ten and eleven were more alertly intelligent and more enterprising than little boys. . . . but in Tchambuli the minds of small males, teased, pampered, neglected, and isolated, had a fitful fleeting quality, an inability to come to grips with anything.

The Tchambuli women, on the other hand, carried on the main economic activity of the people and had a simple, secure life of their own. As Mead describes it:[11]

> Where the Iatmul woman treats her child as strong, as capable of wilfulness and assertiveness . . . , the Tchambuli woman stresses her own strength. She feeds her baby lightly, gaily, either from her breast or with a variety of lollipops, lily-roots, sweet seeds, and fruits. Where the Iatmul mother chases her erring two-year-old with a ten-foot paddle with which she threatens to kill him when she catches him—and never does kill—the Tchambuli mother simply tucks small offenders under her confident arm. In Iatmul, it is the women and children who wear strings of ornaments; in Tchambuli it is the men and the children; the women go with shaven heads, unadorned, deter-

[10] *Ibid.*, p. 98.
[11] *Ibid.*, p. 97.

minedly busy about their affairs. . . . In Tchambuli . . . a young girl enters as a bride the house of her father's sister. As aunt and mother-in-law, his mother treats the young wife well. The women of the house form a great solid mass, always together, working briskly while the little boys tumble unconsidered among them, and the young men sit gingerly on the edge of the women's group and then flee to the men's house.

Cultural influences affect physiological as well as psychological functions

We can profitably supplement what we have reported about the various roles developed for different family members in different cultures by adding some observations indicating that cultural factors affect at least some functions that look as if they were purely physiological.

One example of this is the matter of nausea or morning sickness which pregnant women experience in many different cultures. This is known to be related at least in part to endocrine changes and other physiological changes within the body of the mother during the course of pregnancy. However, anthropological observations show that this phenomenon is definitely not independent of cultural influences.

As Margaret Mead reports, drawing on extensive knowledge of different primitive peoples, ". . . where it is culturally stylized as appropriate for any period of pregnancy or order of pregnancy (such as first pregnancy only), a large majority of women will show this behavior; where it is not, only a very few will. Convulsive vomiting is a capacity of human organism which can be elaborated, neglected, or to a large degree disallowed."[12]

Similarly, it seems that the amount of pain experienced in childbirth is greatly influenced by cultural factors. This has been pointed out by the English obstetrician, Grantly Dick Read.[13] His attention was first called to the matter when he attended the birth of a baby in a poor flat in East London, so poor that the bed was merely some boards put across boxes. As labor progressed, he asked the young mother whether she wished to take an anesthetic. She declined. After the child was born, he asked her why she had refused the anesthetic. "Didn't it hurt?" he asked. She turned to him and said with some surprise, "Was it supposed to?"

That incident started him on a long study of factors involved in childbirth. He found that when women of his own cultural group were given a new understanding of what childbirth might involve and were taught, insofar as any voluntary participation in it was concerned, to go at it in a different way, the great majority of mothers could have much the same experience as this young East End mother. Even when anesthet-

[12] *Ibid.*, p. 220.

[13] Grantly Dick Read, *Childbirth Without Fear* (New York, Harper & Brothers, 1944).

ics were available on request, and even though the women were by no means attempting to set records of heroism, as many as 97 per cent of women in many hospitals would say that the anesthetics were not needed, and they declined to use them.

In part of his work, Read made a trip of investigation almost from one end of Africa to the other, gathering data from mothers and midwives in many tribes. He found that, although there were a few instances where medical help was needed, the great majority of African women apparently found birth a simple experience rather than a painful one to be looked forward to with dread.

In western culture there is a strong tradition to the effect that childbirth is painful. One of the authors heard an example of this in an address by the main speaker at a high school commencement exercise. The speaker urged that young people should have more respect for their bodies. They should keep in mind, he said, at what great cost their lives had been made possible. All of the suffering of all the wars in history, he said, could not be compared with the suffering that had been involved on the part of women in bringing their children into the world, and because of this, children should treat themselves as something that had been purchased at a great price.

In taking this view, he merely reflected what is embodied within our scriptures. In the time of the ancient Hebrews, the Psalmists spoke of painful situations in terms of an accepted simile: "They shall wail as a woman in travail."

When we note this apparent influence of cultural factors on experience in childbirth, we need not suppose that the pain that has been experienced in our cultural group has been merely "psychological." For, even in the view elaborated by Dr. Read, this is not what he means. What he holds is, rather, that the traditional attitudes and childbirth techniques of Western culture have actually produced physiological conditions which, in turn, make childbirth inevitably painful. The muscles of the cervix actually tend to tighten up in a state of anxiety or fear, whereas they might be relaxed instead. Attempts to help the process of childbirth by voluntary contractions of abdominal muscles at too early a stage tend to put the cervix under pressure and create a congested condition there that would not occur if the basic reflex processes of the body were allowed more control during the major part of the birth process. So here, as in many psychosomatic effects, the final effect that is experienced (in this case, pain) is not merely the product of brain processes, but has intermediate physiological links that owe their character to the learned modes of response of the person. And the learning that changes such basic physiological processes may be cultural learning, rather than something derived merely from an individual's testing of the nature of things.

The problem of whether there are any adverse factors in our own Western cultural patterns

When we consider anthropological observations such as we have surveyed, it is easy enough for us to realize that *other* groups of people are influenced by cultural factors. Especially when the cultural factor is clearly at odds with something in our own culture, we can see it as "peculiar." Things that are peculiar are, in our somewhat naive thought, more or less the things that are culturally determined. When we see the elaborate ceremonies of the Zuñi for insuring rain, we say that these ceremonies may be aesthetically interesting, but that they surely do not affect meteorological conditions. We feel sure that the Zuñi's interpretations of conditions surrounding them are superstitious, not realistic, and as such must be the products of their culture.

When the discussion turns to our own culture, however, it is different. We have difficulty in seeing that anything that we do or believe comes from any cultural factors. We tend to feel that what we do is dictated by external, objective realities. We see things in such and such ways because we feel this is the only way a people can see them, if they remain realistic.

Our difficulties here are probably not purely intellectual, but are also motivational in character. This was expressed very clearly by a 15-year-old boy who had been traveling with his family in different parts of Europe. He expressed himself in somewhat these words: "You know, this is sort of upsetting, to find that people live in different ways like this and have different outlooks. It makes it hard for you to know what is really right. There must be some way to live, and some way to think about things, that is really right. But how can you be sure that you have the right way to think about things, or the right way to live, when you see that there are so many people who don't agree with you! There ought to be some way to make people do the same things. Can't they agree, somehow, on what things really are? I don't enjoy this traveling as much as I should. It takes away my feeling of assurance about things too much."

This boy was expressing his reaction more clearly and frankly than most people would. But the feeling he had is common. The culture concept, with its emphasis on the developing, changing nature of culture, is something that challenges the view we built up in childhood regarding the stability and inevitability of our mode of life. Accordingly, this concept tends to produce a feeling of insecurity that makes it hard for us to accept the need for re-examining the basic customs and values embodied in our culture.

However, it may prove costly to us if we continue to neglect this task. The operations of modern society have certainly entailed some hideous consequences. It has become important for us to ask with great seriousness, therefore, whether some of the difficulties and evils of modern society may not come from some peculiar, unfortunate, and unnecessary biases—or perhaps blindnesses—in our own cultural patterns.

This is not the place for any long discussion of this problem. But it may be useful to assess the effect of at least a few features of our own culture.

Perhaps first we ought to point to a few favorable ones. For example, we have come to recognize the possibility of drastic changes and improvements in technological processes and in the material conditions of life. We take this view for granted, but primitive tribes more typically felt that their tools and weapons were the only possible ones they could ever have. For another thing, we have come to recognize how many similarities of capacity and interest there are between men and women, and so at last we regard it as natural to open up to women many opportunities not available to them in earlier stages of Western culture.

A complete analysis of our culture would reveal many other positive features. As we have said, however, we all expect our culture to include such things. It can help us to assess the role of cultural factors better if we can bring ourselves to face up to some of the possible mistakes and dangerous liabilities to be found in our own culture. Three of these may be singled out for mention.

1. *An excessive respect for science and the products of technology to the neglect of human values.* We have allowed much of the rest of our culture to be dominated by the needs or requirements of industry and of science. We have tended to overemphasize training of the intellectual functions and to neglect training of the emotional processes. But emotion and feeling are in one sense the ends of living and not at all the disruptive, disintegrating factors constantly threatening civilization that they are sometimes represented as being.

2. *The tendency to reductionism in our thinking.* As another consequence of our scientific development, our modern thinking tends to favor a *reductionist* interpretation of reality. That is, we tend to interpret everything in terms of the basic presupposition that whatever aspects seem complex or immaterial are not truly real but need to be analyzed or reduced to simpler and more elementary terms if we want really to understand them. All chemical compounds, we say, are after all merely different combinations of a hundred or so elements. All color effects are merely matters of lights of different wave length, and there is nothing in those wave lengths like the greens and blues and other colors we think we see. All thoughts are presumably merely masses of nervous impulses. All nervous impulses in turn, however, are merely chemical processes. All habits are nothing but linkages between stimuli and muscular movements. And so on down the line.

This "nothing but" approach—or this "postulate of an impoverished reality," as one writer has put it—is an approach which we tend to believe is forced on us by the findings of science. But this is hardly true. Reductionism is merely *one* way in which the thinking and findings of science may be expressed. The modern world still needs to learn whether this is generally the best way that they may be expressed. This approach actually may be distorting our experience of the world in much the same way that our conception of a person would be distorted if we took some exaggerated caricature of him and said, "Everyone recognizes the effectiveness of that portrayal—why, the thing looks more like him than he does himself!"

Cultural factors can affect modes of thought as indefinite and generalized as this. They can make certain outlooks on life seem not only natural but utterly inevitable. All the while such an outlook may be in fact only one of a number of possible perspectives, and a seriously unadaptive, hampering one at that.

3. *The terror-and-danger theme in our own culture.* One of the ways to find out about the culture of a people is to study their folklore—to see what stories, themes, and plots run through their literature, presumably because they appeal to a majority of the people. Such a study reveals what it is these people demand. One type of such literary material, a type that appears every day and therefore is in a position to respond to popular demand in an effort to increase its circulation, is a daily newspaper. If we use newspapers as an index of what people want—and newspaper publishers are not likely to be seriously unaware of what people like—what we see is that people want to read about murders, traffic accidents, airplane crashes, people trapped in burning buildings, and children falling through thin ice and being drowned. Those who read about these calamities do not have to know the victims personally in order to be interested. The news from all over the world is combed to get vivid accounts of calamities involving danger, terror, injury, and death.

Another section of the newspaper that suggests the same thing is the comics. These were once what the name implies, portrayals of amusing characters and mirth-producing—though sometimes ridiculous—incidents. There are still a few characters like Major Hoople and Dagwood Bumstead. But one after another of the comics has been replaced by a so-called comic strip in which the main content is far from humorous. Most of these do not evidence such bland disregard of realities as Little Orphan Annie with her hairbreadth escapes from one dilemma after another, each starting out as an apparently peaceful and homelike situation, but becoming one in which people find themselves on the brink of destruction by sinister powers. But the same theme—terror, imminent danger, and escape by a squeak—runs through one comic strip after another.

This theme, in a gruesomely exaggerated form, dominates some of the comic books that are such a prominent part of contemporary childhood and adolescent reading. Fredric Wertham, a psychiatrist who has studied the comic book problem for years, has pointed out how shocking the actual contents of some of these so-called comics have become. One of the reproductions of a comic in Wertham's book shows a baseball game being played with the hacked-up pieces of a human body. The bleeding torso of a man serves as the catcher's body-protector, a head is the baseball, a leg the bat, and entrails mark out the path to bases. The captions to this *horror comic* read as follows:[14]

> So NOW you KNOW, friends, WHY there is a ball game being played in the moonlight at midnight in the deserted Central City ball park. Looks CLOSELY. SEE this STRANGE BASEBALL GAME! See the long strings of pulpy intestines that mark the baselines . . . the heart that is the homeplate. See Doc White bend and whisk the heart with the mangy scalp, yelling . . .
> "PLAY BALL . . . Batter up!"
> See the batter come to the plate swinging the legs, the arms, then throwing all but one away and standing in the box waiting for the pitcher to hurl the head in to him. See the catcher with the torso strapped on as a chest protector, the infielders with their hand-mits, the stomach-resin-bag, and all the other pieces of equipment that once was Central City's star pitcher, Herbie Satten.

The movies are still another contribution to the development of this terror-and-danger theme. Horror movies, crime movies, war movies—what a large proportion of current movies are covered by these three categories!

We often minimize such things by saying, "Of course such things appeal to children and to relatively uneducated readers. Not everyone falls for this stuff, of course."

Maybe not. But the list of readers of mystery stories would be a long one. In addition, at a number of points in the history of the United States and other Western countries, there has been a great deal of the same kind of preoccupation with danger and terror. The country is seen as beset by danger, from without and within. A great amount of time and energy is spent in trying to "free the country from communists," even though the asserted numbers are so few that it appears amazing they would be seen as any great threat by Americans having any confidence in the constructive forces within their own country. Vast sums have been secured for military research and development and for aiding countries that are seen as potential military allies, even when those countries are known to be odiously Fascistic in tradition. It is not merely the common people, but many of the most influential leaders of the country who have tended to see life as fraught with terror and danger.

We need not suppose that such a cultural theme is of recent invention.

[14] Fredric Wertham, *Seduction of the Innocent* (New York, Rinehart & Co., Inc., 1953), opposite p. 212.

In decrying the modern horror comics, we must not overlook the fact that the epic of Beowulf, from the eighth century, is the story of a dangerous and cruel creature that came out of the depths of a dank swamp night after night in order to drag people down to the depths of the swamp and devour them at leisure. Its theme is rescue from this danger by a superhuman man who could dive beneath the waters and fight for days with this dread creature before having to come up for air!

In our religious tradition, again, there is the same theme. Among the Jewish people the greatest religious service was and still is the Passover—the commemoration of the time when the Hebrew people finally were able to flee after their long enslavement in Egypt. Part of this Passover story is that the Angel of Death came to take the first-born son from each family in Egypt except the Hebrew families, to whom the instruction had been given that a certain sign should be placed at the portal of the house to insure sparing of that family. Another part of that story was the tale of how the chariots of Egypt pursued the fleeing Hebrews to the Red Sea, the waters of which parted to permit the Hebrew people to cross but returned to engulf and destroy the Egyptian soldiers when they tried to cross. This terror-and-danger theme ran recurrently through the Hebrew scriptures—witness the Garden of Eden, where mankind so aroused the anger of Jehovah by eating the forbidden fruit that man was almost destroyed; the flood, when Jehovah eliminated all humanity except one man and his family; and the exile into Babylon. Within the Christian scriptures, the Crucifixion theme continued the same note.

The Hebrew people did not lack evidence that life could be marked by terror and danger. They were cruelly treated by others and, when they could, they meted out cruelty in return. They invaded the Promised Land on no excuse except that it was a fruitful country and that they wanted it. When they captured cities they put to the sword all the men, and often also the women and children. When the Romans finally sacked Jerusalem for its rebellious resistance against Roman religious impositions, the records tell of the burning of the city and the massacre of its whole population of about 60,000 people. On down to Hitler's slaughter of perhaps six to eight million of their group, the Jewish people have had reasons for seeing life in terms of terror and either slaughter or escape. And a great deal of the rest of the history of Western European peoples has been marked by dangers—whether violent death at the hands of marauding invaders or death in great plagues or, more recently, from war on a greater scale than ever before in history.

Unquestionably, much of their history can be cited by those who live under Western culture to justify a cultural pattern of preoccupation with terror and danger. But the question we face, with reference to these broad cultural aspects of Western life, is the same sort of question we face when we are seeking to understand our individual personalities. We may be showing the very thing that can be observed in play therapy with children, as we noted in the preceding chapter. There the individual child has more than merely a strong tendency to see things in familiar terms. He tends to act as though he were attempting to coerce the new situation into those familiar terms, even though this sort of situation is one he has been trying to resist or escape! The child tends to create the very effects he has suffered from. His parents often prove ready to respond in a different way when the child's behavior gives them something different to respond to. The child was not responding, therefore, to the full range of realities in his social environment; he was responding merely to part of them.

In the same way, the important question with reference to Western culture is whether external realities really force us to respond by finding such a preponderance of terror-and-danger, or whether our doing this may be the expression of a cultural pattern leading us to emphasize one aspect of life out of all proportion. And it is a question whether, with this theme, we tend to create the very effects that we fear. There may well be some realities in the international scene that ought to be understood in *other* terms than these, such as by a cultural theme of co-operation, helpfulness, or a respectful tolerance of others' ways. There might even be more possibilities of security for a nation that would live on those terms than for the nation that looked with alarm on the world around it.

There is a lot of work to be done before we can know whether Western culture has been unduly dominated by such a terror-and-danger theme. Perhaps there is some other explanation for the prominence of this theme in so much of our journalism and politics and for our endless reiteration of crime and horror movies and wild West battles against savage Indians and wild outlaws. Perhaps there is some other explanation for the fact that our religion has been cast so typically in terms of an angry and threatening God, or in terms of hell-fire and damnation. Perhaps there is some other explanation for the strong tendency in Western culture to cast the act of giving birth to a child in such threatening terms, even though many other cultures have not done so. But to an anthropologist developing his picture of a culture from seeing what consistent theme tends to run through it, expressed in one setting after another, it might seem that terror and danger are too recurrent in our culture to be based on an objective interpretation of events.

In saying all this, we do not mean to imply that Western culture is the only one which has stressed such a terror-and-danger theme. Some primitive groups have been marked by much the same thing. But we do stress the fact that there are almost certainly some parts of our Western outlook on life which are not necessarily expressive of any basic human nature at all and which therefore do not necessarily characterize the life of either modern or primitive peoples. Yet these run through our modern life and determine its character in extremely powerful ways. If this is so, we need to take it into account in our efforts to understand personality, because even the personality of modern man is largely a product of traditional cultural influences, and not of his particular individual experiences or of his hypothetical "original nature."

The problem of what produces cultural patterns

We have quoted anthropological authorities who discovered that even when primitive groups live within 30 or 40 miles of each other and are of closely similar biological stock, as among the New Guinea peoples, the differences of personality and behavior between them can be very marked. Biological factors do not compel human personality to develop always in one narrow way. They create a wide range of potentialities, and it is the culture of a people, broadly speaking, that determines which of these potentialities will be developed and which will be muted.

A further question, however, immediately presents itself when we think about such data as we have reviewed. It is the question as to just which factors are peculiarly effective in producing these differences of culture. This is a question we would like to have the anthropologists answer.

But it is an exceedingly difficult one. One tribe differs from another, not just in some one circumstance which might then be seen as the causative factor, but in a multitude of possible causative factors. For example, if one compared merely the Kwakiutl with the Arapesh, he might be tempted to say: "Ah yes, here it is: where a people have an abundant food supply, they will not use up their energy in wresting a living from their environment and will not focus on the need of co-operative behavior, but will resort to competition and wasteful display."

If one looked only at the Kwakiutl and the Arapesh, this might seem like a plausible hypothesis. But if we turn to the Tikopia, or to the Samoans (whom we have not described), we find that although their food supplies were abundant, these peoples were happy and friendly. So one beautiful hypothesis goes by the board.

The origins of cultural patterns must be sought in more complex factors. But we do not command, as yet, the research methods and the data these provide that would throw much light on this exceedingly important question. It may be that this is a case where anthropology will need to draw upon laboratory studies of thinking and problem solving and perception to pick up clues to the interpretation of complex cultural materials.

One conclusion at least is pretty definitely established by anthropologists—namely, that when a group develops and uses some general cultural theme, it is not necessarily true that they do this in a conscious way and that they can formulate the bases of their actions. Apparently cultural patterns can be developed and transmitted without the members of the group realizing that they are doing anything more than handling specific situations.

Anthropologists increasingly note this phenomenon when they work with primitive peoples. Often, after they have watched a group for some time and talked with many of the natives about their understanding of a situation, they find that the natives are at a loss to explain why such and such a thing is done—it is merely that the particular situation seemed to call for the particular action. Or, sometimes, the people in a culture may insist that what they do is one thing, even when the anthropologists who watch them over some period of time, and who piece their observations together, know that they are doing the opposite of what they say. The anthropologist has learned that he has to work on cultural problems in the same way in which you might study a three-year-old and discover, from his *eated*, *drinked*, and *maked*, that he must have learned the regular means of indicating past time of actions, even though he cannot possibly recognize and describe what he is doing.

In a great many cultural matters, people show evidence of having adopted such unrecognized assumptions. One reason why this is important is that it helps us to see why social problems are frequently hard to solve. We will discuss such phenomena in the next chapter. As we will say there, when people are confronted with difficult puzzles, they work within the limitations of certain presuppositions. Usually they do not realize that they have adopted these assumptions, and they are not able to ask whether they should replace those assumptions with some others. They simply do not realize that their problem solving is so heavily governed by unconsciously-held ideas.

Do cultural influences tend too much to shape our theories of personality?

We have seen that the culture of a group tends profoundly to establish the outlook on life that people have. It makes them accept as inevitable views that are not adopted at all by other groups. This raises some warnings for us. Do these cultural influences affect merely our everyday thinking? Or, when technical workers try to engage in rigorously scientific thinking, are they likely also to be influenced by these presuppositions which their cultural group as a whole tends to use and take for granted?

If this were true, it would not necessarily prove that the principles thereby developed are unsound. As we have insisted, culture does not always consist of unrealistic perceptions and interpretations. The valuable and useful parts of our understanding of the world also are given to us mostly by our cultural heritage.

When one examines some of the technical theories about personality, however, one wonders whether they are really based on facts, or whether they are primarily merely the familiar themes of the given culture dressed up in more scientific garb. We were saying above, for instance, that three main themes can be seen in our modern Western culture: first, the rationalistic emphasis on the picture of what man ought to be; second, the reductionist principle, or belief that some truer understanding can be achieved by viewing a complex thing in terms of properties learned by the study of simpler elements; and, third, the terror-and-danger theme.

Now, when we examine the Freudian or psychoanalytic interpretation of personality, we find that all three of these are represented in it. Freudian theory certainly insists that there are powerful irrational factors in human nature. But it does not see those as something to be trusted, or as something inherently adapted to the needs of civilized man. On the contrary, the nonrational parts of human nature are viewed mostly as something threatening, something posing difficulties which ordinary thought had not been able to face. In the second place, psychoanalytic thought has tended to take seeming psychological realities and to propose that they were "nothing but" the operation of such and such simpler biological influences. Thus, Erich Fromm has the following[15] to say about the thinking of Abraham Kardiner, a psychoanalyst who has attempted to interpret anthropological data in the light of Freudian theory:

> He explains differences in basic personality, hence in culture, by differences in maternal care. But while weaning and sphincter control are mentioned among the main characteristics of maternal care the concept of *love* is not even mentioned. On the other hand we find "constancy of attention" mentioned without reference to the totality of the mother-child relationship. Quite obviously the constant attention of the loving mother has an entirely different meaning and impact from the constant attention of a possessive and dominating mother.

In the third place, the whole theme that runs through psychoanalytic thinking has a surprising degree of resemblance to the terror-and-danger theme which, as we have seen, has been so prevalent in our culture. This general character is well expressed in the biography of Freud written by one of his closest admirers and followers, Hanns Sachs. In it Sachs wrote:[16]

> To look at the Medusa's head is no parlor game. Freud—and this is the sum of everything that has been said in this chapter—was steady enough to stand

[15]Erich Fromm, in S. S. Sargent and Miriam W. Smith, eds., *Culture and Personality* (New York, Viking Fund, 1949), pp. 3-4.

[16]Hanns Sachs, *Freud: Master and Friend* (Cambridge, Mass., Harvard University Press, 1944), p. 123.

firm when he perceived that we are not and never will become the masters of our own soul, even when he made the staggering discovery of what unholy stuff the unknown masters are made. He did not flinch when he had to look down, standing at the brink of the precipice. Most others who followed in his tracks got at first a fit of giddiness and had to hold on to him to steady themselves when the mountains seemed to reel. What could those do who were too proud to be supported by him and yet too weak to stand alone? They covered their eyes with their hands and slunk away.

We can sympathize with Sachs's belief that Freud needed a good deal of courage to explore the sort of view of human personality associated with his name. But, as the childhood saying is, we might keep our fingers crossed on this matter. Freud was not sounding a note new in his culture; he was reiterating an old theme. It might have taken more courage, perhaps, if he had come to see something like this, which might have been justified: "I have come to recognize some very deep hostilities and other disruptive tendencies within myself as well as within others. But I cannot say that this is inevitable. Human nature does not always take this form, and circumstances may have produced something in myself, and in perhaps most other persons in our culture, which is not necessarily the root character of human life."

Such questions as these are not ones to be settled on the basis of who has the most "courage," however. They are questions of what principles are most supported by a very wide range of facts. And, the thing that might make us most uncertain about the psychoanalytic suggestions is that they are not based on any such wide array of facts. Psychoanalysts have generally been professionally trained mainly in medical and biological knowledge, to which later psychoanalytic techniques and theories have been added. Since most psychoanalysts have had little other background, they have had very little appreciation of the need of a cultural or "field" interpretation of what is biologically given in human personality. It may be they have tended to see, as traits of "human nature as such," traits that are characteristic of people in one kind of setting, just as a stone has one weight on the earth and a different weight on the moon.

When a person uses a "field" approach, he becomes cautious about predicting what will be seen under conditions which have not yet been created and tested. A chemist, for example, would say: "Over and over again, whole new ranges of properties of chemicals have been opened out to us. We have found, for example, that compounds can be formed under high pressure that previously were believed to be impossible. We have found that processes which use chlorine rather than oxygen in the intermediate transformations have made possible a whole series of other compounds. Consequently, no chemist would now try to describe the full range of qualities of chemicals. When we develop new conditions—*some of which never exist under natural conditions*—we will learn about properties we had not dreamed of previously."

In the same way, perhaps it remains to be seen what qualities human personality will show when the cultural setting of life takes new forms not previously observed. Our personalities are part of a larger fabric, and as that larger fabric changes, the probability is that what had seemed basic and unalterable in human personality may prove to have changed also.

It might be protested that when we ask psychologists to recognize the dependence of personality on field factors, we are not talking about concepts that are subject to experimentation, and that such an approach would keep psychology from being "scientific." But this seems like a travesty on the task and responsibility of psychology. People do not turn to psychology merely for a summary tabulation of the findings of experiments that have been obtainable to date; they turn to psychology, and quite legitimately, to obtain as truthful and basic a picture of human nature as can be furnished. If, to get this picture, we need to enlarge the kinds of data that we consider, well and good. The aim of the scientist must be the clearest possible thinking and the most instructive factual observations he can find.

Summary

An important question about personality asks, "What characteristics of human beings are inherent and fairly unalterable even under different social conditions?" All groups have a tendency to see their own characteristics as expressive of true, unalterable human nature. Both in popular thought in our generation and in orthodox psychoanalytic theory there is a strong tendency to see human nature in the rather discouraging terms of inevitable hostility, self-centeredness, tendency to prejudice, and lack of satisfaction in living. Relatively recent developments in other sciences, however, suggest the need for a "field approach" and warn us against imagining that we know the properties of anything unless we actually have observed the properties revealed under a wide diversity of conditions.

The science best adapted to learning how human nature operates under drastically different social or cultural conditions is anthropology. Anthropologists have called our attention to the amazingly diverse cultures that have developed where primitive peoples have remained isolated from outside influences. Anthropologists have been slow in shifting from the study of relatively tangible aspects of primitive culture to the phenomena of personality involved in those cultures, but no one denies that anthropological observations of personality give us an increasingly rich field of study.

The conception of the main nature and purpose of human life is extremely different in different primitive groups. The Kwakiutl Indians saw life mainly in terms of competitive, boastful pursuits aimed at humiliating rivals and bringing prerogatives and status to the self. Possessions were valued and used primarily to this end. Ceremonies were conducted without even the pretense of courtesy or consideration, these being replaced by culturally-stylized boasting and ridicule. The Zuñi Indians also had an elaborate ceremonial life, but this was seen primarily as the co-operative social activity whereby the life of the group was served by attempts to secure necessary or desired ends such as rain and fertility. Boasting, competitiveness, and individual display were culturally discouraged; instead, emphasis was put on careful execution of responsibilities to the group and on sharing of resources for group purposes. The Tikopians, occupying a tiny island in the Pacific, mainly stressed the enjoyment of social participation and had customs that tended mostly to knit the people together in a friendly, secure group. Rather complex projects often occupied the Tikopian people, but it was hard for outside observers to understand how this work was organized or rewarded. It seems that the Tikopian culture developed persons who enjoyed such activities primarily for the social participation and other intrinsic emotional satisfactions involved.

Various primitive tribes differ profoundly, also, in the traits they encourage within men and women respectively and in the attitudes they take toward children and encourage in children toward themselves. The Mountain Arapesh of New Guinea developed, both in men and in women, a nurturing and protective attitude which was expressed toward children, in the marriage relationship and in the co-operative economic activity of the adults. Among the Mundugumor, on the other hand, attitudes of quarrelsomeness and self-centeredness are encountered in both men and women. The Tchambuli, also a New Guinea group, developed a secure, comfortable, productive role for the women, but assigned such roles to the men that their lives really were centered in fussy details and in all sorts of petty problems of gossip and status.

Such cultural influences affect even some things which might be regarded as almost purely physiological matters, as the occurrence of nausea in pregnancy and sharp pain in childbirth. Such influences do not come "merely in psychological ways," and it is important to find the intermediate physiological means whereby cultural traditions are transmitted into final psychological effects; but the cultural influences seem clear.

It is unusually difficult for us to recognize cultural influences in our own lives, because, in our limited view, we seem to ourselves to be conforming to the external realities of our lives, rather than to what has been arbitrarily imposed upon us by our particular culture. Not only intellectual difficulties, but also the feelings of insecurity that come from seeing the shifting character of cultural influences tend to hamper our discernment of our own culture. However, such understanding of our own culture is important, because our culture contains, in addition to unquestionably valuable elements, other elements seriously open to question. Of the latter, three such are the excessive respect for rationalism in our Western culture, the tendency to use reductionism in trying to explain things, and the tendency to see life in terms of a terror-and-danger theme. The latter is illustrated by the content of newspapers, comics, and movies and by the ways in which international relations tend to be handled. The terror-and-danger theme runs back into Hebrew times and of course has had plenty of encouragement at many points in history. It is still possible, however, that it is less needed as an outlook on life than we tend to realize in our culture, and that it may operate as personality concepts operate within individuals, tending to make us create some of the very effects we fear.

Cultural patterns cannot be attributed to any simple influences such as abundance or scarcity of food supply, though such factors of course contribute some details of cultural activity. Study of cultural patterns reveals one phenomenon like that seen in the processes of problem solving and concept formation within individuals—namely, that groups very commonly cannot describe or recognize what cultural patterns they have, even though their behavior consistently shows that certain patterns are there.

There is a serious risk that cultural influences will determine, not merely other parts of our lives, but also the supposedly scientific thinking of personality theorists. It is possible, for instance, that the predominantly biological background of psychoanalytic theorists has left them rather blind to the influences of cultural factors. One wonders whether several features of the psychoanalytic theory of general personality, including the tendency to see various factors within personality in threatening and dangerous terms, may not possess an undue resemblance to the culturally-given theme of terror and danger which has been so common with us.

Particularly when we ask what characteristics human nature might have under social conditions which may be developed in the future, we need the same outlook that a chemist would have on the problem of what properties would be revealed in chemical substances with techniques and settings not yet invented. This is one reason why we cannot get a sufficiently deep understanding of personality from observations conducted under naturally-given conditions such as those that are studied by anthropologists. We need also to be looking ahead to the development of new cultural settings for human development and functioning—as, for example, by developing new educational techniques and studying what happens to personality under them.

The data from anthropological observations leave us with a lot of difficult questions even with regard to what has developed under cultural conditions of the past. There are so many variables in these different cultural settings that it is more or less impossible to unravel the causal relations lying back of the effects that are seen. We can, however, reach the negative conclusion that human nature must not be interpreted as having merely a rather narrow range of potentialities. To help in the understanding of anthropological observations—not to mention our need of help for understanding personality phenomena more generally—we need to take advantage of the work of psychologists who have labored to bring different sorts of psychological functioning under observation in deliberately controlled experimental situations. The next chapter will give an introductory picture of some aspects of their work, and at many other points the subsequent parts of this book will build on concepts derived from their work.

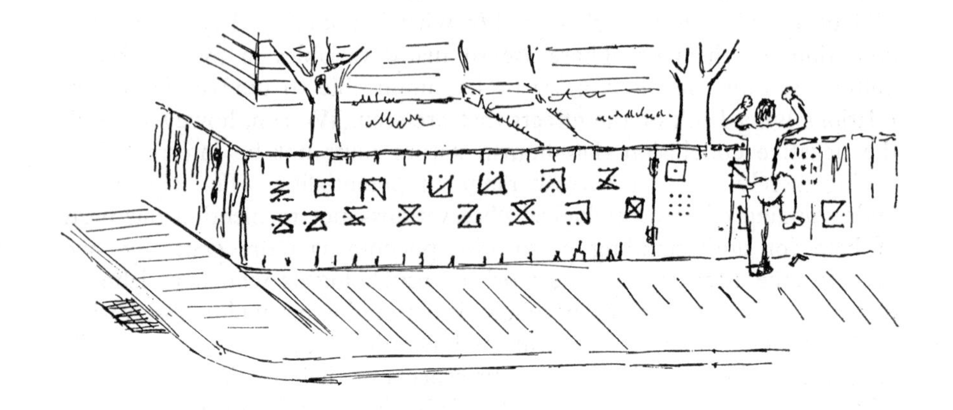

CHAPTER 5

Experimental Psychology as a Source of Understanding of Personality

ONE OF THE CHILDREN Frederick Allen describes in his book on *Psychotherapy with Children* was a 10-year-old girl, May. Allen summarizes in these words the problem that she presented:[1]

> May . . . had maintained for years a severe eating problem. The mother stated that there was no difficulty until she was four, when she began the refusal to eat. She vomited when forced, complained of a distaste for food, and had no appetite. Much time and money were spent on physical examinations. Various diets, tonics and medicines were prescribed, all requiring considerable effort from the mother. No organic causes were ever found. Once started on a regime which assumed a physical cause, however, this was maintained by the constancy and multiplicity of the child's physical reactions. Actually she had become undernourished and that added to the anxiety. The

[1] Frederick Allen, *Psychotherapy with Children,* (New York, W. W. Norton & Co., Inc., 1942), pp. 109-110.

mother was deeply involved in this difficulty and, through her constant concern and overt attention, seemed to be carrying all the responsibility for it. . . .

May's problem had continued for nearly six years, and had now become serious. The vomiting had been worse in the two weeks that preceded the mother's application interview. The area of struggle . . . involved, in addition to May's eating, her dressing, bathing, combing her hair, indeed most routine things in her daily life. The child would go to school for days in an unkempt condition if left to her own initiative. . . .

Although Allen does not go into a description of the child's earlier life, it is fairly safe to assume, from other similar cases, that the mother would have engaged in a great deal of arguing with the child to persuade her to eat, keep herself clean, keep her hair neat, and so on. Not only that, but it is safe to say that the mother must have been greatly puzzled by her daughter's behavior. For, the mother must have tended to say to herself, "What does May stand to gain by acting as she does? I provide good meals for her, and she has nice clothes; but she won't take advantage of them. It would be different if we couldn't give her what she needs. At first, of course, I thought there must be something wrong with her physically. But they tell me there is absolutely no problem on that score. So, when can it be? And why is it that when I explain all this to her and when the doctors have explained it so carefully and clearly to her, over and over again, it doesn't seem to do any good?"

If May's mother had thought in those terms, her basic assumptions would not have differed from those that we usually assume in our everyday thinking about personality. For, in line with what we designated in Chapter 2 as the rationalistic tradition, she would have been assuming, first of all, that all of our important mental processes are conscious processes. Secondly, she would have been assuming that if a person is at least reasonably intelligent, his outlook will reflect whatever clear evidence he has had. "Surely," the mother might have said, "if May is doing all this for psychological reasons, she must know why she does it. And if her behavior is so disadvantageous to her as it seems to be, she certainly ought to be able to recognize this fact when we point it out clearly to her, particularly when she is as old as she is now."

It is not surprising that we make assumptions like this in our everyday thinking. Almost every moment of our lives gives evidence that we can consciously perceive objective facts, even when we have been expecting something different from what we encounter, and that we easily and quickly grasp objective evidence and change our thinking accordingly. When you take your fountain pen from your pocket, for instance, you may confidently expect that it still has ink in it. But you find it will not write. You move the lever at the side of the pen and discover that the pen is empty. It does not matter that you had been expecting something else up to that moment; you now have some clear conscious processes that steer your behavior in a new direction. Such incidents are perpetually happening. Most of life is molded by such conscious, fact-respecting processes. It is no wonder, therefore, that we draw the conclusion that psychological processes—at least on matters that are important to us and that have repeatedly been brought to our attention—would be clearly conscious processes and clearly rational processes.

Of course, even our everyday thinking recognizes that we sometimes learn and use some modes of response that we are not conscious of. Thus, a person may say, "Somehow or other I got into the habit of doing so and so, but as soon as I became aware of what I was doing, I stopped it." That is, we recognize that we can develop faulty ways of pronouncing certain words, of holding a golf club, and so on. Mainly, however, we regard this qualification as applying to muscular responses—as though somehow or other such responses, which rest on frequent repetition for their skillful execution, can be exceptions to the generalization that mental processes tend to be conscious affairs. We confine the qualification to these, rather than questioning the assumption that our main processes of thought and interpretation are conscious processes that easily utilize objective evidence.

The data from anthropology have, of course, brought this rationalistic assumption under serious question. These data indicate that most of the attitudes and values of people have been absorbed uncritically from their cultural environment—have been absorbed in response to cultural pressures that the individuals do not know have been exerted on them. The case histories of the psychotherapists, similarly, have undermined the old rationalistic tradition in several respects. For, as we saw in Chapter 3, the psychotherapists have provided much evidence that people may repress some strong tendencies within themselves, and consequently not be conscious of these tendencies, even though these still find devious indirect expressions.

These conclusions from anthropology and psychotherapy, however, have not been as powerful a challenge of the old rationalistic view as one might have expected. For one thing, the anthropological material has not been absorbed adequately into our everyday knowledge to date. Most people still do not realize that most of their outlook and behavior is culturally derived rather than being some inherent and inevitable way of reacting. Perhaps the psychotherapists' concept of repression has come to be known to a wider number of people. However, even this finding has not constituted as powerful a challenge to the rationalistic tradition as might have been expected, for the persons studied by psychotherapists have experienced profound emotional conflicts. These men and women and children have had strong reasons for not allowing some of their own thoughts and motives to become conscious. The repressed motives were ones that they feared and did not believe they could handle. Consequently, even though psychotherapeutic work requires some revisions in our everyday thought, it is not so difficult for us to believe that such conflicts and such unconscious processes might occur. After one reviews these cases, it still would be possible to believe that, except in the case of such pathological conflicts, our personalities are, after all, *mostly* matters of conscious, rational activity.

Not only do laymen believe this, but also, with quite a high degree of unanimity, the early experimental psychologists used to believe this, too. They defined all the various kinds of psychological processes in terms of their being such and such different kinds of conscious process or conscious experience. They defined psychology, as a whole, as the science of conscious experience. There was a high degree of agreement on this from the beginning of experimental psychology (which is hard to date, but might be set at around 1860) until about 1910.

But even though experimental psychologists at first defined their field of study in this way, their own work in many respects did not harmonize with the definition they accepted. Indeed, one might say that the cumulative evidence from experimental psychology has challenged the old rationalistic tradition even more strongly than has the work of psychotherapists.

Some types of work in experimental psychology which challenge the idea that all psychological activity is a matter of conscious processes

Let us indicate several findings from experimental psychology that indicate the incompleteness of conscious experience as an index of the psychological effects occurring within a person. Particularly it may be of interest to stress some findings by the early psychologists who still thought of psychology as the study of conscious phenomena, because these findings show that the early psychologists were demonstrating the limits of conscious experience even though they had not anticipated that there would be such limits.

1. *Unconscious learning was demonstrated even in early sensory-discrimination experiments.* Some of the earliest of experimental psychological work was concerned with relatively simple perceptual discrimination. For example, a typical study, published by Volkmann in 1858, was concerned with the measurement of the two-point limen, or two-point threshold. The experimenter would touch an area of the subject's skin either with one sharp point (something like a pencil point), or with two points spaced close to one another. The person experimented upon had to report

whether his conscious experience was one of feeling two points or merely one.

A great deal of patience and systematic investigation went into these early studies. They were often carried out with extreme care, testing the same person with thousands of such measurements. Out of this work came one rather surprising result which, for a long time, was not emphasized. This was the fact that even when the subjects were never told whether they perceived the stimulations correctly, and even though they were blindfolded so that they could not check their judgments visually, they regularly became more and more accurate in their perceptions as the experiment progressed. They did not know they were learning anything. Neither they nor the experimenters had thought of these studies as having anything to do with learning. And yet, some process was going on that was not a conscious process and that nevertheless was changing the nature of their responses. Now that attention has been called to it, we can see that such instances of unrecognized learning are very common in the laboratory.

2. *Even in experiments where the subjects deliberately were trying to learn, some important aspects of the learning process were not reflected in the conscious experience of the learners.* Evidence of this sort came from the elaborate and laborious work of the German psychologist, Hermann Ebbinghaus, in his pioneer experimental investigations of learning from 1879 to 1883. Perhaps we ought not to speak of this as the pioneer experimental study of learning, since it was preceded by the work of Volkmann described above and by other similar studies. But such workers as Volkmann did not set out deliberately to study learning, nor did they stress the bearing of their results upon how we learn. Ebbinghaus was the first experimenter who deliberately set out to find whether the so-called higher mental processes, until then regarded as beyond the reach of laboratory experimentation, could also be subjected to careful experimental study.

In a monograph in 1885, Ebbinghaus emphasized his detailed empirical findings rather than their general theoretical significance. But the theoretical implications were there, nonetheless. Take, for instance, this fact: when Ebbinghaus tried to memorize a list of 12 nonsense syllables (such as *zap*, *bif*, *nim*, and *dal*), he found that it required, on the average, about 16 trials to bring himself to the point where he could recite the list without error. After several additional trials, he could tell, introspectively, that he was recalling the items of the list with greater ease and assurance.

But after a few more of such "extra" trials, he could no longer tell, subjectively, that any further learning was occurring (just as when a student, after going over some material a few times, feels that he has learned it as well as he possibly can). But when he tested his memory for such lists of syllables after long intervals of time—such as four weeks—

he found a different story. The more overlearning (the more the extra trials), the better the retention at a later time. Learning, in other words, was not equivalent to making consciously recognizable changes in oneself; it was something that could be demonstrated in an exact and complete fashion only by objective measurements of the performance of the person under a variety of conditions.

About two decades later Bryan and Harter expanded the work of research on learning by studying how men who were being trained for telegraphy learned to send and to receive messages in Morse code. In such work, the learner tends to think that he is learning merely to deal more skillfully with the patterns of dots and dashes that constitute the individual letters of a message. But Bryan and Harter proved that the men were not learning merely letter-habits, but also word-habits and phrase-habits. They proved that the skillful telegrapher depends on higher units of response, as they termed them, that he does not know he possesses.

3. *Experiments on mental set showed that there are complex directing processes which can work without awareness.* In these studies, initiated around 1900, the subjects were given certain instructions as to what they were to do. A person in one such experiment might be told: "You will be given a series of words. In each case, give another word that is synonymous with the word that is given. Thus, if you are given *swift* you might say *fast.*" Or, at another point in the experiment, the subjects might be asked to give words opposite in meaning to the stimulus word or, again, words subordinate to the word presented (as *trout* is subordinate to *fish).*

In these experiments, the subjects were questioned from time to time as to the nature of their conscious experiences during work on these tasks. The general conclusion that came from their testimony was as follows: At first there was a rather clear consciousness of the instructions that had been given, and this conscious process seemed to be used to help locate an appropriate response word. As the testing continued, however, the consciousness of the nature of the task seemed to fade away more and more, until finally it was not discernible at all. What occurred, instead, when the experimenter gave such a word as *big*, was merely that the word *huge* flashed into the subject's mind and he spoke it. Under the instructions to give antonyms, if the experimenter gave the word *big*, the word *small* would appear from nowhere.

In other words, the instructions seemed to set up some process or mechanism in the person that could remain dominant for long periods of time—hours, say—and yet not operate consciously. These guiding factors could be rather complex and precise, so that there seemed little doubt that they should be regarded as part of mental activity. And yet, they did not fit the notion that all mental activity is *conscious* activity.

4. *Experiments on concept-formation showed that we can form and use concepts unconsciously.* The influence of unconscious processes showed up also in more complex thinking. Here we refer to work which sought to learn about concept-formation, but which was conducted without informing the subjects of the nature of the experiment. In one of these studies by H. J. Rees and H. E. Israel,[2] the subjects were asked to solve a series of 30 anagrams such as the following by rearranging the letters so as to make, in each case, a familiar word.

nelin	raspe
nedoz	klsta
ensce	nolem
sdlen	dlsco
lecam	hsfle
slfal	naorg
dlchi	evoli
neque	egsta
frsca	tnsai
peshe	epslo
nitra	naoce
macre	tesle
elwha	maste
ytpar	egran
htmou	eltab

In the left-hand column, each anagram has only one possible solution. *Nelin,* for example, can make *linen,* but nothing else. But in the column on the right, each anagram might make two or more words. *Maste* might make *steam, meats, mates, tames,* or *teams.*

When people were tested with these last 15 anagrams without giving the other anagrams first, it was found that all of these different potential words were about equally likely to occur. But, when the subjects had worked on the other 15 anagrams first, they gave, with a high degree of unanimity, the same word for a given anagram out of the several possible ones.

Some subjects did this for clear, conscious reasons. With the first 15 words, they had learned that each anagram could be solved by treating the letters as though the first, second, third, fourth, and fifth letters of the sought-for word had been placed in the anagram in the arrangement 54123. They quickly rearranged each anagram in this easy form.

Even in these cases an important point is involved. The preliminary stages of their learning finally caused consciously-recognized concepts to

[2]H. J. Rees and H. E. Israel, "An investigation of the establishment and operation of mental sets," *Psychological Monographs,* Vol. 46 (1935), pp. 1-26.

appear, but these preliminary processes, which led these subjects to recognize the recurrent pattern that could be used, were not conscious themselves. However, the role of unconscious processes in concept-formation is shown even more clearly in the other subjects. About half of the subjects solved the right-hand column of anagrams in the 54123 fashion; but when asked how they had gotten these solutions, they had no inkling at all of the mental process that, from their performance, we can tell they must have used. Questioned, they would merely say such things as: "How can I tell you how a person solves anagrams! You look at an anagram, you try to think of what word it might make; you maybe get the notion of using any *s* as a means of creating a plural word; you think of the vowel as coming in the middle, of course. But that doesn't help you very much. . . ." "But," a subject sometimes says, "I did notice that the list got easier as I went along, though I don't know why!"

In other words, when a person is told merely to solve a series of problems in which one common factor or relationship recurs in each problem of the series, he is likely to learn a *generalized* way of handling the materials. This takes the form of an abstract *concept* that guides his further responses. Often the concept is sufficiently simple that any of the subjects could, and some did, formulate it in a clearly conscious way; but still many of the subjects formed and used the concept without conscious recognition of what they were doing.

This type of finding is not a rare one. It has appeared in one experiment after another on concept-formation. The fact that people may use and depend upon such unrecognized concepts is a frequently observed and normal phenomenon.

This is the sort of thing that must have happened in the case of May, whom we mentioned at the start of the chapter. Somehow or other, out of the experiences that she had in her relationship with her mother (and perhaps with some other significant persons), May apparently had decided not merely that she ought to reject the demands that her social environment made on her, but also that her technique of resistance ought to be one of sabotage by refusal to care for her own needs, rather than a technique of frank rebellion. Or her concept may have been that the only kind of attention she could get from her mother was the attention brought about by such unco-operative behavior and that such attention was better than no attention at all. In order for May to have learned and retained such a concept, it would not be necessary at all that she be able to formulate it or be conscious of it, even if no repressions were involved. As the experiments on concept-formation indicate, it is quite possible for people to learn highly abstract ways of dealing with situations and yet not know what they have learned.

5. *Experiments on problem-solving learning reveal the fact that unconscious sets or directions often affect this type of activity.* A great deal of

human activity is directed toward finding solutions for baffling problems with which we are presented. For example, for six years May's mother had been confronted with a problem of this sort. She knew it would be good for her daughter to eat more heartily and to act as though she had some pride in her personal appearance. And the mother must have used a good many different lines of approach to try to get her daughter to change her behavior. Her efforts were of no avail—if anything, May's problem got worse as time passed. Yet the mother would have been inclined to say, "I've tried everything that could be tried."

When subjects have been studied in experiments on the solving of difficult problems, they similarly tend to believe that they have explored every possible means of approach. What proves to be the case, however, is that all of their efforts have stayed within the limits of certain presuppositions they had not realized they had accepted. Take, for example, the work that N. R. F. Maier conducted.[3] In part of his experiments, for example, each person is given a sheet of paper marked with sets of nine dots arranged in a square, as in the drawing used on p. 134 as the headpiece for this chapter. Each subject is told: "Your task is to draw four straight lines, each one beginning where the previous one ends, and the four of them placed so that they will go through all nine dots." When confronted with problems like this, a person may work and work, trying one solution after another, until he finally declares that the problem is absolutely insoluble, because he has tried *everything* that could be tried. He is likely to have tried the same inadequate solution three or four times over at different parts of his work. He really has tried! But all of the trials have been conducted within the limits of some set of presuppositions that the person did not realize he was using. In Maier's terms, he worked under the influence of a direction (or, as we might say, a mental set) that he did not know he was using.

In the problem above, he never said to himself, "Of course the lines must stop at the edge of the figure—I'm not allowed to draw straight lines that reach farther than that." In fact, if he *had* said that to himself—if he had clearly realized this self-imposed limitation—this very thing would have tended to make him see that the instructions did not prevent his drawing lines of greater length and that these ought to be tried also. Not that the latter clue would have given him the solution immediately. But it would have paved the way for a possible solution, whereas the unconsciously-held limitation would forever prevent him from getting an answer.

Not only May's mother but also May herself must have been hampered by this same phenomenon of "directions." May was confronted with a situation calling for problem-solving learning. Her technique of inter-

[3]Norman R. F. Maier, "Reasoning in Humans, I., On Direction," *Journal of Comparative Psychology*, Vol. 10 (1930), pp. 115-143.

action with her mother and with other persons must have been causing her a lot of needless disappointments and frustrations. It was by no means a necessary and inevitable technique that she was using. And yet, as happens over and over again in the field of personality processes, she was not able to see that all of her attempts at problem-solving thinking were staying within the limits of certain unconsciously-defined directions, and that her most basic need was to get some fundamentally new mode of approach to the problems of her life.

The general significance of such experimental findings

Such facts as we have reviewed were accumulated over a long period of time and by many different workers. Sometimes their significance has been obscured because certain psychologists have given up any attempt to talk in terms of conscious experience at all. These psychologists have asserted that the only possible way to do research in psychology is to treat people in a thoroughly behavioristic manner, as if no scientifically-meaningful statements could be made about conscious experiences, and as if psychology must talk merely in terms of relationships between training conditions and overt behavior.

In the present book we are recognizing, and even insisting, that conscious experience has its limitations. We are saying that psychological processes are much broader and richer than a person can recognize, introspectively, within himself. And we are saying that this greater breadth may exist even when there are no emotional conflicts to keep some processes from becoming conscious. But there is a difference between recognizing the *limitations* of conscious processes and disregarding conscious processes altogether!

From the standpoint of the present writers, it would seem foolish to abandon interest in the conscious experience of people merely because it is not the full range of psychological activity. For, even though conscious processes are merely part of what goes on, they are a part that possesses extreme interest for us. Especially in the field of personality, some of the main effects that we wish to understand are changes in the conscious experience of persons. After all, when a person has a great deal of discouragement, bitterness, or unreasonable sense of guilt in his life, we are not interested in this merely because it affects his public behavior in certain ways or because it influences his physiological functioning—we are interested in these properties of his life because of their character as conscious experiences of the individual. Or conversely, when a person has become able to experience life with some deep appreciation of the beauty, intellectual interest, or grandeur of the world, this is important not merely because of the behavior that such conscious processes help to produce—there is value in these conscious experiences for their own sake. In fact, what we might well say is that the conscious experiences of human beings are the only clear ultimate values in human life. They are the goal to which all else is a means. So a main thing that we want from the psychology of personality is some better understanding that will help us to predict and control conscious experiences in ways that we can see are desirable.

If a person is interested in understanding human personalities, it therefore seems unnecessarily restrictive for him to adopt a purely behavioristic approach, casting aside all thought about the conscious aspects of various personality processes. Definitely, in this book, the writers are not advocating such a behavioristic approach, even though they grant that it can be used with considerable effectiveness on many problems. Yet, on the other hand, when they accept the view in psychology which regards consciousness as a reality, which seeks to learn more about conscious processes, and which assigns a place of great importance to them, this does not mean that we interpret psychological processes as if almost all of the content of such processes must necessarily be conscious. The data from experimental psychology do not endorse any such conception, but lead instead to the conclusion that Wolfgang Köhler has expressed in the following words:[4]

Without the observation of direct experience we should be in great danger of constructing an artificially simplified system of psychology, as is that of current behaviorism. On the other hand, it seems absolutely impossible to me to develop psychology as a science of direct experience or of "consciousness." For the development of that science, the field of actual experience alone is inadequate, especially when compared with the totality of those processes in the nervous system, a few of which are at each moment accompanied by experience, but *all* of which seem to be more or less interdependent. How can one pretend to contruct an adequate theory of psychological events using experience alone, if the processes underlying experience are merely a dynamical province of a much larger functional whole? It is almost impossible to deny this fact nowadays. Therefore, we cannot hope to understand experience itself from its own aspect, any more than one could hope to learn and understand the game of chess through watching only the moves in one corner of the board the whole time.

In this latter case the observer of the game would soon become aware of the fact that something important was going on beyond the narrow field of his observation, that evidently the moves in it referred to something beyond, since they even seemed to come from there and to disappear again into the unseen. Exactly the same is true of experience.

[4]Wolfgang Köhler, *Gestalt Psychology* (New York, Liveright Publishing Corp. 1929), pp. 269-270.

Some portions of experimental psychology indicate that psychological processes tend to operate by quick organizations that then resist modification

In the previous portions of this chapter, we have seen that experimental psychology tends to disprove one important part of the rationalistic interpretation of personality that we generally employ in everyday thinking. For, whereas such a rationalistic interpretation assumes that almost all of important mental activity is conscious, the experimental psychologists have been finding that psychological processes cannot be understood merely in terms of what is conscious, but must be dealt with in terms of background unconscious processes as well.

Now we turn to another aspect of the old rationalistic conception of human nature. This conception also portrayed psychological processes as what we might call *fact-respecting processes*—as processes that would take all of the evidence and, within the limits of ability of the person and except for certain chance errors that might occur, would draw the conclusion that ought to be drawn from that evidence. In a very important respect, however, experimental psychology gives a different portrait. What experimental psychology suggests as outstanding about the human mind is not that it uses factual information carefully and gets the resultant advantages, but that it tends to draw hasty conclusions and get the somewhat different advantages that come from this mode of functioning. The point is not merely that human beings make errors in using information; it is that they have certain systematic ways of operation that tend to yield certain predictable kinds of efficient functioning and certain predictable kinds of errors, with both the gains and the liabilities coming from the same basic tendencies!

To illustrate what is meant, let us note the contrast between psychological processes and the work of certain machines. With ordinary calculating machines and computers, for example, it should make no difference whether we feed the information into the machine in one order or in another order. For example, it should make no difference in the product obtained whether we multiply 6 x 8 or 8 x 6. If we want to figure the average height of a group of men, we expect the calculating machine to yield the same average regardless of whether we give the measurements in this order: 6 ft.-2 in.; 6-4; 5-10; 5-4; 5-11; 5-2; or in the reverse order. Calculating machines are made so that they will utilize information to arrive at the same conclusion regardless of the order in which the information is fed into the machine.

However, human beings do not work in this way. We are more like a calculating machine that reaches one conclusion if the data are fed into

1
2
3
4
5
6
7

it in one order of presentation and another conclusion if the data are fed to it in another order. And this occurs not just as an occasional, chance-governed effect, but as a fundamental quality of all we do. It is the way we are made. It is the way we *had* to be made if we were to become the marvelously adept creatures we are. We could not be built on the model of the order-free calculator and survive in the competition for existence. We had to be built on a better plan.

Let us illustrate our point with the drawings on the opposite page. The fourth picture of the series is a fairly neutral and well-balanced one. If the people who look at it have not been biased with regard to it beforehand, approximately equal numbers of them will see it either as a young woman with her face turned far enough away so that her mouth is hidden and only the tip of her nose can be seen, or as a rather old woman with her chin buried in her fur collar and with a large Roman nose seen in profile.

In other words, if a person were to see the middle picture *as it is*, he would see it as having both of these possible patterns. But the psychologists who developed and used these pictures found that the mode of seeing the pictures in the middle part of the series depended on which pictures you showed a person first.[5] If you started with No. 1, then proceeded to No. 2, you might be able to go to No. 5 or No. 6 with a given subject before he would begin to see anything except the old woman. But, on the other hand, with another subject, if you began the series by showing him No. 7 with its clear representation of the young woman, and then showed him No. 6 and so on, you might have him go clear through to No. 3 or No. 2 before he would realize that any of the pictures could reveal anything except that same young woman.

If a photographer's camera worked the same way, you might well say to the photographer, "Please let me come back for my picture another time. I just saw your last customer go out as I came in, and I don't want my picture to look like her!"

You don't need to worry about the camera. It is a rational, objective, order-free instrument. It doesn't operate in later situations partly by virtue of what it had photographed previously. This fact has its advantages. But it also is true that the camera never learns anything. It never gets better at catching the smiles on people's faces, or their scowls. If there is any improvement in these things, it has to come about through changes in the photographer, not in the camera.

There is an important point in all this. If we are to have a fundamentally sound idea of how human beings operate, we must come to see how their functioning is determined by factors that come with *order of presentation*

[5]From unpublished research by Solomon E. Asch, Martin Scheerer, and Henry Gleitman. Personal communication to the authors.

in a way not seen at all in the simpler sorts of mechanical devices with which we generally are familiar.[6]

Let's illustrate with human beings again. Suppose you see a person working with this task: "You are given some measuring devices that hold respectively 3, 64, and 29 quarts. You are asked to measure out three quarts of liquid. How would you do it?"

You would surely expect this person promptly to say, "Fill up the 3-quart container with the liquid, and there will be what you want. You will not need the other two containers at all."

You might expect him to say this and you would be right, if he were given the problem in just this form. But give him a series of about eight other problems to work on, beforehand, and you are likely to find that he will give you this solution instead of the easy one above: "Fill the 64-quart container. Out of it, fill the 29-quart container twice; then pour out another 3 quarts by means of the three-quart container, and you will have left, in the 64-quart container, the 3 quarts that you want."

If you found a person solving the problem in this way, you might imagine that there must have been something in the instructions that required him to work in this very indirect fashion. Otherwise it would seem incredible that people would go through such involved procedures. But A. S. Luchins[7] found that, under certain circumstances, people do go through such complicated roundabout procedures, even when the instructions explicitly allow the obvious short solution. The possibility of

[6]Lest we be accused of trying to bring some mysticism into psychology, let us hasten to remark that, as several persons have pointed out, it would be possible to construct electronic computers that would work in the same basic way. It would be possible to build mechanical devices that would work, not in an order-free way, but in the fundamentally different fashion we are describing. It might seem that it would be useless to construct such devices. But whether they would be useful would depend altogether on what is wanted. The machine that is merely approximately correct could work in flexible, economical, almost "intelligent-like" ways that are utterly beyond the capacity of the order-free machines. It is all a matter of what one wants.

[7]A. S. Luchins, Mechanization in Problem Solving: The Effect of *Einstellung*," *Psychological Monographs*, Vol. 54, No. 248 (1942).

the short solution is not even noticed by most subjects. In different groups of high school and college students, Luchins found that from 52 per cent to 85 per cent of the subjects went through the complicated procedure.

When one first reads Luchins' monograph, one can hardly believe that people could be thrown off so seriously as this, but when one of the writers tried these problems on different members of his family who were available—his wife, 16-year-old daughter, father, and younger brother—they all did the incredible.

The way in which Luchins' material leads to such a response is this: The subjects are first confronted with a simple problem: "Given containers holding respectively 26 quarts and 3 quarts, measure out 20 quarts." This gives them the idea of measuring by pouring-off liquid. They next are given a series of six problems of this sort: "Given containers that hold respectively 5, 35, and 9 quarts, measure out 12 quarts." Again they find that the "pour-off-and-discard" solution works well with all this series. When they meet the problem that *could* be solved by simply filling the 3-quart container, they go right on using the pour-it-back-and-forth approach. They solve the problem, but by the very complicated route.

The subjects are usually rather stunned when they find out how "stupid" they have been. One of them, who saw himself as a victim in such an experiment, chased the writer out of the house after he found out how he had been "tricked." Even though he came from Texas and is perhaps too close to traditions of the violent frontier, he ought not to have gotten so excited. For, while it seemed to him to be an idiotic mistake, he had done it for a wonderful reason—he went about his task as he did because one quality that gives human beings their great problem-solving capacity is that they *do* carry over to later situations the concepts and methods that worked in earlier ones. This in part insures our resourcefulness in exceedingly complex situations. It is also what tends to blind us too much when the method we originally learned is unduly limited and not at all the best method of dealing with what turns up later.

The basic consideration in the case of both the electronic computer and the human brain is that they are limited in their storage capacity. However, we want them to carry the lessons of a terrific amount of experience and previous information. To permit them to do that, we can't ask them to store everything just as concrete, specific detail. That would be inefficient. For example, you would have a hard learning task if you tried just by rote memory to learn and retain the following list of numbers:

581217233038475768809310712213815517319221 2

George Katona showed in some very interesting experiments that it was much easier for people to remember rather complex materials like this if they could store just a *few* things, such as "*(a)* there is a series of numbers that starts with 5, *(b)* the next number after the 5 will be 3 greater than it, the next one 4 greater than that, and so on, *(c)* the series ends at just past the 200 mark."[8]

Whether in electronic computing machines or human brains, information can be stored more efficiently with the aid of such abstract ideas or categories, or "recoding," than just as raw information in all of its original detail. When previously obtained information, recoded and stored, is to be used again, it can be translated back into its original detailed form. But it is carried—in the meantime—through the generalized categories, rather than in its original detail.

The reason this is helpful in animals and human beings is that life situations rarely recur in just the same form. Thus, suppose that a baby meets a series of situations where some adult calls out to him the word "Hot!" One time it is his mother, another time his older sister, another time his father. In each case the word will probably be pronounced in a different way—there will be a difference of pitch, timbre, and loudness, or whatever. Furthermore, in one case, the word is given with reference to the piping-hot cereal in the dish before him; in another case, with reference to the radiator; in another case, the kitchen stove. If the child is to live efficiently, he must group these occasions together as essentially alike, despite their differences. Even though some of these objects are hotter than others, even though the part of the body exposed to the heat is the mouth in one case and the hand in another, and even though the warning words are given in distinguishable ways, what the baby needs to do (and does) is to group all of these experiences as being in some respects the same. He must be made so that he won't treat each new situation as distinct from previous ones because it has some distinctive features. The child must be constituted so that he will recognize similarities or recurrent features even though there are differences in detail. Every child must operate in this way; so also must every adult. It is our basic means of efficient adjustment.

How personality concepts that are learned early tend to carry over because they are not corrected by ordinary social experiences

There is another aspect of the formation and use of concepts that we might illustrate by asking you to memorize another series of numbers:

711162229374856663697478

In a case such as this, even though neither the beginning numeral nor

[8]George Katona, *Organizing and Memorizing* (New York, Columbia University Press, 1940).

subsequent additions are the same as in the other problem, you are likely to carry over to this problem, or at least try out, the principle of an increasing series such as you met in the previous case. Not only that. You have a tendency, on this second problem, to economize effort. You check the first part of the series and see that it follows a rule of "start with 7, add 4, then 5 to that, etc." And you note that the series keeps going until it ends with 78. But there is a temptation not to check the series all the way through. The temptation is to check the principle with the first nine or ten digits and then to conclude that the same principle holds throughout. If this is what you actually do, you fail to discover that more than one principle is involved in this case, and that, at one point, the series is quite arbitrary.

In later chapters, when we return to a specific discussion of personality, rather than the more inclusive principles of learning in general, we will see that this number-series problem differs in one major way from the situations related to personality. A number-series like this is quite clear-cut and verifiable; if the learner is careful enough, there is no need for him to make mistakes. In most life situations in which personality characteristics are formed, however, there is no such clarity. A small child starts to school, for instance, and is thrown with a new group of associates. He tends to carry over, into his dealings with them, the habits that he has learned by acting with his parents, brothers, and sisters. He expects praise for some kinds of conduct, disapproval for other kinds, and no special reaction at all for still others. He carries over such modes of conduct because he fails to see that the new situation differs in some important details from the situation at home. At home his parents may have been taking a lot of pride in his accomplishments and may have showed him a lot of favor when he boastfully demonstrated to them how much he knew. He fails to see that the other children also want recognition for what they are learning and are not interested in admiring him. He fails to see that the teacher, although she wants him to learn, is also interested in preserving an impartial situation where all the children will be just as confident of getting recognition as he is. His reaction is the same in kind as if, in the last number-series we referred to, he analyzed only the first portion of it and failed to see that the second part introduced a new principle.

Also, when he carries over his old principle into the new situation and uses it there, he will generally fail to see what results he is securing by doing this. This is not so surprising. What his behavior evokes in other people will not be a clear and unambiguous set of reactions. His teacher, for instance, may actually make a mental note to the effect: "This child, I can see, is going to create some problems for me; I'll have to try to help him learn to feel more secure and self-respecting and to get over his feeling that he must be competitively successful." But she does not show this clearly in her behavior. Instead, when he says, "You know, I read ten books last summer—hard ones, too," she is apt to murmur, "Oh, that's fine, and you enjoyed them a lot, did you?" From your standpoint you might suppose he would thereupon ask himself, "What did she signal by that?" But he doesn't. He can't tell just what she meant. But he does know what he got, earlier, by such boastful statements as this, because this is the sort of situation where his mother swept him into her arms, told him she was proud of such a bright son and that she was sure he would become a great scholar some day. He doesn't expect that the teacher will do just the same thing. But he gets just a few clues from her and infers the rest; as a result, he is strengthened, rather than altered, in his belief that this is the way that he can get along most effectively with other people. Actually he is getting an unfavorable judgment from her. But he doesn't see that, any more than the subjects with Luchins' problems saw that they were behaving ludicrously in trying to get 3 quarts by filling a 64-quart container, dumping 29 quarts out of it two times, dumping out another 3 quarts, and ending triumphantly with the desired 3 quarts as the product of all this unnecessary effort.

Summary

In a number of ways, the experimental psychologists have been doing the groundwork for a basically different way of thinking about personality. Their findings supply evidence that even in situations where no repressions are involved, our thinking and acting are often dependent on mental processes outside of our awareness. If we are to understand ourselves or other persons, we must be prepared to search in an area broader than that of our conscious experiences. And, if we are to understand ourselves or other persons, we must see that our mental processes do not depend simply upon the experiences we have had, or upon the data that life has provided us with, but also on the *order* in which things were given to us and on the organizations or concepts that we carried over from them, often to the serious neglect and misrepresentation of the reality around us. We are not like order-free calculators. We are like a much more complex type of computing machine that is designed to identify recurrent themes in whatever material comes along, but that is not required to work with absolute accuracy in future situations in which such materials may recur. We make the same kinds of mistakes (even in utterly nonemotional situations) that such a special sort of computing machine would make.

The kind of experiments by which such conclusions have been established include Volkmann's early experiment on distinguishing between one and two points of pressure on the skin, Ebbinghaus' experiments on rote memorizing, early experiments on the influences of mental set, Rees and Israel's experiment on learning to solve anagrams, Maier's experiments in problem-solving thinking, Scheerer's observations with ambiguous figures, Luchins' experiments on mental set, and Katona's experiments with tasks that could be learned either by memorizing or by grasping more abstract properties of the material to be learned.

The sorts of data that we have been considering in the last three chapters perhaps have fairly revolutionary implications for our understanding of human personalities. It seems that they require something more than merely corrections of minor details of our everyday thought. It may be that they call, instead, for some rather drastically new basic ways of conceiving of personality. In the succeeding chapters we will attempt to see whether this is the case and, if it is, what new conceptions of personality ought to be employed both in technical research and, in a more general form, even in our day-by-day lives.

Part III

THE EMERGING UNDERSTANDING OF PERSONALITY

CHAPTER 6

Personality as a Matter of How We Perceive Life Situations

IN THE LAST THREE CHAPTERS we have glimpsed some methods and findings of three important fields of work in which a basis for a new sort of understanding of human personalities has been laid. Now, in the main part of the book, our task is one of determining what better concepts might be developed from all of these sources. Our task is one of finding concepts that may have scientific origins and that may be absorbed into our everyday thought and life. In other spheres of thought, our everyday views have been significantly changed by new conceptions that were originally achieved only with great difficulty; it may be that the work in psychology can bring about a similar change.

The main theme the succeeding chapters will develop is that we need

The headpiece illustration is from C. M. Mooney and G. A. Ferguson, "A New Closure Test," *Canadian Journal of Psychology*, Vol. 5 (1951), pp. 129-133.

particularly to understand personality as a matter of perceptual processes and of perceptual habits. This interpretation is suggested by many converging trends in the research and thinking both of experimental psychologists and of other workers who are engaged more specifically with the study of personality.

There are many different modes of thought and terminology in psychology that do not seem to harmonize well with such a proposal. Psychology is still so young that it has not had time to integrate all of the ideas which have converged upon it from different directions. We are proposing, however, that there are common perceptual principles of far-reaching significance, not ordinarily brought together, that would take advantage of many different kinds of evidence if assembled and studied as a possible means of increased understanding of personality. As this discussion proposes some new integrations, it may require that you reconsider some of your usual ways of looking at things and some of the definitions of terms that you have taken for granted. We will need to proceed carefully, therefore, so as to help you find grounds for deciding whether or not the proposed concepts are reasonable and useful.

The need of focusing on representational processes within the individual

There is much discussion today about psychology as a "behavioral science." It might seem from this that our primary focus of interest ought to be on the outwardly observable behavior of people. This overt behavior is important, of course. But by itself it does not give us any penetrating understanding. Only when we consider a larger range of facts about the individual—only when we figure out what lies back of his overt behavior—can we get a satisfactory understanding of his behavior.

Consider this example. A number of years ago one of the writer's children, about three years old, used to enjoy each evening carrying firewood and helping to make the fire in the fireplace. One evening the writer had carried in a huge chunk of wood that contained so many knots it could not be split. It was a wedgeshaped piece, not very thick, but so broad that it almost filled the length and breadth of the fireplace, entirely covering the paper and kindling. When the writer lifted this chunk of wood on the fire, he noticed that the boy was almost crying. The next night, when another large log was placed on the fire, the boy was even more troubled. Then he explained directly: "Daddy, you're hurting the fire; don't do that!" On other evenings, the smaller pieces of wood had brought no such effect from him; but with this big piece, apparently, he could get some idea of the pain it would bring if it fell on his fingers or toes, and he was responding to the situation in these new terms.

In this case there were overt responses, of course, such as his facial expressions. But these could not be interpreted directly. The child might have been upset because he had not been allowed to help lift the wood onto the fire; he might have been troubled because there was something in the fireplace he wanted to remove first; or it might have been something else. *To understand his behavior and deal with it, one could not have dealt with his behavior as such.*

This may seem like a simple illustration, but we submit that the point is basic. One has to go back to the child's representation of the situation and try to deal with it—as the author attempted to do (though perhaps his specific way of doing this was not necessarily the best way)—by saying to the boy that the fire liked to have such a big log because it gave the fire something to burn for a good long time.

Perhaps another example would help to make clear that when we speak about a need of focusing on inner representational processes, we are not proposing that the explanation of behavior should be sought merely in verbally reportable experience. On another evening, when the same boy was about four-and-a-half years old, the writer and his son had been looking through a copy of *Life* magazine. A little later, the boy was tucked in bed. He soon came out again. "I'm thirsty; I want a drink of water." It was given to him and he was shooed back. Soon out again: "The blankets have come off; come and fix them." They were fixed. Soon he was out again to say that he needed to go to the toilet. False alarm. Then some other pretext. After that, the writer finally got the point. He realized that when they had been looking at the pictures in the magazine, the boy had noticed a cartoon showing some savages dancing around two captives and around a fire with a big pot on it. The boy had asked what this was. Without taking thought, the writer answered that these dancers were cannibals. "What are cannibals?" "Well, a long time ago, way off on the other side of the world, there were savages who ate some of their prisoners. In this cartoon, this is what they are showing. But there aren't any cannibals any more . . . ."

In this case, as in the incident with the log, it was the boy's overt behavior that impelled the writer to try to understand the personality processes of his son. But he could not make sense out of the outward behavior directly; for it was so diverse in its specific goals. The thing that had to be turned to was the question, "What is the background representation from which this diversity of specific responses is coming?" And, even though the boy could talk fairly well, the writer still had to assume that the child's verbal expressions of his wants were not necessarily good indicators of the important representational processes within him.

The writer therefore had to stop and realize several things. He had to recognize that a four-and-a-half-year-old child is quite capable intellectually of understanding that there might be a custom of killing people, cooking them, and eating them. These are simple, concrete concepts. Enough to make anybody a bit nervous. But the writer had to come to see, too, that there were some facts basic to his own sense of security that he could not get across to his son. "The cannibals lived only on the other side of the world, across the ocean, thousands and thousands of miles away." The writer knew what all these words meant. But "thousands?" A four-year-old can hardly count to five yet. "Miles?" "Ocean?" "Other side of the world?" These words lack meaning for a preschool child. All attempts to explain that cannibals lived only in jungles, in hot parts of the world, far, far away might merely leave the child with the idea that cannibals live off in the woods at the edge of town. When the writer sent his son back to bed after the fourth sally, he said, "Move over, there, and let me lie down beside you for a while." And, since this was "security language" that the child could understand, he soon dropped off to sleep. As far as could be seen, that was the last of the cannibals.

This second example points in the direction of a very complex effect that is often disclosed by the work of psychotherapists. For, it happens frequently, even in the case of intelligent adults, that an individual may not be able to identify and describe the representational processes that lie back of his behavior and back of his more superficial conscious experiences. You will recall the case described earlier (pages 75-76) of the young man who had developed a fear of going into barber shops. The long, slow work of the therapeutic interviews finally revealed that this effect was a disguised consequence of a powerful background representation of his older brother as a hateful person. Until this young man had been helped to take a whole series of steps toward better self-understanding and greater self-acceptance, he could not recognize this crucial representational process lying back of his symptoms. Nevertheless, this was what had to be dealt with. It would have been useless to have afforded him recurrent experiences of going into barber shops without being hurt in them; he really was not afraid of barber shops or barbers as such; his fear was a fear of his own hostile impulses toward his brother. The basic problem was his idea that his brother had behaved insultingly toward him under the guise of pretending to be helpful.

Hence, when we say that any attempt to understand personality ought to penetrate to the way in which the individual represents his life situation, we are not proposing a task that is always easy. Sometimes quite the reverse. But in any case it is necessary. The real key to a person's life lies in how he experiences his life situations, or how he represents them to himself, how he interprets them. Out of the fullness of these representational processes perhaps only fragmentary expressions are apparent in the behavior of any given moment. This behavior is important. But, as we have said, we cannot understand that behavior—we cannot know the goals toward which it is directed or really what it means—until we attain some realization of the background representational processes.

Therefore, even though psychology is a "behavioral science," we cannot focus our interest solely or primarily on behavior. We have to go back of behavior to the fundamental processes.

Inadequacies of rationalistic interpretations of these representational processes

In daily life, we often realize the value of trying to deal in terms of the individual's representations or experiences of life situations. But the way that we go at the task of understanding these representational processes is poor because, as we saw in Chapter 2, it is a *rationalistic* mode of approach. Such an approcah means we assume that psychological processes tend to be accurate reflections of external, objective realities—provided, of course, that the individual in question is not a small child, a psychotic, or a feeble-minded person. The rationalistic view assumes, too, that a person may not correctly reflect objective realities because he suffers from lack of information. But this is the same as holding that if the individual is intelligent, not obstinate, and not perverse, he will respond quickly by shifting to the correct representation provided the objective facts are clearly demonstrated to him, and provided the necessary abstract arguments are given with sufficient force.

As we saw in Chapter 2, this is the way Rockwell Kent tried to help the neurotic patients who had been referred to his farm household by the psychotherapist whom he knew. It is the way that a friend might have counseled Jean—the girl described in Chapter 2 who, though definitely winsome in appearance, suffered so poignantly from feelings of being homely. Approaching the problem rationalistically, such a friend might have said, "Now look, Jean, be sensible. Here you've been spending all this time being miserable about your appearance—trying not to see yourself in the mirror, lest you be faced with a realization of how 'homely' you are, crying into your pillow night after night, and so on. This is crazy. The fact is that you are one of the best-looking girls around here. If you have any doubt about that I'll ask a bunch of the other students. But you know it yourself. You know the boys like you. You know you are not overweight. You know that you have beautiful hair and that the compliments you get about that don't need to be inspired by any difficulty in giving you compliments on other scores. Good heavens, Jean! Start thanking your lucky stars, and get out and enjoy yourself. There's absolutely nothing wrong with you."

In other words, the rationalistic interpretation of personality prompts us to proceed as though personality were naturally under the control of highly-efficient intellectual processes, processes that can easily grasp and utilize the plain-as-day facts of a person's life situation.

There are a lot of reasons why we tend to use such a rationalistic approach. Our mental processes or psychological processes often do prove to be wonderfully quick and accurate in registering and using evidence from environmental realities. Even when strong emotions are aroused, there may often be quick readjustments as new objective evidence is met. A very good example of this has been described by Rufus Jones, who was for many years a professor of philosophy and psychology at Haverford College and who carried great responsibilities after World War I as director of Quaker relief work in Europe. In a book in which he tells of his childhood, Jones says:[1]

> Everybody, everywhere I went, told "scary" stories and frightened me with what *might* happen to a boy. The climax came one evening while I was waiting in the post office for the mail to come. Some loafers who were sitting there waiting for mail that never came, began telling of "warnings" which often came to persons just before they died. One man said, and I listened breathlessly, that you often saw mysterious lights in the road, or in your room, and that was a sure "sign" that you would soon die. He told how a friend of his was driving home in the dark, late one night, and as he went to turn into his dooryard he saw two strange lights burning like candles on each side of the road. After he got out of his wagon he went back to look at the lights but they were gone. A few days later the man died.
>
> I went home that night badly scared and for some days I dwelt upon that tale with a morbid fascination. A short time after this, I awoke in the night and saw a light burning about three or four feet from the ceiling of my room. There was nothing there to burn. It could not possibly be a "regular" light, it must be a "warning" light. I covered my head up under the clothes and felt terrified. Then I looked again and there it was burning on, though there was nothing there to burn.
>
> Then I did the most heroic act of my life. I got up, drew a chair under the mysterious light, got up in the chair, and grasped at the light with my hand. I caught hold of a long ear of seed-corn which I found afterwards that father had hung up in my room the day before. A beam of the moon through a hole in my curtain had struck the ear of corn and made my terrifying "light." I went back to bed a "new" boy. I was never again afraid of "mysterious lights." I had taken a momentous step toward freedom from foolish fears.

In our everyday life, when we are trying to deal with personality problems either in ourselves or in other persons, we usually try to use this same method of introducing the person to some objective facts that he apparently had not grasped clearly enough, and we expect him to make the same quick utilization of them that Rufus Jones made after his hand touched the ear of corn. "What else could one do?" we tend to say. "Here is this person—feeling afraid, or guilty, or depressed, or inferior, when actually his objective situation ought to give him a deep sense of confidence, self-respect, or achievement. What could he possibly need except to have the objective realities clearly demonstrated to him!"

[1]Rufus Jones, *Finding the Trail of Life* (New York, The Macmillan Co., 1926), pp. 36-38.

That's what we ask. But in so many cases clear, logically-adequate demonstrations do not work. Somehow or other, even though at times the rationalistic conception of man as a creature that can use objective facts to make quick intellectual readjustments is confirmed, this conception somehow is too seriously in error to serve as a general picture. In a way, it is like the statement, "If you want to start a campfire, you put some paper and sticks together, touch a match to the paper, and in a few minutes you'll have a roaring campfire." Such a statement is true provided a lot of supporting conditions exist that are not specified by the statement —provided the paper and the sticks are dry, provided they are arranged in certain ways, provided the paper is of a kind that burns easily, provided some of the sticks are small enough so that they quickly heat through, and so on. This is the difficulty with the rationalistic interpretation of personality. It proposes as typical something that occurs only under special conditions which the rationalistic interpretation does not and cannot specify.

What we need, instead, is some much more adequate formulation to help us understand why quick intellectual processes suffice in some cases and why, at other times, even with highly intelligent persons, recognizing objective realities may involve almost insurmountable difficulties. In the knowledge we have received from everyday observation, we have not found any adequate interpretation of these difficulties. We need to ask, therefore, whether any of the scientific discoveries have made possible a better way of thinking about personality.

A good many considerations suggest that we may find the answer in an integration of certain discoveries by the psychotherapists, on the one hand, with some main contributions from the experimental psychologists, on the other. There are a number of fundamental similarities between the principles developed by these two groups, and a richer understanding of each field might be secured by recognizing and developing these relationships. In general, these two groups of workers have made no effort to explore the fundamental kinship of ideas that exists between them. Indeed, psychotherapists have rather commonly taken the view that experimental psychologists deal either with remote or trivial matters, far from the richer issues of life. The experimental psychologists, on their side, particularly when their own interests were concerned with research on perceptual phenomena, have taken very little interest in trying to relate their concepts to problems of personality.

Even though most psychologists interested in perception and in perceptual theories of learning have taken this view, the writers believe that the most promising concepts for the understanding of personality are the concepts that interpret personality in perceptual terms. Before our discussion is ended, it will be apparent that the writers believe that the term *perceptual* has to be reinterpreted in a much broader way than the experimental psychologists have generally recognized. But even if the term is used in the narrow, traditional sense still favored by many psychologists, it seems to us that some principles absolutely indispensable for an understanding of personality have developed out of the traditional experimental work in perception.

To explore this point, we could proceed by first describing some perceptual principles and then indicating how these principles apply to problems of personality. However, this would be a difficult order of procedure for most readers. We propose, instead, to turn first to a rather full, and certainly vivid and human, document in Lillian Smith's book, *The Journey*.[2] It is an exceptionally discerning account of personality processes as a part of real life, and in its concrete content alone it has a great deal to say about personality. In addition, however, it can make a great contribution through helping us to understand a number of highly abstract principles that are basic for achieving insight into personality. Let us launch into this case and try to grasp it, first, as a concrete account. We will then turn to the abstract principles that apply both to it and to the field of personality generally, but which would not be easy to recognize in many other cases.

Lillian Smith writes:

I asked her the question for I had known her since she was a child.

She said, "I didn't find my way. Not for a long time. If John had been here—but he was in Korea. His letters—I couldn't have done without them—and there was Bill's surgeon, a wonderful man—and friends. All of it helped. But I was lost. And I failed Bill.

"It's the suddenness of it. He was skating with the neighborhood children. I called to him as he left the house to be careful, something might happen. I never believed it would. You don't. You just say it. When the telephone rang I was washing my hair. I let it ring until I had rinsed the soap out, thinking it was one of the girls. Then I ran downstairs to answer it.

"Sometimes, even now, it wakes me in the night—the ringing."

I was visiting in Marty's home for a few days. And as we talked, we were on our way to the school to pick up Bill. She did not say more until traffic cleared.

"I had nothing inside me to meet it," she said. "I had always believed it could never happen to me. And when it did, there was nothing there—not even a little mental first-aid kit."

The boys were racing. A truck swerved around the corner. No one was hurt but Bill. His arms were so injured that they had to be amputated close to the shoulders. For a few days the doctors were not certain that Bill could

[2]Lillian Smith, *The Journey*, (Cleveland, The World Publishing Co., 1954), pp. 160-180, 188-193, 194-195, 197-200.

make it. There had been severe concussion, much loss of blood, a long wait for an ambulance. But finally things leveled off and he was out of danger.

"When I knew what the score was, I—it will shock you. Bill's surgeon told me it was natural—at least, other people do it, sometimes—and I've tried to believe him. I—left Bill. I went to the hospital every day, my body did; but deep down in me I wasn't there. I had gone to look—"

She told me how she searched her life through, looking . . . for two little lost arms. Asking herself why it had happened, what had she done or failed to do, dragging out memories, turning them over, raveling them out to find an answer. As if, once an answer were found, then somehow, in a magic way, those arms would be restored.

She had spoken to him at breakfast that morning about his table manners. And then, as he dashed off to skate with the other children she had called to him to be careful. "I began to think—crazy things." If she had not told him to be careful, maybe it wouldn't have happened. Maybe she had nagged him too much. Maybe he had to show her he could be reckless to keep her from ruining him. The sensible part of her, the sane part, told her she was not a nagger. *But why did I tell him something might happen! Did I know it was going to happen—did I want it to happen—was that why I warned him?* The sane part told her that, though skating is a reasonable risk for children to take, and Bill was alert and careful, it was right, even so, for her to warn him of danger.

"But they were like somebody else's words. Not mine."

And then she began to go back to that breakfast, raking over its small events. It was as if the room had frozen. A streak of sun across the table—a spot of jam on the checked cloth—Bill's yellow cereal bowl—the clock ticking. Nothing changed in that "still life" for months. "I went back a thousand times to find what I had done, or failed to do," she said. "As if I had to touch every small part of that morning again and again."

Bill had gulped his cereal, and she had scolded him. Then Bill tilted his bowl and slurped the milk. She thought, If he does it again, I'll— She spoke sharply. And he stared at her—even the little cowlick brushed back slick and wet stared at her as if both believed her their mortal enemy. And then he said in a low voice, "I wish Daddy would come home. I do wish it! I wish it, I wish it!" And she wished it, too, for she was dead tired of being mamma and papa both, but it had hurt to hear him say it.

After he left to go skating, she felt that she could not go on alone, another minute, without John.

"I was breaking up like the pieces of a puzzle and knew I'd better do something quick. So I washed my hair. When the phone rang, I didn't answer at once because—well, I didn't feel very gay and my friends always expect me to be on top of the world. As I say this to you, it could be something I read somewhere. It still doesn't feel as if it happened to me. . . ."

Her question kept on. . . .

"I'd be in the kitchen cooking, forgetting for a moment—and it would start. I felt compelled to answer—as if Teacher were there, or something—a presence—I don't know—that would not leave me alone. Was I a morbid kid? Too guilty about things? I don't remember that I worried much." She glanced at me quickly. "Or maybe I did and forgot it. I don't know. But they kept on, the questions."

". . . it went on and on, for a long time. Like a dream in which you are caught. You try to wake up. You can't." . . .

"And Bill's surgeon, bless him, just kept talking to me. . . . He is the kind of surgeon who doesn't leave you after an operation. He stood by, operating on Bill's life until he was sure it was worth living again." And as he worked with Bill and fitted his new arms, he kept operating on Marty, too, telling her in his calm, sure voice how the human body restores its functions if only the mind and heart will help it a little, building a picture of human strength, trying to cut away her fear.

"It's a strange thing," she said slowly, "how you hold on to fear. I didn't want it amputated—even though it was poisoning me. But he kept talking, so calmly and quietly."

He explained to her the process of making small canals through the muscles of chest and shoulder—cineplastic canals, he called them—and fastening the new arms to the pegs inserted in these canals, so that the muscles—the pectoral and others—can control the arm's movements. And he took her to see people who were using their new arms, all the while quietly reminding her that Bill, some day, would control his as skillfully. "He will be able to do miraculous things," he told her. And he told her more: how the brain has many resources for a hurt body to fall back on. Emergency reserves that most of us never need and never use. But they are there, waiting: nerves, ready to set up a new system of communication, of movement; ready to go to work when we say the word. "And it meant nothing to me," she said. "I heard the words but they had no meaning."

As the physical therapist exercised Bill, he talked to her, too, telling her what a fine strong son she had, how the muscles in chest and torso had grown hard, what a beautiful balance he had acquired, and so quickly. "Losing your arms does tricks to your balance, much as the loss of wings does to a plane." Bill was determined to play ball again and worked long hours on his exercises—

"And instead of feeling proud, I didn't feel at all. It was as if things were on two levels: on one I could see and hear, I knew what was going on but I couldn't feel it; on the other I was feeling but I didn't know what was happening.

"I got up one morning with the same nagging pain between my shoulders that had been there since the accident, and ran downstairs to make a cup of coffee. While the coffee was dripping, I went to the window. The trees were bare. I don't think I even looked at first. Then I saw that the buds had begun to swell, and it was raining—a slow soft rain like we used to have at home in the hills. I stood there, leaning against the cold windowpane, remembering how Mother would let us make candy on rainy days, and how I'd run out to see about my calf. I'd bring the little wet thing inside the barn if it had strayed out, and it was always warm and good in there. . . . And I remembered suddenly a crocheted throw—made of purple and yellow and black and red squares, not very pretty but I loved it—which Mother would wrap around me when I was sick—

"And then it happened. Somehow I was looking in a different direction and I saw—everything. How do you explain it? I can't. It was as if I had awakened from a deep and terrible sleep. Maybe that is what I did. I knew where I was. I was *here* and Bill was *here*, I could touch him."

And she began to feel for the first time, that morning, what Bill was going through. This was *his* ordeal that she was engaged in, not hers. It was as if she were inside him, feeling what he felt, looking at what he saw ahead of him. "I felt the distance"—how far away everything seems to you if you have no arms to touch it. And the little things—what it was like to want to pick up your knife or turn the radio dial, or run a comb through your hair. "I realized all he would miss, all of it." . . .

And slowly it came to her: it didn't matter what she had done or failed to do; only one thing mattered now and that was Bill; Bill, this minute, and the life he was going to live.

"So I came home." She smiled and parked the car across the street from Bill's school. "I still don't know where I had been."

We waited for the children to come out of school and neither of us talked for a while. Then she said, "He knew." . . . She had gone to the hospital and, as usual, Bill was staring out of the window. He slowly turned when he heard her. And quickly his eyes reached out and caught her and held on as if they'd never let go, just as he used to do when he was little and she had been away all day.

That was the hard moment. "When I saw how completely I had failed him I almost forgot him the second time, worrying over that." She smiled quickly to push back the tears. "It's like flypaper—once you get on it."

Bill came running across the school yard with his books and his kite and his little friend, Jenny.

"She was with him when it happened," Marty said.

They stopped, searched the cars, found us, dashed across the street. It was spring and a fine, soft day and we were going on a picnic down by the river.

The two of them climbed into the back seat, Bill checked to see if his fishing tackle was there, we turned into the river road.

After lunch, the youngsters went off to dig bait. Marty picked up a book, settled down under a tree. And I sat under another tree, not reading but thinking of her, of those questions which had kidnapped her—and Bill too—

and left them on a lost road; thinking of that little memory which, like a firm, loving hand, had brought her back to her real world again. Rain . . . a limb of a tree . . . buds swelling . . . the cool windowpane against her cheek . . . and suddenly she had access, once more, to the love within her nature. All because a memory had the mysterious power, somehow, to set off chain reactions of memories, of beliefs, until at last the way cleared to the creative, fusing, loving part of her and she found the strength to accept her future—and Bill's.

Beyond us, I could hear Bill and Jenny calling to each other, counting the worms, dashing from one place to a better.

As I looked up, Marty laid her book aside and told me about the two:

Jenny lived next door. She was a shy, withdrawn little thing when they first knew her, who found it difficult to do the things other children do easily. So Bill took over as teacher. He would put her up in front on his bike when he was eight and she was six and take her around with him. He taught her to ride her bicycle when it was given her that Christmas. He taught her to skate and swim and to ride his pony. It was Jenny who gave the policeman Marty's telephone number. And Jenny who gave him quickly and clearly the other information he needed. But when her mother told her about Bill's arms, she did not say a word. She got up and went to her room and began to read a book. She did not mention it when she was with her parents. Days passed and she did not ask to see Bill. It was as if she had wrapped herself up and laid "the package" away where all that had happened could never touch her again. But they know that each of us has his way of fitting himself to the sharp edges of a disaster like this, and being wise parents, they did not press her.

One night, shortly afterward, a storm came up. Jenny's father went into her room to see about the windows. When he came out, he said, "I want you to go see Jenny."

They went in quietly and by his flashlight they looked at their child, asleep, covers half off, her arms tied down to her body with a heavy cord, from her shoulders to her wrists. She had to find out what it felt like.

At breakfast, they did not comment on the red lines on her arms. They told her they were going to see Bill and invited her to come along. "I have a friend," said Jenny's father, "who is a fine tennis player. It happens that he lost his right arm when he was young. But he can beat me any day on the courts."

Jenny did not ask one question but her father answered all of them that had been written on her face for days.

"My friend has a cineplastic arm," he said. "A hook is on it. He wears a hand when he wants to." He told her about cineplastic arms. About wearing a hook. About "cosmetic hands."

"It all depends on Bill's nerve, how he comes through this," he said. "And that of course depends a lot on Bill's friends."

After a little more talk, Marty returned to her book. And I sat there remembering her when she was ten, twelve, fifteen, for she had spent many summers as a camper on our mountain. Had I been asked to choose from among the children in my camp those for whom one could reasonably predict success in meeting a trouble as big as this, Marty's name would not have crossed my mind. The little black-haired girl with the big eyes who was scared of thunderstorms? So pale when she saw someone hurt? Who used to say, when we talked of books, "Has it a happy ending? If not, count me out." When not frightened of life, she was busy playing tricks on it. And like the little clown she was, she never smiled at her own jokes. After the camp was asleep, one night, she hung all her cabin-mates' shoes and her own on the limbs of trees. The next morning, she slept late, apparently unaware of the excitement, came to breakfast with feet bound with Grecian thongs, her wonderful long black hair in a Psyche knot, and a volume of Emily Dickinson's poems in her hands. Everyone loved this child for her foolery; it was a façade that served her well, though it was of tissue-paper thinness and easily ripped to the anxiety beneath.

It was the custom, at this camp, for children and counselors to talk frankly about themselves and the world they live in. And there were, among them, many who understood as much about those feelings that bind us together or sometimes tear us apart as they did about tennis and swimming. They had traveled a little way, at least, into the two worlds we live in, and talked about it with humility and insight and humor. But not Marty. During these talks, she was evasive and restless. Or she would begin to giggle—so infectiously that all of us would join in her laughter and that would be the end of seriousness for that day.

Even in those years, there were traces of strength in her, character prints that a good sleuth might have looked for. Marty gave up quickly on a job but always went back and carried it through. On the tennis court, in the sculpture room, down would go the racquet, the clay. A walkout. Then her return, grimly determined, as if there were another little girl in her who could not fail. . . .

It was her curious rhythm of failure-success that I thought of now. There was the day she was thrown from a horse. Rather badly shaken up. Cried for a long time. Next day, she was back at the stables, ready to ride, insisted on the same horse when the instructor suggested a more amiable nag, and saw it through successfully—white to the lips. This was the Marty underneath the mask so frivolously painted, underneath the easy fear and panic that often showed through.

I sat there, listening to the children's voices, to the *shush* of turning page as she read her book, thinking of what she had told me. Yes, she had run away—from her responsibility and a future she could not bear to face. She had "left Bill."

But it seemed to me that, this time, it was not so much a flight as a search. Something in her beyond words, primitive, irrational, but human and natural, had rushed out after those arms just as a mother would leave her other children to find the child who is lost. The rest of Bill was *there*. It could wait. What was lost had to be recovered. So that he could be whole again. So that she could be whole again. For Marty thought of herself not only as the reflection she saw in her mirror changing but seeming to remain always the same; not only as the girl loved by John, and her parents' child, but as the mother of Bill, too. On a shadowy wordless level, as deep as those somatic processes which keep one's heart beating and lungs breathing, he was an extension in time and space of her image of herself. And so she "left" him, in order to find the old image of herself *and* him—that could never exist again. What an ancient drama it is! Human beings forever trying to make whole what is broken; so often destroying their future in a desperate effort to restore their past. It is so easy to call it "self-destructiveness." But I don't think it is. Marty was trying to create something. The trouble was, she worked with unreal materials. It was as if she were an artist trying to paint a portrait with fantasy tubes of color. The canvas, after all her effort, was still blank.

One day, she realized this. She began to see that she had tried to make with the materials of childish guilt what can be created only out of mature love. And she came back from the past in time to help Bill grow a real life for himself.

Jenny had caught a fish; she was squealing, she wanted help to get it off the line, and Bill was taking it off for her. . . .

"John—" Marty looked up from her book. "From the beginning, he was different from me. It was Bill that he thought of, not himself, not me. Bill's life." She could not get in touch with him at first; he had gone up to one of the islands on a mission. At last he heard and phoned her. "I shall remember his voice as long as I live, coming from another world—it seemed to me—so steady and easy, telling me that he loved us. Then in his quiet, detailed way, he told me what to do to get Bill going again. The practical, down-to-earth things. I never knew what a fine grown-up man I had married until that day. He made it seem not simpler but smaller—set against other people's trouble. It had happened; we could handle it. He had no doubt of Bill's strength, of mine, of his own; just love—and determination that nothing should keep Bill's life from being good and right for him.

"And all the time I was crying in the telephone, not saying a word."

For a moment she did not go on. Then:

"They kept him flying the Hump a long time in the last war. I was afraid he couldn't take it. But after he called me that day, I knew he could take anything. There is something in him that doesn't give an inch. It is as if he decided long ago what he values. I can't say it well—it is simply that he believes in life as people have to live it on this earth. He accepts it, not just the good part but death, trouble, pain, all of it. Not as evil which one must be resigned to but as experiences without which human growth would be inconceivable. When something happens, John doesn't waste a minute resenting it. He gets to work on it."

"And you?"

"Me. . . ." she sighed, and smiled quickly. "There are two: one does the wrong thing; the other runs fast to catch up and mend it. Always late. I've never been quite glued together. But you know that, don't you?

"Once," she said, "while things were hard, I thought of a talk we had, long ago, on the hill at camp. One Sunday morning. We were talking about our fears and dreads, learning to face up to a few of them. And someone asked you what you feared most—and before you could answer, they began to tell *you.*"

One said, to have your face burned and left scarred. Another said, No; to be paralyzed would be worse; not to be able to dance. Another said it would be, for her, the forgetting of the past and her own identity. Another said she could take anything but the death of those she loved. One said she could not accept being poor—"losing our house and cars and my horse and all that; I'd rather be dead." And several agreed with her; they'd rather be dead, they said, than separated from their things. An older girl said, "It wouldn't be *things* for me. What would be hard for me would be to lose faith in the people I believe in. There are only a few," she said quietly, "but I need my belief in them."

Yes, I remembered that talk. And I had wondered, as we sat there together under the trees that Sunday morning, what life would ask these protected youngsters to take; where the breaks would come; out of what resources of intelligence and memory and belief and love, and hope, each would make her bridge. And Marty? Marty had said nothing. She was, as usual, playing with a beetle, or tickling the girl next her with a leaf.

"And all the time," she said now, "I was thinking of a woman who lived on the street back of us at home. She had lost her hand. It seemed to me the most dreadful thing: to lose part of your body. I remembered the old story about the woman with the golden arm—how she died and someone stole it from her grave and her ghost came back to earth searching for it. I suppose it means something different to each child who hears it. For me, it was a wind whistling around the darkest corners of my childhood. And as I sat there on the hill listening that day, it seemed too unbearable to speak aloud. And I thought, if anything like this ever happens to me, I'll die. It never occurred to me . . . that, when something happens to you, *you* in turn happen to it. It is *you* who make the next move, *you* who decide what meaning the experience is going to have for you."

"You are wise if you have learned that."

"I haven't," she said with her quick candor, "not yet. I am still trying to learn."

She told me more of John's across-the-sea telephone calls to her, of his letters to Bill. Once, when things were rough for Bill, when he had gained enough of his strength to begin to look into a future he dared not see, she had written John of his discouragement and John called her from Tokyo and told her to tell Bill the story of Guillaumet.

"Guillaumet—I couldn't even remember who he was. And John said, 'Saint Ex's friend, darling!' As if they were his closest companions."

Antoine de Saint Exupery. Of course. Though he knew him only through his writings, Saint Ex had been to John an intimate friend as he went on his lonely journeys through the sky. And Marty knew this. "But I could not remember about Guillaumet," she said, "I found the story in *Wind, Sand and Stars,* and that night I told Bill of Guillaumet's journey across the Andes, of his crash-landing in weather twenty degrees below zero, his walking his way out day after day, three days and nights, four—

"—Doing what no one thought he could do. He had come up from Patagonia, and with Exupery and others in those early years of aviation he was opening up the first mail routes across the sky. They had been exploring the Andes, making their maps as they went across the vastness of snow and ice and silence. This day, he was alone. The sky did not look good; the winds were not friendly. But he had a job; to deliver the idea that, in good weather or foul, mail could be brought across the Andes. And he went on, as those early pilots did, with few instruments to help him. It was not long before the way closed up behind him. Then it closed up in front of him. There was nothing to do but slog it out with the clouds, and he climbed as high as he could.

"Then things began to happen: it was as if the winds had emptied the sky, leaving the plane in a vacuum; there was a moment when it seemed suspended between time and space then was caught and pulled like a slip of paper between the peaks and out again. He did not know how long the struggle had gone on when he felt the plane sucked down and rolled over and over like a hat in a road, he said afterward, from eighteen thousand feet to ten. Somehow he righted it and saw that he was trapped in a gorge flanked by sheer walls of ice and rock. At the bottom of it was a tiny glacial lake, beautiful and serene. He flew around it, again and again and again. There seemed nothing else to do. And he kept circling—until the petrol was exhausted and then he slid the plane down softly on the snow.

"There was no way out except to walk and no path to follow and for two days the winds were too strong to walk against. So he sat in the shelter of his plane and waited. On the third day he began that incredible journey through snow, ice, along narrow ledges. He walked four days and nights. He had no food, the cold made him sleepy, the glare burned deep. It would be so easy to lie down.

"Then the fight inside him began. All the forces gathered on one side or the other in battle for a man. His lungs wanted to stop breathing in the thin air, muscles stiffened, joints ached, hands grew numb, and he began to leave things: his knife, his glove, the equipment he needed to see him through. It was as if one part of him were ready to give up and die. But on the other side of the battle line, fighting back hard, were memories of his fellow-pilots, his wife; sudden scraps of talk, laughter; and belief that the sky belonged to men and men had to open it up, *he* had to open it up. If he failed now it would be harder for the others.

"Another day passed. He was fighting his body's fatigue with two fixed ideas: his wife waiting . . . 'she would expect me to come back'; his fellow-pilots waiting . . . 'they would know I would keep on walking.' So he kept on walking. But after a time he could not walk. He would lie down and sleep, he told himself, he had done all a man could do. It was at that moment that he remembered his insurance. His wife would not receive it for four years, according to French law, unless his body were found. She could not do without it four years. And he knew his body would not be found where he now stood, for when the snows melted in springtime it would be washed into a crevasse. Ahead of him, fifty yards ahead, was a large rock. If he could walk that far, his body would be found by shepherds when summer came. So he took a step, and another, and another.

"When the peasants heard that his plane was down, they said it was impossible for him to come out of such ice and snow. 'The Andes never give up a man in winter,' they said. And Exupery, who had flown to his assistance, believed it impossible, too, though he went up day after day to search for him. And other pilots searched. And somehow, though they knew it was impossible and said so, as they drank coffee together in the cafes of the Chilean towns, they expected Guillaumet to do it—as they would have expected themselves to do it, even though it could not be done."

"It became our bedtime story," Marty said. "Bill reserved a few lines for himself. *The Andes never give up a man in winter*—that was his to say." And always at the last—when Guillaumet was spotted near a remote village, having taken that one step and the next and the next, and Saint Exupery had flown there and brought him back to the hospital in Mendoza and he lay half dead, starved and nearly blinded, with both hands frozen—it was Bill's turn to say those spine-tingling words when Guillaumet told Saint Ex, "I swear I have been through things no animal could come through!"

And each night after the story was done, Bill's mother said they would sit there without a word. Then Bill would say, "Gee . . . and he walked out of something nobody could walk out of just because Saint Ex expected him to and those other pilots; he knew they did; and his wife expected him to—"

"—and he expected himself to."

And Bill would say softly, "Yep. That's it."

She told me of a letter John wrote on the eve of Bill's leaving the rehabilitation center. Bill had been there a long time, among people whose bodies had been stripped of strength or broken or altered by accidents or illness. He had grown used to that upswing of body and the soft down-thud of crutch on floor of a paralyzed girl walking down the corridor; to the people in wheel chairs working, playing, eating their meals; to the contour of men, women, boys, girls, without limbs, to the metallic sounds of braces, locking, unlocking and the glint of prosthetic arms and legs; as used to all this as a medieval warrior was used to armor. But outside, he would be the only one on his street without arms; the only "cripple" in his schoolroom. He would be different. And that would be new; that would hurt.

So John wrote his son a letter. He told him, in words as simple and plain as those he used in making his reconnaissance reports, about a man's rights. He said he was fighting in Korea for those rights, for his own, for Bill's, for Marty's. "For everybody's rights, Son, no matter where they live. But sometimes a guy gets mixed up. You hear so much about rights these days you begin to think you have a right to everything. Even to a body with two legs and two arms and sight and hearing and so on. But you don't. No one has a right to that kind of body. It's a gift. God gives it to you or nature gives it, or you can call it the evolutionary process, or however you want to speak of it. In big words or little words, it is a gift. And not everybody is given it. For accidents happen before birth, as well as afterward. I know a great chap who was born without arms and legs. . . .

"And sometimes," he said in this letter, "even when we have a gift to begin with, it gets messed up. You know about that. And I know too, out here, because it has happened to some of the bravest men I've flown with. It's funny how a guy can get mixed up about things. He loses a leg, say; or his arms, or his sight; he begins to feel he hasn't had a fair deal; things are raw; he's been gypped; somebody's taken his right to a whole body away from him. He's all wet, Bill.

"But there is a right that you do have; everybody has; and that is the right to a whole life, whether you have legs and arms, or not; no matter how different you may be. And I mean by a whole life, a life full of fun and interesting experiences (along with the hard things), and people you love, and a girl some day, and a job you like to do, and sports, and making things better for others. We are going to do our best, Bill, to help you hold on to that right. To see that nobody takes it away from you. But you have to walk to it, boy, like Guillaumet. All your mother and I can do is stand by, and help when we can."

Bill read that letter to pieces. He did not comment on it. He handed it to his mother to read, then asked for it back and read it again and again. Marty could not be sure how he was taking it. Perhaps it is over his head, she thought. Maybe you can't understand about having no right to a whole body, when you're just a kid. Then one day, Bill said to her, "I'd like to meet a man born without any arms and legs. Gee . . . it must be wonderful to be born that way and yet learn to walk and do things."

"So we went on a little journey, too," Marty smiled. "We visited rehabilitation centers, talked to people who had 'done things no animal could do.' It was an amazing and humbling week for me—and thrilling to Bill. He was with friends. They spoke the same language, laughed at the same jokes. For weeks after we came home, he practiced them on Jenny." . . .

But there were nights when Guillaumet walking his way out of that twenty-below-zero trap in the Andes could not help; and John's letters could not help, and Bill's dreams of what he was going to be could not help. And Marty, in her room, across the hall, would hear the low sobbing begin. Sometimes she let him fight it out, knowing there is one kind of strength that can be found only within the lonely center of you. But at other times, she could not, herself, bear the loneliness and she would go in and sit by his bed and sing to him, binding him back to her, letting him be the little boy he had to be, now and then; and finally he would hush and she would hear him quietly breathing in sleep. . . .

The children were looking at television. Marty was preparing dinner. After a little, she called them to come help her finish things up. Bill set the table; Jenny beat a meringue—to such fine high peaks that she rushed in to show me. The Hump, she said, Bill's father used to fly over; it must be wonderful, she dreamed aloud, to fly over it at night and watch the sun rise—does it come up under you? like this? And then she tipped the Himalayas and they slid on to the rug and as we cleaned it up Bill came to the door to jeer at the mess and Jenny rubbed meringue in his face and Marty called them to go wash up. "If you're fighting her, Bill, watch out for your hooks."

It was impossible to believe that in this cheerful household there had ever been disaster, or could be.

"John's feeling—his acceptance of life—where did he learn this?" I asked Marty. . . .

Marty did not answer for a long time. "I have spoken very freely for him," she finally said. "More so than I have a right to do.

"I think his sureness with life comes because he loves so surely. But how does one learn to love like that? I almost hated him, once, because of it."

And then she told me. It happened while John was at home:

She had wished for him every day. But when the news came that he would have a four months' leave she began to dread it. Things would be different. It was strange that Bill's losing his arms could change her relationship with John and his with her and theirs with Bill. But it had done so. This she suddenly knew.

The only part of this feeling that her mind could put into words was her realization of the shock John would have when he saw Bill. No matter how many facts he knew, his eyes had not seen; a new image would take the place of the old; in one instant would destroy it. To look on as this happened—

The night before the plane came in, she did not sleep much. Against a background of feelings impossible to fit to words flashed questions. Should she suggest to Bill that he wear his hands? Or let him do as he wished? He liked to wear his hooks, they were convenient but John was not used to—no, let him do as he wished. Should she have sent pictures? It would have been unfair. Maybe she should go alone to the airport, talk it over—but Bill wanted to see John too, it would not be right to leave him out of this important moment. But would John be able—

It kept on all night.

The next morning, early, she heard Bill up, walking around; now in the shower; now pulling out the bureau drawers. He came into her room dressed to the hilt. Hair wet, slicked back with a high-smelling lotion on it. Neck scrubbed. One hand on; one hook. A big red handkerchief in his hip pocket. A purple tie. A yellow sweater. His school patrol badge.

"He was wonderful to look at," she said.

The morning was sunny and cold and fresh-blowing from the Sound as they drove to La Guardia Airport. They had only a few minutes to wait. The plane was overhead; it taxied down the strip; passengers began to leave it. She was trembling all over. She would not look at Bill; it might be easier for him—for her—so she looked straight ahead. She saw John wave—and Bill was in front of her now waving back.

"Gee, Daddy's grown a lot," Bill shouted. And he did look taller than his six-feet-two as he stooped through the door of the plane and came down the runway. She laughed. And Bill laughed, realizing that he had said something funny and they were laughing when John came up to them. He took Bill by the shoulders, gave him a shake and kissed him, and said, "I got something for you." Then, "Gee, Bill, what you been doing to her! She looks wonderful." The things you'd expect a man to say. It was only when he took her in his arms that she knew he was trembling too. But it was all right. Everything was natural and right. "Why is it that we try so hard to hide our most decent feelings?"

They went to the car laughing and talking, now and then one of them wiped away tears. But no one minded. "We were just glad to be together." And they went home and had a big breakfast of waffles and ham and eggs, and Bill had a cup of coffee to celebrate.

For a few weeks they skidded along on sheer excitement. Then things happened. "One day I touched something very disagreeable in myself."

The feeling was quickly gone. John was in Bill's room at his worktable helping him. They were building shelves, planning to make a stool, many things. She thought *This is just what Bill has needed.* Then the feeling slid back over her. Across the whine of the electric saw, she could hear them talking. "Listen, Daddy," and Bill would talk to John. Talk, talk—as if he had been saving it up. *As if she could not understand,* she whispered the words to herself. "Had I screamed them I could not have been more shocked."

The next day she was cleaning John's study, running the vacuum over his shelves. Their voices kept coming through. *Listen Daddy . . . Boy, you're somep'n* . . . thin voice, deep voice. *But Dad, you see.* . . . She could not hear all the words but she tried to. "I cleaned those books a hundred times as I stood there, snooping on my two."

She had had Bill to herself so long. All the pain and responsibility—and satisfaction had been hers. It had not been easy, she had made plenty of mistakes, she knew. But she had brought him through; he was doing all right. Now she felt as if her job had been taken over by a superior officer.

"The point was, I knew John would do a better job than I had. And it burned me up." She had never been jealous before—of anyone as far as she could remember. But it seemed so easy for him—coming home—seeing Bill—she felt she had worried unnecessarily about, well, everything. And now Bill had turned to him. She wasn't in the picture—

It seemed impossible to accept this new look at herself. Bill needed John's humor and ease and masculine know-how. Without it, he would not learn what a man can be. A boy must have this image. This was clear to her. Her brain had not shrunk. "It was my heart," she said, "I had not known I could be so small."

She put away the vacuum, left a note, took the car and went out to the river where we had been on this day. Where John and she had gone many times; where they used to camp in the summers; long ago he had told her here, as they cooked over a camp-fire, of his dreams to go to M.I.T.; and she had told him one cold windy day as they walked along the river's edge that she was pregnant; and when his mother died they had talked about his childhood under these same old trees. All the little things not thought of for years had tumbled out that day, his memories, hers. Everything, almost, in their life together had been talked over, out here. "I guess I thought it would come back; if I could see the trees, the old rock, I'd see the whole design, maybe, and fit this piece in with the rest. Maybe it would not seem so evil to me. But I could not think it through. All I could hold to was the knowing that if I began now to compete with John for Bill's love and esteem, it would tear our lives up. Bill would lose something far more important to him than his arms." . . .

"Isn't it strange," she said after a time . . . "that I could have envied John the very qualities I love in him and depend on?

"Envy is hardly the word—I hated him that day. It seemed to me he had done everything right from the beginning of our trouble. He had made no mistakes. And I had made so many! I knew I would make more—and some of them would be hard for Bill to forgive and for me to forgive. I hated John because of his success. I knew it came because of his capacity for tenderness and concern, and I hated him for that, too. I ached that day with the unfairness of it!" . . .

They were waiting for her when she came in, that evening. They had cooked dinner and set the table and were in the kitchen trying to figure out a way to keep the food warm. The kettle was boiling and John was saying, "Now what do you think of trying a little hot water under the shrimp, Sergeant?" She stood at the door a moment, looking at them. Each had on one of her aprons, faces were flushed, they looked as if they had had quite a workout—

"But we don't have to warm it up," yelled Bill, "she's here."

"Hi," said John, as if she had just stepped around the corner to the store. And Bill, taking his cue, said, "Hi."

And then she helped them take up dinner. When they went into the dining room she saw that they had put a few red roses in her little white bowl—the one she kept in her bedroom because she loved to look at it. And she felt warmed by this wordless effort they were making and close to tears for a moment. But John kept it easy and gay and casual by telling her the small absurd events of the day. And as they sat there, eating the shrimp stew he had made, she realized how thin he had grown since his return and how tired, really tired, Bill looked—worn-out from trying to stretch up as tall as his father. And she knew suddenly that they had found it as hard as she: each had been hurt by a different thing, maybe, had suffered in a different way, but battle fatigue was on all their faces.

After supper, they played Canasta. When it came time for Bill to go to bed, he told them good night and went to his room. And she and John sat there, smoking, not talking, now and then smiling at each other, questions in John's eyes—she did not know what was in hers.

And then Bill called her. He was standing in the middle of his room. He had taken off his arms though he still had on most of his clothes. As she walked in, he sort of grinned and waited a moment, then said very low, "Mommy, will you help me to bed?" And she knew as if he had written her a long letter how he felt about her, and about John. She winked at him and said, "Sure," and then he ran to her and began to cry hard trying to smother the sobs against her shoulder, so his father would not hear. After he was in bed, she sat by him, stroking his hair now and then, and he stared out the window and did not say a word.

When she went back to John he was in the study smoking his pipe, and reading.

She wanted to tell him at once all that had troubled her. But he began to tell her what had troubled him:

It was not so hard in Korea, he told her, to take it. About Bill. He could see it, out there, set against the suffering of the whole world. It was his boy, yes; and he hurt for him; and for her; but there was distance—the distance that comes not as much from geography as from a totally different setup where the size of personal disaster changes, somehow. He could be philosophic about it out there—enough to keep his bearings, keep his mind clear. But when he came home, and saw, actually saw Bill—"I became a little boy, too, I reckon." He had to fight harder than he had ever fought against storm or mountain or the enemy—and there she was, he said, going about things easily, calmly as if nothing had happened. He'd watch Bill put on his arms—his daily routine—"and the sweat would pour out of me and she would be telling Bill to hurry, the others were waiting, voice casual, easy," he wrote a friend in Korea, who sent her the letter . . . "I was a raw recruit and she the veteran, taking it, determined to treat him like a boy, not like a cripple—and not like a hero either. And as I watched her I was humbled by this courage of women—only the word is not courage, precisely, nor is it creativity; our language has no word for it because, perhaps, we do not yet know it for what it is: they go about so quietly cutting tragedy down to a size that they can fit into a home. And we? we males set it on a stage, turn all the lights on and strut our little piece—or else we wholly deny it. And sometimes we make great poetry of course, but they make life. And what is better than life, Bob?" . . .

He said that night only enough for her to understand how he felt about her and Bill. But she knew he had guessed her trouble so truly that there was little more for her to say.

"It was then that we began to feel it, think it together"—to see how one's problems change as one's framework changes. John's problem changed when he came close to it. Then it was that it slipped from his mind, where he could handle it objectively, into his heart and blood stream and nerve endings, and he suffered as if the accident had happened that day. And she had acquired her problem by maturing a little: along with this new independence came a new pride. She had invested heavily of herself in their ordeal—it was natural for her to want to clip the coupons. "But neither of us could clip them, rightfully; only Bill," she said. "And not even Bill." That night they began to see this: to see that somehow theirs and Bill's trouble must be shared with the world, just as one shares one's good fortune: They had to identify with all children who had lost their arms; had to give of their hurt and experience to help these others; had to do something to make it more difficult for accidents to happen; had to fuse their unique ordeal with every man's ordeal. Only by doing so, only by assuming the heavier burdens of mankind could they bear the light weight of their own.

"Things have been leveled off now," she said. "When John comes home, we are going to do something—I don't quite know what—but something to help all children. We want to, we feel we must.

"But you will think me unteachable," she smiled, "when I tell you I still wish there could be a happy ending, though I know there can't be."

"But something—more real?"

"Yes," she sighed. "Maybe. Understanding . . . sympathy . . . (the words came slowly as if heavy with nights of thinking) acceptance . . . knowledge . . . forgiveness—all the learning that gives men their flavor and strength—you don't know how often I say the words to myself, trying to believe them."

The fundamental perceptual principles involved in personality

This case of Marty, beyond all doubt, involves profoundly significant human experience. It involves far more than we can ever fully illuminate by laboratory experiments. In fact, it might seem impossible that laboratory experiments could apply to any such experiences at all, because laboratory experiments, particularly within the field of perception, usually deal with small-scale samples of experience that seem utterly trivial from a motivational point of view. Contrastingly, the various experiences of Marty and the others in her family were profound, motivationally speaking.

However, when we seek to understand significant experiences like these, we need to remember that the history of science makes it quite clear that little, unimportant-seeming phenomena have often been the means whereby a better understanding could be achieved of something massive and important. For example, when the early physicists started to work with electric sparks produced by rubbing a comb on a piece of silk, it might not have seemed possible that they were already close to an understanding of lightning and that they were laying the foundations of a field of knowledge which would transform modern life in innumerable ways. Abstract knowledge has a way of permitting us to see resemblances between different things that at first blush seem utterly unrelated. Perhaps this is true of personality, on the one hand, and the relatively simple phenomena of perception, on the other hand. Let us see what we can learn from some simple examples of perceptual activity.

Before we begin this analysis, however, it might be well to explain that experimental research with perception usually has been of two main types. One type might be described as *sensory-organization* examples of perception, the other as examples of the *perception of meaning*. Of these two classes of perception, perhaps the simpler or more primitive is the first—the sensory-organization type of perception. It is this type of example to which we will refer through most of the rest of the chapter. Toward the end of the chapter we will make some references to the types of perceptions that are matters of changed meaning; but through most of our discussion we will be talking only about principles that appear in matters of simple sensory organization and yet also apply to very significant phenomena of personality. Five of these basic principles run as follows:

1. *Most stimulus situations are vieldeutig.* Figure 2 shows a number of drawings such as have been used in research on the sensory-organization type of perception. Perhaps you are familiar with these from previous study. If not, it might be worthwhile for you to spend some time with

these drawings, staring fixedly at each of them for a minute or more. What you find with each figure is that it seems to have some one natural and inevitable way in which it should be seen. You see the figure in that one way, and then you tend to say, "All right, I see it clearly, and that's that. But what of it?" But this matter is not as simple as it might seem. For one thing, if you compare notes with some other person, you might find that he sees *A* as a row of rather fat goblets standing upside down, whereas you perhaps see the same representation as a row of

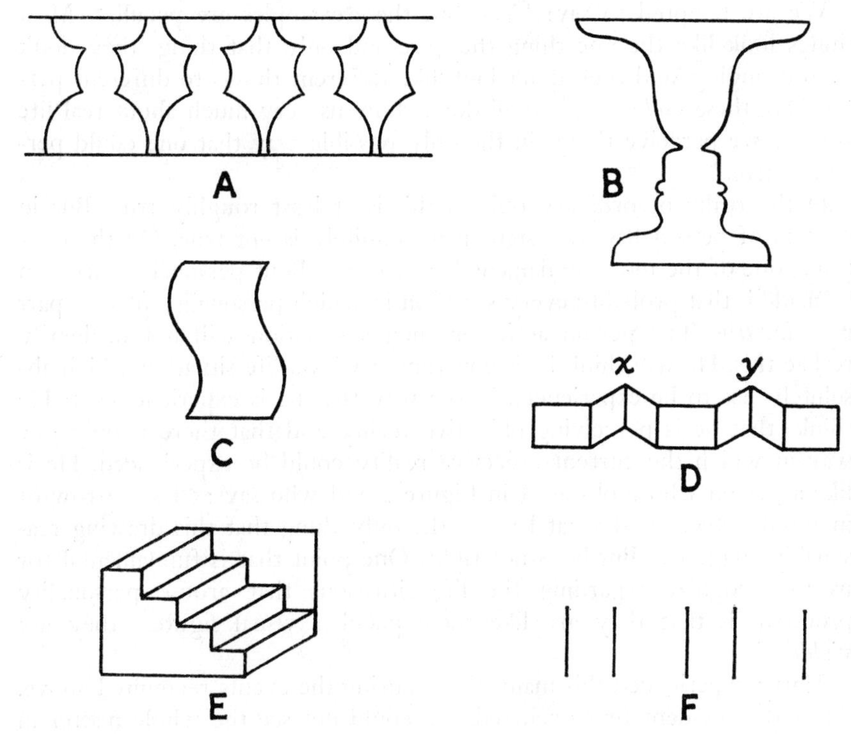

FIGURE 2. *Examples of Ambiguous Figures.*

sharp-pointed holly-leaves. You see *B* as an urn or bird-bath; he perhaps sees it as two persons looking at each other. For another thing, if you continue to stare at any of these figures, you find that it changes. You yourself receive drastically different impressions from each at different times.

In English we do not have any good term for this, though the terms *ambiguous* and *equivocal* are partly satisfactory. German does better. In German, a situation may be *eindeutig* (having one possible value or character), *zweideutig* (having two good possibilities), or *vieldeutig*[3] (hav-

[3]Pronounced "feel-doi'-tig."

ing a number of possibilities within it). Our English term *equivocal* has overtones of meaning that are inappropriate. Thus, the dictionary asserts: "that is equivocal which conveys (often with intent to deceive), along with a given idea, another quite different one with equal clearness and propriety." This sort of meaning is unacceptable in our discussion of perceptual materials. There is no intent to deceive with such drawings as in Figure 2; it is simply a fact that each of these drawings can produce quite different effects in different beholders, or in the same beholder at different times.

We are tempted to say: "Yes, but these examples are peculiar. Most things look like the one thing they are and only that thing; they don't keep changing, and they don't look like different things to different persons. So, these *vieldeutig* stimuli don't show us very much about real life —there we perceive things in the only possible way that one could perceive them."

In the realm of ordinary objects this is at least roughly true. But in matters of personality, this statement definitely is not true. On the contrary, one of the most fundamental statements about personality that can be made is that probably every situation in which personality plays a part is *vieldeutig*. The person active in such a situation will not ordinarily realize this. He will think he is confronted with a life situation which absolutely has to be experienced in the way that he is experiencing it. He thinks that he is perceiving objective reality and that there is only one way in which the current objective reality could be experienced. He is like a person who looks at *A* in Figure 2 and who says: "I see a row of inverted goblets, and what I see is the only thing that this drawing reasonably suggests." But he is not right. One point that is fundamental for us to recognize regarding the life situations that arouse personality processes is that they are like these peculiar visual figures—they are *vieldeutig*.

Marty experienced this many times during the events recounted above. After the accident first occurred, she could not see the whole matter in any way except in that first fashion that made her so preoccupied with the question of what she had done wrong. But this was not the only way that the situation could be seen, and she was able later to perceive it in a way that made her vastly more helpful to her boy than she had been at first. To her son, too, life presented a *vieldeutig* situation. It was more or less inevitable that the situation at first seemed almost unbearably bitter. But though his loss was grave, it was also true that he could face his situation in terms like these: "I still can see as I did before; I still can hear music and everything else; I still can know the great things that friendship can bring to life; I still can be a husband who can make his wife truly happy and grateful; I still can win the love and gratitude of my children; I still can do useful and valuable work; it is even true that I can still be physically vigorous at many things. I am handicapped in certain ways, but most of the things that make human life potentially great are still open to me!"

Over and over again one sees that when people have personality problems, they fail to recognize this *vieldeutig* character of their life situations. They believe they are experiencing life in the only way that it might possibly be experienced. But they are wrong. Every personality situation is *vieldeutig*.

2. *In an important sense, in such vieldeutig situations, the person lives only in terms of his dynamically-organized perceptions, rather than in terms of the objective realities.* Almost as soon as a person looks at such simple designs as those in Figure 2, a dynamically-organized perceptual process results. Thus, when a person looks at *D* in Figure 2, this may appear at the outset like a flat, two-dimensional figure, but it soon becomes a three-dimensional figure and may never return to its original (and *actual*) two-dimensional character. However, at each instant, the perceptual process that is evoked is what may be called a dynamically-organized process. That is, it is a process in which things influence one another so that some consistency or harmony among the parts is produced. Thus, if the right-hand edge of *C* is seen in one way, the left-hand edge will be seen in a way that is congruous with it. Or, look at *A* in the same Figure 2. If one part of the drawing becomes a goblet, all of the row becomes goblets. In *D*, if *x* stands out toward the person, so also does *y*; when *x* moves away, then also *y* moves simultaneously with it.

In consequence of this factor of dynamic organization, perceptual processes have a highly selective or abstractive character. It is as if the objective situation exists for the person virtually only as it is perceived by him—as though, for the moment, the objective stimulation has no other qualities than those that are represented in his perceptual process of that moment.

After her husband returned on furlough from the South Pacific, Marty perceived him as handling the situation without strain or difficulty, and she perceived her son as having shifted his interest and dependence entirely to the father, leaving her as though she had no function in the family situation any more. She was not perceiving the situation correctly, and eventually the actions of her husband and son compelled her to alter her perception to a more valid organization. But, as long as her perception remained unchanged, she lived only in terms of what she thus perceived. In this case, therefore, as in the earlier examples cited in this chapter, we see that any attempt to understand another person must seek to find what representational processes are occurring within him. What governs the rest of his activity, once a certain perceptual organization has been achieved, is the *perceived situation*. It is not some external reality composed of unchanging lines on a sheet of paper; nor is it some unambiguous set of facts in his social situation.

3. *With vieldeutig situations, there is the possibility of drastic shifts in perceptual organization.* You have already met this phenomenon in reacting to the various drawings in Figure 2. It is not necessary, in order that such a reorganization should occur, for you to realize that there is another possible organization that might be achieved. Even during the period while one perceptual organization prevails, conditions develop that tend to prevent its continuance and that tend to make it possible for some second or, later, a third sort of perceptual organization to occur instead. And sometimes, at least, as in the case of the drawings in this figure, the changes occur with dramatic suddenness.

Marty experienced such changes at several different times. You will remember, for instance, her account of how she stood at one time by the window, looking out at the soft rain, "remembering how Mother would let us make candy on rainy days, and how I'd run out to see about my calf . . . . And then it happened. Somehow I was looking in a different direction . . . ." Later she felt she no longer had any really important role in her son's life and she had to go out alone where she could try to fight the forces of jealousy within her. But when her son, in going to bed, called to her to help him, and when he showed so clearly that he needed someone besides just his father, and when her husband revealed so clearly in his comments what unsuspected emotional struggles had been occurring in him, she naturally changed her perception of her life situation in as sharp and dramatic a way as ever happened with our simple visual figures.

4. *These drastic reorganizations, however, do not always come swiftly and do not always come easily.* You may have been puzzling about the drawing that we used as the headpiece for this chapter, on page 157. Unless you are unusually good with such incomplete figures, that headpiece possibly still puzzles you. Most persons find, even when they stare at it for quite a while, that it continues to look like a lot of confused, chaotic marks. This does not mean that the perception is not "organized," because each of the marks can be seen clearly and sharply. But there is no sensible, familiar pattern in the drawing. Then, as you stare at the figure long enough, perhaps after having been told to look on the right for a small boy who is bending over, left hand on his knee, right hand reached out to pick some flowers from the ground, and to look on the left for a young girl who is sitting on her heels and who also is reaching out to these flowers, you may finally see the two figures—the boy with his overalls, the girl with her long bobbed hair, and so on.

One further point of special interest is the fact that even though this "correct" organization is hard to achieve, it thereafter tends to persist with remarkable tenacity as the only organization. It becomes virtually impossible for you to see the drawing as the same collection of meaningless, unrelated marks that you perceived originally.

Some other examples show that perceptual organization sometimes changes only gradually, without any sharp changes at any point. Thus, consider the sort of perceptual learning that is required before a person can listen skillfully to music. A person may become highly skillful in following any voice within a quartet or any of the instruments within a symphony orchestra. But this skill with music is not something that can be achieved in a few minutes or few hours—it is something that has to be built up over years of training.

In our everyday thinking we are relatively unfamiliar with this idea of the gradual acquisition of perceptual skills. However, every person has been acquiring a great many of these skills in a number of different areas. His life would lack much of its fineness if he had not gone through such training. For example, most persons have become so good at hearing different voices that they can identify hundreds of different persons by the slight differences of quality in their voices. They have become so expert at recognizing the cast of people's faces that they could learn to recognize thousands of different persons. In our everyday life we don't regard this as any special accomplishment. "After all," we say, "the faces of different persons *are* different; why shouldn't we see them as different?" When we say this we are making the old rationalistic, externalistic assumption about our psychological processes. The mere presence of external differences does not in itself produce the ability to perceive those differences. This fact shows up in some experience that the psychologist Dr. Donald Hebb has described. When he was working at the Yerkes Primate Laboratory in Florida, he found that he and the other workers became able to recognize the faces of chimpanzees as being as distinctive and characteristic as the faces of human beings. Not only were they able to distinguish between the various chimpanzees they were working with in the laboratory, they could also easily see striking differences in the facial appearances of new animals. For most of us, however, chimpanzees all look alike except for obvious differences in size.

In fact, where one has the capacity for quick shifts of perceptual organization, as with the old-woman–young-woman figure discussed in Chapter 5, the chances are that this is possible only when the individual has previously gone through the long, slow development of perceptual skills that offered him the alternatives between which he could shift. Thus a tremendous amount of perceptual learning goes on in human life, even though, because we have not deliberately pursued such learning, we take it completely for granted.

In the case of Marty's son, we find an example both of the difficulty of achieving a new organization and of the gradualness with which new organizations sometimes must be developed. To get the new outlook on life that Bill needed after his accident—to get some perception of the fact that he could still live happily and richly—was no easy, simple thing for a boy of his age, particularly. He was helped by talking with other patients who had had serious physical injuries. He was helped by the heroic way in which the flier, Guillaumet, had faced his crisis. He was helped by Jenny and many other persons. But it was a long, hard struggle. When we talk about the development of perceptual organizations, we are not always talking about processes that can be transformed in the twinkling of an eye—we are talking about cases, too, where the task is the long, slow one of the person who wants to become skillful in some complex new field in which, at the start, he completely lacks adequate habits.

5. *Whatever perceptual organization is achieved first tends to resist later influences that would tend to produce an alternative organization.* To illustrate this point, we might consider again the ambiguous drawings given in Figure 1, page 147. If the middle drawing in such a series has been prepared properly, so that it does not favor either of the possible patterns more than the other, it seems it is almost a chance matter as to whether a given person, if allowed to look first at this middle drawing, will perceive it as a pert young woman with her head turned far enough away so that the mouth is hidden, or as a quite different head seen in profile. But if a person has been shown a simplified drawing first that emphasizes the characteristics of either the young woman or the old woman, he is almost certain to see a similar head in the composite drawing. Also, after having been led—without any special effort on his part—to see one of the possible organizations, most of such persons experience a lot of difficulty in seeing the other possible organization, one which would have been quite easy for them if they had happened to be prepared to see it originally.

In a talk given in 1952 as president of the Western Psychological Association, one of the present writers spoke of this type of development as a "seed-crystal effect," comparing it to an effect produced in chemistry. With any of certain chemicals, a supersaturated solution can be prepared that will crystallize very quickly when a tiny "seed crystal" is dropped into it. But the type of crystal that is formed, and that must be redissolved before the other sort of crystal can replace it, depends on the shape of the tiny "seed" that starts the action.

Another example of perceptual organization—though now an example of perception of meaning, rather than an example like those of the sensory-organization type—illustrates still more effectively the point that perceptual organizations may be extremely resistant to change even in cases where they were established in the first place with very little effort. In the town of Eugene, where the University of Oregon is located, the position of the Willamette River and of the neighboring hills is such that both the railroad and the main highway have to take a broad bend as they come toward the town. This means they have to go through the town along an east-west line, rather than along their main north-south direction. When people first come to Eugene, either from California to

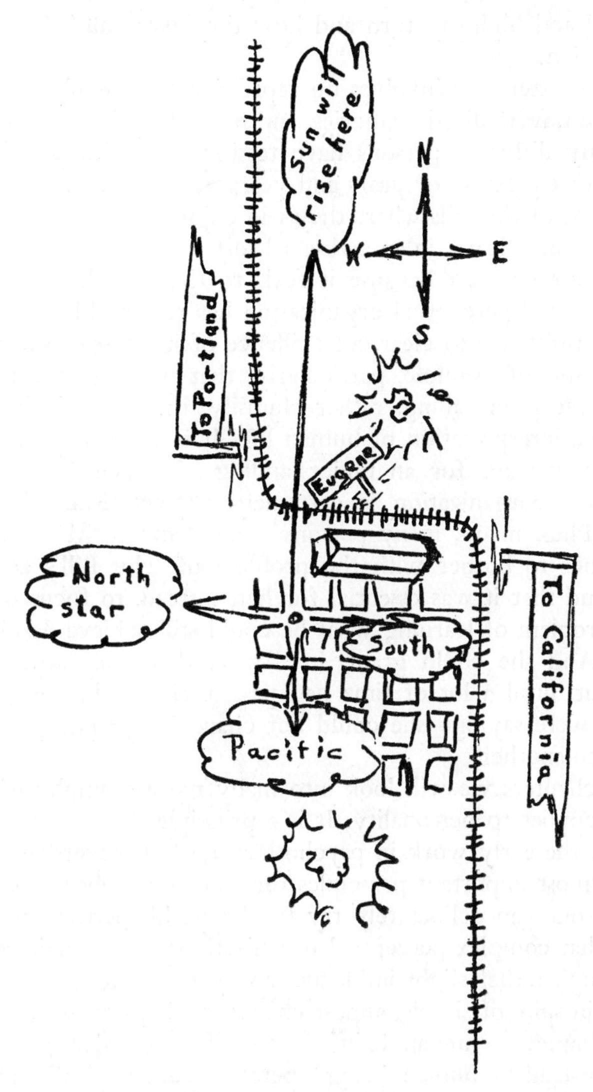

the south or from Portland or Washington to the north, they seldom notice that the direction of the highway or of the railroad changes as it goes through the town. The result is that if visitors take their geographical orientation from the portion of the railroad that goes through town, they get everything twisted around by 90°. Sometimes it is only a few days before they notice that the sun is setting over a range of hills (the Coast Range) which they thought lay to the north of Eugene. They find that streets that seem like north-south streets have such designations as East 13th Street. They get out at night and find that the North Star seems to be in the east. And perhaps they get maps that show them how the railroad and highway turn and how they were misled in their ideas about direction.

This is a matter that involves no repressions, no highly emotionalized attitudes, no unverbalized memories, and no early childhood origins. And yet, as many different persons have testified, this faulty orientation is something that persists for years and years, even with persons who build homes on one of the hills where they can enjoy the sunset day after day. Such persons may learn, in an awkward sort of way, to say that a certain direction must be west because it feels to them as though it is north; but their original perceptual organization has remarkable staying power, remarkable resistance to clear-cut evidence of its incorrectness.

It is this sort of example, particularly, that warrants our rejection of what we have been calling, rather clumsily, the rationalistic or the intellectualistic interpretation of human life. It is a sort of example that is extremely important for an understanding of personality because this resistance to reorganization is extremely characteristic of personality processes. Thus, many, many persons pointed out to Marty that it was futile for her to bother with the problem of why Bill's accident had occurred and that it was essential for her, instead, to focus on the constructive problem of learning what he could still achieve despite his new handicap. And she could grant, in a way, that their arguments were sensible. But, until a lot of time had passed, she could not really grasp what they were saying—she could not change from one perceptual organization to another.

In later chapters we will look into many more examples of this principle as it applies to personality. It is a principle that seems not to have emerged in the early work in psychotherapy; but, nevertheless, it seems one of the most important principles for us to remember when we think about how one can deliberately try to change his personality. We need to realize that complex perceptual organizations can sometimes be established through rather slight influences and yet tend to have terrific staying power in spite of simple, almost chancy beginnings. As we said in the previous chapter, a human being is not like an order-free calculating machine. Instead, a human being operates more typically by forming quick perceptual organizations which then can operate under less favorable circumstances and which resist modification even when the person encounters many objective influences that should change them.

Some necessary changes in our conceptions of perceptual processes

We have followed the path, in this chapter, of suggesting that personality processes may profitably be considered as perceptual processes. So far, we have not had occasion to develop the parallel notion that the enduring features of personality—personality *habits*—may similarly be thought of as *perceptual habits*. Such a suggestion is needed to round out the fundamental idea proposed in this chapter.

Before proceeding farther, however, we need to examine several points in connection with the definition of the terms *perception* and *perceptual*. For, as these terms have most generally been used in psychology, they are not as broad as they would need to be to apply to personality. We are not proposing that we or anyone else can arbitrarily extend the meaning of these terms. But we do think it is legitimate to conclude this chapter with a discussion of four respects in which thinking about perceptual matters ought to be enlarged in order to incorporate some matters of fact from psychological research.

1. *Perceptual processes may be either conscious or unconscious.* In the older tradition in psychology, as in most of popular thought, there was a strong tendency to assume that all important psychological processes are conscious. Thus, even recently most discussions of perception have assumed such definitions as this: "Perception is an awareness or consciousness of present objects and events."

In view of what we now know, however, it hardly seems desirable to continue to use this definition. We know that various psychological processes follow much the same laws and serve much the same purposes whether they are conscious or not. As an example, suppose we give a person a long series of numbers, telling him to multiply them. If we give 8 and 6, he says 48; if 7 and 3, he says 21; and so on. From our observation of his behavior on such a task, continued over a long time, we can tell that he is maintaining a tendency, or set, to multiply. But, as we know from the research mentioned near the start of Chapter 5, this set toward multiplying may be either a conscious or an unconscious steering process within him.

In the same way, after some important new influence has made an impact upon the personality of an individual, it is not necessary that he should continue to perceive this new factor in conscious terms. Such was the situation with Marty—even when she was asleep it was as though she were unconsciously experiencing her life situation in a new way after the accident had happened.

It is worthwhile to realize that when psychologists have defined perceptual processes as conscious processes, they have been swayed very heavily by considerations of expediency in research. Psychologists interested in perceptual processes have usually worked with *conscious* perceptions because it is relatively simpler and more economical to handle introspective data than behavioral data of the kind they have to use with animal subjects or with human infants, who cannot give introspective reports. But it would be foolish to continue to define a type of psychological process merely on the basis of what is easy to observe. The whole point of laboratory research would be missed if we proceeded in such a way.

The purpose of experimentation is to get an understanding of all phenomena that obey the same laws and that consequently ought to be classified together. To get such understanding, experimenters naturally seek to work, first, with those examples of a class that will be best adapted to their task of discovering relationships; then they will need to check these hypotheses with other examples that may be less economical to work on, but that also seem to belong with the simpler examples that they used at first. To see the full meaning of their findings, however, experimenters need to avoid defining their phenomena merely in terms of the distinctive characteristics of the simple examples with which they originally work.

Therefore, what we can mean by *perceptual process* is any dynamically-organized process that shows most of such properties as are shown by the processes, say, that are stirred up by the drawings in Figure 2. If we want to indicate that such a perceptual process is a conscious one, we can add the adjective and speak of *conscious perceptual processes.* But otherwise we can use the bare term *perceptual process* to refer also to that great host of psychological processes, whether conscious or not, by which we continually represent our surrounding environment.

2. *Perceptual processes may have a strong motivational character.* We can readily understand the fact that laboratory workers in the field of perception have usually worked with perceptions of a neutral, nonmotivational sort. It is easier to get subjects for an experiment, for instance, on the discrimination of lengths of lines than on discriminations of differences in temperature between various hot objects. One would have to enlist a group of stoics if he wanted to do perceptual experiments on the perception of different patterns of electric shock.

But this practical consideration of expediency in experimental research does not mean that perceptual processes are all of this neutral, colorless sort that lends itself so readily to laboratory demands. For example, when a person perceives the taste of something, he does not perceive it in some neutral, nonmotivational way—and yet his process does not stop being a perceptual one just because it also has a motivational character. Or if a child perceives that he has slipped beneath the surface of his bathwater and that he has gotten soapy water into his eyes and mouth and nose, his experience is motivationally powerful and yet still a perceptual process as well.

Throughout, therefore, we need to realize that perceptual processes can be motivational processes at the same time they are perceptual processes, just as it is true that a person is living in Pennsylvania at the same time that he is living in Philadelphia. In particular, the processes that are involved in personality are simultaneously both perceptual and motivational processes.

3. *Perceptual processes may be* "conceptual processes" *or* "concepts." Generally, psychologists make a major distinction between perceptions and concepts, chiefly along the line that perceptions are processes having reference to objects or events that are, at the moment, stimulating the person, whereas using a concept, or conceiving, is a process that refers to things that may or may not be present. For example, according to this distinction you could have a concept about the relation of pyramids to the old Egyptian ideas of immortality even though you didn't happen to be standing in front of a pyramid; but if you stood looking at a pyramid and saw it as something built as a sepulchre for one of the Pharaohs, that process would be a perceptual process since it would be related to a present perceptual stimulus.

Actually, this distinction is impossible to apply in many matters. Take the phenomenon of one's orientation with reference to the points of the compass that we discussed previously. Is this a matter of perception or of concepts? Traditional usage in psychology would say that when a person was actually looking at something in Eugene and saw it in an incorrect way, he would be having a perceptual process because he was experiencing a present object in an organized way. But, we may notice two facts. First, the way he developed his faulty perceptual habit was by a bit of deductive, syllogistic thinking—"I'm traveling on a train that goes north, the main street of Eugene runs at right angles to the railroad; therefore it runs east and west and the butte that I see off past the end of this main street must lie to the west of the town." Hence, this "perceptual habit" developed in the same way that we think of many concepts as developing. Second, once a person has thus learned to perceive a presently-visible town in this way, it also is true that he cannot *think* about the town, even when he is thousands of miles away from it, except in the same fashion.

In this book, therefore, we shall use the term *perceptual process* as a very inclusive one that covers all of the means by which people experience or represent anything, whether present or absent. We can recognize that some perceptions are simpler than those we might refer to by the term *concept.* Thus, when you looked at the last of the drawings in Figure 2, you probably saw the five lines grouped into two pairs that were close together and a fifth line that stood by itself. Such a response-process is a dynamically organized process, as is indicated by various considerations, and shares a number of properties that are found also in more complex perceptions that we would speak of as concepts. But concepts also are perceptual processes, just as a highly industrialized state like Massachusetts is one of the United States even though it may also be described as an industrialized state and, grouping it in a somewhat different way, may also be recognized as more markedly a northern state than is New Jersey.

4. *Perceptual processes may be either transitory or long-sustained processes.* On this point, too, psychologists have been influenced too much by considerations of expediency in laboratory research. Since they found it easiest to work with motivationally-neutral perceptual processes, psychologists were working with perceptual processes that tended not to continue after the external stimulation ceased. But note what happens when we assume, as we have above, that perceptual processes sometimes are motivationally significant processes and sometimes are relatively complex conceptual processes. Suppose a physician informs a person that he has some particular symptom that the individual had barely noticed and then promptly forgotten, and adds, "Now, this may not be serious, but there seems to be a growth here and we ought to do a biopsy to see whether it is malignant. Probably it isn't. So, don't you worry about it. You go about your life as usual, and we'll find out." The physician might say this, changing the person's perception of the small lump that he had hardly noticed previously. But suppose that this warning comes to a person who has had no occasion beforehand to build up some stoicism on the matter, and who has seen what cancer could do to some other member of his family. Suppose the person does go back solely to his usual "stimuli." He avoids discussing the problem with anyone else; he avoids looking at the calendar, which now has acquired quite a different significance to him; he tries to busy himself merely in his usual responses. But he can't do it. When he walks or rides home, the after-effects of this discussion do not vanish merely because a few minutes or hours have passed. All of the objects and situations he meets now have a new effect on him because of the long-sustained responses or long-sustained representations he is carrying with him. It may turn out that his fears are groundless. But that doesn't matter. Hour after hour he lives in a different way because he carries within himself, somehow, an active representation of changed objective realities in his life.

This capacity of the organism to represent objects and events that are *not* present as stimuli has a very important role in life, and those very simple animals that lack this capacity are seriously handicapped by their deficiency. For, in contrast with the kaleidoscopic way in which stimulation changes from moment to moment, our environment has actually a much more steady, continuing character, and the individual needs to live in terms of this stable environment, rather than in terms merely of current stimulation. Suppose, for example, that a child looks down the street and sees first that a car is approaching, and then sees that the ball he has been playing with is rolling into the middle of the street. The life of the child may depend, in this case, on his continuing to perceive the approaching car even though now, with eyes on the ball, he is no longer looking at it. Behavior has to relate to the *environment* more than to the momentary *stimulations* from that environment. The processes involved in the totality of response to the environment are so similar that it would be foolish to adhere to the old definition that a person's perceptions are merely the processes touched off by objects actually stimulating him.

This phenomenon of long-sustained perceptual processes is illustrated by many different aspects of the case of Marty. You will remember the occasion when she and Bill were to go to the airport the next morning to meet her husband—how she continued to worry, even seemingly during her fitful sleep, about the question of how her husband would take the meeting—whether she ought to have sent him some photographs, whether she ought to have Bill use one of his prosthetic aids rather than another, and so on. This type of long-sustained response is a very important phenomenon in personality. In thinking of personality we cannot get along unless we free ourselves from the idea that psychological processes are merely transitory processes. Personality processes are most often enduring activities within us.

5. *Perceptual processes commonly are "reintegrative" in character.* That is, the way a person experiences any situation (consciously or unconsciously) is a consequence not merely of the stimulation that he is receiving currently from his environment, but must be understood also as a re-experiencing of psychological realities that had existed for him on previous occurrences of the same or similar situations. Almost every incident in the story of Marty and her family illustrates this point. When Marty looked out of the window and saw a soft rain falling, for instance, she re-experienced certain psychological realities. Nor did this situation give her the reintegrative effect that it might have produced in another person—in others the scene might have aroused feelings of sadness and lonesomeness. Instead, her psychological processes were definitely altered because of the happy and lively experiences previously experienced in connection with such a physical setting.

This matter of reintegrative influences is so important that we will need to take it up in detail in a later chapter, Chapter 13, devoted specially to it. In the meantime, however, it might be worthwhile for you to note the brief explanation that we have given here for this term "reintegrative," because it will recur at intervals before Chapter 13.

What is needed for a full conception of personality

At the end of this chapter, now, we may need to indicate the breadth of what has been suggested. For one thing, since we have talked so much in terms of perceptual *processes* and only occasionally in terms of perceptual *habits,* we may need to mention specifically that these two expressions do have a different reference. Most of the perceptual habits of a person are not in active use at any one moment—are not functioning as perceptual processes. Thus, you may have habits that make it possible for you to hear music as an expert musician does, or habits that permit you to grasp a great deal of detail in a football play; but these habits, in most of your life, are merely a reserve stock of equipment kept in readiness for situations where there will be an opportunity to use them. In its enduring, long-range aspect, personality is mostly a matter of such perceptual *habits*. We can learn about them only through studying their use, but these habits are such powerful determinants of perceptual processes that they are one of the main things to try to understand if we wish more understanding of human personalities.

This idea about the importance of past learning for perceptual processes does not fit very well with the ideas that some psychologists have favored regarding perception. In fact, many psychologists may be surprised, in view of the obvious sympathy of the present writers for much of the work of Gestalt psychology, that they put so much emphasis on the contribution of learning to perception. But, even within Gestalt psychology this point of view has been recognized. Thus, speaking of the perceptual organizations that develop in the small child, Kurt Koffka wrote:[4]

> . . . it should be emphasized that the configuration, which we have assumed to be the first phenomenon of mind, must be thought of as very simple indeed—merely as a quality emerging from a uniform ground. Accordingly, we must not think of these phenomena as being at all like the experiences we adults have; at the beginning, only the slightest degree of complexity and definiteness can be ascribed to them. . . .
>
> Out of these rudimentary phenomena of dawning intelligence, our richly furnished, multi-colored, and finely organized outlook upon the world must evolve. . . . The requirements which the adult's life brings to bear upon his behavior are so numerous that they can in no wise be satisfied by the primitive phenomenal configurations of infancy.

Furthermore, as we have made clear in the preceding section of this chapter, we understand the term *perception* in a broader sense in some other respects as well. When we say that personality is a matter of how the individual perceives his life situation, we want this idea of perceptual processes to include processes that are highly motivational, that sometimes are conceptual in character, that sometimes are unconscious, and that frequently are long-sustained processes. Consequently it is obvious that, if we are to understand personality in perceptual terms, we must

[4]Kurt Koffka, *Growth of the Mind*, 2d ed. (New York, Harcourt, Brace & Co., Inc., 1928), pp. 158-159, 161.

go beyond the kind of materials that psychologists have traditionally used for the study of perception. In this chapter, we stayed mostly with those traditional materials—with things that appear to be trivialities of experience. We hope we have demonstrated that even with these, there are some laws which are indispensable for understanding even the most complex and profound of human experience. But these traditional materials of perception do not provide, by any means, all of the understanding that we need. There is a risk, too, that our emphasis on perceptual processes as factors in personality will leave the impression that motivational factors are unimportant in personality. We have tried to guard against leaving any such impression. For, as we have said, we regard motives as one kind of perceptual process—and as a type of perceptual process of fundamental importance for personality. This concept needs to be developed further, and we will therefore turn to it in the next chapter.

Summary

This chapter has been a long one, but it is of central theoretical importance for the understanding of personality. To understand personality, we cannot think merely in terms of the outward behavior of the individual. The same outward response may come from many different sources, and what is necessary is to make such extensive observations of the person as will help us to learn what inner representational processes lie back of his overt behavior. It is only in these representational processes that we can find what the overt responses mean.

In our everyday thinking, we generally try to understand these representational processes in a rationalistic way. We assume that in any reasonably mature and capable person, the psychological processes ought to be able to make quick and efficient use of data regarding objective realities. This rationalistic view is, of course, partially correct. Under some circumstances we can and do respond in this way. But there are many other situations, particularly in the field of personality, where people cannot respond in the way that rationalistic theory holds. We need some more inclusive interpretation.

Within the fields both of psychotherapy and of laboratory psychology, many converging lines of thought lend support to the idea that personality may profitably be understood in terms of perceptual processes and perceptual habits. Even if we take some of the simplest of traditional experimental materials from perceptual research, such as the old ambiguous figures, we find a number of principles that possess fundamental importance for the entire field of personality as well. Thus, simple experiments in perception indicate that (1) stimulus situations usually have multiple potentialities, or are *vieldeutig*, instead of being capable of being seen in only one way; (2) in many important senses, the person lives only in terms of his perceptual response to such *vieldeutig* situations, rather than in terms of objective realities as such; (3) there are possibilities of drastic shifts of perceptual organization in response to such situations; (4) even though these reorganizations can often come easily and swiftly, sometimes they are achieved only with great difficulty, and sometimes only through long, gradual developments such as are seen in the development of capacity to hear complex music in a skillful way; (5) whatever organization is achieved first tends to resist transformation into some alternative organization, even though the latter might originally have been equally easy. Particularly in matters of direction-orientation, it is found that faulty perceptual organizations can persist for years and years despite frequent and clear evidence of their inaccuracy. These principles do not hold true merely for simple visual materials, however; they possess fundamental importance with reference to profoundly significant personality matters as well.

If we are to use a perceptual approach in personality, we need to abandon the traditional conception that psychologists have had about perceptual processes. This traditional conception has been dominated unduly by certain limitations arising from the nature of research material perception-psychologists have used. Thus, the usual meaning of the term *perception* needs to be extended by recognizing that (1) perceptions may be either conscious or unconscious processes; (2) perceptual processes may be powerful motivational processes; (3) perceptual processes sometimes have the character of what are traditionally termed *concepts*, and these may be of great complexity; (4) perceptual processes are often long-sustained responses rather than merely transitory; and (5) perceptual processes often are primarily determined by past learning and need to be understood in terms of the past formation and present use of perceptual habits—that is, as reintegrative phenomena.

Finally, we might add a concluding note that was not stressed in the chapter above, but that was abundantly illustrated in the stories of Marty and of the aviator Guillaumet. This is the point to emphasize: Even though perceptual processes, as motivational processes, may tend to press for immediate expression in corresponding behavior, it still remains true, too, that human life often has to involve tremendous processes of striving and effort on the part of the individual himself. It was only so that the downed flier, Guillaumet, fought his way out through the snows of the Andes. It was only so that Bill was able to find a new way to live after the accident that made such a change in his life; it was only so that the members of his family were able to handle their own problems.

When we say this, we are not implying that there is necessarily some uncaused, unlawful element that comes into personality. We are saying merely that one of the links by which the chain of cause-and-effect operates in human life is through a type of process that fits our notion of what is heroic. We can hardly bring such things into the laboratory, but so much the worse for the laboratory. When we suggest that personality processes are perceptual processes, we want in the same breath to emphasize the idea that personality processes may at times contain all of the richness and grandeur and heroism that men reveal in real life. Our conceptions of personality processes need to be broad enough to include these finer things. We all know that they are realities. We cannot hope that our present knowledge of motivation will carry us as far toward an understanding of this aspect of human life as we would like to go. However, this is part of the content that we will be trying to understand in the several chapters which follow.

CHAPTER 7

The Motivational Aspect of Personality

ONE OF THE MOST important principles coming from many different lines of research is the principle that personality processes are *organized* processes. In the previous chapter we considered one of the main respects in which this is true. The influence we dealt with there is one that we rather generally fail to appreciate in our everyday attempts to deal with personality. When we find a person with some outlook on life that we recognize as unjustified, we expect him to change this outlook if we put before him enough specific facts that call for some desirable change. We expect the person to be able to grasp one of these facts after another, and we expect that when he has grasped enough of such separate facts, these should produce the necessary change in his over-all view.

We do not realize to what a degree it is true that until a person has succeeded in changing some very general aspects of his reaction to the problem in question, he will find it almost impossible to grasp, in their true significance, the separate details that are inconsistent with his over-all response. He is like a person who sees only the young woman in the fourth drawing in Figure 1 on page 147. He may be told that what he sees as the chin could be seen as the nose, instead; that what he sees as the ear can be seen as an eye; and so on. The person who is trying to help him arrive at the other perceptual organization of this figure may feel that if he can point out enough of such details, the person then should be able to reorganize his perception. But the difficulty is that the person cannot see each of these details, perhaps, except in the manner consistent with his over-all organization. So it is hard for him to take advantage of what is said to him. He cannot treat like isolated details the things which are parts of some larger organization he has developed. There is really a very fundamental importance in this fact that personality processes, therefore, are like the perceptions of some relatively simple visual designs.

The present chapter will be concerned with a second respect in which personality processes are organized. This second type of organization in part overlaps the type of organization we already have considered. But it involves some additional problems because it is organization exerted by an influence that certain major perceptual responses (ones that represent the goals that must be served by the person) have over the rest of the psychological activity of the person. It is a sort of organization, in other words, that comes from the motivation of the person.

This second sort of organization is one which we also have found difficulty in using in everyday life. It calls for some changes in our ideas about cause and effect along some rather fundamental lines. More than we realize, the general ideas that prevail in our everyday tradition about matters of cause and effect have been drawn from familiarity with what we might call *one-phase machines*. Most of our devices are still of this sort. The effect in them depends upon a direct causal factor. If you hit a typewriter key harder, it makes a darker letter. If you step harder on the brake pedal of your car, the brake operates more powerfully (and even with power brakes the same thing still is true). All such machines are under the constant control of the human operator, and his decisions at every turn must control the main changes in their operations.

In part, our own bodies and our psychological processes work in this same way. When you speak to a person and he can hardly hear you, you speak louder and then he hears. A light slap can hardly be felt, but a stronger and stronger slap becomes more and more painful. A listless attempt to lift something may not budge it, but with greater effort up it comes. In such matters we are like one-phase machines.

Most of mankind's ideas about cause and effect have come from such things. They have given us our basic concept of causation. And it is a good concept, too, where it applies.

However, as the inertia of man's preoccupation with one-phase machines has been broken, another type of machine has become more and more common to the point that it is transforming our modern world. This is what we might call a *two-phase* or *self-regulating machine*. It is built with some controlling or regulating mechanisms that govern the operation of the rest of the machine and make possible some fairly steady output even under rather remarkably diverse conditions.

Imagine the bewilderment of a person who had no idea about thermostats but who was trying to study the heating of a house where the furnace was governed by such a device. "I can't understand this," he would say. "The furnace seems to change the way that it works in just such a fashion as to keep the house at almost the same temperature all the way along. But sometimes this means that the furnace works almost continuously, and sometimes it means that it does not operate at all for long periods. And yet, no one is changing the drafts or turning on the motor to carry fuel into the furnace. I don't see how this can be."

The oldest of such regulated devices are perhaps clocks and watches; in them the speed is governed by an escapement mechanism rather than by the tightness with which the spring is wound. Another relatively early example is the old-fashioned steam-driven hoisting engine, with its governor that depended on metal balls which flew out by centifugal force and changed the opening of a valve if the engine started to operate too rapidly. But it is only within the last half-century or so that mankind has glimpsed the boundless possibilities that lie in this sort of causal system. In a great part of our everyday thinking, we have not yet had time to incorporate the new concept of possible causal relations that these two-phase machines illustrate.

Nowadays such devices have become fairly common. Radar-controlled bombs have been developed which can alter course and accurately pursue a battleship, even if the ship twists and turns to avoid bombardment. Volume-control devices on radios operate so as to keep the output of sound at some constant level even though the strength of the waves arriving at the antenna is variable. Automation in industry is made possible by control devices that keep the processes flowing at an even rate, producing a constant output in spite of variations in the raw materials or other operating conditions. The modern world, in short, is being profoundly changed by the development of machines in which the mode of operation is no longer like that of a typewriter but is like that of a thermostatically-controlled furnace.

Now, obviously, with such machines, we are still talking about cause-and-effect systems. No spirits have been introduced anywhere—no animism and no magic. Yet here is a type of device that calls for a new sort of understanding—that requires us to understand such devices somewhat in terms of cause and effect in self-regulating systems.

Partly because our generalized ideas about causation come so much from our experience with machines, and partly because the accelerated use of self-regulating systems is very recent, it has taken mankind a long time to realize that the bodily processes of organisms are very often of this same self-regulated sort. And yet, in some respects at least, this is obvious. Though the air about us ranges in temperature from below zero to 120° F., our internal body temperature keeps near 98.6° except under rare circumstances. The rate at which we breathe and our rate of heartbeat likewise vary with the requirements of the organism. Somehow or other there are some "thermostats," or regulating mechanisms, that control all of these processes. In effect, the assimilation of this concept of regulating systems has been transforming the study of physiology. Physiologists are developing an astonishing picture of the vast array of means by which physical processes are controlled by various mechanisms that keep conditions within some narrow range of variations. We walk a narrow path, it seems. There must not be too much calcium in the blood, for instance, or too little, however the calcium content of our food may vary. If the variations are too great in one direction, convulsions result; if the variations are too great in the other direction, a state of coma results—the same with variations of blood sugar, of phosphorus, of thyroid secretion, and of a long series of other aspects of body chemistry. It does not matter that mankind has invented self-regulating machines only in the last few centuries; in the processes of the body, even the most recent "inventions" go back millions of years, and the more basic inventions go back hundreds of millions of years. If we try to understand physiological problems, we cannot possibly get along, today, without including the distinction between regulating and regulated mechanisms and without using the idea that there is a sort of *goal-directedness* in the operation of many phases of our life.

These are important background concepts for our discussion of motivation. Let us move on, now, and see how they apply.

How goal-directedness is seen in psychological processes

One of the two respects in which regulating processes are seen in our psychological functioning is so omnipresent that we take it for granted, never realizing what a marvel it is. This is the way that our muscular responses are governed not only by our perceptions of what we are trying to accomplish, but also by our perceptions of what we *are* accomplishing. Thus, when you see a pencil on your desk and reach for it, your reaction of reaching is not a consequence merely of your original perception of the pencil and of your body in relation to it; instead, there is a continuing perceptual guidance of your reaching movement, with minor corrections of this movement if the perceptual process indicates that this is necessary. When you are driving a car, playing a musical instrument, or speaking, there is a perpetual feedback that helps to adapt your muscular response to the requirements of the situation. Consequently, the technical concepts of psychology in general are coming to be phrased more and more in terms of these previously unappreciated contributions of perceptual guidance of responses.

In the field of personality, we are not concerned about those details. But the concept of regulating processes is, nevertheless, of revolutionary importance for the understanding of personality. This is because the regulation of psychological processes also is accomplished—and in some exceedingly fundamental ways—by the *motivation* of the individual.

Psychologists now are wrestling with these problems in an effort to get an adequate interpretation of human life. They have inherited many concepts that tend to picture motivation only in terms of relatively tangible factors because psychology, just as other fields of thought, has tended at first to overemphasize what could be perceived easily and relatively directly.

In this book we would have little reason to be concerned about these matters of psychological theory if they were merely specialized, technical matters. But they are not. In our everyday life we need to use a new mode of thought that will take advantage of our new knowledge of human life as something given stability and direction by inner self-regulation. This newer mode of thought is more complex than older ones, but it is the only mode of thought that seems to do justice to the actual nature of man.

An analysis, first, of the operation of a motive clearly accepted as a motive

Let us begin by taking an example of the influence of hunger, which all psychologists accept as a clear-cut instance of motivation. In the following paragraphs from his book, *The Heart of the Antarctic*, Sir Ernest Shackleton[1] is speaking of the final part of a trip that he and three other men made in 1908-09 in an effort to reach the South Pole. On this trip, they traveled over 1700 miles from their base camp. At first they had the aid of four Siberian ponies; later, after the ponies gave out, they had to haul their sleds by hand. The terrain was often very rough, and the weather intensely cold.

> We would make the biscuits last as long as possible. . . . If one of us dropped a crumb, the others would point it out, and the owner would wet his finger in his mouth and pick up the morsel. Not the smallest fragment was allowed to escape.
>
> We used to "turn backs" in order to ensure equitable division of the food. The cook would pour the hoosh into the pannikins and arrange the biscuits in four heaps. Perhaps someone would suggest that one pannikin had rather less in it than another, and if this view was endorsed by the others there would be

[1]Sir Ernest Shackleton, *The Heart of the Antarctic*, Philadelphia, (J. B. Lippincott Co., 1909), Vol. 2, pp. 2-9.

a readjustment. Then when we were all satisfied that the food had been divided as fairly as possible, one man would turn his back, and another, pointing at one pannikin or group of biscuits, would say, "Whose?" The man who had his back turned, and therefore could not see the food, would give a name, and so the distribution would proceed, each of us always feeling sure that the smallest share had fallen to his lot. . . .

During the last weeks of the journey outwards, and the long march back, . . . we really thought of little but food. The glory of the great mountains that towered high on either side, the majesty of the enormous glacier up which we travelled so painfully, did not appeal to our emotions to any great extent. . . . We could not joke about food, in the way that is possible for the man who is hungry in the ordinary sense. We thought about it most of the time, and on the way back we used to talk about it, but always in the most serious manner possible. . . .

On the outward march we . . . had to keep some distance apart in case one man fell into a crevasse, . . . and the blizzard . . . from the south made unnecessary conversation out of question. . . . It was on the march back that we talked freely of food. . . . The wind was behind us, . . . and . . . we were able to keep close together. We . . . could take turns in describing the things we would eat in the good days to come. . . .

It is with strange feelings that I look back over our notes, and see the wonderful meals that we were going to have. . . .

On a typical day we would be beginning to march with some degree of comfort, and one of us would remark, "Well, boys, what are we going to have for breakfast today?" We had just finished our breakfast as a matter of fact, but the question would receive our most serious and careful consideration at once, and we would proceed to weave from our hungry imaginations a tale of a day spent in eating. . . .

We did not smile at ourselves or at each other as we planned wonderful feats of over-eating. We were perfectly serious about the matter, and we noted down in the back pages of our diaries details of the meals we had decided to have as soon as we got back. . . . All the morning we would allow our imaginations to run riot in this fashion. Then would come one o'clock. . . . We would drop the harness from our tired bodies. . . . An hour later we would be on the march again, once more thinking and talking of food, and this would go until the camp in the evening. We would have another scanty meal, and turn into the sleeping-bags, to dream wildly of food that somehow we could never manage to eat.

The experiences of these men show some concrete ways in which hunger operates as a regulating mechanism in our lives. We need to rephrase these effects in more abstract language, though, so that we can use this example to help us see whether other processes exert essentially similar influences. We note the following effects:

1. Hunger modifies perceptual processes, particularly in the direction of

making relevant things stand out focally. Thus, as was said, the men's attention would pounce on tiny crumbs of biscuit that got dropped. There has been a great deal of research work in psychology in recent years exploring the hypothesis that motivation tends to distort our perceptions, making important things look bigger to us. This is a minor influence, if a real one at all. Hunger did not make the crumbs look bigger to Shackleton's men; it merely made the crumbs stand out vividly.

2. Hunger tends to determine the content not merely of direct sensory processes, but also of the thought processes or associations. Even between meals, when no food was present in the sense of stimuli, it was still a case of "Well, boys, what will we have when we get back to civilization and can have anything we want?" Even in their sleep, they dreamed about food.

3. Hunger tends to make men learn new ways of trying to satisfy their motives. All their ritual of dividing up equal portions of food, for example, was a new tactic that they learned because they were so strongly motivated, as were all the magnificent culinary inventions they jotted down on back pages of their diaries.

4. After men have learned new ways of trying to satisfy hunger, the hunger motive tends to guarantee that they will *use* these new habits.

5. Hunger tends to determine the choice of positive goals. Shackleton's group was traveling through a country of magnificent beauty. They were men who, under other circumstances, would have gotten great aesthetic enjoyment from the landscape. But even though they knew that all of their talk about food could not increase by one crumb the amount of food available among all these snow-swept valleys, they focused their attention on everything connected with food rather than on enjoyment of the scenery.

6. Hunger makes men willing to endure hardship and undergo penalties. It was not easy for Shackleton's men to haul the sleds that carried their food. They were so near exhaustion that, sometimes, when they tried to lift their arms to set up their tents, their hands would start to become frostbitten because the circulation in their arms became less with raising them. But none of them would have dreamed of leaving their food behind so that they could lighten their loads. They might have been glad to have a chance to haul ten times as much!

In short, we see that hunger serves as an energizing and directing influence in our lives. It arouses, sustains, and directs activity—not just any activity, but activity directed toward the goal of serving that particular motive. Or, somewhat more specifically, we may say that hunger (1) modifies perception, (2) influences thinking, (3) leads to learning new ways of motive-satisfaction, (4) leads to the use of new habits, (5) affects goal-choices, (6) and compels work and the acceptance of penalties to satisfy the motive. These six influences of hunger illustrate our chief means of knowing whether or not a person or an animal is motivated. We do not need to depend on the person's introspective report that he is intensely motivated (though this is often an important and reliable guide). We can watch the individual's activity and, from his behavior, determine whether or not he is motivated.

How the same criteria apply to emotional processes

It has been relatively easy for us to see, both in technical psychological discussions and in everyday life, that hunger operates in a manner fairly analogous to the way a thermostat operates in controlling a furnace. For even though extra food is on the table, a person tends not to eat after his hunger is satisfied. And, on the other hand, it does not take the sight or smell of food to stir him into food-seeking behavior. He may not be able to get food through his goal-seeking activity, just as was the case with Shackleton's men, but his behavior is concerned with a goal of eating, nevertheless. And this behavior is obviously related to some definite physiological processes and mechanisms within the body. We do not have much difficulty in getting the idea that hunger, thirst, and similar physiologically-based motives are directing, organizing, steering processes.

But it has been more difficult to see that perhaps we need to think of emotional processes as motives. A few psychologists have even proposed that emotional responses are just the opposite of motives—that, whereas motives are organizing in their influence, emotional processes are intrinsically disorganizing.

Let us examine emotions, however, in the light of the six influences that we enumerated above. If, indeed, we grant that these influences identify a process as a motive, and if their operation in the case of emotional processes is also evident, then it would follow that emotional processes must be included within the larger class of motives. They might be motives somewhat different in character from physiologically-based motives like hunger, but still belong within the large, important category.

Before proceeding farther we need to have a concrete instance of emotion before us, like the following account of the behavior of one family during a fire-bug scare in their community:

> When we returned from a trip, we heard much neighborhood talk about a fire bug. There had been such a scare several years ago when arsonists burned up over $500,000 worth of barns in the surrounding countryside.
>
> Sunday evening I was putting the children to bed. They too had heard all the neighborhood talk of the fire bug's weekly burnings, as well as our own family conversation over the newspaper accounts. Just then the fire siren sounded.

"Would he burn our house, Daddy?" asked one child fearfully, as the shrieking siren died away in the distance.

I reassured the children that it was unlikely, since only uninhabited buildings, barns, and cars had so far been burned.

"Did he burn the building across the street, Daddy?" asked another, referring to a recent dramatic fire of unknown origin that the children had seen the previous Sunday.

"No one knows," I replied, "but there weren't any people in that building, so we're sure he wouldn't burn houses with people in them."

My wife and I talked about the children's fears. We were uneasy too. We talked about the need for an escape ladder from the second floor and about the pattern of recent fires, drawing comparisons with the arsonist burnings of the previous year.

To reduce our fear, we bought several fire whistles that would go off automatically when heated, and distributed these around the house. A neighbor bought a ladder partly as a fire-protection measure and showed us where he stored it in the garage if we needed to reach the second floor, so we gave up the idea of a rope ladder. We also arranged with our neighbor to leave an upstairs door into the adjoining apartment unlocked as a fire exit, and told the children about this.

I remember my thoughts as I locked up the house one night: "He hasn't burned inhabited houses, but fire setting is a crazy impulse, what is to stop him from burning homes? Our basement door is unlocked at night. How easy it would be to come in and set a fire! It would be an inferno before we even awoke, two floors above." Images of leaping flames surrounding the children flashed through my mind. I could see us struggling to reach them, cut off in the end room as they were!

I decided to lock the cellar door and did so every night until the fire bug was finally caught.

Here are "emotional" responses. Do they show the properties our analysis of hunger in the Shackleton case revealed?

1. Fear affected the perceptual processes of the parents in making relevant things stand out in a focal way (they saw the firetrap nature of the children's room; the father saw the unlocked basement door in a different light).

2. Their thought processes were strongly influenced by the fear (the family and the whole town talked about the fires).

3. The parents learned new routes of expression for the motives now active (they pored over catalogues and discovered that they could buy fire sirens that heat would trigger and so warn of a fire in the basement or attic).

4. They used the new habits (by actually buying and installing the sirens).

5. They used old habits in service of the motive (as by locking doors and leaving exit passageways unlocked).

6. The fear led them to choose between goals (they spent much time in the evenings discussing this problem rather than on more pleasant things, and they gave up buying some needed household things to get the warning sirens; a neighbor spent over fifty dollars for a ladder; the father took pains to go down every night to lock the basement door).

What differences can be found between the hunger motive and the emotion of fear? Apparently both hunger and fear operate to arouse, sustain, and direct activities in these six important ways that are the mark of motivation!

Or, for that matter, it seems that emotional processes sometimes exert these influences so strongly that they countermand the influences of physiologically-based motives. Look again at the behavior of Shackleton's men. Suppose we ask whether their behavior was more powerfully directed by the motive of hunger than by any other process.

When we raise this question, immediately we can see that some other motive must have been involved. These men were "intensely, fiercely hungry." But what they did through the first half of their trip was steadily to work their way into a barren region where they knew they could find no food and where they were getting farther and farther away from the food stored at their base. And yet they kept moving on. Why?

We examine their behavior in the light of the six criteria analyzed above. All of these criteria indicate that they were motivated by more than just hunger. When they came to a fork in some valley they were traversing, they did not choose their route at random, or on the basis of the easiest travel or the most beautiful scenery. Each day, they were bent on putting the maximum distance between themselves and their well-stocked home base. They willingly endured the discomfort of intense hunger in the interests of another goal. Their behavior does not become understandable until we realize how desperately they wanted to reach the South Pole, with all the glory and other fruits of being the first men to do so. (They failed by only 97 miles!)

What were these other values or other goals? One could not say for sure without knowing the men individually. Perhaps in one case the main goal was professional prestige. In another case a highly personal curiosity or love of adventure, regardless of whether the trip later would ever be discussed with others. In another case perhaps a love of meeting and overcoming obstacles or of surpassing others. Perhaps an interest in geographical exploration from many other trips elsewhere in the world. We could decide between such alternatives only with extensive further observations of what choices these men made, what situations produced new learning in them, what choices they made of perceptual content, and so on.

In any case, we may be certain that the motivation would not have originated in tissue-states within their bodies; also that the motives that led them on toward the South Pole must have been stronger than their intense hunger, stronger than the need to terminate their exertions, stronger than any other motive springing from a bodily condition.

Or suppose we look at two other aspects of their behavior. We might ask, "Why didn't they eat more heartily? Actually, at each meal, they had more food with them than they prepared and consumed. If they were so hungry, why didn't they 'dig in'? Or, if they were so hungry, why didn't they try to steal food from one another?"

There apparently were regulating factors that controlled the men on both of these scores. Fear in the one case, perhaps; sense of honor or sense of comradeship, perhaps, in the other. From a behavioral point of view, we are compelled to recognize that apparently there were either some emotional processes in these men, or some representational processes, or some thought processes, that exerted effects characteristic of motives. Not only that, but when hunger pulled in one direction and these other processes pulled in another, these men acted more in accordance with these other processes than in accordance with their fierce hunger.

There is one difficulty. "What about the fact," you might say, "that the men talked and thought incessantly about food? It was only at intervals, at the most, that they thought about the fact that they were trying to reach the South Pole or that they needed to conserve their food. But they seem almost perpetually to have been conscious of their hunger."

Our answer to this question depends on how much we want to restrict the idea of motivation to the field of *conscious* mental activity. It is only in that sense that hunger was a more omnipresent motive than the desire to reach the South Pole. For if we deal with this matter *behaviorally*, rather than just in terms of conscious experience, we see that wherever food-seeking behavior competed with Pole-seeking behavior, Pole-seeking behavior won. Only at the last heartbreaking spot, where they estimated they were only about a hundred miles from the Pole, but where they had to admit that their resources of strength and food were so depleted that they could not extend their journey except at the certain cost of their lives, did they subordinate the Pole-seeking to anything else. Indeed, in most of their journey, even though they were not consciously thinking "We must struggle toward the Pole," there must have been some long-sustained processes within them that made them take one weary step after another in a direction dictated by this goal. And when the exigencies of the situation demanded especially careful choice of routes, they would then momentarily turn their attention consciously to topographical matters rather than to the allurements of food.

Emotions, therefore, are motives, though different in some respects from physiologically-based motives

The conclusion of this first step in our analysis, therefore, is that emotions or emotional processes *are* motives. There are other things that can be said about emotions, too, as some psychologists have pointed out, such as that they can add color and vividness to life. But the main point to be understood about emotional processes is that they arouse, sustain, and direct activity in basically the same ways that hunger and thirst do.

To say this does not say that all motives are emotions, any more than we could say that because all typewriters are machines, therefore all machines are typewriters. Instead, emotions are merely one subclass of the larger category. The other main subclass, contrasted with emotions, is composed of physiologically-based motives. Some of these are cyclical, such as hunger, thirst, and fatigue, which depend on a gradual development of conditions that finally produce such motives in a strong form. Some other physiologically-based motives rest on specific stimulation that need not be cyclical at all, as in cases of pain aroused by a burn, an electric shock, or a toothache. In the case of all physiologically-based motives, however, the motive exists only as long as some rather definite physiological condition continues to affect the central nervous system. Thus a toothache persists so long as certain sensory stimuli arouse nerve impulses that proceed from the tooth to the brain. When the dentist injects novocaine into the nerve and thus blocks the passage of nervous impulses, the toothache-motive stops.

Emotional processes, on the other hand, are matters of relatively long-sustained representational processes. They are matters of the individual's perception of his situation. And, as we said in an earlier chapter (p. 192), perceptual processes can continue without steady support from external stimuli. Thus, suppose a person who is very fearful of dentists has finally been driven to the dentist's office by a bad toothache. Suppose that the dentist has anesthetized the nerve and yet the person is still pale and trembling. The dentist might say to him, "Now, look—the toothache is gone, isn't it?" "Yes." "Well, why not relax? If you don't like the sight of my instruments or me, close your eyes and shut us out. I'll turn on the radio and all you will hear will be music. At least while I'm studying these x-rays, you ought to feel comfortable."

No dentist would try any such argument, of course, because he knows better. But if one did, the patient might well reply: "My toothache is gone, and I'll admit that I can shut out all the external stimuli that would make me feel afraid. But that doesn't matter. I can't kid myself. I *know* that I'm in your office and that you're going to start drilling pretty soon, and I hate it. You might as well turn your music off, unless you want it, and I might as well keep my eyes open and watch what you do." Emotions don't depend just on what stimuli are being received at the moment; they depend on what the person perceives as his real situation.

Emotional processes, in other words, are like processes of mental set for multiplying or adding—they are processes that can be aroused by rather slight cues, but that can guide other aspects of psychological activity in significant ways, and that can continue to operate over long periods of time even if the person does not continue consciously to hold the same mental set that was aroused in the first place.

The biological advantages of emotional motives

Ever since Charles Darwin published his book, *Expression of the Emotions in Man and Animals,* in 1872, psychologists have granted that emotional responses have certain limited biological advantages. Many animals respond in ways that make them look more dangerous when they are attacked, just as house-cats snarl and make their hair stand on end and so look bigger and stronger. The internal physiological effects of anger, rage, and fear frequently have biological value. A man or animal running away from an enemy can run faster and longer because certain of his emotional processes accelerate his heart beat, drive the blood supply from his digestive organs to the large muscles of the body, and release extra blood sugar, which is a source of energy, from the liver. Physiologists and psychologists have long recognized the advantages in these so-called emergency responses.

This is an instance, however, of the point that we were making near the start of the chapter—that people develop an understanding of relatively tangible matters long before they come to understand other more subtle relationships. Thus, in the present instance, the physiological by-products that appear with such emotional processes are much less important in the whole economy of the organism than is the fact that emotional processes are motives—that they influence the other parts of the *psychological* functioning of the individual in ways that also are characteristic of physiologically-based motives.

Emotional motives have the following four special advantages as compared with physiologically-based motives:

1. *There are advantages in the fact that the emotional motives do not possess the strongly cyclical characteristic so typical of many, though not all, physiologically-based motives.* This cyclical character is appropriate for many physiologically-based motives. Thus, after hunger has been satisfied, it is appropriate that the organism should pass through a period of quiescence before becoming hungry again. In the case of the sex motive, a period of quiescence permits replenishment of the glandular products involved in a renewal of sex activity.

But in matters related to emotional activity, there is typically no such advantage in this cyclical phenomenon. Thus, if a hen has frightened away one cat that threatened her chicks, this does not mean that she can safely abandon, even for a short period, her readiness to respond in the same way to any other prowling cat. The hen is dealing with needs created by *environmental* factors rather than by any developments within her own body. Consequently, a kind of motivation that may operate continuously for long periods is needed, one that also may remain latent during other long periods merely because, under other environmental conditions, this motivation is not needed.

2. *Emotional motives can be touched off by much more delicate stimuli, and by much more precisely differentiated stimuli, than are required for the arousal of physiologically-based motives.* This is obviously true with regard to situations that are emotionally significant because of past learning. In these cases, it is easy to see that emotional processes can be excited by stimuli as slight as anything that the organism can differentiate perceptually, as in cases where deer have learned to respond with fear to the scent of cougars. But this principle is also seen in cases of unlearned emotional responses. If animals did not have such unlearned emotional responses, they would have to start their learning from some experience in which they actually received physical injuries from an enemy. But with unlearned emotional responses, much slighter cues can operate. Thus, Tinbergen has shown that young goslings will hide when they see a cardboard model with the silhouette of a hawk soaring overhead, but are not disturbed when something with the silhouette of a goose soars above them. Anyone who has observed quail knows that the warning cry of the mother bird causes her young to scatter and "freeze" and remain so quiet that, with their protective coloration, it is almost impossible to find them in the dried leaves and grass, even right at your feet.

3. *Emotional motives constitute the sort of motives that are developed by learning, and they are the ones, consequently, that can be elaborated for the particular circumstances of the given individual's life.* It is important, particularly in the case of the more complex organisms, and outstandingly in the case of man, that motivation should be highly variable from one individual to another. Thus, in a highly specialized civilization, there would be a lot of discontent if it were not possible for different persons to take delight in quite different sorts of vocational activity. It is because of this that the surgeon, the coal miner, and the political leader may each love his own work, despite the enormous differences of activity. Because of their susceptibility to learned modification, emotional motives also get shaped to suit slightly different situations, so that a beekeeper, for instance, can work comfortably with bees under conditions where it is sensible for him to open up the hive, though he stays adequately motivated *not* to disturb the bees at other times when they would really "give him the works."

4. *Emotional motives have the advantages of operating as positive feedback mechanisms.* Perhaps you have encountered the phenomenon of *positive feedback* that is heard when the loud-speaker of a public-address system is too close to the microphone. The person speaks into the microphone, and the loudspeaker amplifies his voice; the increased sound comes back to the microphone, and is intensified still further. Once such a vicious spiral is started, the howl can get worse and worse, right to the upper limit of sound-production by the system.

The occurrence of such a phenomenon is a nuisance in most physical systems. Therefore, when engineers build complex systems that are intended to operate in self-regulating ways, they build them with a *negative feedback* or *reverse feedback,* instead. Thus, as we mentioned earlier

All right, suppose a saber-tooth tiger is coming. Why should I run? I don't feel any pain yet!

Well, stay if you wish, but you'll never have any chance to become an ancestor.

in the chapter, when the load on a steam engine gets lighter, and the engine starts to work more rapidly than it should, a governor reduces the amount of steam going to the pistons instead of increasing it (as would be the case with a positive-feedback system).

In these physical devices, however, there is some supply of energy already present in more or less optimal amount. The only thing that needs to be done is to increase or decrease the utilization of this energy to suit the changing conditions. But an organism is not like that. The organism does not have its different motivational energies already mobilized and pressing for expression. There isn't one "head of steam" that corresponds to "aggressive energy" and another "head of steam" that corresponds to "sex energy." Within the organism, instead, although there are potentialities for arousing any number of emotional processes in very strong form, these potentialities remain latent most of the time. At most moments, the potentially-intense emotional processes are like smouldering fires that have been carefully banked.

It would be wasteful for an organism to function otherwise. Energies would be unnecessarily squandered to maintain a considerable number of different emotional processes at full strength when only one or two were appropriate to the immediate situation. But at the same time it is true that an organism needs to be able to mobilize quickly any one of these energies when it really is relevant. When a deer approaches a water hole, it may be fairly quiet and unfearful at the moment (though probably, as a wild animal, never entirely devoid of some active fear). But when a sound is heard that indicates possible danger, there is a quick focusing of the eyes and of the perceptual processes generally on the spot from which the sound came, rather than on the water ahead. By this focusing the deer sees a cougar or hunter that otherwise would not have been perceived. And this perception will arouse an even more intense emotional response than that stirred up by the original sound.

In such situations we have the essentials of a positive-feedback system. Emotional processes seem to do the very sort of thing that engineers try to avoid in their mechanical devices. Emotional processes are a means—through such successively clarified representational processes, and through the working of reintegrative mechanisms—of quickly developing a strong motive out of what was merely a latent potentiality a moment before.

In each of these four respects, then, we see that emotional processes are not luxuries or frills from the standpoint of the fundamental life-needs of the organism. They sometimes create problems, of course, just as it is true that a person's struggles to obtain the air he needs many cause him to drown, whereas had it not been for this motive, he could have reached the surface before his need for air became too desperate. However, we ought not to derive our general picture of emotional processes only from situations in which emotions work disadvantageously, any more than we should regard fire or winds or rainfall as basically harmful because of the damage they can do. We need to see that, on the contrary, emotional processes are efficient mechanisms for the energizing and regulating of activity with reference to long-range objectives. They are indispensable in complex organisms. Human beings have survived, in the long course of evolution, partly because they are such emotionally sensitive and responsive creatures.

Emotional motives as perceptual processes

In the preceding discussion, there is one difficulty that may have been cropping out repeatedly in your thinking. You may have been saying to yourself: "True enough, the examples of emotion cited in this chapter have been instances of guiding, directing, organizing processes. The family worried about the arsonist, for example, certainly showed some well-organized thought and action. But what was described about that family was primarily their *perceptions* and *thinking*, and not their *emotional* processes as such. So, I am not sure that this chapter has been talking about emotions; it has been talking about perceptual processes for the most part."

If you have been bothered in some such way, you have been sharing much the same view that has prevailed rather extensively among psychologists regarding emotional processes. The most common views have drawn quite a contrast between emotional responses, on the one hand, and perceptual and conceptual processes on the other. Thus, some psychologists have hardly conceived of emotional responses as psychological processes at all, but have described them as primarily reactions of the visceral organs (of organs in the main body cavity and of the circulatory system more generally). Many other psychologists have tended to view emotions in somewhat the same way we do in everyday thought when we think of emotions merely as feelings, or affect. Thus, this way of thinking about emotions finds expression in statements about conflicts between intellectual processes and emotional processes (such as, "I knew what I should have done, but my emotions got the better of me").

Our ordinary language encourages this kind of view. It includes a host of terms such as *fear*, *hatred*, and *delight* that refer to emotional processes as if they were merely generalized, diffuse processes. And we often use the names of emotions in this way. Thus, we say that it is fear that makes an elderly man pick his way carefully down an icy street, it is fear that makes a man run from a bull, it is fear that makes an inexperienced person afraid to speak before a group of people.

But before we decide to follow this everyday tradition, we ought to look more closely at such examples. We ought to check (either by introspective reports or by extensive behavioral observations) to see whether the "fear" that makes the elderly man move slowly down the street is the same "fear" that operates in the other cases. We find, of course, that it is not. The fear that operates in the elderly man is a specific, definitely-structured thing. It is a process that pictures his situation and its possibilities in quite particular terms. The fears that motivate the man being chased by a bull and the man who gets weak knees when he tries to speak to a group are different fears, and they too picture the situations of these men in precise ways. What follows from this, therefore, is that *emotional processes*, rather than being something outside of and distinct from perceptual processes, *are one type of perceptual process*. They are processes that represent realities, just as other sorts of perceptual processes do, but they are perceptual processes that are motivationally significant.

To clarify this interpretation of emotional processes, we might use this analogy: we may say that perceptual processes are like motion pictures. That is, they are processes that have some detail and fullness as representations of objective realities. Some of these motion pictures are merely in black and white. These might be compared to the perceptual processes that have no motivational character. But other motion pictures are in color. We might compare these latter movies to emotional processes. The fact that color (or motivational significance) is present in these perceptual processes does not mean that they are any less detailed, any less "perceptual" than those neutral perceptual processes usually employed in perceptual experiments. They do not have any less detail or less ideational content about them than the motivationally neutral perceptions; the difference is only that something has been added. (In the case of movies, of course, the pictures are either definitely black and white or definitely colored. A closer analogy with emotional processes would be suggested if we imagined that the movies virtually always have some color in them, but that the color varies from a virtually-absent shading in some perceptions to intense and vivid coloring at the other extreme.)

When we say all this, one objection has to be met. Both in clinical work and in everyday life, we see many examples of emotional responses where there is little that can be observed introspectively except some vague state of feeling. For example, people speak of having moods: "I don't know why I feel so gloomy—there isn't anything in particular that I'm gloomy about, but I just can't shake off the feeling." Or "I don't know why I'm feeling so happy today, but it's just that I seem on top of the world." Clinicians describe states of worry that they sometimes see in patients and speak about them as matters of "free-floating anxiety." The intimation in this phrase is that there is affect or feeling that is devoid of ideational content.

We have already met this same problem with regard to other processes, however. In Chapter 5, for instance, we saw that when subjects were asked to find a solution for Maier's problem of connecting nine dots by four straight, connected lines, these subjects did not realize that they had made any assumptions that limited their mode of attack on the problem. But Maier's research showed that people in problem-solving situations *do* have "directions" in their thinking that they are not conscious of. In these other areas, therefore, we know that we cannot take the introspective observation of the person as necessarily indicating the full nature of his psychological processes.

In the same way, when moods or "free-floating affects" are studied carefully enough, as in long therapeutic work, it becomes very clear that in the unconscious parts of the responses of these persons, there is actually a lot of specific perceptual detail. For instance, the so-called "free-floating anxiety" shows up with a given person only in certain sorts of situations, or it is related only to certain ways of acting on his part. Therefore, the full emotional process of the person or full perceptual process of the person is *not* one merely of affect, but has the larger character that perceptual processes have.

The problem of whether emotions are basically disorganizing

There is one further difficulty that we should mention, but that we will not consider in detail. A number of psychologists have interpreted emotional processes as being basically different from motivational processes because they have portrayed emotional processes as being basically disorganizing. They have cited examples like this: when a boxer gets angry he starts to box more wildly and lays himself open to attack; when a person is in love it is hard for him to think about his work; when a person is worried about a sick child at home it is almost useless for him to try to enjoy a concert that, at another time, would please him very much; and when a person is afraid that he will be criticized for mistakes there is little likelihood that he can work as creatively and effectively as he might if he were not apprehensive of criticism.

Admittedly there is disorganization in these cases. But this does not prove that emotions are basically different from physiologically-based motives. When Shackleton's men were so hungry, it was this very physiologically-based motive that made it impossible for them to attend to many of the things around them that otherwise they would have attended to. From a more generalized theoretical standpoint, we can see that any process of an organizing sort, by that very fact, has to be also disorganizing in its effect upon some other processes. When a nation is organized for war, it has to disorganize or interfere with many, many peacetime activities. When a group of people meet as a committee, they may begin by swapping a lot of interesting personal remarks; but when the chairman wants business to start and calls them to order, the organized activity has to interfere with the free talk that would have gone on longer.

Sometimes organized activities are ill-chosen. A gang of criminals does not become socially valuable merely because it is organized. Similarly, when a person becomes so afraid of forgetting in a piano recital that he cannot play well, this fear has unfortunate consequences. It would be better if the person were organized in a different way. But the trouble is merely that the person is organized in ways that he ought not to be; it is not that he is not organized.

All of this needs to be seen from another standpoint, however. The thinking that people have done about emotional processes has hit first on the emotions that are dramatic and easy to see—processes like those of intense fear, or anger, or profound feelings of guilt. But a knowledge of these emotions which could be appreciated easily is not necessarily the most important knowledge.

In other words, the most significant emotional motives are not those that usually make the headlines in newspapers or that furnish the content for sensational movies. Instead, they are the powerful, steady motives that keep a man happily at his work day after day and year after year. They are the motives that make it possible for a woman, year after year, to do the work that is involved in caring for a family and yet experience that work as a privilege rather than as a burden. They are the motives that underlie our friendships, our life as citizens, our enjoyment of the world as a fascinating and wonderful place. And these motives are not primarily the physiologically-based motives; the motives that support the main activities of human life are the less tangible and perceptible from among the emotional motives.

The development of emotional motives, therefore, results from the formation and growth of neural systems that the individual originally did not possess

The view of motivation sketched in this chapter suggests a conception of human motivation quite different from that entertained by many psychologists at the present time, including those who favor the Freudian or psychoanalytic interpretation of personality. A widely-held view is that motivation is a matter of a relatively limited number of biologically-given mechanisms, and that learning operates merely to link these with new situations, changing the channels through which they are expressed in the thought and behavior of the person. Thus, the Freudian idea is that even though a person may be engaged in some very complex artistic or scientific pursuit and be intensely motivated in what he is doing, this motivation is merely another expression of the same basic energizing mechanisms that underlie the thumb-sucking and other erotic and aggressive activities of infancy and childhood.

We can agree that the individual does have some simple motivational mechanisms to start with. We can agree that these are, in part, such motivational mechanisms as the Freudians have proposed, even though Freud saw only the more tangible of human motives and hence his theory is no more a complete account of innate motivation than are those endless series of movies which are written as if all of human motivation is summed up under the three items of sex, aggressiveness, and fear.

But as these motivational mechanisms come into play in different situations they do not continue to be the same motivational or perceptual mechanisms that they were at the start. They cannot remain the same. They are changed with use, just as the individual's capacity to hear musical sounds or speech sounds is changed as he listens to such sounds, to the point that later he cannot possibly hear musical sounds in the same fuzzy, undifferentiated way that he did originally.

This does not mean that every way in which motivational mechanisms develop is desirable. The individual may develop some hampering, embarrassing, handicapping emotional reactions, just as, physiologically, he might acquire an allergic reaction he did not have previously.

These unfortunate cases, however, should not give us our sole picture of the nature of motivational development. We need also to recognize that out of the equipment with which human beings are born, motivational habits of affection, altruism, intellectual curiosity, and aesthetic interest can grow, yielding motives that the small infant does not have at all, except in rudimentary forms. When we get the idea that emotional processes are perceptual processes, rather than merely matters of affect or vague feeling or visceral activity, we have the means of envisaging this basically different conception of human motivation. Psychological research has helped us get away from excessively-strong nativistic theories with respect to other sorts of psychological activity. A realization that emotions are perceptual processes can help us to bring to bear on our interpretation of emotions all the ideas about reintegrative processes and about perceptual learning that we have been able to develop in other instances of perception—the ones that were worked on first because they were easier to study.

These ideas about emotions involve some additional considerations, however. For while we are proposing that emotional habits are perceptual habits, and therefore need to be related to our general conceptions of learning, we need also to relate them to the regulating mechanisms that we discussed at the start of this chapter. It might be well to put the matter this way: what we need to see is that whenever an individual is learning anything (which almost means "whenever he is doing anything"), he will be learning two different sorts of habit. On the one hand, he will be learning the particular skills, or the arrays of information, that he and his teacher may have selected as valuable. But, in addition, he also will be learning some other perceptual habits that have a motivational quality to them, and these latter perceptual habits, later on, will be decisive factors in determining what other habits he will use and what ones he will want to avoid. In other words, in any particular learning situation the person is all the while building up regulating mechanisms or motivating mechanisms, and not merely acquiring the specific habits by which he can carry out what he is motivated to do.

Consider this description, for instance, of the kind of training a certain young boy was getting:

Some of us visited the winter quarters of the Ringling Brothers Circus in Sarasota, Florida, this afternoon. At a training tent we saw three boys about ten years old and one older boy in his late teens practicing bareback riding and somersaulting.

As we watched, it became clear that the trainer, a man in his fifties, was an ex-acrobat, and that both the teen-ager and youngest boy, Romulo, were his sons. Fifteen or twenty visitors were watching.

Tony, one of the other trainees, took a turn. He was buckled into a safety belt and tried to leap up on the galloping horse. He managed it after several awkward attempts and stood shakily on the running horse's back.

Andy, a rather overweight boy, had to be pushed up on the horse after a dozen unsuccessful leaps. He stood on the horse's back for a few turns around the ring and fell off when he tried to dismount, swinging ignominiously in the air on the safety belt.

Romulo pranced about during this time, cartwheeling and somersaulting, yelling "My turn!" He was smaller than the others, stripped to the waist, wiry, sun-browned, and good-looking, with a shock of tumbling black hair. With obvious confidence he leaped up on the horse and rode cockily around the ring, doing a double somersault after he dismounted, to the cheers of the small audience. He sauntered over to the fence nearby with nonchalant pride.

The father's attitude toward Romulo was severe and demanding as compared to his treatment of the others. He criticized some small mistakes that he let pass when the others made them, but there was pride and care in his concern. Romulo was good, and it was obvious that the father had spent many long hours working with him.

In the somersault-training that followed, it was the same story. Even his grown brother could not outdo the saucy little Romulo, who insisted on doing three somersaults where he was supposed to do only one. Again there were cheers from bystanders and criticisms from the father, whose pride showed through his anger at Romulo's running unnecessary risks with his knees by landing stiff-legged after the third somersault—a feat actually beyond his ability to execute safely.

Now suppose, years later, we visit the circus and see Romulo when he is 20, and later at 30. From our point of view, outside the circus, we might wonder what Romulo can see in such a life. But a reintegrative conception suggests a much more understandable picture. At 20 or 30, Romulo will not be merely his present self, hearing the applause of the circus crowd. The applause is a reward, but it is pale stuff compared to his inner emotions, for he is in part again the 10-year-old daredevil surpassing his playmates, even his older brother, winning the proud criticism and attentive training of his father—he is this and hundreds of similar significant childhood experiences. These have left him with a tremendous emotional potential that becomes aroused automatically in circus work and that functions to make the life of the acrobat an emotional thrill beside which any inducement we might offer him to go into something "sensible" in life would be pale.

So with the mountaineer with his mule and shanty, the isolated rancher in the desert. So with hundreds of seemingly humdrum, sometimes dangerous and bizarre jobs that we find people drawn to. People are not held to their work by mechanical "habits" that come from mere frequency of past use. Habits they are, but *emotional habits,* habits with a tremendous motivational punch never suspected by the outsider.

Similarly, if we lacked an understanding of motives as reintegrative habits, it would be impossible to understand the lives of persons in cultures very different from our own. We saw in Chapter 4 some of the diversity of events that can come to have central emotional significance in the lives of persons reared under cultural conditions widely different from our own. The emotional meaning of a Kwakiutl potlatch or a Zuñi rain-dance rest on the reintegrative residues of innumerable previous childhood, adolescent, and adult experiences. To us, Tikopian *mokos* are merely curious-looking, kettle-drum-shaped pieces of metal, but to the Tikopians a display of mokos has strong emotional meanings of great wealth, power, and influence. The filed-down and blackened teeth of their young people arouse in us emotional meanings more akin to revulsion; to them a young girl is not beautiful without these whittled-down stumps of blackened teeth.

In our own culture, we have not given much thought yet to this matter of developing the motivational habits of children and adults. The difficulty in part is that we haven't even seen that there are any such possibilities, just as ancient man did not see that there was any possibility of deliberately increasing the prevalence of food-producing plants. Part of the difficulty is that, in our interpretation of motives, we see only what is relatively spectacular and dramatic, just as even the oldest of ancient tribes mastered the art of fire, but failed to master other more prosaic matters. Our thinking about motivation has been dominated too much by an emphasis on tangible physiological factors which, though a part of the whole picture, are not the main part. Because of all of these limitations, we have formed views of human nature that have failed to do justice to the possibilities of human life and have been blind to the magnitude of the task that is before us. Motives are not something that are "in us just naturally." There are biologically given beginnings for the motivational life of the mature and finely developed man or woman. But the motivational capacities of the adult are not biologically given in the small child any more than the trunk and branches and leaves and bark of the mature oak are present in the acorn. What is given biologically to start with has to be developed and inevitably gets developed in one way or another, and after such developments have occurred, the acorn no longer exists.

Even though there are some matters like this where knowledge has developed only recently, still, once a clear perception is achieved, this knowledge is clearly usable. Thus it does not matter whether mankind lived for perhaps 98 per cent of its history before learning to practice agriculture—still today we can see agriculture as an obvious means whereby we can make our earth a better place on which to live. It does not matter that out of a possible human history of about a half-million years, it took 99.99 per cent of that period before mankind could see that mosquitoes had anything to do with malaria—it still is possible for us, now, to use this knowledge whenever we need to use it to free our world from much human misery. And it does not matter that it has taken mankind a long, long time to see that complex systems do not all work like one-phase machines of a typewriter sort, but often must be understood in terms of the combination of regulated and regulating processes. In our own day, because this is such a relatively new idea, we are still struggling to assimilate it into our personal and social thinking. This is hard to do. It is hard to keep in mind that a human being is to be understood in terms of motives that work as quietly and inconspicuously, often, as the thermostat on a furnace. But, if this is the way a human being is made, there is no possibility of our getting a good understanding of this complex creature unless we do make our thinking correspond to these objective realities.

Summary

Just as it is true that a small child learns some things much more rapidly than others, so also is it true that in the course of human cultural development, man has reached an understanding of some aspects of the world at a much earlier point than he has reached an understanding of other matters. Factors like tangibility of cause and effect, closeness in time and place of cause and effect, and dramatic quality probably helped to account for the fact that man learned, perhaps 500,000 years ago, to use fire, and yet learned to practice agriculture only 10,000 years ago and learned only within the last 60 years or so that mosquitoes transmit malaria and yellow fever.

Among the concepts that have proved difficult for mankind to develop has been the idea that devices could be constructed so as to be self-regulating rather than to require constant supervision by a human operator. It has been difficult for scientists to recognize that physiological and psychological processes involve this feature of self-regulation that we have come to understand only so recently. Within recent decades, however, not only our industrial processes but also our physiological knowledge have been profoundly changed by the development of the concept that cause-and-effect systems do not have to follow the simple model of typewriters or cash registers, but can function like a furnace with a controlling thermostat.

When we turn to the psychology of personality, we discover that this concept of regulating mechanisms applies particularly to the phenomena of motivation. It has taken psychologists a long time to take up the study of motivation, and particularly to see that we need to think about motivation in terms of something more than merely the operation of physiologically-based motives such as hunger. A number of functional properties distinguish such physiologically-based motives. Such motives, for example, control the perceptions of present objects, influence the content and course of thought processes, induce new learning, govern the use of habits, and govern the selection of goals.

When the role of emotional processes is considered, we see that they exert these same influences (as in the fear-about-an-arsonist example). This suggests that emotions are one kind of motive. It has taken psychologists a long time to develop an appreciation of these effects of emotional processes; most of the attention that psychologists have paid to emotional processes has been directed to the relatively tangible physiological effects of emotion, to the physiological mechanisms of emotion, and to the conscious feeling tones that we know as emotional. It is also true that psychologists and psychoanalysts have tended to pay most attention to the more dramatic emotional processes, such as hostility and fear and those related to sex, to the neglect of the more quietly operating motives from which ordinary life activities spring. Ever since Darwin's discussion of emotion, psychologists have recognized that emotional processes sometimes have biological utility, but it has been hard for them to recognize the motivational character of emotional processes, which is, after all, their main significance.

Emotional processes have several main advantages as motives. They are relatively free of the cyclical characteristic of so many physiologically-based motives, and hence can correspond more closely to motivational demands of the organism's current situation. Emotional processes can be touched off by very slight stimuli and by stimuli that have been very precisely differentiated from other stimuli that mean something else. They are particularly subject to development by learning, so that they become more highly adapted to the individual circumstances of each person's life. Emotional processes operate as positive-feedback mechanisms that can pick up slight cues from the environmental situation and lead to more carefully focused responses that, in turn, will perhaps produce very powerful responses. They are an indispensable type of mechanism, therefore, in complex organisms.

We must not think about emotional processes in terms that make a great contrast between emotional processes, on the one hand, and perceptual processes (including conceptual processes), on the other. It will often happen that an individual does not consciously experience an emotional process in any full form, but can report merely that he has a vague mood, such as the "free-floating anxiety" that clinicians talk about. But the individual often knows well enough that what arouses him is not, for example, just "fear in general," but a fear that such and such parts of his environment will produce such and such effects. And even when emotional processes are known only very incompletely by introspective means, a careful study of the behavior of the individual still reveals that emotional processes have a quite specific and detailed character in these instances as well. We are driven, therefore, to conclude that all emotional processes are perceptual processes, even though not all perceptual processes are emotional processes, and even though emotional processes are not always *conscious* perceptual processes.

Emotional processes more or less inevitably produce some disorganization of those processes that are inconsistent with themselves; but this does not mean that emotional processes are basically disorganizing. Sometimes the organizing influence of emotional processes is undesirable, just as it is true that a gang of criminals may be all the more dangerous because it is organized effectively. But the basic influence of emotional processes, as with any motives, is an organizing influence, and disorganization occurs because any strong organization must be purchased at the cost of interfering with what is inconsistent with it. Emotional processes often show themselves able to control behavior even more powerfully than do the competing physiologically-based motives.

Psychologists also have been inclined to overstress the degree to which motivational mechanisms are innate. There are innate origins for emotional processes, of course. But learning modifies those innately-given mechanisms just as learning modifies other perceptual mechanisms, such as those involved in hearing sounds or discerning visual forms. The emotional life of the individual particularly depends, therefore, on the reintegrative mechanisms that he develops. These are the processes that provide the great bulk of the motivation of modern man. In view of this fact that motives depend so heavily on learning, and in view of the great differences of desirability of different motives, it is important for us to have some better idea of the range of main types of motives that may operate in different personalities. It is to this question that we turn in the next chapter.

CHAPTER 8

The Basic Motives in Personality

A CERTAIN PROFESSOR of the social sciences taught in a very small college in his first year of teaching. Part of his pay was board and room in the house of the president of the college. He soon noticed that at one meal after another, there was a conflict over how much the two small boys of the family should eat. The parents were concerned because they thought the boys did not eat enough. They felt it was particularly important that each boy should drink his glass of milk before he left the table. The young instructor won the parents' gratitude by making it a game to see whether he or the boys would drink their milk first in the course of each meal. The parents, much relieved at the success of this stratagem, told him that previously they often had to have the boys (particularly the older one, then about seven) remain at the table for an hour or more after the meal before they would drink their milk.

They were also concerned over several other things about the boys. The older one, especially, seemed too prone to daydreaming. Sometimes he would stop with a sock half on when he was dressing and would sit staring into space for fifteen minutes or more unless someone insisted that he get going again. Also they had noted that when this boy had been given a small puppy by some of the students, he had treated it so cruelly that the parents had had to give it away. "I can't understand it," the mother said, "because I've taken him to Sunday School ever since he was two or three years old, and he has been taught that he should be kind and gentle, and yet he does things like that. What's wrong?"

The behavior of these parents is a good example of what we mentioned at the start of the preceding chapter. As we said there, people generally come to recognize and emphasize the relatively tangible factors in a situation before they get around to sizing up the less perceptible or more subtle factors. And, as part of this one-sidedness, people have difficulty in recognizing and dealing intelligently with motivational processes.

A small boy is basically like a colt or a calf or a dog or any other animal when it comes to the question of whether he will eat enough or not. He has some built-in mechanisms of hunger that guarantee that he will eat as much as he should, and he needs no more urging than does any other animal. The parents did not recognize or trust this motive. They were trying to run this eating process themselves, rather than trust the built-in "thermostat" they should have trusted.

But their problem was more complex than this. You can make anyone dislike any food by waiting until his hunger is satisfied and then forcing him to eat that particular food. This is what the parents were doing with the milk. They had built up a new motive of distaste for milk which was not at all necessary. Furthermore, they were creating conditions that would inevitably produce feelings of humiliation and resentment in the meal situation, because, instead of making this a happy and pleasant occasion, they were scolding, fussing, and inflicting punishment. Imagine what your feelings would be if you were compelled to remain sitting at the dining table after everyone else had left, with an ultimatum hanging over you that you would have to stay there until you drank your milk. The parents were tending to establish reintegrative habits that would almost inevitably work against a hearty appetite and the enjoyment of food. It is a safe bet that the boy's treatment of the puppy was not unrelated to this; probably any person would want to have something on which to take out his pent-up resentments after such a long series of disagreeable and humiliating situations. Yet the parents were mystified about all this. They could see the relatively tangible factors of food-needs and food-intake, but they were not able to think in terms of the motives that were really the crucial factors in the poor eating of their children.

The materials reviewed in the previous chapter suggested that human beings are basically self-regulating mechanisms, rather than systems analogous to the old-fashioned sorts of machine that must constantly be regulated from the outside. Those materials suggested that from a psychological point of view, this regulation is particularly a product of motives within the individual. If we fail to take these motives into account, we are like persons who are trying to understand how a thermostatically-governed furnace operates, but who do not recognize that there is such a thing as a thermostat and who try to make predictions without taking its influence into account.

If this argument is sound, it must be very important for us to have the clearest possible understanding about what motives operate in human lives and what effects they produce. This is true particularly in the field of personality where different individuals operate from vastly different motives, though under the same immediate objective conditions, and where they tend to live, consequently, in quite different ways. Admittedly this is not an easy topic to explore, and the ideas we shall advance in this chapter should be considered somewhat tentative. But these are not excuses for failing to explore the problem.

The broad distinction between positive and negative motives

One of the important distinctions that gradually has been developing out of the observations and thinking that people have done about motivation is a distinction between positive and negative motives. It is becoming increasingly clear that, although both of these types of motivation have important qualities in common, still it makes a really profound difference in an individual's life which kind of motive he has developed most as the mainstays of his approach to life. Negative motives, we now see, are usually somewhat easier to use in trying to control a person's immediate behavior. But it is also becoming clear that an undue development of negative motives may be the chief factor making for personality maladjustments and for personal unhappiness, and that the development of positive motives is essential for a healthy personality.

Take as an example the two boys we have just been talking about. If their parents had let them decide for themselves how much they should eat, and had made the family meals a happy occasion for everybody, the boys would have had a healthy, positive motivation to eat. A growing boy naturally enjoys good food, right up to the point where he has taken aboard all he should. He will naturally drink all the milk he needs, partly because he likes it anyway, and partly because it helps to wash down other food without too much chewing (all of which, in turn, according to recent nutritional studies, is no disadvantage anyway, as dogs might have taught us since they don't chew their food any more than they have to). Instead of trusting such positive motives, however, the parents, by scolding and arousing fears of sickliness or of not growing up to be tall men, were trying to get food eaten by making noneating unpleasant. In the course of doing this, however, the parents were unknowingly forming additional negative motives. They were building up aversions to some of the most valuable types of food. They were creating resentments and hostilities that cropped out elsewhere in the lives of their boys.

Negative motives do have value as protective factors. In fact, they often play an indispensable role. Thus, when small children compete with one another to see how high a place they can jump from, the sharp pain they feel in the soles of their feet makes them properly cautious about trying jumps that are too high. When a child plays carelessly around the kitchen stove, the pain he gets from touching part of the stove serves as a negative motive to teach him caution, a certain amount of which he needs permanently. When a person neglects his visits to a dentist, a toothache may guarantee that he won't continue this neglect indefinitely.

However, even in these matters, it is to be noted that negative motives possess value merely because of what they coerce the person into avoiding. They do not, in themselves, add to the happiness and satisfaction of life. It is merely that they goad the individual into conduct that has value on other grounds. Activity based on negative motives is therefore like the activity of a man who spends time patrolling his farm so that the fruit won't be stolen by small boys or neighbors, or who spends time sprinkling his barn so it won't burn down or plowing a strip around his fields so that fires won't spread into his grain. All such things may be necessary at times. But they don't raise food for the farmer and if done to excess will cause his bankruptcy.

In many situations, however, people actually do not have to depend on negative motives. They rely on negative motives merely because often it takes less thought to use them or because a habit of relying on them is in keeping with their general personalities. A person can, indeed, be motivated (and quite strongly) by fear of failure, fear of reproof, sense of guilt, feelings of inferiority, fear of illness, and other negative motives. But when negative motives are used as the main basis of the person's life, they exert severely crippling effects on the personality. Even when they lead a person to get some work done that is socially valuable, they do so at heavy cost.

Remember the histories of Ann and Beatrice in Chapter 1. When Ann's uncle poked fun at the playsuit the little girl was so proud of, he thought it was a harmless bit of ribbing, one the child would get over in a few minutes. But, as Ann said, "The hurt has never been entirely erased." When she was afraid to climb the shaky ladder to the haymow, her step-father and uncle urged her on—"They kept laughing at me and my mother told me to go on." After all, one could say, a child will get over such fears, and ridiculing her a bit will help her to see her fear is groundless. But, said Ann as a grown young woman, "I often think of this incident today and hate those men for laughing at me."

To keep her from becoming "boy crazy," Ann was scolded until "I was afraid to speak to any boys." Earlier she had been told she would never marry. Probably as a reprimand for some small misdemeanor. Harmless? Ann's small brain was busy at work: "I . . . concluded that maybe I was different." Her healthy excitement after the thrilling game was reproved: "I gradually learned to try to keep my true feelings to myself."

What was the outcome? As a college-age girl, Ann said of herself:

> I've grown into a person who is afraid to do anything for fear of being laughed at or not doing it correctly. I am very self-conscious and find it hard to make friends of either sex. I constantly find myself distrusting people, thinking they don't like me. . . . It seems every year, as I grow older, that my mind comes to be more in a state of such confusion that I don't know which way to turn.

Beatrice was spanked at times, but the over-all treatment she received was of a very positive kind. When she threw sand into the little girl's eyes, her mother did not say a word to Beatrice, but rushed to help the hurt child and took the little girl away with her, leaving Beatrice alone. The mother's actions were saying, in a way that a small child could understand, "This little girl is precious, too, and should be allowed to live with a sense of dignity, rather than be treated unjustly." The father, too, did not scold or whip Beatrice, even though, with a child like Beatrice, this would have stopped such incidents. Instead, he listened to her side of the story and, treating her in an adult way, told her that God had created everyone equal. His words and attitude not only stopped the sand-throwing, but helped Beatrice to develop some positive feelings about herself and others: "I am a respected person whose story is listened to. I am someone whom Father cares a lot about, to talk to me this way. Father thinks I am a person who can learn grown-up ways of looking at things. He thinks I'm basically good, even though I did this bad thing."

What is the outcome? At Ann's age, Beatrice says: "I believe my personality is positively developed; I have high morals, ideals, I can get along with all people. All in all, I am a happy, contented person."

More systematic investigation confirms this impression of the unintended and unforeseen effects of using predominantly negative motives. Alfred Baldwin and his group at the Fels Research Institute observed a group of some 67 four-year-olds in free play and in their homes. Some of these children came from homes where severe discipline was the rule, others were from "democratic" homes which children were treated with respect, talked to a great deal, and given plenty of explanations about the reasons for family rules. Baldwin found that severe control over a child has much more widespread consequences than merely enforcing obedience. Severely controlled children did show less disobedience, aggression, and noncomformity in nursery school, but—and here's the rub —they were also less curious, less playful, less sociable, and less spontaneous in many ways.

Positive motives may have a great deal of strength. They possess the additional value that they contribute something of intrinsic value to life. For example, a person may play golf because he enjoys the game very much, rather than because he fears he may get sick from lack of exercise. When he plays with such enjoyment of the game, he is getting more than mere physical benefits from exercise and fresh air; he gets a greater general measure of happiness and emotional stability in his life as a consequence of the kind of motivation that produces his golf-playing. If a student has had some positive interest kindled in literature or science, this means something more than that he has been motivated to learn certain facts; it indicates that he has acquired the means for a sort of emotional response to literature or scientific work which will impart an intrinsic value to any reading or study he does in these fields.

It often takes planning and skill to decide how best to motivate people in positive ways, particularly when they do things we so dislike or fear that we tend to respond defensively. For example, it has proved very difficult for people to see that problems of delinquency and crime ought to be approached through creating more favorable community conditions in which young people would develop so many and such strong positive interests that it would become virtually impossible for them to turn to delinquency or crime. It has seemed much easier to attempt to control crime by depending on negative motives such as fear of imprisonment. This negative approach has proved terribly costly and terribly ineffective. Yet, it is hard for people to turn away from traditional negative-motivational approaches toward the required, more complex, farsighted development of a positive-motivational attack on this problem. In much the same way, the large nations are diverting staggering amounts of money and manpower into attempts to achieve national security by measures that, in proportion as they seem successful, are simultaneously arousing panic—and therefore accelerated efforts of the same kind—in the nations they fear. It is certainly true that no attempts of comparable strength, or anything approaching it, are being made to try to handle the problems of precarious international relationships by evoking and developing positive motives instead. It is taking mankind a long time, perhaps a fatally long time, to see that reliance on negative motivation in this field is miserably poor policy, but that another kind of motivational approach might succeed!

One fact that makes it difficult for us to appreciate the difference between these two types of motivation is that, in everyday situations, either one of them may be the basis for external behavior of much the same sort as the other. Thus, suppose a woman is extremely careful about all the physical details of taking care of her baby. Her outward behavior may not, in its grosser characteristics, indicate what her motives are. Suppose we speak to such a woman, meaning to compliment her because she is so careful with her baby. "Yes," she replies, "I don't dare to do anything else. What a sharp-tongued mother-in-law I have! My husband, too, for that matter—he is just his mother over again. Or, really, I don't suppose I could act any other way even if they didn't care. I feel so afraid of making mistakes with the baby. I know how much I resent some things that my own parents did with me, and I hate to think that maybe this baby will grow up and look at me in the same ways. It's a lot of unpleasant work taking care of a baby, all right. But you're just caught; that's all."

We speak to another woman, complimenting her on how careful she is with her baby and commenting on much work she is doing for it. We ask her if this isn't an unpleasant responsibility. "Oh," she answers, "sometimes there are things, of course, that I'd like to get out of. Like, sometimes, when I'm tired, I wish the baby's washing were simpler to do.

But there's not much that is like that. No, it's fun, after all, this taking care of a baby. I can't explain it very well. But it just warms you up inside. It's as though I had been hungry for something, and now I have it. You'd laugh at me, though—the things that I enjoy. But why shouldn't I? What is more wonderful than to see a good, wholesome human being developing and to know that you are helping to make it possible?"

In such a case, surely, the distinction between positive and negative motives is important.

The positive motives important in healthy personality

If our principle is correct, it follows that one of the outstandingly important tasks of a person's life is to foster the development of positive motives in himself and in other persons. To do this, he needs to have some ideas about what positive motives are possible in human life, and particularly about which are of greatest importance for healthy personality. In the following chapter, we will point out some positive motives that are rather shoddy in character and ought to be used less often in our culture. In the present chapter, however, we shall first examine seven positive motives which are possibly the really valuable ones to develop. We shall then look briefly at certain negative motives which can strongly influence personality.

We turn, first, to two positive emotional motives so greatly interrelated that perhaps they ought not to be listed separately. In some respects they seem to need separate discussion, and we will take them up separately on some scores. But in most respects they are interdependent, and we will discuss them together. These first two motives are:

1. *The motive of feeling accepted, respected, and loved by others.*
2. *The motive of self-respect, of pride in oneself, or of self-acceptance.*

One of the outstanding facts about human beings is that, generally speaking, they have to live in groups. Even biologically, they are hardly fitted for a solitary type of existence. The helplessness of an infant and the dependence of a small child demand that he occupy a secure place within at least a small social group. Every human being depends greatly on the step-by-step transmission to him of the cultural heritage of tools, techniques, and customs developed in previous generations. Even with the most primitive men this was the case.

There are probably two ways in which this necessary social character of human life produces certain socially-oriented motives or needs within human beings. Certainly to some extent it must be that the infant or small child learns by experience with other persons that he gets various important advantages when others are favorably inclined toward him, and, conversely, that he is in danger of punishments or frustrations or neglect when he arouses hostility or impatience. However, it also is quite possible that, in the long history of mankind, there has been a kind of biological selection which has helped to produce a type of creature so constituted, instinctively or innately, that the positive approval of other persons is enjoyed and their disapproval and rejection is a source of distress. Just as it is true that men have exerted a genetic selection among dogs so that modern strains of dogs are capable of a closer attachment to man than is possible with wolves or foxes or coyotes, it is quite possible that man is, to some extent, instinctively a social creature.

Whatever the relative weight of the different origins of this social orientation, it can hardly be questioned that one of the most important positive motives needed for a healthy, well-functioning personality is a feeling of acceptance and warmth from other persons.

This feeling of being accepted and loved by others is not to be understood as a matter of receiving praise or rewards from other persons, though such things might constitute clues by which the individual would sense the emotional attitude of others.

Often the treatment that the small child receives does not create the feeling of genuine acceptance that the parents feel it should, but tends to produce, instead, a different effect. The child comes to feel that he is (or that he might be) loved and cherished by others only on a conditional basis, as one might say. And he may develop the conviction that these necessary conditions for securing affection or acceptance are rather hard to meet. Thus, the child may experience a great deal of affection, but with the added perception that this is given him on condition that he remains well-behaved, clean, neat, mannerly, and obedient to the wishes of his parents and, later, of others who fill similar roles. Or the child may feel loved on condition that he continues to be unusually beautiful and attractive in appearance. He may feel that the affection he is given is dependent on whether he shows himself unusually bright and successful in competition with his age-mates. Partly as an illustration of this point, and partly because it throws some light on psychoanalytic theory, it may be worthwhile to note that Freud's childhood apparently brought him this sort of provisional love. According to Ernest Jones's biography,[1] Sigmund Freud said, referring to himself: "A man who has been the indisputable favorite of his mother keeps for life the feeling of a conqueror, that confidence of success that often induces real success." But even the way in which Freud puts this gives some indication of the particular nature of his feeling of acceptance by others. He does not speak merely of the warmth and security of affection that he felt—he introduces terms of relative or competitive position—*indisputable*, *favorite*, *conqueror*. Such terms hardly express confidence in being loved for oneself. And, actually, the great warmth of affection that his mother and

[1]Ernest Jones, *The Life and Work of Sigmund Freud*, Vol. 1 (New York, Basic Books, 1953), p. 5.

others in his family showered on Freud as a child was apparently colored —in a way the boy could readily grasp—by the evidences they gave of their confidence that he possessed unusual powers. The economic position of his parents was not very good, so that the home was crowded and poorly furnished, but Sigmund had a room to himself. It became obvious to Sigmund that the family hoped and expected him to become a famous scholar of some kind. Thus, to quote further from Ernest Jones's biography:[2]

> The "cabinet," a long and narrow room separated from the rest of the flat, with a window looking on to the street, was allotted to Sigmund. . . . There he lived and worked until he became an interne at the hospital. . . . In his teens he would even eat his evening meal there so as to lose no time from his studies. . . .
>
> An illustration of the esteem in which he and his studies were held in the family is a sad story related by his sister. When she was eight years old their mother, who was very musical, got her to practise the piano, but, though it was at a certain distance from the "cabinet," the sound disturbed the young student so much that he insisted on the piano's being removed; and removed it was. So none of the family received any musical education, any more than Freud's children did later. Freud's aversion to music was one of his well-known characteristics. One well remembers the pained expression on his face on entering a restaurant or beer garden where there was a band and how quickly his hands would go over his ears to drown the sound.

When we speak about a "feeling of acceptance and affection" as one of the sound and wholesome bases on which a healthy personality can rest, we are not speaking primarily of any such feeling of provisional or conditional affection as Freud experienced. Such a feeling of provisional affection may lead, as it did in Freud's case, to tremendous efforts to achieve, but it is a positive motive of a precarious and not altogether satisfactory sort. It makes the individual uncertain within himself as to whether he will continue to receive the affection of others. It also makes him less sympathetic and appreciative of the good qualities in others, just as it was difficult for Sigmund Freud to be sympathetic with the musical activities in which his sister and mother took an interest but in which he had no part.

This distinction between two sorts of acceptance and affection is one of the most difficult for people to understand. The parents who bestow such provisionally-expressed affection do not see themselves as saying to the child, "Do this or else. . . ." They feel that their praise and encouragement of the child is merely showing him how high is their regard for

[2] *Ibid.*, pp. 17-18.

him. But the child is apt to experience the affection, not as an affection for his real self, but as an affection for a self that is hardly his own.

There is a saying attributed to Victor Hugo: "The supreme happiness of life is the conviction that we are loved." Provided this statement is properly understood, it might well be taken as descriptive of one possible foundation for a healthy personality. Particularly these two observations might be stressed: First, it is noteworthy that Victor Hugo used the term *conviction*. This is in line with the view elaborated in this book that emotional processes are not matters merely of affect or diffuse feelings; instead, they are complex perceptions or representations of objective realities. Second, it is noteworthy that for a child or adult to have the conviction that he is really loved, he must have the feeling that he has revealed himself pretty completely, honestly, and spontaneously to those whose love he needs, and that they hold him in deep respect and affection despite the fact that they know him for the person he is. Otherwise the individual tends to feel, "They are expressing affection for what is after all only the external appearance that I keep up. I doubt if they would love what is really myself."

What is the difference between these two modes of treatment of children or others—between such provisional love and a more understanding love? It is hard to state. It can be illustrated, though, by the difference between the way that children are dealt with by some skillful nursery school teachers and the way that the same children are dealt with by their own parents. For example, one of the writers remembers a trivial incident on one occasion when he went to the ocean shore with a friend and the friend's small son. The father helped his five-year-old boy don his bathing trunks and get into the water. The water was a bit chilly, and partly because of this and partly because of his degree of unfamiliarity with the situation, the boy was merely stooping over and splashing and playing in the water. "Go on, Philip," the father said, "get down into the water and show how you can swim. It isn't too cold. Show what a man you are."

A nursery school teacher would not deal with a child that way. She would assume that the child was doing what interested and appealed to him most. She would respect his right to keep on doing that or to shift to something else when he felt so inclined. She would not run the risk of undermining his feeling of self-respect and his feeling that he was accepted by others by implying that the play that he naturally engaged in wasn't as manly as it should be. One timid nursery school child that the writer knows about was allowed by the nursery school teacher to "sit on the sidelines," as it were, for more than two months when he first attended school. There was no pressure put on him to join in the activities pursued by the other children. There were no comments from the teacher such as, "Don't you want to do this too? You're missing a lot of fun by not doing this!" Instead, the teacher was expressing by her actions and manner that she respected the child *as he was* and that she had confidence in him. And, in fact, the parents reported after a month or so that the child actually was initiating such activities with neighbor children at home, even though he still was abstaining from them at school. Before he started to nursery school, they had been greatly worried because he had been so excessively timid in his social contacts, but all their urging him to participate had only made matters worse.

This does not mean that the nursery school teacher or the parent or anyone else needs to let the child "do anything he wants to do" or "get away with murder." The child needs to feel that his parents respect themselves and respect other people as truly as they respect him, and that when he attempts to do something that would sacrifice other people for his own pleasure, they will interfere. But this is a different matter from letting a child who wants to wade in the ocean, rather than immerse himself totally, do what he wants to do instead of attempting to coax or order him to do something that the father, for some reason of his own, prefers!

There are perhaps no other influences that are so fundamental, however, with regard to the healthy emotional development of a child as are these influences that decide whether a child develops a conviction that he is unconditionally loved, in the sense that we have spoken of above. Karen Horney expressed this matter well in the following statement in her first book, although here she was speaking more of the effects of absence of such affection than of its presence:[3]

> In examining the childhood histories of great numbers of neurotic persons I have found that the . . . basic evil is invariably a lack of genuine warmth and affection. A child can stand a great deal of what is often regarded as traumatic—such as sudden weaning, occasional beating, sex experiences—as long as inwardly he feels wanted and loved. Needless to say, a child feels keenly whether love is genuine, and cannot be fooled by any faked demonstrations. The main reason why a child does not receive enough warmth and affection lies in the parents' incapacity to give it on account of their own neuroses. More frequently than not, in my experience, the essential lack of warmth is camouflaged, and the parents claim to have in mind the child's best interest. [Such camouflages] . . . are the basic factors contributing to an atmosphere that more than anything else lays the cornerstone for future feelings of immense insecurity.
>
> . . . Observation shows beyond any doubt that children, as well as adults, can accept a great many deprivations if they feel the deprivations to be just, fair, necessary, or purposeful. A child does not mind education for cleanli-

[3]Karen Horney, *The Neurotic Personality of Our Time* (New York, W. W. Norton & Co., 1937), pp. 79-82.

ness, for example, if the parents do not put an undue stress on it and do not coerce the child with subtle or gross cruelty. Nor does a child mind an occasional punishment, provided it feels certain in general of being loved and provided it feels the punishment to be fair and not done with the intention of hurting it or humiliating it. . . . What matters is the spirit in which frustrations are imposed rather than the frustrations themselves.

3. *The motive of affection and friendliness for other persons.* Though we are speaking of affection and friendliness—we can take them together—as if they could be thought of as a separate positive motive, it seems safe to say that this motive occurs in conjunction with the two preceding motives (respect from others, and respect for self) and is perhaps hardly to be distinguished from them. True, there has been a stream of thought within the Christian tradition that has encouraged profound guilt feelings within the individual toward himself, something almost akin to hate of self, and at the same time enjoined the individual to make love of others the main motive of his life. This is hardly the place to discuss whether this is an authentic representation of the original teaching of Jesus, but we might point out that the commandment, "Love your neighbor as yourself," implies also that you basically respect yourself, else your neighbor too will fare badly.

One reason why we speak of such friendliness as a valuable asset is that it makes for so much more happiness within the person himself than does hostility or distrust. There is also another aspect of the matter, one we have commented on at other times: that processes within the individual help to create in the objective environment the very qualities that he anticipates. Part of the reason that a friendly person finds other persons worthwhile is that his own personal atmosphere helps to produce what he values in them.

It is important to realize, though, that what an individual may think is his affection for others may not really be any such positive motive. When we come to discuss different patterns of personality in Chapter 14, we shall see that a not uncommon type of personality organization is one built mainly around the attempt to get protection and security and the indirect satisfaction of one's wishes by subordinating oneself to others, always trying to appease and please them, making them the dispensers of the favors one really longs for. The individuals who have this pattern of personality tend to praise affection as the greatest value in life and tend to emphasize emotional processes within themselves which they take to be deep affection for others. Such affection, however, is an alloy, at best. Far too much of it is but a disguised expression of fear, anxiety, and self-distrust. True affection, true friendliness, can exist only in limited ways in the basically insecure person.

4. *Healthy sex motivation is another important positive motive in sound*

personality. The sex motive, one of the positive motives that we are discussing, has some special characteristics because it rests in part on definite physiological factors. This does not mean that the sex motive is solely a physiologically-based motive and not in any important degree an emotional motive. It is a motive that shares the characteristics of both of these two large classes of motive that we distinguished in the preceding chapter. It is both a physiological and an emotional motive.

In the long history of mankind, and before that in the long evolutionary development that eventually produced humanity, a strong selective influence apparently operated to perpetuate the sort of human being whose sexual motivation was strong and vigorous. In all forms of life, evolution has favored those factors that insure a considerable margin of safety in the reproduction of the species. In trees this comes through the production of vastly more blossoms and seeds than could possibly find an opportunity to develop into trees. Salmon and most other fish produce a vastly greater number of eggs than could ever reach maturity. In higher forms of life, where the number of offspring is reduced, the margin of safety is insured by different means, such as the protective care that is lavished on their young by parents, as in the case of elephants, with a single offspring at each birth. In most animals, too, the margin of safety is increased through the existence in both sexes of a powerful motive to secure mating and the fertilization of eggs. Whereas in most animals a mating urge occurs only in limited seasons, in human beings, outstandingly, there is no marked seasonal variation in the intensity of the sex motive corresponding to the limited periods during which fertilization might occur. Reproduction in the human species has been insured partly by a strong sex motive that tends to produce recurrent sexual behavior pretty much independently of ovulation cycles in the female. It is as though evolutionary factors had favored the selection of motivational characteristics that would tend, at least in rough degree, to favor such sustained and even permanent association between two individuals as is needed to insure the co-operation of both mother and father during the long period of infancy and childhood when the child needs training and care.

We may suppose that there is a tendency for sexual motivation to favor the development of tender, affectionate, protective motivation, but it is only a tendency at most. Where there are such protective tendencies with regard to the young, they have had to arise primarily from other motives than merely the sex motive. The sex motive, as such, does not necessarily lead to altruistic behavior. In persons who have enjoyed the most favorable life circumstances, there comes to be a fusion of sexual interests with aesthetic interests and with affectionate tendencies, so that the positive enjoyment of sex activity ministers to some of the most important emotional interests and satisfactions of the individual. But there is nothing in the sex motive as such which insures that it will assume this valuable role in a person's life. It is a motive that can press for expression even when there are no factors of affection or protectiveness in the situation. In the history of war, for example, record after record will be found of armies that raped and pillaged indiscriminately, with the one activity showing no more altruism or protectiveness than the other. In peacetime life, too, an all-too-common happening is that sexual interests lead persons to enter into hasty or ill-advised marriages, or to rush into extramarital affairs, or to pursue other means of sexual satisfaction that they know are prejudicial to their own interests and to the well-being of others. The sex motive is in certain ways like fire. It may add enormously to the enjoyment and beauty of life. It is one of the most essential processes. But, like fire, the sex motive can be overwhelmingly destructive in its effects if used inappropriately and thoughtlessly.

It is far from easy, therefore, for a parent to discover how he may help his child develop proper emotional habits with reference to sex. The child must learn that this is a motive to be guided and used with discrimination and foresight, just as fire should be used intelligently, and this has to be done without developing habits of morbid fear or a sense of guilt. Such habits cannot easily be developed suddenly out of nothing during adolescence, partly because the individual, if unprepared beforehand, tends to be startled by the depth and vividness of the sexual feeling that sweeps over him, often making him feel that there must be something unique and abnormal about himself. An adequate program of sex instruction, therefore—and this includes introducing *pre*adolescents to certain facts about the psychology of sex, not just facts about the anatomy and physiology of sex—should be considered an essential step in the direction of sound personality development.

The first steps of preparatory training in these matters must go back to early childhood, even to situations where emotional habits are established long before verbal communication with the child has become important. The evidence is—though it had long been conveniently overlooked—that even the infant and the small child have feelings and impulses that are erotic in some degree. Right then the building of wholesome attitudes, rather than feelings of shame and guilt, should start. One reason for this ought particularly to be understood. It is the fact that sexual feelings and some other valuable emotional feelings (as friendliness, affection, and aesthetic delight) are sufficiently similar perceptually that if the individual builds up habits of guilt and fear about sexual feelings, these habits will tend to be evoked by these other perceptually similar feelings. This may happen even though the parents had not the slightest intention of making the repressive training they gave apply to anything except sexual feelings specifically.

These are difficult problems. The greatest of the difficulties arises, almost certainly, because sexual maturity comes in early adolescence, whereas in modern society it is only after another decade or so of development that the individual has secured the vocational preparation and attained the degree of personal independence and self-understanding and the breadth of experience in life that makes it appropriate for him to marry. Quite possibly, in consequence, society will need to recognize that healthy personality development through adolescence may require a much more frank acceptance of auto-erotic satisfactions as a feature of adolescent experience than has been the case previously.

One conclusion, one that will be developed further in a later chapter, has come with our increased knowledge of sexual motivation. It has been found, especially through intensive psychotherapeutic work, that sometimes where the sex motive seems to have become disastrously strong, the motivation is not strictly sexual, but is a combination of sexual motivation and other motives such as intense anxiety, intense hostility toward others, excessive guilt feelings, or even the general hunger for rich emotional experience.

5. *Enjoyment of activity for its own sake as another really major positive motive.* As we have said more than once, it has been easier for man to fix his attention on relatively tangible realities than to come to grips with the intangible and subtle realities of his world. In line with this principle, one striking feature of the work of psychologists on motivation is that they have done much more investigating of physiologically-based motives than of motives of other sorts. Thus, the chapters on motivation in textbooks of general psychology usually devote most space to discussions of the role of hunger, thirst, pain, and other physiologically-based motives. Even when Freud, in order to deal with personality maladjustments, felt he needed to broaden the range of motives to be taken into account, he turned to the sex motive, which might well be regarded as the next motive down the list in order from the more tangible to the less tangible ones. The other motives stressed in psychoanalysis (hostility, and fear or anxiety) are only somewhat less tangible. Almost any movie-goer, regardless of his level of intelligence, can appreciate the presence and operation of sex, aggressiveness, and fear.

A sufficient development of any science, however, cannot be achieved merely by the recognition of the more obvious phenomena. The things that possess crucial significance as causes are often obscure—witness the dietary-deficiency diseases (beri-beri, pellagra, scurvy, and others), the causes of which proved so difficult to detect and understand.

Perhaps the chief motive that we have been slow to appreciate is a relatively imponderable motive—interest in activity for its own sake rather than as a means of getting food, security, comfort, sexual satisfaction, or some other tangible objective. Even the animal psychologists now have demonstrated that much of the activity of rats, monkeys, chimpanzees, and other higher animals rests on an enjoyment of activity as such, including sometimes merely the activity of looking at or perceiving something. An example of activity for activity's sake may be found in the behavior of dolphins studied by Hebb and McBride at a huge aquarium at Marineland, Florida. As they report,[4] a dolphin will sometimes find a feather floating on the water and make it an object of playful activity for a half-hour or more—blowing it into the air and catching it again, racing to keep it away from other dolphins or to retrieve it from them. On one occasion, a dolphin had been removed from the tank for a while and then was returned to it. Another dolphin that had often played with it previously came out to meet it with great excitement, and the two of them spent most of the next two hours racing together, side by side, around the tank. Visitors to the Marineland exhibit have reported that the dolphins regularly make a game of tossing a small rubber football to the crowd surrounding the pool. The visitors catch the ball, and the dolphins wait expectantly for it to be thrown back. They then rush after it eagerly like playful puppies chasing a thrown stick, often catching it in their teeth in mid-air and flipping it back to the crowd for another throw.

Activity which can be enjoyed for its own sake seems to be related particularly to the possession of more complex brains and the resulting increase in capacity for complex psychological processes. Cows and chickens, on the one hand, seem to be able to live happily and healthily under conditions of extremely restricted activity. Some chicken farms now limit the hens to small individual compartments where they have almost no chance to move around and explore, yet egg production is maximal. In many dairy farms, the cows spend most of their lives with their heads held in stanchions above their mangers. But many other forms of animals, and particularly those with greater brain capacity, can hardly endure such restrictions of their activities.

We might well think about this matter in the following way: Among the more complex animals—those with more highly developed brains—the greatest biological advantage they possess is their capacity for learning. This implies, in turn, a greater capacity to perceive things and adapt to them in more diverse and complex ways than are possible in the case of animals lower in the developmental scale. And whenever there exist such biological means of adaptation, the processes of evolutionary variation and selection have operated to produce forms of life motivated to make vigorous use of these special means of adaptation. Thus, even in young animals that are well provided with food and water, and that have all their other physical needs met, there remains a strong drive toward

[4]A. F. McBride and D. O. Hebb, "Behavior of the Captive Bottle-nosed Dolphin, Tursiops Truncatus," *Journal of Comparative and Physiological Psychology*, Vol. 41 (April, 1948), pp. 111-123.

various types of activity merely for the sake of activity. No one can doubt this, sensibly, who has ever watched small puppies or dolphins at play, or who has watched human children closely enough to note how many and what sorts of goals are being achieved by what they do. The exploring child often encounters lots of bumps and even burns and bruises that he could avoid if he were less active. But security and comfort are not the main things he values—the keenest motives, once his simpler physical needs have been met, are his motives of enjoyment of activities for their own sakes.

Here again, however, we need to guard against some oversimplified interpretation of what activities are involved in such motivation. Some of the problems of modern civilization may be due to the fact that we set our attention only on the more tangible and recognizable of our motives. Thus, we don't stop often to give much thought to the idea that some of the values we need are the values which appeal to the relatively more imaginative or poetic aspects of our natures. People build cities, for instance, as if little more were needed in housing than to protect human beings from cold and rain and to provide for efficient transportation. The fact that man may have some perceptual hungers—that he cannot live well and responsively without some surroundings of color and beauty, things less machine-like in their qualities—is indeed rarely considered. The time way well come, however, when the civilization of the twentieth century will be judged to have been fearfully blind to the subtler motivational needs of human life, just as some of the diets of peoples through long stretches of time were deficient in meeting man's nutritional needs.

We will go into some further discussion of this motive in the next chapter. For the present, therefore, let us say that a healthy person must find room somewhere in his life for the motive of activity for activity's sake. For some persons, it may even become the chief motive. The individual may be defective on many other scores and may be burdened with some seriously handicapping negative motives, and yet it may be that some strong development of this motive of enjoyment of activity for its own sake may be a basis for a tremendously effective life. Frank Barron, a psychologist who has been engaged for almost a decade in research on unusually creative persons, has told how strongly this was called to his attention recently. He participated in a conference of psychoanalysts, psychiatrists, and psychologists on the goals of psychotherapy. The group was fairly well agreed, Barron writes,[5] that the traits indicative of psychological health are:

(1) accuracy of perception of reality, (2) stable body functioning and

[5]Frank Barron, "The Psychology of Imagination," *Scientific American*, Vol. 199 (September, 1958), pp. 150-166.

freedom from psychosomatic disorders, (3) absence of hostility and anxiety, (4) capacity for friendly and co-operative relations with other people, (5) spontaneity and warmth, (6) social responsibility.

Barron adds, "An excellent combination, I said to myself." He goes on:

However, as I continued to listen in comfort and mild edification, I suddenly realized that my thoughts had drifted off to a description I had recently read of Robert Hooke, the brilliant 17th-century scientist whose achievements place him second only to Newton among his contemporaries, and whose prolific originality in experimentation has remained unsurpassed. Hooke suffered throughout his life from severe headaches, from indigestion so troublesome that he noted gratefully in his journals any meal that happened to agree with him, from giddiness and insomnia, and from fearful dreams during the few hours a day he was able to sleep.

Images of other figures drifted through my mind: of the apocalyptic rages of Beethoven, the savage indignation of Jonathan Swift, the terrible loneliness of Van Gogh, the criminality of Rimbaud, the shameless preenings of Baudelaire, the stoical despair of Emily Brontë, the excruciating physical and spiritual pain endured by Heine. I felt distinctly uneasy. . . .

In his work with contemporary creative workers, Barron has found that this same diversity of traits exists, with some creative thinkers not well developed with respect to other positive motives. A feature they strikingly share, however, is a need to work each in his own complex, challenging medium, a need to *create*.

6. *The motive of a sort of healthy aggressiveness, enjoyment of competition, and confidence in the value of effort and hard work.* Anyone who has watched young roosters knows that at some time before they are sexually mature, they begin to take a major interest in combats among themselves. Later on, some advantages come to the stronger birds from this, such as easier access to food and more opportunities for mating with hens, but the interest in combat could not be said to develop because those advantages are to be gained; it comes from a positive and doubtless inborn tendency to engage in such battles for their own sake.

The motivational life of roosters is much simpler than that of human beings, but still it seems that one of the motives that also exists instinctively in human beings to some extent, and that can be developed considerably by learning, is the positive enjoyment of struggle and competition and overcoming of difficulties. It is undeniably a positive motive, yet it is not altogether unrelated in character to the retaliatory anger that perhaps is classifiable more essentially as a negative motive. At least it is similar to the point that if a child is to remain capable of a kind of healthy aggressiveness and self-assertiveness, he must be protected against feeling guilty or afraid because he has angry impulses inside himself. Otherwise a habit of reacting negatively to anger within himself may spread to the healthy aggressive tendencies as well. This, of course, does not mean that a child should be allowed to express anger in any way that pleases him. He should learn to discriminate and to know when expressions of anger are appropriate. But he should not be made afraid of anger as such, lest he be robbed as well of this self-assertive sort of positive motivation, one that he may well need if he is to be effective in fighting wrongs.

It is a real question as to whether Western civilization has not over-encouraged this enjoyment of assertive, competitive, effortful activity, and perhaps organized far too much of life in these terms. It is only one among a group of positive motives, one not to be overstressed. However, even if this is the case, we must not go to the other extreme and fail to recognize it as a reality in human motivation.

7. *Feelings of adequacy as a basic motive.* This positive motive is one that psychologists do not often list, even though they often speak about "feelings of *inadequacy*" as a hampering or negative motive. The writers suspect that the chief reasons why this motive has been listed so infrequently are that (1) a "feeling of adequacy" obviously is a matter of fairly complex judgments on the part of the individual, (2) it is a type of emotional response that operates quietly and undramatically, and (3) psychologists have tended to see emotional processes as restricted to simpler and yet more dramatic processes.

Actually, however, it seems safe to say that a feeling of adequacy is one of the most important motives that might be fostered in a child or adult. It is a kind of process that needs to operate as a sort of steady background process for the major life-activities of the individual.

The individual's feeling of adequacy depends in part on his development of his own concepts of himself in terms of the kind of role appropriate to his sex. The individual needs to have a confidence that he has the qualities needed for the place in life that his biological characteristics will make essential for him, his cultural group being what it is.

Negative motives often become important in personality

Paired with at least most of the positive motives are corresponding potentialities for negative motivation. We will speak only briefly of these. It should be realized, however, that they can be developed into motives of great strength and can be the dominant forces in a human life, sometimes producing results of considerable social value, but remaining always a risky sort of motivation for society to count upon, and certainly intrinsically costly to the person himself.

As contrasted with the feeling of acceptance and respect from others, the negative feeling of being rejected, of lacking respect, and even of being despised by others may become obsessively strong with some persons.

Along with such feelings of being the object of unfavorable attitudes in others is likely to go a similar feeling of self-contempt or self-hate. The strength that this feeling may attain is sometimes appalling, as with one unfortunate student who described himself in these words:

> I think of myself as a dwarfish, grotesque, dirty, and unshaven figure—perhaps two to three feet tall. The kind of person who wears clothes that don't fit; who doesn't wash behind his ears. A rat-like, ferret-like creature in movement and thought. Someone who is regarded by others as untrustworthy. I feel that they don't trust me, but I know that they do.
>
> The other variation in my picture of myself is a feeling that comes when I am with people smaller than I am; then I conceive of myself as very, very tall, awkward, stumbling—a big boob, except that a big boob is usually likeable, and I am not.
>
> I have no conception of myself except this cartoon-like thing. I often ask other people what sort of person I am, but I never know no matter how much they tell me.

It is hard to imagine that the fellow who wrote this self-portrait was a rather striking-looking, even handsome young man whose appearance almost any man would jump at the chance to have. But such was the case.

At the other extreme from the positive feeling of affection and friendliness toward others is its opposite, hatred and resentment, which tends to accompany feelings of being spurned or neglected by others. Resentment and hatred came to the surface in a boy called Harry, the slightly crippled son of a surgeon who had made considerable efforts to help his son overcome his bodily handicap, but who had done so in a way that made Harry feel as if his real interests had been ignored. Harry described his father as "a domineering man, and one of the best surgeons in the East." The father was considered by others to be "lacking in appreciation of other people's feelings and accustomed to running things." When Harry was between age 7 and 15, the father subjected him to 12 operations, one after the other, in an effort to correct his deformities. Harry spoke of these operations with intense feeling. He often wished they would amputate his legs and be done with it, he said.

Harry developed into an unco-operative, stubborn, angry boy who sometimes smashed up his room. As a young man he became fond of drinking. He loved to get into arguments and debates in which he could best his opponents. He had fantasies of assaulting others, spent money well beyond his earnings, and grew into a skeptical, suspicious person, afraid of taking anyone into his confidence. He said there were only two ways of getting on with people—either beat them or be beaten. He seemed to do everything possible to hurt his family through his irresponsible behavior, even to the extent of getting arrested for passing bad checks.

Contrasting with the positive motive of enjoyment of activity there may exist either a relative lack of such motivation, which is a handicap in itself, or a negative motive of ennui or boredom. Perhaps the most tragic outcome of poor teaching is not that it fails to develop positive interests in literature or art or science or whatever, but that poor teaching builds negative motives that actually repel people from what might have been of great interest to them.

Another of the most important negative motives, and one that often provides the basis for some other negative motive, is fear. The importance of this motive in the life of animals has been well indicated by H. Hediger, director of the Zoological Gardens of Zurich, a man who has recorded extensive observations on wild animals both in their native habitats and in captivity. At one point Hediger quotes the following aphorism from Schiller:

> For the present, and until philosophy runs the world,
> Its driving force it gains from hunger and from love.

Then Hediger comments:[6]

> This poetic conception of the maintenance in nature of living creatures has strangely enough become almost a dogma in biology. Even the study of behaviour and animal psychology have been so bedazzled by the predominance of these two mighty urges that for long enough they have almost completely ignored another superior element in the struggle for life throughout the animal kingdom, namely, the all-important escape tendency, *i.e.*, the urge to avoid enemies continuously.
>
> "Hunger and Love" take only the second place. The satisfaction of hunger and sexual appetite can be postponed; not so escape from a dangerous enemy, and all animals, even the biggest and fiercest, have enemies. As far as the higher animals are concerned, escape must thus at any rate be considered as the most important behaviour biologically. The primary duty of the individual, to ensure its own existence, and thus the preservation of its kind, lies in being prepared to escape. By far the chief occupation of the free wild animal, therefore, is constant watchfulness; eternal alertness for the purpose of avoiding enemies.

Hediger then proceeds to document in fascinating detail how true it is that most animals, under natural conditions, live in almost perpetually

[6]H. Hediger, *Studies of the Psychology and Behaviour of Captive Animals in Zoos and Circuses* (London, Butterworths Scientific Publications, 1955), p. 39.

alert fashion, even responding during sleep to stimuli that betray the approach of enemies. He tried at various times, for instance, to make observations on the sleep of elephants. But, no matter how quietly he tiptoed into their quarters at night after having left the doors ajar so that he would make no noise in opening them, he always found that they had scrambled to their feet and were trumpeting in warning when he arrived. He was able finally to make observations on sleeping elephants in a circus where long experience with the confusion of night-time breaking of camp had habituated the elephants to having human beings around at night. With elephants, Hediger says:[7]

> One of the most surprising results . . . was that these great beasts would suffer the most severe disturbance from their fellows without ever being wakened up, while they immediately started up from sleep at the least disturbance from human beings. This fact proves that the central nervous system functions properly during sleep. But the incoming stimuli are filtered, so to speak, *i.e.*, divided into biologically harmless ones from the members of their own species, and potentially dangerous ones from human beings or other enemies.

Men are not elephants, of course, and it may seem to you that we have plenty to think about in human reactions without bothering about fear in animals. But mankind, too, has had a long, long history in which it somehow managed to adapt and survive despite the same insecurity and perpetual danger that wild animals have. Out of this past have come the important mechanisms that make man capable of being strongly motivated by fear. This is not to say that learning is unimportant in determining what things will be feared and, indeed, whether any appreciable amount of fear will be experienced in a particular human life. But it does mean that this is one potential capacity that can be a terrifically strong force in human life.

Summary

At the end of the preceding chapter, we suggested that two of the most important means of adaptation in human life are the capacity of human beings for emotional response and the capacity of human beings for developing different motives under different circumstances of life. In this chapter we have explored this matter further by considering the crucial differences, psychologically, between positive and negative motives, and then by taking up some of the most important motives in each of these two categories. For the most part, in this chapter, we have been talking about individual motives separately.

[7] *Ibid.*, p. 27.

In this chapter we considered seven positive motives that play important roles in healthy personalities: (1) feelings of acceptance and respect from others, (2) feelings of self-acceptance and self-respect, (3) affection and friendliness for others, (4) healthy sex motivation, (5) enjoyment of activity as such, (6) healthy aggressiveness and feeling of the value of effort, and (7) feelings of adequacy.

Among the negative motives that may become powerfully developed are a number that are simple opposites to the above. The negative motives include: feelings of rejection by others, feelings of self-rejection and self-hate, hostility and resentment toward others, feelings of ennui and boredom with reference to particular sorts of activity, fear, and feelings of inadequacy.

Many of our efforts to motivate other people and even to change our own motives tend to place undue reliance on negative motives. These should be seen as having a legitimate role in those situations where they operate as emergency or protective mechanisms. They are ill-adapted, however, to become the main motivational basis for a person's life. They are intrinsically costly in the life of the person, since they are all too likely to produce side effects of an undesirable sort. The various positive motives have been more difficult to appreciate. They are less dramatic in character than the negative ones, and hence were not recognized as quickly or seriously studied as early by psychologists. They typically require more forethought and more complex behavior to develop them than is the case with negative motives; but they are valuable in human life both for their intrinsic contributions and for the consequences to which they may lead. It would be very desirable, therefore, if we could come to think of personality situations more commonly in terms of the possible positive motives that might be developed in them.

Some motives are sufficiently similar to one another perceptually that, if an individual has learned to fear or be guilty about one of these motives, he will tend to respond in the same way to certain other motives as well. Adverse conditioning to the sex motive, for example, tends to spread to other motives. Adverse conditioning to anger tends also to bring inhibitions and the avoidance of healthy self-assertiveness.

In the chapter that follows this we will move on to the question of what *general* motivational influences lead either to conditions of emotional poverty or emotional richness within the life of the individual.

CHAPTER 9

Emotional Richness and Emotional Poverty

LET US SUPPOSE an investigator from another planet visits us for the purpose of inquiring about our motives. He observes a person eating steak with great relish. "Indeed I do like steak!" says this person to our visitor's inquiry. "I think it's the best food in the world."

The observer writes in his notebook: "People on earth put pieces of beef in their mouths and chew them; they like beefsteaks more than anything else."

Of course only a short time later he finds someone devouring a fried chicken and recommending it with the same enthusiasm; and so on with ice cream, lemon meringue pie, and chocolate cake.

When he finds some Europeans giving the same preference to snails, sour cream, spaghetti, red peppers, and sauerkraut, our observer's notes begin to puzzle him. When he comes to people in other cultures who smack their lips over grasshoppers and various kinds of grubs, he is inclined to throw up his hands. "What food *do* these people like? What a barrel of motives are involved here! Everyone gives a different answer!"

Since our visitor's brain is a concept-forming organ like our own, however, he finally concludes: "Ah, I see. It isn't that grasshoppers or steaks or sodas are really fundamental. The general truth is that these people like to eat. The man who said he likes steak was perfectly right. For him it is the one best-liked food. But when I look at all these individual expressions of what is the fundamental craving or need, I can see that it isn't for this or that particular food; the motive back of the eating of all this diversity of foods must be some general motive of hunger and of enjoyment of eatables in general. Some extra touches, it seems, can be added by learning. But, apparently there is some very general need, not for any one kind of food, but for food of any of a wide variety of types. And, depending on circumstances, this need may develop into one more specific motive or another."

Since our visitor comes from a highly developed culture where they have learned to apply experimental checks to lovely hypotheses (otherwise they never would have developed their flying saucers), he proceeds to test his hypothesis that eating depends on a motive that can be satisfied with any kind of food. He takes the person, for instance, who says that lemon meringue pie is the finest possible food and makes it possible for him to eat nothing but lemon meringue pie for two weeks. He finds, after a while, that the person refuses to go on with this diet because he longs for something else. "I thought you said lemon meringue pies were the best possible food." "Yes, I did, but not too many of them; what I'd like now would be a beefsteak or a hot dog."

The investigator therefore concludes: "It must be that things like beefsteak are really the best human food." So he feeds another person solely on beefsteaks. After a while he gets complaints from him: "I'd like a salad, maybe, or a baked potato, or something like that."

Out of all such attempts, the visitor might come to see that apparently eating rests both on a very general motive of hunger, which might be satisfied by any of a huge number of foods, and also on certain more limited motives such as a craving for proteins, a craving for foods rich in phosphorus and calcium, a craving under some conditions for foods rich in fats, and so on down the line.

"Still," he might say, "I was right when I concluded that the motive involved in any particular person's eating is not his craving for just that one specific food, even though he has learned to like it better than anything else. There are general components to hunger. There are underlying needs that determine which specific things people like. Except as I use this hypothesis, I cannot make sense out of my notebook entries. It would be a good thing if people knew more about their basic motivational needs!"

Our need for emotionally rich experience

Are we not driven to a similar conclusion with respect to human motives generally? Are we not driven to the conclusion that human beings apparently have a need for motivational satisfaction in general, so that different activities of the most diverse sorts may at least partially substitute for one another? And yet, are we not also driven to the conclusion that there are certain more restricted kinds of motivation, more or less distinct from one another, each of which must be served as such if the individual's motivational needs are really to be served? Furthermore, are we not driven to the conclusion that our modern life is perhaps leaving us motivationally starved in some important respects, even though it has provided us with many things that are very satisfying and that compensate to some degree for these other things in which our lives are deficient? Or, putting the matter even more bluntly, may it not be that human beings in our modern society typically suffer from some degree of *emotional* starvation or *emotional* poverty?

We are likely to react with surprised disbelief to the idea that modern living may often leave us emotionally starved. We so habitually evaluate the adequacy of a culture in terms of its industrial development or of material wealth that we are sure anyone who disputes this self-evident goodness must have some peculiar and cranky streak in his nature making him want to belittle what we have achieved.

Our complete conviction that the world "never had it better" shows up especially in the wonder and pity with which we look at primitive peoples. For instance, *Life* magazine once published a series of articles on man's history. These were very good accounts of life in precivilized ages, but the emphasis was completely on the utter material primitiveness of life in periods before our own. At one point the Australian bushmen were described as a "contemporary Stone Age people." The starkness of their material lives is symbolized by a picture of a nearly naked black man trotting home to his family with a fox slung over his shoulder, one he had killed by throwing a crude spear.

In effect, the beautifully-photographed pictorial story said "What a life!" This theme is explicit in a small book for children about a boy who is called "You now." "You now" is today's child, and his modern life is pictured on the right-hand side of each double page of the book. On the left side there is always a corresponding picture of how a Stone Age child had to live and do the same things. Thus, the modern "You now" child crosses the ocean in a large ship, whereas the poor Stone Age child is pictured as using a crude log raft to cross a small pond. The one sleeps in a modern house, the other in a cave with a fire in front to protect him from animals. The intent of the little book is basically good—it tries to tell a small child in simple terms that man once lived in a very different way, and that there has been progress in many respects.

The article in *Life* and the "You now" book epitomize our general appraisal of our own culture. We see it as having made progress in satisfying human needs at almost all points. But something about this attitude needs to be questioned sharply. For while we have made great progress in serving our needs for food and shelter, transportation, and medical care, we had perhaps better look again to see if we may have lost some of the values primitive man enjoyed. It may be that there were more genuine, vivid emotional satisfactions in certain areas of primitive life than we have succeeded in providing in modern times.

For example, think again about the Stone Age Australian bushman with the fox that he has killed. If a man has been fiercely hungry and has stalked a wary animal for hours and manages to kill it by throwing a handmade spear, he has done a highly skilled thing. If he has a family waiting hungrily to acclaim his success, if he grew up as a boy admiring and intently determined to master good hunting techniques, then killing that fox could give tremendous satisfaction. Or consider the Stone Age boy on a log raft. Is it more fun to be up on the deck of a huge ocean liner, or might navigating one's own crude log raft right down in the water be far more of a thrill for a small boy?

One does not need to belittle the material accomplishments of our society (incidentally, these are *not* our personal accomplishments, yours and mine) to see that there can be intense motivational satisfactions in ways of living that look extremely meager to sophisticated eyes. Nor do we need naively to urge man to return to the life of Rousseau's noble savage. In fact, in primitive life, the very lack of material resources must often have resulted in an existence dominated by fears and bitter frustrations. Our material achievements are not to be depreciated. They conceivably can yet give us the means of a life richer, even in most emotional respects, than any primitive could ever have known.

To say that such a thing is possible is not the same as conceding, however, that we have achieved this result so far. Great numbers of people brought up in modern civilized surroundings are showing, either directly or indirectly, that something is wrong. It is as though they were saying (and sometimes actually they do):

> I've only one life to live, and the days and years are slipping away. In that life I have wanted to live richly, vividly, significantly. As it is, I feel I've been cheated. What I've known have been minor, colorless, unappealing experiences and activities, and there should be something richer and more vital than that! Life ought to contain more satisfactions than I've found; it ought to have more in it! And yet, how can it without running into things that bring serious disadvantages with them, or risks of such? It seems that vividness of experience can be purchased only at the cost of too many fears and penalties.

Ultimately this may be what lies back of many of our difficulties in modern life. If so, it may explain, to a considerable degree, the selfishness and competitiveness that creep into so many situations. People may be seeking for big incomes, for instance, not because they enjoy great wealth as such, but because they have been badly frustrated in their hunger for a meaningful life, and they know that a large income has been one means of securing such a measure of emotional vividness as they have had. But if we knew more how to secure such emotional satisfaction in ordinary living, then people would be freer to act altruistically and with social wisdom toward others. We know how to get plenty when it comes to food and other material things. But somehow we have missed wholeheartedness and depth of emotional meaning in our ordinary civilized life. Perhaps such lacks are at the basis of the present exaggerated interest in sex, or even in aggressive behavior typified in the extreme case by the Nazi movement. In such matters perhaps the crucial motives have not been what the surface appearances seem to suggest, but rather a deep hunger for vividness or emotional "aliveness" or just the positive emotions in general.

Sometimes we find, in the direct testimony of people, evidence that such suppositions may be correct. This testimony often comes from people who have enjoyed a great many advantages. Thus, one observant person who has a good job of his own choosing, his own home, a fine family, and many other reasons to feel satisfied, expressed his experience in this way:

> I see life situations in terms of a more or less endless series of jobs that must be done, none of them too satisfying, but rather the opposite—in fact, with tenseness and worry connected with them, and fear of criticism for not doing as good work as ought to be done, and a feeling that they have to be hurried or they will not be done in time. It is a pattern of a lot of "must jobs" that leave a lot of hungers. It isn't that I can't carry the responsibilities that I'm supposed to. I can, and I will. But it is dull and tasteless. There is something left out, and I don't know what it is.

Some indirect expressions of this feeling of emotional poverty

Right now a lot more effort might be directed toward meeting this need for emotionally rich experience if more people saw clearly, and admitted, that there is something lacking in modern life. But, most often, the feeling of lack does not express itself in such clearly conscious form as in the words of the person just quoted. The discontent shows up more in indirect ways. It may be worthwhile looking into some of the indirect forms that emotional poverty may take. Let us examine six of these, even though this list is surely far from complete.

1. *Pseudo-hungers for food as an expression of emotional poverty.* One of the simplest indirect expressions of emotional poverty is a craving

for food that the individual does not really need and would not eat were it not for his emotional hungers. Thus, one college teacher observed this about himself:

> This fall the office staff was moved to temporary quarters while their building was being remodeled. All the staff was crowded into one building. There was space for all but one person. Being only a temporary member of the group, I volunteered to take an office in a nearby building, entirely apart from everyone else. I liked my work and was engrossed in it, but I would get the strongest craving for sweets during the day. Once I went out and bought a half-pound bar of chocolate and gulped it all!
>
> I remember the last time I had such a craving. It was in 1942 when I was drafted and found myself a private in an infantry division just being activated. We were all strangers to one another and felt uprooted and lost. For the first month we were confined to the post. Not even visitors were allowed. During the week we were too tired to feel much, but weekends were intolerable. We used to go to the P.X., and those of us who didn't drink beer would sit at the ice cream counter and drink endless sodas and milkshakes in succession, often finishing off with several big bars of chocolate!

The same man noted that, when his wife went out without him, for some reason, in the evening, he showed this same tendency to make up for the lack of companionship by eating:

> It's not very long after Jane is gone that I often get intensely hungry. I wander around the house for a while, maybe, and get my desk organized for an evening's work. Sometimes, then, I feel suddenly tired. Other times I get hungry for cornflakes and milk. It's absurd. I've had a good dinner; but that insistent craving starts, and I can't get to work until I pour myself a huge bowl of the stuff and eat it while arranging my work. Once I get started, the work carries itself along, and time passes quickly. But, particularly if the work is a bit of a chore, or something I can't too well see my way through, I'm likely to get hungry, no matter how recently I've eaten.

Here you have only one case, but what it reports is typical of a good many persons—in short, it is a good instance of an expression of emotional deprivation.

2. *An exorbitantly increased demand for closer human relationships as one effect of emotional poverty.* Emotional hungers may find an outlet through our dependence upon and demand for more satisfaction from our close human relationships than we can reasonably expect. In marriage and in other close relationships, some people tend to want others almost to revere them and to share with them all their ideals, ideas, and interests. Such a demand is exceedingly egotistical, not wholly unlike that of a

small child who feels that his mother should think only of him. In all soberness we have no right even to imagine that any other person would respect us on some matters, love us for some reasons, or share some of our activities, because each of us is complex and each of us inevitably will differ somewhat from every other person. One wonders if it is not some unfulfilled emotional hunger on our part that makes us expect more from a marriage or from any other relationship than it can be expected to yield except under the rarest circumstances—except when both persons involved are of the most unusual fineness and when their natures are complementary in some fullest sense.

3. *Overdependence on sexual satisfactions as a consequence of emotional poverty.* No one would think of denying that the sex motive is a strong one simply in its own right. The satisfactions of sex are vital in themselves, just as the satisfaction of hunger is vital in itself. Given its proper development and place in relation to all the other components of a full life, the sex motive becomes part of an enduring and profound love-relationship. As such it is part of a complex of motives that is anything but simple.

Even when this profound and more inclusive relationship is achieved, the sex motive tends to press for much more frequent expression than would be required for reproduction of the species under ordinary circumstances. The basic biological nature of man was laid down in those long ages when human life was extremely precarious and difficult. The skeletal remains from ancient man indicate that early primitive people rarely had a lifespan of more than about 30 years. Their conditions of life, even during such a lifespan, must have been arduous in the extreme. Under such circumstances, one of the means by which some margin of safety was secured in the perpetuation of the species was the development of a sex motive that reached great strength early in adolescence and that tended to insure frequent mating thereafter. If there were some individuals who, by hereditary variations, were less strongly motivated sexually, they probably tended, under conditions when life was not easy, not to have offspring. So our hereditary traits tend not to be derived from such individuals. All of the present forms of life inevitably are derived from those earlier ancestors who were constituted so that they were suited to secure, not merely the survival of themselves as individuals, but the survival of the species.

Because the sex motive has a strong physiological basis, it is a rare person who, as an adolescent and adult, has not depended to some considerable extent either on sexual relations with others or, if his upbringing and social ideals or his situation have made that sort of expression inappropriate, on autoerotic satisfactions. One fact tending to work in this direction is that, unlike many other motives such as the enjoyment of music that requires long training to develop adequately, the sex motive provides intensely pleasurable effects even when the richer forms of satisfaction of this motive—its fusion with the rich emotional elements of shared lives—have not been achieved.

However, even when all this is recognized, it must be definitely recorded that the sex motive is not as imperiously strong as it sometimes seems to be when its expression occurs under those conditions we have termed conditions of emotional poverty, or when it is accompanied by fear, sense of guilt, or some other intense and negative motive.

Two sets of observations upon animals seem definitely to support this hypothesis. Thus, G. V. Hamilton, in his very interesting book, *An Introduction to Objective Psychopathology*, tells of some observations he made of monkeys and chimpanzees. No one could accuse these animals of having any puritanical traditions with regard to sex activity, and when both sexes are living together, there is a considerable amount of mating behavior. However, Hamilton made this further observation: Under conditions of wild life, the sex motive of these animals seemed to find adequate satisfaction in ordinary mating behavior. But, when he kept them caged within limited areas, even within pens of several acres' extent, their heterosexual activity seemed not to be sufficiently satisfying to them, with the consequence that autoerotic activity was general also. Hamilton's hypothesis is that these primates possess a drive to activity that would more naturally find expression in exploration than in sex activity but that, frustrated in finding its natural expression, it caused the animals to seek alternative satisfactions of this other form.

An animal psychologist, Otto Tinklepaugh, reported at a meeting of the American Psychological Association that chimpanzees and monkeys often turned to sexual activity when they became badly frightened. When he created situations that were very upsetting, but that did not permit the animals to express their fear by flight, he found that one animal would often mount another animal, as though sexually motivated, all the time trembling violently in a manner that betrayed the fact that fear was the main source of the activity.

Many psychotherapists have come to the conclusion that most of what appears as excessively strong sexual motivation in human beings must be similarly explained. Karen Horney was expressing the views of many of such workers when she wrote as follows:[1]

> . . . just as "all is not gold that glitters," so also "all is not sexuality that looks like it." A great part of what appears as sexuality has in reality very little to do with it, but is an expression of the desire for reassurance. If this is not taken into consideration one is bound to overestimate the role of sexuality.
>
> The individual whose sexual needs are enhanced under the unrecognized stress of anxiety is inclined naïvely to ascribe the intensity of his sexual needs

[1]Karen Horney, *The Neurotic Personality of Our Time* (New York, W. W. Norton & Co., Inc., 1937), pp. 157-159.

to his innate temperament, or to the fact that he is free from conventional taboos . . . an individual who needs sexuality as an outlet for the sake of allaying anxiety will be particularly incapable of enduring any abstinence, even of short duration.

. . . a great deal of sexual activity today is more an outlet for psychic tensions than a genuine sexual drive, and is therefore to be regarded more as a sedative than as genuine sexual enjoyment or happiness . . . .

It is one of the great achievements of Freud that he contributed so much to giving sexuality its due importance. In detail, however, [within psychoanalytic views] many phenomena are accepted as sexual which are really the expression of complex neurotic conditions, mainly expressions of the neurotic need for affection.

It is not surprising, then, that the research of Kinsey on sex hehavior in human beings should show, in a somewhat similar vein, that the socially and economically underprivileged classes in our society are more sexually active than is, for example, the professional class. The difference may not lie in the greater virility of lower class groups, or in some supposed repression of sex in professional groups, but in the over-all differences with respect to emotional satisfactions that their everyday lives provide.

4. *The powerful and insistent demands for material comforts and material products that characterize our society may be an expression of emotional deprivation in other respects.* Many persons who study our society come to feel that our interest in the material products of our technology far exceeds their value as the means to a fuller life. Material goods, they feel, come to be wanted with an irrational intensity bewildering to the detached onlooker.

There is, for instance, our tremendous itch to own the newest, biggest, most powerful, and showiest car, an urge that goes far beyond any simple need for going places. One automobile executive remarked that if sales appeal were the sole basis for deciding what next year's car was to be like, it would have 500 horsepower and be made of solid chrome.

No one denies that a car is what most people need for getting quickly to work; it may allow a family to live in beautiful country though the breadwinner works a long distance away. It is wonderful for a trip to the coast or mountains on weekends, for vacation exploring. Going up 12,000 feet over Trail-Ridge Road in Rocky Mountain National Park, or over Tioga Pass in Yosemite, can be a never-to-be-forgotten thrill—an experience alive with adventure and beauty. But why must one have a car loaded with expensive chrome? Why must one have 285 horsepower rather than a mere 250 or 150? Why a new car every second year?

Yes, automobiles in our society serve emotional needs far beyond their immediate functional uses. Of course, their power and speed do have great intrinsic appeal. Adults enjoy these no less than the child who loves to roll or slide swiftly down a hill on his wagon or sled. But such thrills gain in attraction for the person whose ordinary way of living is pretty meager. A vacuum cleaner salesman who talked to one of the writers had had his motor especially tuned up for extra speed and power. He admitted he just couldn't resist the thrill of driving over a hundred miles an hour. Four times he had gone off the road in accidents that all but cost him his life, but still he went right back to the old speeds. Might it be that his emotional life was such a void that he had to seek foolhardy thrills?

Often it seems that people are misled in judging how much emotional value they can get from the ownership of material goods—cars and other things—acquired at great sacrifice. Some questions need looking into. Is it true, for example, that we especially enjoy and like people who own luxury homes and big cars? Do we feel any unusual sense of warm human interest in them when we are with them? Can it make a difference in the quality of friendship they extend to us if we arrive in the latest and biggest model of a car?

Or do we remember and like those people who are most human, friendly, and interested in us, and who are unpretentious, and warmly and simply welcoming and hospitable? Isn't it likely that if we go in for exaggerated material ostentation, it will arouse envy and competitive counterreactions rather than the kind of humanness we really want from others—despite the reactions that advertisers lead us to feel we will surely get if we arrive in a Cadillac?

Here, it would seem, is a fine instance of how basic, unfilled human hungers for companionship and appreciation, for being wanted, liked, valued, for feeling close to others, get sidetracked and replaced by a need for material things that we want so desperately as supposed means of gratifying these basic desires. But somehow the supposed means turn out to separate us even further from the kind of fundamental human responsiveness we want from others.

5. *Much interest in violence (directly or through phantasy) may be an expression of emotional poverty.* It is sobering to look at the activities of many teen-age gangs in cities such as New York and Philadelphia. One news item told about a teen-age youth, the leader of a street gang, who had shot and killed an innocent boy. He had mistaken the boy for the leader of a rival teen-age gang that his group were fighting over the question of whether the other group could wear jackets colored like their own. As he was led away by police, a group of teen-agers followed him, cheering him loudly. The girls in the group shouted, "We love you, Tarzan!" Several days later they assembled at the funeral of the innocent victim and booed and threatened the police there, loudly defending the act of their leader. That he had killed someone added to his stature in their eyes. Another report told of an unbelievable incident in which some boys drenched a child with gasoline and set fire to their screaming victim. One youth, arrested for knifing a perfectly innocent

person, was asked why he had done such a horrible thing. He replied that he wanted to feel the thrill of his knife going through bone! Unbelievable? One need only read the newspaper reports to find similar incidents every week among teen-age gangs in our cities.

What fiendish impulses are these that we harbor? Is there any hope for man if he can come to this? One needs to pause before replying and ask whether such inhuman behavior is so different from some of the best motivated acts that we admire. The day that the Tarzan story appeared in the local paper, a geologist friend told of taking a group of 60 teen-age boys on a river trip down a deep gorge of a relatively unknown but beautiful stream in the West. They floated in rubber boats between towering, majestic cliffs for nearly a hundred miles. It was a thrilling adventure for these teen-age boys.

Do we have two different kinds of beings in the Tarzan gang and the river-boating boys, or is it that we are all not only inherently good, but also have innate murderous impulses that come out in the open in certain gang activities? Or is either answer right? Perhaps we should ask whether there is a common denominator in the need for satisfying emotional experience. In recognizing such a possibility, we need not assume that violence is innately satisfying. There certainly seems to be an innate tendency to be aggressive in the sense of protectively fighting back when one is attacked, but the enjoyment of violence looks more like something that can be developed as an emotional interest when most other outlets are blocked. If the inhuman acts of these gangs seem fantastic, perhaps the emotional poverty of their lives is just as unbelievable.

It seems not to be merely slum children who are fascinated by thoughts and portrayals of violence. This is obvious from the degree to which movies and TV programs have emphasized this sort of material. Thus, the National Association for Better Radio and Television reported the following program content for seven television stations that they watched for a week:[2]

Killings	223
Suicides	2
Attempted murders	192
Robberies	83
Kidnapings	15
Conspiracies to commit murder	24
Jailbreaks	21
Attempted lynchings	7
Dynamitings	6
Extortions	11
Arson	2
Physical torturings	2

[2]From the *Denver Post,* July 27, 1958.

As this report commented: "That figures to a total of 588 killings and/or other crimes—84 a day, or one every 17 minutes, day and night."

6. *It may even be that war appeals to us because we are emotionally starved in peacetime.* Many writers have pointed out that it is not the whole truth to say we fear and hate war; in many ways we like it. Some of them have concluded, as Freud did, that man is equipped with a fundamentally aggressive need that is almost bound at times to find an outlet in war if it cannot be successfully drained off by less horrible substitutes. Another possibility may be, though, that wars come partly from other indirect emotional sources. In war some men attain their deepest emotional experiences—in heroism, generosity, companionship, courage, and self-sacrifice. One need only read Winston Churchill's account of the "finest hour" of the British people subjected to Hitler's all-out bombardment of London in World War II to realize what wars can bring in the way of emotional values that continue to be celebrated in movies and fiction for long afterwards. When people so docilely support the aggressive military programs of their countries, it may not be entirely from a feeling of helplessness in the face of such a waste of treasure, but rather because the idea of a struggle for national survival has its positive emotional appeal, particularly in view of the dearth of meaning in much of peacetime existence. If so, the transforming of modern life to make it emotionally more rich is not something of merely individual concern, but is one of the major social needs of our modern world!

It would be possible to mention a number of other indications of emotional poverty in modern life. The high frequency of alcoholism may be one such indicator. The increasing reliance on cocktail parties as a means of making social life "sufficiently interesting" may be another. Sensationalistic newspapers may be still another.

The problem is extensive and serious enough, at any rate, that it is well worth our asking about the factors that produce emotional poverty in modern life and about the resources that we might use to foster emotionally rich experiences, instead.

Factors productive of emotional poverty

1. *Conformity pressures.* In a country founded in part on a belief in rugged individualism, it is a curious fact that, with every passing year, it seems to become more difficult to be one's own individual self. It is commonly pointed out that we have been moving rapidly toward an "organizational" society where the individual tends to become lost in the large-scale unit such as a corporation, union, bureaucratic government, university, or church. The structure of such organizations is designed to meet the goals of the group, and before he knows it the in-

dividual finds himself falling in line with group pressures regardless of whether it is in his own fundamental interest to do so or not.

The young executive may want to live in New England where he grew up and where he deeply enjoys living, but he knows he has to take the offered transfer to Kansas if his career is not to be blocked. He wants to spend his evenings and week ends with his wife and children, but instead brings home a brief case full of work in order to meet the pressures that come down on him from above. He enjoys good literature and the theater, but the circle of associates who hold the reins to his future favor evenings of canasta, bridge, and social drinking. He dislikes parties, but knows that not to be seen at the organizational gatherings would be fatal.

The scientist is subject to the same forces. We may have always thought that research flourishes in proportion as the individual genius is free and that the fundamental premise of the laboratory is that the inquirer must be his own judge of what he considers the most promising line of work. But it is the relatively rare scientist who can do just what he wants. He too must conform to views of the large foundation or government bureau as to what deserves research funds. Too often our scientists find themselves offered large grants to work on something considered valuable by someone else but are unable to get a few thousand dollars for research on their own ideas.

These influences tend to dry up the wells of rich emotional living. It is the essence of such full living that the particular nature of each person and his interests serve as the basis for decision in choosing what he should do or not do. This does not mean that we are each to develop without contact or influence from others. But it does mean that we must have freedom to be attracted to this or that work or person in accord with the character of our own selves, rather than according to the dictates of conformity to an external value-standard set up by authority.

An interesting expression of this respect for individual differences occurs in a recent article by Marlin Perkins, whom many people have know through his popular TV program, "The Zoo Parade." Perkins says:[3]

> My life has taught me that the surest path to success is to find out what you most *enjoy* doing—then set about to do it.
>
> I decided young that if a man is going to spend most of his waking hours earning a living, he ought to spend them doing what he likes best. Today, in my 50's, I believe this inexperienced decision was wise and practical. I am doing precisely what I chose to do. I have not yet met the man with whom I would trade places. . . .
>
> As a little boy in Carthage, Missouri, I loved to explore the countryside for

[3]Marlin Perkins, "Do What You Want to Do—Now!" *Family Weekly*, Oct. 19, 1958, pp. 4, 5, 7.

wildlife, particularly snakes. I'd ride into the country on my bicycle, collecting water snakes, blue racers, anything I could find. I was almost thrown out of Wentworth Military Academy (where we weren't permitted to own pets) for keeping snakes in a cage at the top of my closet.

By the time my father sent me to the University of Missouri, I knew I had to quit acting like Huckleberry Finn and decide what I was going to be. This was when I learned how some people plan their lives.

One of my friends, about to graduate as an engineer, told me he was going to become a bond salesman. Another, majoring in agriculture, was planning to take over his father's store. Two fellows in geology were planning to go into business—and forget all about geology. This, I thought to myself, was pretty ridiculous. What were they studying specialties for? What appeared even worse, they didn't really *want* business careers. They seemed pushed by vague notions of what they thought they *ought* to do. They seemed to be wasting their time and their money and, in the long run, their lives.

I'm not trying to imply that a business career is a waste. Far from it. Business can certainly be as fascinating as collecting snakes, if that's what a man wants to do. All I'm saying is that a fellow ought to *choose* it, not fall into it nor let it fall on him.

Right then and there I assumed naïvely—but, I insist, quite correctly—that if a man made up his mind to turn his chief interest into his livelihood, he could do so. . . .

So I decided, if you'll pardon the wisecrack, that I belonged in a zoo. . . .

I knew that my father, who was a circuit judge, deeply wished that I would follow law. He had tried several things himself in his early days—railroading, carpentry, farm jobs—but on Saturdays, he'd wander into the courtroom just to watch the judge and the lawyers. Then he began to spend the nights studying law (he never went to college) until he felt he could pass the examinations.

Dad encouraged me to go ahead.

I rented a room in St. Louis, went to the zoo where I had often gone as a visitor, and asked a keeper in the monkey house whom I should see about getting a job.

Then the story goes on about how he was tried out first for about three weeks on manual labor around the zoo—cutting grass, trimming hedges, possibly to see whether his protestations about interest in work were really earnest—then he was assigned to look after the reptiles; then he helped to prepare an exhibit of snakes that aroused great interest and resulted in the building of a special reptile house. This led on to field trips for collecting animals, then to his television program, "The Zoo Parade." His interest spread to include the archaeology of early man and man's relationships to the animals around him, and to work on a TV program on the history of early man. And all along the way he kept up an absorbing interest in photographing animals. Perkins concludes his article:

> I am truly sorry for those people who have always dreamed about doing something else, but surrendered before they ever tried. My decision to spend my life enjoying wild animals was unconventional, maybe even outlandish and impractical. But I have made it come true, and I wouldn't trade places with anybody.

2. *Blue-ribbon motivation and emotional poverty.* The following conversation was reported by a father of a girl who was near the end of her first grade in school:

> "Daddy," she said, "you have to get me some books that I can read myself."
>
> The father, pleased at such an early interest in reading, smiled benignly, "Well, if you like reading that well, we'll certainly have to get you some books."
>
> "Yes," little Marguerite went on, "Dorothy's already got five stars on her reading chart, and I haven't got any yet."
>
> "Reading chart? Stars? What's that got to do with wanting books to read?"
>
> "Well, you see Daddy, I'm in the fast reading group, along with Dorothy Harlan, Sally Evans, and Jeanie Scott—those three are the best readers—and they're in our 'sharp eye' group, which is the best in the first grade. This week the teacher put up a big chart on the wall. She said that now that we could read, we would all have to read books on our own, outside of class. Everytime we read a book, we tell her, and she marks another star by our name. Dorothy gets two or three stars every day, and I haven't got a one yet."

While this is a schoolroom example, the practice of giving recognition to those who are to be considered first in any activity is not limited to child education. In our culture the question too often is: "Are you *first?* Are you the *top* in your field? Are you the *best* there is?"

This is "blue-ribbon motivation." The character of the work itself, its interest for you, its importance to society, are all secondary, or not even asked about. The only question is whether, by some external, tangible criterion, you have, in some sense, won first, or at least ranked high, in competition against the rest of the field. To some extent, it doesn't even matter too much what the competition is about. It may be for making the best pie at the fair or the best model of a nineteenth-century sailing ship, for being president of the largest manufacturing plant in the whole country; or it may be that you came in first in a hamburger-eating contest.

Throughout our whole society it is remarkable to what extent such extrinsic, tacked-on, blue-ribbon evaluation is the main basis for undertaking what people do. Listen, sometime, to parents talking about their children who are away at the university. You will find them telling of their son's or daughter's being elected to class presidency, or some club presidency, or being on the honor roll, or getting a prize for being the best freshman engineering student, or what not. How rare it is, instead, to hear a parent rejoice because Mary or Ronnie has a brand new area of interest that fills her or his letters home—just that, and no blue ribbon!

It is very hard, in our society, to continue to like doing something for itself, for its intrinsic merits. Such an interest is regarded as an indulgence. Even hobbies too often become competitive. Sometimes we allow art to become an intrinsic interest, providing it is understood to be distinctly amateurish. But, most of us are a little mystified by the person who says he is doing something merely because it is interesting. He doesn't make money at it, he isn't very good at it, but he likes it—something surely a little odd about such a fellow!

One difficulty about blue-ribbon motivation is that it guarantees that most of the group will be losers. When it is used in the schoolroom, the majority may be left with a lifelong distaste for what they think of as "school*work*." In adulthood those who felt themselves losers rarely take up again any of those studies as worthwhile just in themselves. Few want ever to read history again. "Good literature" is forever put aside.

But even the winners are doomed to lose. Let's look at what happens to the few who manage to be model pupils and win first consistently. Typically they are the ones who go on to college, and maybe, after that, graduate study. Years of hard study that look meager indeed to an outsider are not only endured but enjoyed by such a person. The enjoyment has the same kind of reintegrative basis as in the example of the circus performer—it depends on a background of satisfying past experiences, the emotional accompaniment of which is automatically reintegrated as part of the feel of that activity whenever it is engaged in.

The lot of the scholar, however, is not necessarily one to be envied. They do have some reintegrative enjoyment that comes from past "being first" experiences, along with whatever intrinsic enjoyment they have managed to preserve against the influence of the blue-ribbon evaluation system. But too much of this reintegrative enjoyment is conditional on continuing to be first. After being first in grade and high school, the "A" student is sent to college. Here the proportion of other former firsts is higher. In some small, select student bodies, the student may find himself in a population made up chiefly of high school firsts. Graduate school intensifies the situation even more—even many high school firsts have fallen by the wayside. Of this new group only a handful are destined to be acclaimed by their teachers as "really topnotch." The rest leave with their Ph.D.'s and a puzzling new experience that is peculiarly intolerable —the experience of being quite average, or even on the poor side.

The young Ph.D. then starts afresh in a large competitive field where there is a handful of recognized top positions and a great mass of anonymous strugglers. He is occupied with something that should be fascinating in itself. Fortunately, most men retain a surprising measure of intrinsic satisfaction for their special areas of study, in spite of all hindrances. But the professional person often works in an emotional atmosphere that negates whatever intrinsic satisfactions remain, an atmosphere of self-doubt and of doubt on the part of others as to the value of his efforts. These are doubts that only further blue ribbons can erase: a brilliant discovery, a Nobel prize, or election to the presidency of a professional organization.

As the net result of relying on such tacked-on motivational devices, we teach all but a very few top people that they are "not good enough." Consequently, the work experiences which emerge are powerfully motivated but unsatisfying.

"Here I am," said one scientist, "working at the job that I've spent my life preparing for. It's great; I should be happy, and, in a way, I am. It's fun to work in this area, there are endless problems that are challenging, and I know I can contribute to their solution.

"But it isn't what I expected. There's something wrong. I'll sit down at my desk and try to write something, and soon an uneasy feeling inside gets so strong I have to get up and go out in the hall and pace up and down.

"I don't feel that what I'm doing is worth working on. It seems unimportant. I know that it is just as important as what hundreds of others are publishing every day in the journals, but I don't feel as though my own effort is important. I feel as though I ought to have ideas that are better than theirs, but I am perfectly aware that what I'm doing is not outstanding.

"I realized this after my experience with my Ph.D. thesis. I started out with a design that I thought would allow me to make a final and definitive test of the half dozen most important theories in my special field—like the fairy tale about the fellow who killed seven dragons at a blow. Wham! And they'd all be either proved, or done for, and no remaining arguments!

"When it was all over, I found my grand setup couldn't test the theories at all, and I had to settle for writing my data up into an average sort of thesis—good enough, but nothing to startle anybody.

"I see now that, with such work, I *am* about in the middle of my professional group. I know a lot of so-so researchers are doing just that kind of thing, but the thought of being just another passable scientist isn't much reward for all one's preparation and lifelong hopes.

"Sometimes I get lost in pursuing a question that looks interesting. Then it's fun. I forget myself. But when I come back to my everyday self, back comes this old feeling of 'not good enough,' and I start just fussing around in a way that doesn't get much of anywhere—just a lot of busy work that leaves me tired and grumpy at the end of the day."

Blue-ribbon motivation is becoming increasingly inappropriate in proportion as the scientific and technical work that characterizes our society becomes more and more consolidated in massive organizations. Several hundred scientists may be employed in the research laboratories of one large oil company, or on a huge development project. Consider the dramatic campaign to find a polio vaccine that culminated in Dr. Salk's finding a successful protective innoculation. This was a nationwide research effort involving an army of scientists; yet Dr. Salk won the only blue ribbon. Developing a vaccine calls for trying out scores of possibilities, nearly all of which the scientist is pretty certain, ahead of time, will prove to be false leads. It takes just as much training and intelligence to follow up an inadequate lead and to demonstrate clearly that this possibility is *not* the answer as it takes to follow the one-in-a-thousand that turns out to be correct. Any one research scientist in medicine may have worked five or ten years on polio, may then have turned to studying heart disease for another decade, and still later may have spent the same length of time on cancer research. The chances are probably a thousand-to-one against his turning up a single blue-ribbon finding in a lifetime of devoted, imaginative, and well-done research. If he has been conditioned to find his work satisfactions in rewards that he has such a remote chance of getting, his life will be disappointing, even though he may actually play an essential role in a massive team-hunt for polio, cardiac, and cancer cures. We are glad, of course, to see Dr. Salk's brilliance recognized. Our point is that the main motivation for a lifetime of such work should and can rest on a more substantial basis than the possibility of winning blue ribbons.

3. *Oversatiation of major interests.* Pressures to conform and to succeed have another insidious effect. Even when they do not keep us from pursuing our major interests, they tend to produce an excessive concentration on one single activity and tend to have corrosive effects on the emotional satisfactions inherent in this activity.

Professional activities tend to be self-chosen, and when a person has gone into science, teaching, business, or the ministry as something he preferred to do above everything else in life, it is hard to imagine that doing it could have harmful side effects. In fact, if such activities were limited to a 40-hour week, they wouldn't. But whereas the 40-hour week is standard in working-class lives, the professional and business-managerial groups in our society are fortunate if they have less than a 60-hour or 65-hour week.

Any mother of three or four little children can tell you about satiation effects, though she may not call it by that name. For, in our contemporary kind of servantless middle-class society, where families live long distances from any relatives who could help, and where the husband typically is gone from breakfast time until the children's bedtime, the mother may find that she has spent well over 80 hours per week in caring for her children and running her home.

She loves her children. But still it is true that any activity, when engaged in too persistently, tends to lose its interest, except when a person has unusual emotional resources.

The husband, likewise, is likely to report in a similar vein—if he can be made to spill over. If he doesn't complain he may say: "Sure, I work a 60-hour week, but I love my work, and you have to do it to get ahead. Hard work never hurt anyone!" But satiation effects are an impartial foe. They do not corrode only the harassed wife and leave her husband untouched, though he usually isn't aware that satiation is a factor in his professional problems. For satiation effects appear as qualities of the man's work and environment: things seem to go unaccountably slowly; problems seem larger and more difficult; his own abilities seem small in relation to taxing requirements; he becomes irritable and antagonizes people whose good will he needs. Over-all, the net effect is reduced achievement instead of the resounding success he looked forward to. His solution, though, is to work harder. If things aren't going right, the obvious fault must be that he isn't trying hard enough! Understandably, the resulting increase in satiation effects operates to magnify the already considerable emotional dearth that resulted from having pushed aside many other interests in order to devote himself completely to his job.

4. *The neglect and belittling of concrete perceptual experiences is another source of emotional poverty in our culture.* Modern Western society is highly advanced in technology and scientific understanding. Our culture has laid stress upon abstract knowledge and standardization. These things have some real emotional value for us, and they are not solely the servants of material ends. But they fall far short of serving our emotional needs in a full way. Some of our emotional experience must spring from things around us that impinge directly, immediately, concretely upon us, that are perceived as having color, warmth, and vitality and are likely to be down-to-earth—as the play of color and form in the fireplace, the feel of the winds, and skies, the alternation of lights and shade in a forest, being surrounded with friends.

There is even a lot of tacit disapproval of living in the present in our middle-class culture. It is as if we had some leftovers from past religious prohibitions against investing too heavily in present earthly pleasures. Of course, we need abstractions, we need to have a future orientation, and so on, else we would be a nation of sensualists bent only on immediate pleasures. But we also ought to be able to shuck off regularly all these necessaries and immerse ourselves in fuller realities and concrete joys of life.

5. *Emotional poverty may spring from the failure to develop the neural mechanisms for some satisfactions.*

A vacationing family had climbed up to a beautiful alpine lake. After some hours spent enjoying this unusual spot they met another visitor, a tired-looking mother whose small child was sleeping exhausted on the grass nearby. The two families fell into conversation.

They were camping, the woman said, and she made it plain she had had enough of it. "I haven't had a bath for six days," she said in disgust. "We've never camped before. We read about it in magazines, and it looked like a lot of fun—something everyone should do—so we bought a lot of equipment and came up here. It's awful; it just isn't any fun at all!"

Here, potentially, were rare enjoyments and not one of them had been realized. Everything turned out sour. Why? The answer was that this woman just didn't have the necessary habits to enjoy camping. Those require a certain kind of childhood, some training in perceiving natural beauty, a few outdoor skills, and a breadth of experience that ranges beyond life in city streets. We can see that an airplane pilot needs years of technical training, but, perhaps like this woman, we tend to suppose that one can read in a book about some interesting activity and at age 30 promptly go out and start enjoying it.

It is amazing how we seem to assume that our children will grow, without any special help on the part of the older generation, into adults who will have the motivational mechanisms for a resourceful and satisfying adult life. Here is the family of another vacationer whom one of the writers had a chance to observe:

They were a family of three staying in a cottage among the mountains for several weeks. The father was a college professor. He and his wife were never seen outside their cottage except as they emerged in order to get into their car periodically, drive into town, and back again.

On the first day, their 11-year-old boy appeared outside carrying three toy rifles, a cartridge belt, and two cap pistols. Each day he appeared, armed to the teeth, and proceeded to play, as best he could, with his guns.

Across the road there was an inviting-looking livery where even small children could learn to ride horses. There were plenty of fishing streams nearby, a lake, beautiful trails. Never once did the father take his boy out to sample any of these interesting activities. The boy happened to be playing among rocks that would have been fascinating to collect and study, with trees and flowers around that fairly begged to be observed in their beauty. The general scenery was awe-inspiring, or so it seemed until perhaps we chanced to remember that it isn't the eyes that see, but the habits of the beholder. As far as we, his neighbors, could see, those five guns were the sole interest that boy had.

What will such a boy be able to find deeply satisfying at age 30 or 40? What is he prepared for except to sit and watch some of those 588 killings and other crimes that the National Association for Better Radio and Television workers tallied in one week of watching seven TV stations?

How are people to be made less blind to their responsibilities for helping their children to develop, to *grow*, psychologically? Rich positive motives do not simply unfold by themselves without somebody's making the effort to care about them, to implant and foster them. The development of strong and diversified motives is one of society's main tasks and it requires stupendous efforts in comparison with what we as a people have done in the past.

Summary

Somehow or other, we need to develop our modern life so that we can walk through life with a combination of greater dignity and greater enjoyment. The world is an infinitely rich place, and our experiences of its physical, intellectual, social, and emotional opportunities should make living a really great experience. We need to learn respect and love for our friends, our husbands or wives, our children, and our associates for being what they really are, for the ultimate values that they embody. But too often, instead, our home life becomes a matter of pale convenience-relationships, with far too much friction and faultfinding mixed in. It is not as often as it should be a warm, affectionate, radiant center in our lives, a place where a certain spirit and quality of relationships has been so built up that it can be counted on for warmth and beauty of affection and the mutual sharing of significant experience. Instead, we lapse into dull routines, like creatures on a treadmill. We treat the materials of life as though they have no potentialities for variety and excitement and color—as though the meaning of existence, as in the life of clams, is only security and safety. We do not dare reveal our capacities for emotional responses and interests. Our too-common motto is, "We have got to live in terms of getting and keeping the mechanical externalities of urbane existence—to hell with the rest!"

The consequence is that our peacetime life lacks stability and depth. The world topples into war because it resembles a pyramid standing on its point instead of on its base.

We know that we need adequate food and shelter and protection from insecurity, and we assume that if we have these things we shall be content. But material satisfactions serve to fulfill only some of our motives.

Modern life overemphasizes these material values and underrates the human being's hunger for emotionally rich experience. Out of the emotional poverty of our lives seems to come not only directly-experienced discontent, but also indirect manifestations such as excessive demands on our closer human relations, pseudo-hungers for food, excessive craving for material goods, excessive dependence on sexual satisfactions, outbreaks of violence and war, and many other evidences of human failing.

The reasons for the emotional poverty of modern life include our lack of respect for individuality, our lack of appreciation of the value of concrete perceptual experiences, our dependence on competitive motivation that tends to draw people away from their intrinsic interests and leads them to a precarious quest to outdo their fellows, our tendencies to oversatiation of some of our own best interests by one-sided life programs, and our failure in general to develop those habits that bring the greatest satisfaction. It is clear that, if we are to solve many of the problems of emotional poverty and richness, we must have a more adequate understanding of personality development in childhood. It is to this topic that we turn in the next chapter.

Perhaps, at the conclusion of this chapter, we ought to make plain that we are not suggesting that everyone ought to go off on one-man canoe trips across the Atlantic Ocean, as Erich Lindemann did in 1957. A person sitting quietly under a fir tree in a dripping rain may be having just as rich an emotional experience as one who is mountain climbing, provided he has learned how to make it so. Even the feel of soapy dishwater and the experience of filling up the dishrack with clean sparkling glasses can be strongly satisfying to some persons. But the basic idea of what we are trying to say is that man must somehow find the means to make his life more emotionally significant and vital than it commonly is today. Man is a powerfully emotional creature. He is inevitably hungry for emotional richness of some sort or other. If a culture does not help those who live in it to get an emotional richness in ways that are valuable and growth-promoting, individually and socially, then that culture is hardly likely to achieve the stability and health it needs in order to survive.

CHAPTER 10

Personality Development in Childhood

THE DEVELOPMENT OF personality continues all through a person's life. There are several important reasons, however, for taking a special interest in how personality develops in childhood, particularly in early childhood. As we will see in the later chapters, it is easier for many reasons to establish good personality habits in the first place than to change bad ones later. The preschool period is a time, furthermore, when parents have a proportionately greater measure of responsibility for the personality development of their children than they will have at any later time, since the older child comes increasingly under the influence of his age-mates, his teachers, his favorite TV programs, and many other things. Though parents never cease to be important for what they do and do not do for the child, the period of really special opportunity for them is early childhood. The subject of the present chapter is therefore close to some of the greatest practical responsibilities for influence upon personality and character that most people will have. This is the field where they have to function as experts, as persons dealing responsibly with very significant problems.

Childhood is the period when the fundamental characteristics of personality are being laid down. For this reason, if we want to understand personality in general, or especially as it appears in adults—even if we are not interested in children as such—we can hardly get such understanding without learning more about the period in which the most decisive influences upon personality development are at work.

Both motivation and learning occur from birth on

In some ways, the most striking fact about the newborn human infant is inequality of development. Thus, in comparison with the body proportions it will have later, the infant is grotesque (or, to avoid being too egocentric, let us say that from the standpoint of the infant, the *adult's* bodily proportions are grotesque). The infant's head is bigger in diameter than its chest. The legs and arms seem awfully small and shriveled by comparison with what they will be later.

There are marked inequalities also in the baby's capacities for different sorts of responses. He can sneeze, yawn, and swallow about as well as he ever will be able to. If you get him to close his hand over a small stick, you will find that he can swing by one hand perhaps for even as much as a minute of two, which is something that most adults cannot do (in fact, one of us, who thought he was in pretty good muscular condition, just tried this himself and found to his amazement that he couldn't manage more than about five seconds with his right hand and couldn't do it at all with his left). When it comes to the complex co-ordinations required for nursing, the infant can make 70 or more sucking motions per minute, interspersing breathing reactions in between these, and managing very precisely to send the air down one passage from the throat and the milk down the other. Unless it was prematurely born, the newborn infant is fairly well equipped with temperature-regulating mechanisms. But in some other ways he is fairly helpless. He isn't able to roll over from back to stomach if he gets uncomfortable in one position and won't be able to do so for another five or six months. It will be about equally long after birth before he can reach for anything. Even several months after birth, if a rattle held before him excites his interest, all that he can do is to make some excited movements, such as arching his back and kicking or slashing with his arms. Until six weeks or so after birth he won't be able to make any sounds except when he cries. What his visual and auditory perceptions are like, it is hard to say, but it is a fairly safe bet that they are extremely primitive at first, so that his mother's face against a dark background may produce a fuzzy, indistinct bright patch against a darker surrounding area; but that would be about all.

There is little capacity for learning soon after birth and there are strong anatomical reasons for this limitation. At birth, even though all the nerve cells of the brain are present, a great proportion of them are still merely little rounded cells without the long, branching arms that reach out to permit the passage of nervous impulses. The "lower" parts of the nervous system, those concerned with reflex activities, are mostly well developed, but the part of the nervous system that particularly is involved in learning and in complex perceptual processes is still markedly immature at birth. And, of course, most of the knowledge and understanding that we take for granted in adults is not included in the baby's repertory.

Suppose a mother has been told, somewhat unwisely, that she ought to stick to a strict schedule of feeding, and suppose her baby has taken too little food at one feeding and awakens and starts to cry an hour or so before the next scheduled meal. The mother, obedient to the pediatrician's recommendation, tells him, "Now, little boy, you had better not cry; it won't be time to feed you for an hour yet." Out of all this, what does the infant, several weeks old, experience? Merely some blurred sounds, blurred patches of light and dark shifting around, plus a very powerful and uncomfortable feeling of hunger. Consequently he does the one thing that he can do before food is given him. He yells. Even at four or five months, if the same thing happens, all that he can do is yell. At that age he may hear sounds in somewhat less-blurred ways and be able to distinguish more precise visual patterns around him, though perhaps not yet precisely enough to see the difference between one person and another. And he perhaps gets some additional feeling of frustration because he can recognize that the adult whom he sees could provide him with food, but doesn't. Muscularly, he still can't do much except yell, but he does have a powerful process to support that type of behavior. In fact, it may be that he will never ordinarily be as hungry later in life as he is as a baby. He is growing with terrific speed—ordinarily doubling his birth weight in the first five months and tripling it the first year. He will never grow as fast again and never again need food so keenly. Therefore, even though his development may have been leisurely in some respects, it has provided him not only with reflex mechanisms for sucking, swallowing, and yelling, but also with the motivational mechanisms that guarantee his use of these reflex mechanisms when they should be used.

Consider another motive that can operate early in life. Some friends of one of the authors had a good chance to observe the operation of this motive when their first baby was about two months old. The baby started to cry at about 10 o'clock in the morning and gradually picked up more and more volume. They fed the baby, but this stopped the crying only momentarily. At first the parents felt that there was no special reason for concern, but when they tried to correct all of the conditions they could think of and the baby still kept crying, they became more concerned. Late in the afternoon they called their old family physician. "Well," he said, "all babies cry a fair amount; it's good for them, gives them exercise. But, if he cries too long, give him some paregoric, and that will soothe him." Somehow or other this sounded to them like rather outdated advice, and they refused to follow it. In the evening they called a young pediatrician they had heard of. "No," he said, "a baby should not cry indefinitely like that; I'll be out." Arriving at the house, he sized up the situation, reached under the covers and felt the baby's feet, lifted him out and held him near a fire that was burning in the fireplace, and in about a half a minute the baby was sound asleep. That was all that he did, except to send them a substantial bill to help underline the suggestion that babies like to be comfortable; that was all that was needed.

It would be good if we had vastly more research information about what motives are ready to function innately in human infants. These motives are of tremendous importance for the life of the infant and for his later learning. The motives of an organism give it one of its most fundamental characteristics, as we have already considered in Chapter 7—

namely, the characteristic that an organism operates in self-regulating ways, rather than like a typewriter that waits until the environment does something to it to make it respond. With an infant, it can be easily shown that the sucking response is not produced just by the touch of the nipple on the baby's lips or by the taste of milk in its mouth. The baby has to be hungry to take food, and when he has taken as much as he should, no amount or urging and encouragement will make him take more. Long ages before adults ever figured out how many ounces of milk they thought a baby ought to have, the motivational mechanisms of hunger were on the job to take care of this decision.

A splendid piece of research by Dr. Harry Harlow was described by him in his address as president of the American Psychological Association in 1958.[1] Harlow chose to work with infant rhesus monkeys because he wished to explore their behavior under a great variety of conditions. For instance, instead of leaving the baby monkeys with their real mothers, he substituted two kinds of artificial mothers both shaped very roughly like the trunk and head of a monkey. One type of mother was covered with sponge rubber and with soft, furlike cloth over that. The other type of mother had only hard wire netting stretched over a framework similar in shape to that of the "soft" mother. The wire-netting mothers were something that the baby monkeys could easily climb and hang onto but, needless to say, they were not a very cozy type of mother. The infants got their food from a nursing bottle placed in the upper part of the trunk. Sometimes it was a wire-netting mother that provided the food for the infant, sometimes the terry-cloth mother, sometimes both.

The main thing that Harlow found was that the infant monkeys formed strong attachments, not to the wire-netting mother even when it was the only one that fed them, but to the terry-cloth mother. Their preference showed up most dramatically when the monkeys were put into a small room with a lot of possible play-objects scattered on the floor around them. In this strange (and hence for the monkeys somewhat frightening) environment, the baby monkeys would show a great deal of active exploration provided the terry-cloth mother was in the room, too, so that they could cling to her at first and occasionally return to her. But if only the wire-netting mother was present, the tiny monkeys would huddle on the floor, screaming and crying as though in terror, or try desperately to achieve some reassuring sort of contact with the wall of the room or with some other object.

Harlow concluded that a chief motive in infant monkeys is a "contact hunger." This was hardly satisfied at all by clinging to the wire framework, even though this was rounded roughly into monkey form, but did

[1]H. F. Harlow, "Love in Infant Monkeys," *Scientific American*, Vol. 200 (June, 1959), pp. 20, 68-74; and H. F. Harlow, "The Nature of Love," *American Psychologist*, Vol. 13 (December, 1958), pp. 673-685.

seem to be satisfied in high degree when the sponge-rubber padding and the soft texture of the terry cloth was added to the same basic framework of the artificial mothers.

It cannot be concluded with certainty that human infants have a similarly strong contact hunger, though observations do seem to suggest that this motive is present in human infants at least in some degree. Monkey life is such that the babies must cling to their mothers while the mothers are climbing around in trees, and it is altogether possible that genetic selection has developed in monkeys (by elimination of those that fell off, to put it simply) a type of monkey that innately has a strong craving for contact with something like the mother's body (and not just with rocks or tree trunks), whereas this same craving may not be very strong in human infants. After all, we do know that there are different innate cravings in different species. Ground squirrels love to store nuts; pigs are equally interested in food but show no such tendency. Goslings are frightened by the sight of a hawk soaring overhead; some other species of birds have no such fear. Some breeds of dog seem almost insatiable in their enjoyment of having someone throw a ball or stick that they can retrieve and carry back to the thrower, but this is not true of all breeds of dogs. But, nevertheless, Harlow's work does provide a significant illustration of the point that the behavior of young mammals is to be understood partly in terms of their powerful innate motives.

Motives in human infants

We have spoken of a few innate motives of human infants—motives related particularly to the needs for food and warmth and perhaps also for some degree of bodily contact such as appears in infant monkeys. Thirst is another motive that might be mentioned; pain is another. Evidence of innate fear, too, is shown when a neonate human infant is subjected to a sudden loud noise or the sudden removal of support.

From birth on, in human infants, there seems to be another very important motive, too, even though it is vague and diffuse at first, and one might well ask whether it operates originally as a "motive" or merely as a matter of general physiological condition. As Margaret Ribble and some other authors have pointed out,[2] the human infant at birth is not altogether ready for an independent existence, even in some respects where we ordinarily would not have suspected his limitations. The circulation of blood and lymph through the body, for instance, is accomplished not only by the action of the heart, but also by virtue of body movements

[2]Margaret A. Ribble, *The Rights of Infants* (New York, Columbia University Press, 1943), pp. xi, 118; and Margaret A. Ribble, "Infantile Experience in Relation to Personality Development," in J. McV. Hunt, ed., *Personality and the Behavior Disorders* (New York, Ronald Press, 1944), Ch. 20.

and contractions and relaxations of the big muscles of the body. When an older child or an adult is sleeping, and the circulation gets congested in the muscles on which he is lying, the individual can turn or roll over and get things going well again in those parts. But the infant on his own responsibility gets less of such movement than seems to be needed for adequate circulation. Before birth, this was not the case. The foetus gets a lot of movement just from the activity of its mother; furthermore, since the unborn infant is virtually floating in the amniotic fluid, it can turn and twist and move in a vigorous fashion that any mother can tell about, and that can be observed externally as well. After birth, there is a big reduction in the amount of movement. What Ribble found, even though her observations were rough in some respects and need to be repeated, is that infants who are left in their cribs with a minimum of being held, or rocked, or turned over, tend to show in several ways the adverse effects of this loss of movement. Some infants who were subjected to a minimum of physical movement tended to become over-tense muscularly but changed to a much more relaxed state and slept better when they received a good deal more physical stimulation from outside. Other infants under minimal stimulation showed frequent periods of markedly stuporous reactions, as had been noted in some earlier experiments aimed at establishing conditioned responses in very young infants.

In addition to the effect of lack of activity upon circulation, or perhaps in good part in consequence of it, Ribble observed also that a program of minimal physical stimulation seemed frequently to produce disorders in two other aspects of bodily functioning of infants—namely, in breathing and digestive activities. With minimal physical stimulation, the breathing tended to be more shallow and irregular than otherwise. The program of minimal stimulation seemed to cause more regurgitation and an inefficient utilization of food. With somewhat older infants, Ribble noted also that minimal outside stimulation tended to induce such behavior as tossing the head back and forth, or tossing the whole body from side to side violently, before falling asleep. It seemed as though the infant, not getting sufficient physical stimulation from outside to satisfy his needs, was forced to provide it for himself.

Some psychologists have criticized Ribble's work because she used the term *mothering* and said that one of the main needs of the infant is a need for mothering. To them, her account seemed like an overly-sentimental interpretation of infancy. Actually, however, it would be difficult to find a less sentimental hypothesis than the proposition that *movement* is one of the main motivational needs of human infants. Indeed, instead of saying that the infant needs *mothering*, we can just as well speak of the baby as needing Plymouthing or Buicking, because its essential need, according to Ribble, is for such physical stimulation as might be given by a ride in a car.

When one of the psychologist-authors of this book first came to Oregon (this was before Ribble had reported her observations), one of his children was about two-and-a-half months old. This child had shown a strong tendency to regurgitate after being fed—even when you burped him carefully after a feeding, put him down softly, and tiptoed away, as like as not a geyser of milk would come shooting out, over the low side of the crib and over everything. When the psychologist's wife contemplated the trip by car to Oregon, she moaned. "Even with a washing machine here," she said, "I can hardly keep up with him; what will we ever do when we have to stop in motels!" But the trip had to be taken. So, a big cardboard carton was secured, padded with blankets in the bottom, the youthful imitator of Old Faithful was placed therein, and off the family went. At the time, it seemed as though some patron saint of travelers must have been taking charge, because there was no regurgitating during the trip and, besides, the baby abandoned his tendency to wake up in the middle of the night for a feeding. But on being settled in Oregon, he reverted to both of those performances, and the only advice that the pediatrician could give was: "Get an old smock to wear when you feed him and just wait for him to outgrow all this. We don't know of anything that causes it; you'll just have to wait."

This is just a minor example, but several different investigators since Ribble have reported observations supporting her proposal that the human infant has a powerful need, both in a physiological sense and in a psychological sense, for such physical stimulation as comes from being picked up, held, rocked, turned over, and so on. This is the sort of program that a fond grandmother of the old school would give just because she would enjoy it. It was the puritanical tradition that anything enjoyed that much by an adult must be bad for the baby; but these various observations do not seem to support the puritanical tradition on this point.

This need of human infants for physical stimulation, it must be emphasized, is not merely a physiological need. Unquestionably it is partly physiological, but the hampering effects of minimal stimulation and the favorable effects, on the other hand, of more adequate physical stimulation seem to be matters of general emotional reaction as well. If this is true, as it seems to be, the conclusion follows that the original influences starting emotional development of the infant in one direction or the other are matters that can hardly be differentiated from physiological processes. It seems that the human infant's nature calls originally for very simple physical factors of stimulation, even though these are not the same physical factors that infant monkeys appear to rate as the highest values in life.

As the infant gets a bit older, some other motives develop that were not apparent at birth. One of the most important of these is the craving for activity for its own sake. We might almost call it a craving to function, using an expression that Hornell Hart proposed. But that term is excessively broad, because the infant does not show a craving to function in ways that are painful to him. However, the infant does want to explore, even at the cost of encountering some pain. He wants to chew on things and find out what they are like in that way. He wants to bang on things and make noises. He wants to creep up and down stairs. If he is given a newspaper he wants to crumple it and tear it and hear all the noise that this produces. He wants to pull all the pans out of the kitchen cupboard and climb into the cupboard himself. Even when he is still unable to sit up, he wants to be where he can watch things go on and hear people talk. When he is being fed he may be more interested in blowing bubbles with his applesauce than in swallowing it. It is as though he says to his parents by this behavior: "You are such materialistic creatures—you think a man lives by food and sleep and safety and that one should never do anything that might make him lose some of these. But you're all wrong; the great thing in life is the poetry of experiencing things. Take these bubbles with my applesauce, or look at the beautiful splashing that I can make with a plateful of stewed tomatoes when I slap my hand into that. These are the great things in life!"

Other motives in the infant are connected with some other aspects of physiological functioning. It seems, for instance, that the baby gets some satisfactions from sucking on things even aside from any need to satisfy hunger—it is as though the organism had been given a double mechanism to help insure that it would be sufficiently interested in taking nourishment. The baby probably also gets some satisfactions out of the activities of urinating and defecating, though it is likely that the psychoanalytic theorists have greatly overstated the importance of these satisfactions. The older types of toilet training tended to make infants very self-conscious about their excretory processes, because parents attempted to force infants to learn control of these within the first year of life, despite the fact that this is a difficult requirement and the child is not ready to meet it with reasonable ease before he is 18 months old, or older. The traditional methods of training could hardly have been more skillfully devised to make excretory processes of major emotional interest to infants, as when a suppository was used every day that a baby did not have a bowel movement at the expected time, and when punishment or praise depended upon the baby's being able to make the fine discriminations of time and place that the parents were trying to insist on. Except when there are such rigid training conditions, however, it seems that the infant takes only a very transitory interest in his excretory processes. Something of the same sort shows up later when the child is several years old, for then it often seems that the chief difficulty connected with his toilet habits is to get the two- or three-year-old to desist from other activities long enough to go to the bathroom. Of course, the psychoanalytic interpretation of this matter has been that the small child actually has been magnifying his satisfaction from excretory sensations by all of his stalling techniques. The simpler and better interpretation, however, seems to be that excretory pleasures are not really major satisfactions or anxieties for the small child unless an overhasty and oversolicitous program of training has accentuated his natural degree of interest in, or concern over, such experiences.

Another motive that may operate only in minor ways, or that, on the other hand, may become really a major problem for the child, is the motive of anger. The child inevitably runs into some situations which he perceives as attacks by others, and to these he can respond with aggressive tendencies about as powerful as any of the rest of his motivational potentialities. Sometimes this arousal is only brief. One of the writers remembers witnessing an instance of this when an older brother interfered with the activity of a nine-months-old child as they sat side-by-side on a bench at the kitchen table. So quickly that the startled older boy could not dodge, the baby stuck his head out and chomped down on his brother's cheek with all eight of his teeth, and bit so hard that the marks of every one of them could still be seen a day later. The small child is a part of that large array of nature which has survived partly because it has the potentiality of fighting back and defending itself if and when this seems necessary. The motives of resentment and hostility can operate instantly and can develop tremendous strength under some circumstances.

How learning modifies the motivational life of the child

One of the greatest mistakes that could be made would be to imagine that just because there are powerful innate motivational mechanisms in the infant, the operation of these motives continues to be a matter solely of the innate mechanisms. This is not the way that human development proceeds. Instead, with functioning, or with the lack of it, the innate mechanisms get modified in lesser or greater degree and thereafter exist only as modified. In fact, this is what we ought to mean by the term *habit*—habits are "more or less modified innate mechanisms."

Thus, as Kai Jensen showed in a very careful study of infants of only a few days of age,[3] the infant will stop his sucking movements if he finds that the temperature of the milk lies above or below a relatively narrow range. No ice cream for him! But quite a bit later he will enjoy cold foods and, as an adult, he may insist on having his coffee or tea so hot that it will almost take the skin off the inside of his mouth. He didn't

[3]Kai Jensen, "Differential Reactions to Taste and Temperature Stimuli in Newborn Infants," *Genetic Psychology Monographs,* Vol. 12 (1932), pp. 361-479.

start wanting it that way, but his innate motivational mechanisms with regard to the acceptable temperatures of food get changed.

At first, too, there are only a relatively few tastes that seem good to the infant. But having been started on very small amounts of different foods before he is a year old, he learns to enjoy the taste of orange juice, egg, and nearly every other ordinary food. If he is fed cod-liver oil with a spoon, he will even insist on licking the spoon, much to the mystification of his parents. If he is fortunate in the way he is dealt with, he also learns to enjoy resting and going to sleep. Such things change from "mere happenings" to things that feel good and are sought out. He learns to enjoy pleasant bodily contacts with others. He learns to enjoy different sorts of play. He learns to enjoy doing things in the ways he sees others doing them. In mentioning this last, however, we are jumping ahead into a somewhat later period.

Let us go back now and speak of what is probably the first important motivational learning of the infant. As we have said, this is probably a learning of just general emotional feelings of well-being and happiness—or of discomfort and restlessness—that depend on the presence—or absence—of such things as food, warmth, and the conditions that Ribble described as mothering in the early weeks and months after birth. We do not mean that the baby shifts over entirely to a dependence on learned cues in this matter in these early months and does not depend also on a continuance of the simple physical realities from which such habits started. But the experiences of being held and moved have more than merely a temporary physiological and emotional effect. They cause a beginning of personality development of one sort or another that might, indeed, be reversed later, no matter which way it started, but that would proceed most easily and happily if the environmental factors were favorable from the start.

We need to recall that, as we said in Chapter 7, most motivation is not a matter of the operation of innate biological mechanisms that can be only slightly modified, at most, by learning. There are some such mechanisms, of course. The reflex mechanisms that compel us to breathe, for instance, are probably only slightly modifiable by learning. The same seems to be true of the mechanisms that govern the changes of size of the pupils of our eyes, judging by the difficulties that several experimenters have had in trying to establish conditioned pupillary reactions, trying to teach different individuals to enlarge or contract the pupils of their eyes when some signal was given.

The fact that some mechanisms are fairly inaccessible to modification by learning does not prove, however, that all or even most of the innate motivational mechanisms are thus inaccessible. Most of the motivational life of the small child, in fact, shows a great deal of development as time goes on, partly as a consequence of physiological maturation, but primarily because of the development of the perceptual-and-emotional mechanisms by learning.

For example, the very small infant does not react differently to his mother or to some stranger who holds him in some comfortable way. But by an age of about 4 or 5 months the child commonly will have learned to differentiate familiar persons from strangers and will respond fearfully to the latter. Particularly if the child has not had much diversity of experience, its emotional responses of security and confidence will be tied very strongly to a limited setting.

Working in England with children of three or four years of age, Anna Freud and Dorothy Burlingham[4] encountered such effects during World War II. In the case of small children who lived in areas subject to frequent bombing, it had been thought that it would be best to relocate such children in safe rural regions, placing them for the time being with foster families. But, instead, it was found that generally it was emotionally disastrous for such children when they were suddenly removed from their usual physical surroundings and usual family contacts and placed in such other settings, no matter how kind and conscientious the substitute parent-figures were. Anna Freud and Dorothy Burlingham found that such transfers could be wisely made if the mother went along with the child for a short span of days and then gradually retired to a less conspicuous role as the child acquired a sense of security in its new setting. But these psychologists were forced to conclude that, except as this was possible, children three or four years of age were much more upset by such transfers to areas of safety than they were by all the uproar, confusion, and danger that they experienced through bombings in their familiar environment.

Any such emotional development, however, must not be understood as merely some tying of innate emotional mechanisms to particular stimuli. As we suggested in Chapter 7, the mechanisms of emotional functioning are perceptual mechanisms and are profoundly modifiable by learning. Thus, the child's enjoyment of music is not to be understood as a matter of the operation of some "pleasure center" that can come to be activated by more complex patterns of sound. The development of enjoyment of music is a case, instead, of the development of neural mechanisms that originally existed only in very crude and primitive form. The same seems to be the case with the child's development of enjoyment of physical exercise, of affection and friendliness, of feelings of adequacy or inadequacy, of play interests, and of all the other main emotional processes.

[4]Dorothy Burlingham and Anna Freud, *Young Children in War-Time* (London, George Allen & Unwin, Ltd., 1942), pp. 1-81.

Learning in the small child, its main features, and how these affect the course of personality development

There is a curious double character to the learning capacity of the small child, especially in the period from about one year to five or six years of age. On the one hand, during this period, the small child is an exceedingly capable learner. He can learn a host of things that adults can learn. The most amazing demonstrations of this ability occur when small children are taken to a foreign country and are thrown into surroundings where they need to learn a new language. They greatly surpass their parents in the speed with which they acquire the new vocabulary and in their pronunciation of the new tongue. No one who has ever seen this marvel would speak belittlingly of the learning capacity of small children!

But, on the other hand, the small child is handicapped in many matters because he does not have the background of related knowledge that would help him respond realistically and appropriately in many situations. Consider the following example:

For quite some time a family had been discussing a trip they were planning to make from Pennsylvania to Florida. The three-year-old in the family asked repeatedly where "Florida" was. The parents and older children did their best to explain. One day the boy drove a short distance to another house with his parents. Upon entering it, he asked, "Mummy, is this Florida?"

This child had had some actual experience of long trips. When he was two-and-a-half years old, he had traveled by car from Oregon to Pennsylvania. In spite of this real experience, he frequently asked, in the weeks after the trip, whether he could go and play with Nicky, an Oregon playmate. He seemed to think that Nicky must live a few houses away.

In other much more immediate matters, the same childish difficulties showed up. When he was five years old, he received a letter in the mail before his father came home to lunch.

"Daddy!" exclaimed Billy, in a tone of suppressed excitement, "I want to whisper a secret to you!"

The father leaned over toward Billy. "If you want to keep it a secret, let's wait until after lunch. If you try to tell me now, everyone else at the table will hear you."

"That's all right," replied Billy complacently. "They already know." He then proceeded to whisper the secret about his having received a letter.

This sort of difficulty in grasping concepts of distance and other complex concepts leads to a good many special emotional problems in the small child. He can form many concepts regarding dangers in his world, even in cases where the danger is not actually real, but his concepts of how to protect himself against these dangers are often most inappropriate. Thus, after the above-mentioned family went to Florida:

The little boy awoke one night and called out in fear, "There are crabs in my bed!" The father reassured him that there were none. He turned on the light, and they looked. No crabs. "But still, they *might* come in my bed," the boy insisted.

"But the crabs are way up at the end of the island where we were yesterday. It's seven miles from here—a long, long way. They couldn't come here. Besides, they wouldn't like it here, they like to be near the water."

"Still, they *might* come in!" was the tearful insistence. The father sat down on the bed. This was not going to be an easy problem, he could see. "Look, son, remember how far we had to drive to get to the place where all the crabs were. Even Daddy couldn't walk that far! A crab couldn't come from there to the cottage here. It's far, *far* away."

"About this far?" inquired the boy, spreading his two hands a foot apart.

"No, no, it's *very* far, you'd even need a car to go there!"

"About from here to here?" asked the child, touching the father's wrist at one point and measuring from there the distance to his shoulder.

Fortunately, the boy's mother, who was listening through the open door, said, "Bring him in here." She put him down between them in bed. He soon fell asleep and was carried back to his own bed.

The following example further illustrates the difficulty a child can have because he does not yet have the background knowledge necessary for making an understanding response.

A small boy, about four years of age, was very cautious about going down into the playroom on the lower floor of the house unless the door into the furnace room was shut. "There might be some tigers in there," he would say. The father granted that it was dark in the furnace room, but he said that he doubted whether there were any tigers there, and that perhaps they might check by turning on the light and poking around in all of the corners. So, they would look. They would find no tigers. "But," the boy would finally say, "You close the door anyway. There *might* be some tigers!"

And why couldn't tigers appear anywhere—don't pictures and voices appear on television out of nowhere?

In other words, if adults want to understand the emotional life of a three- or four-year-old child, they need to take into account the fact that his intellectual processes inevitably are developing unequally in different matters. He is starting to know about new dangers—tigers, wolves, cannibals, fighter planes, burglars, death. He can see the fearful possibilities of these just about as well as his parents can. Perhaps even more vividly. But he is not developed sufficiently to understand the things that give his parents a sense of protection from at least most of the things he is worried about. Such adult security often depends upon abstract considerations extremely different from giving a frightened child security by taking him into one's bed.

These limitations of the child's background explain why it is that personality maladjustments may arise just as readily in unusually bright children as in other children of much more limited intelligence. Psychologists have often conducted studies to discover how much correlation there is between intellectual level and amount of personality maladjustment. The recurring finding is that there is no tendency for brighter persons, on the average, to be either better or more poorly adjusted than other persons. One of the most notable studies in this area was conducted by the psychologist Anne Roe, who made intensive personality studies of scientists recognized as among the leading score or so in the respective fields of biology, physics, anthropology, and psychology. As she has said, summarizing her years of work:[6]

> Scientists are people, not rational automatons. They differ from other people in terms of what they do, in the things that give them satisfaction, more than in terms of completely special capacities. There is nothing you can say about them as persons that you cannot also say about some people who are not scientists.

This type of finding does call for some explanation, however. If personality is rather heavily a matter of generalized concepts, as we have been suggesting, and if some persons, as scientists, show a remarkable level of ability in developing accurate concepts within their professional fields, we also should expect that they would be able to use their high intellectual ability to form good concepts in the field of personality. We would expect that their generalized ideas about themselves, about life, and

[6]Anne Roe, *The Making of a Scientist* (New York, Dodd, Mead and Co., Inc., 1953), p. 230.

about their interpersonal relations would be remarkably sound generalizations, just as their thinking in chemistry or genetics is known to be of unusually high quality. We would expect outstanding scientists, therefore, to be unusually well-adjusted persons. But, instead, while some of them have remarkably fine personalities, these seem to be the exception, just as they are the exception in the general population. In their personality adjustments, scientists seem to be a good cross section of the population at large.

But there are a number of considerations that we need to recognize. First of all, scientists, as scientists, commonly deal with questions that have not been of any special concern to them until they have developed a considerable intellectual background. The small child of three or four years of age is not forming strong convictions about igneous rocks as contrasted with shale and limestone. He meets ideas like these much later in life. Furthermore, a great portion of the conclusions he then accepts come from the carefully screened work of his whole professional field. He has to have a high degree of intelligence, of course, to be able to understand those concepts, but he meets them at a point where circumstances favor sound thinking.

When it comes to personality, on the other hand, many issues are met early in life. Even at three years old, the future scientist may hear his mother ask him, "Why are you so slow and clumsy? Why aren't you like your big brother? You can't ever seem to do things right!" Here he is handed a generalization or an abstract concept by his mother, just as a university student is handed a concept in a course in chemistry. In the first case, however, a generalization or concept comes from the particular personality and prejudices of his parent, rather than from the accepted store of knowledge of a professional group. Furthermore, the concept is handed to him at an age when he has almost no background for evaluating it independently. No matter how high his IQ, there is no likelihood that a child three years old can answer: "Yes, mother, but you aren't thinking in terms of proper age-norms. I may seem clumsy in comparison with my older brother. But I have watched other three-year-olds, and I know that I am not clumsy and slow." He cannot respond in this way. He is forming or accepting abstract concepts about himself which are related to very vital matters in his life, but which he cannot see in perspective.

Sometimes the parents play a part in the formation of unfortunate self-concepts in the child through misguided attempts to be nice to him. Thus, as one of the keenest memories of her childhood, one college girl related that when she was about four years of age, she had wanted to help her mother do some housework. She was an only child, and housework appealed to her as something interesting and intriguing. It actually could have had a lot of value for her by giving her some confidence that she could be helpful and, more specifically, that she had the qualities which later would permit her to carry out the role of a grown woman. Her mother told her, however: "You don't need to help. I can do this work faster by myself. You run along and play and have a good time." Run along and play and have a good time!—the lack of sensitive understanding of the processes of the child's mind kept the mother from seeing that she was excluding her child from the very experience that could have had the values she craved for her daughter.

Another example shows how inadequate a child's intelligence may be to provide sufficient understanding of some situations. One of the writers remembers an incident involving a small child of about 22 months of age whom he had been studying in a learning experiment. The mother of the little girl was all ready to go to the grocery store. It was late winter, and the sidewalks were covered with puddles and melting snow. The little girl, when she saw her mother preparing to leave, came to the door and made it plain that she wanted to go along. The mother told her she couldn't go because she was not wearing a coat and it was cold outside. The child had sufficient language ability to understand this and started to tug at the mother's coat, which was a short leather jacket.

The mother said, "Oh, all right, if that is what you want, you can have my coat. But of course you can't go with me."

Thus saying, she slipped her coat off, put it on the child, and went and got another coat for herself. But the child of course still wanted to push through the door. The mother insisted she couldn't go, because the sidewalks were wet and the child had no shoes on. The little girl, at that, sat down and tugged at her mother's shoes. The mother went through the same ritual again: "Well, you can have the shoes if that will keep you happy; but, you understand, you can't go with me." Soon the child was standing by the door wearing her mother's high-heeled shoes and a leather coat dragging on the ground. Then the same episode was repeated with the scarf that the mother was wearing.

With the child thus arrayed, and still wanting to go, the mother finally said, "Listen, I've told you you can't go; now I can't take any more time with you—I just *have* to hurry to the store. You'll have to stay here."

And so, after all this, she went out the door, leaving the child behind. The child stood at the door, with all this grotesque garb, crying for ten minutes or more before she could be diverted to other things.

The daughter was an intelligent child, for, since then, she has graduated with high standing from Stanford University. If she had been given an intelligence test at the time of this early incident, it is fairly safe to say that she would have demonstrated a definitely high IQ. Suppose it were even an extraordinarily high IQ of 175. Expressed in terms of mental age, this would have meant that she had an MA equivalent to that of the typical child about three years and three months old—enough mental ability to understand what was meant when the mother said she couldn't go because she didn't have outside shoes, or a coat, or a scarf. But not enough mental ability to understand what in the world was going on when, after she had been helped to don the same clothes that her mother had planned to use, and which her mother had said were necessary, the mother brusquely pushed her back and went off alone.

Constructive factors in childhood personality development

Many difficulties, we see, may occur in the course of personality development throughout childhood. Probably no child entirely escapes all crippling influences. Even though we recognize such difficulties, however, this ought not to blind us to the fact that there are also some remarkably powerful constructive factors that operate in childhood in the direction of a healthy, positive sort of personality development.

For one thing, the child benefits from the vigorous urge to explore and to experience. This motive, which he naturally possesses to some extent, can become a major motive under favorable circumstances. It is almost as though, in his behavior, the child asserts that the main purpose of life is to get a deep, extensive, sympathetic knowledge of reality. Some psychologists have expressed this by saying that the child has "an urge to grow." To the authors that seems a bit too vague. Admittedly, it is also rather indefinite to say that the child has a basic craving to experience reality deeply and appreciatively. But we need to have, somewhere in our lives, some ideas of what the fundamental objectives of human life are. A number of thinkers have proposed something like the vivid experiencing of reality as the one objective that can best guide adult life. Such is the thought, for instance, in Joyce Cary's recent book, *Art and Reality: Ways of the Creative Process.* It is only in a simpler form, of course, that this hunger for reality exists in the child. And yet, when you watch any small child closely, you will see him acting as if he had some grasp of this formulation of human purpose, a formulation that has lately taken its proper place in philosophical thought.

For another thing, the child does not shape his life solely by his own experiences. He shows a powerful tendency to take over, from his parents and others, a lot of conceptions about what goals are worth trying to reach. As the psychoanalysts have expressed it, he "identifies" with them. That is, he builds up an urge to model after them, not for the sake of the specific advantages that he sees their conduct brings them, but because he wants to be like them. It is hard for parents to appreciate the depth of this influence. It is hard for them to realize how much the child has been building into his own outlook and into his own goal-mechanisms the qualities and modes of life that he has seen in the parents, and how much stability this imparts to the child's development. The child, of course, does not need to know he is doing this.

The process of development of personality in the early years is probably like that of acquiring a distinctive mode of speech. This apparently goes on without any deliberate intent to learn, and yet it is unquestionably a very complex phenomenon in the development of the child. A person may be impressed with this when he lives in some region where the accent is different from his own, as when one of the present authors taught for a year at the University of Aberdeen in Scotland. He ought not to have been surprised, of course, but it never ceased to amaze him to hear little Scottish children of two or three years of age speaking with all of the special intonations and shadings of sound-production of the typical Aberdonian, even to the burred R's and the "och," both of which impressed him particularly because he couldn't copy those sounds himself. In such instances one wonders, "How could these youngsters ever get these fine shadings of sound! The parents certainly don't drill them in this, and they wouldn't even know how to teach such speech to another person if they were to try. So, where does it come from?" One is therefore driven to hypothesize that probably even before the infant begins to speak, he is forging a general mental picture, or perceptual norm, of the proper mode of speech. It is as if he is getting some idea of goals to be striven for. And, as he struggles to produce speech sounds himself, more or less on a trial-and-error basis, it must be that what he counts as success within himself and hence tends to repeat and keep are those sounds corresponding to what he has heard from others. In this process, too, there must be amazing delicacy and accuracy of perceptual discrimination, because the speech sounds in one part of Scotland or England are frequently different from those of places only 20 or 30 miles away. Yet, somehow, the children learn the slight shadings that give all of this local character to their speech. In matters of personality the case seems to be the same. The parents cannot know at how many points they are creating normative pictures in the small child; nor can they appreciate how much, when it comes to shading of personality as truly as in matters of speech, the child is influenced by what he perceives in the lives of others.

It would be hard to disentangle the effects of these two influences of exploratory interest and of identification in the following series of small incidents from the life of one small child. Fortunately, it is not highly essential for our present purpose that we should achieve this separation. These incidents, taken from a series of notes made by the father, will at any rate drive home the point that childhood has a lot of constructive forces.

One day when seven-month-old Roger was having a bath, he lifted the soft hunk of soap to his mouth and took a substantial bite. He screwed up his face in extreme distaste and pushed the soap away. On the next day he started to lift the soap to his mouth, and then made the same wry face without tasting the soap, and turned his face over his shoulder. But, for several months after this, quite often he would nibble very tentatively on the soap, not making any very screwed-up faces except once when he happened to get some yellow laundry soap instead of the more mild soap used in his bath. With all this exploration, he more surely knew the taste of Ivory soap at nine months —knew more about this property of his environment—than most adults.

At about 10 months of age, he became much interested in a light bulb plugged in a wall socket in one of the bedrooms. Soon after he learned to creep, he climbed toward this bulb one time when it was lit, grabbed the hot globe, and then of course jerked his hand away and cried. For some days after that he would not touch the bulb, though he still would creep toward it and move his fingers to within a few inches of the globe. Still later, he grew more bold. He would reach his hand tentatively toward the globe, hover over it for a while, and then very gingerly bring his hand into contact with it. When the bulb was cold he would then work with it, pulling it out, screwing and unscrewing it, and so on. When it was hot he would jerk his hand away and shake it, but not cry. He did not learn, in other words, that the bulb could be handled unhesitatingly when it was not lit and that it would surely burn him when it was on. But he learned, nevertheless, that the properties of the bulb were different at different times and that these could be determined by exploration, and he had learned pretty precisely what amount of pain was involved when the bulb was hot, so that he did not get a strong emotional reaction from it as he had on his first experience.

When he was 16 months old, he wanted to climb up on a chair when the rest of the family was having supper. His mother brought his high chair and put him in it. He had previously picked up a regular knife and fork from the table. She removed those and gave him his baby fork instead. He pushed it away and turned his face toward the wall of the room and cried as though his feelings had been bitterly hurt. She offered a regular table knife to him, but he pushed it away likewise. Then she offered a big fork. His face cleared immediately and he started to eat with it, though the way he ate was to pick up a handful of mashed potatoes or whatever, push this onto the end of the fork, and then put the end of the fork into his mouth.

At another time, when he was about a year and a half old, I came home one evening and found him fretting hungrily in the kitchen. It was past his usual supper time, but his mother was engaged in the solemn ritual of peeling potatoes, and there was no interrupting her. So, after I got on my old clothes, I encouraged the little 18-month-old to come out with me to see if he would forget his troubles. There was some work that I needed to do to repair some cold-air-return pipes under the house. So I got some tools and started to crawl under the house through one of the little ventilating openings in the foundation. I had wiggled no more than halfway through when I felt something on my legs outside. Turning my head, I saw that the baby was trying to climb in after me even before I could get through the hole. The space under the house was not high enough even for him to stand in, so every once in a while, after he got in, he would sock his head on a joist. But, though his face clouded sometimes from these bumps, he never even whimpered. It was not too comfortable for his knees, either, because the ground was uneven and hard. We worked around for a while, crawled out again, and went in through another ventilating opening. This time again the baby could hardly wait for me to get in first and was climbing in over my back while I was still inching my way through the hole. Altogether it was about half an hour before his mother came and asked me to get him out somehow through one of the openings so he could be fed. Thus, even after another half hour since he started fretting from hunger, his opportunity to explore this new world had made him forget his hunger and ignore all the bumps, and he could scarcely be persuaded to leave.

These are illustrative incidents from a very early portion of the child's life. They do not adequately suggest the complexity of the task that confronts the child later, when he tries to develop an adequate concept of himself and of the opportunities and problems arising in the larger world at school, in his social relations with his age-mates, in his developing concept of his own proper roles as a boy and as a man, and in finding some form of adequate and congenial vocational support for his adult life. There are a host of such later situations in which the child's personality has to keep on developing. But, partly because they are drawn from such an early portion of the child's life, these examples do illustrate the point that the child is not waiting passively for things to come along and happen to him. On the contrary, both because of the craving to explore and experience and because of his identification with other persons, there exist powerful, massive forces within the child's personality that help him to move toward the rich, extensive, and sympathetic experience of reality that we might well describe as the goal of personality development.

Summary

It is particularly important for us to understand the learning of personality characteristics in childhood. This is the period in which the major lines of development are first blocked out. It is the period in which parents have their greatest opportunities and responsibilities. It is the period that we need particularly to understand if we want to understand the sources of adult personality.

A very important factor in the personality processes of the infant and small child is the high degree of inequality in the rate of development of different sorts of function at early ages. Many reflexes are ready to operate with full efficiency at birth. Some motives also are powerfully operative then. But there is little capacity for precise perceptions, and of course any understanding of the more complex features of his environment is something that the child will achieve only with years of learning. Even at four or five years of age the small child will not be able to understand the factors that protect him from dangers of tigers and many other things, though he will have developed sufficiently to understand many dangers that did not exist for him when he was an infant.

The newborn human infant seems to be in need of some considerable amount of physical movement and stimulation from the outside. Such stimulation seems valuable on several physiological scores. It seems also to be conducive to the production of favorable emotional states, and possibly it is the first significant factor in determining the main direction of the child's personality development. As the infant grows, his enjoyment of exploratory activity can become an increasingly important or even the major motive. Some of the motives that have been emphasized by Freudian theory, such as interest in excretory processes, do play some role in the infant's life, though these are hardly major motives when the parents do not forcibly direct the infant's attention to such matters by premature efforts at toilet training. The motive of anger or resentment is another example of an emotional potentiality that may be aroused and developed by certain types of life situations.

Learning operates, not by building up some new mechanisms that then exist alongside of the innate emotional mechanisms in the small child, but by modifying the innate mechanisms. Our best way to conceive of habits is to regard them as those mechanisms, now more or less altered, that originally existed as innate mechanisms. Such modification starts early. At first, the tiny infant will accept milk only if its temperature lies somewhere between rather narrow limits, and he will accept foods that have only a small range of tastes. But learning modifies these likings for food and greatly expands the child's responses on many other matters as well, including his general feeling of well-being or discomfort, his interests in play, and his needs of social attention from others—already a very significant factor in the emotional life of the infant and small child.

The learning involved in personality development, even in early childhood, is often a matter of forming rather general concepts. This does not mean, however, that children of unusually high IQ are likely to have any easier time in developing a sound personality than children of lower IQ. For, no matter how bright the child of two or three years of age, he still lacks the background and perspective that would enable him to discount and reinterpret any faulty methods of care to which he is subjected. The small child does not lack learning ability in some things, as witness the terrific speed of language development of children. But learning at that period necessarily encounters some special problems arising from inequality of background on all sorts of different matters.

Even though the course of early personality development never runs without at least some difficulties, it should be recognized that there are several factors that tend to create fortunate results even at an early period. One of these factors is the tremendous interest the small child easily can develop in exploring and experiencing his environment despite the fact that his explorations may sometimes cause him outright pain. The other main factor is the strong tendency of the child to learn by identification with his parents. He develops a very strong tendency to copy them, not for the sake of any specific advantages to be gained by such copying, but because of his general desire to be like them. Much more stability comes into the child's life from this factor of identification than the parents are likely to recognize.

When we try to understand the personality development of children, we can see that obviously many important aspects of personality development must be understood as consequences of learning. Our earlier discussion of motivation more generally suggested the same conclusion. It seems, therefore, that the phenomena of learning are so important in matters of personality that they deserve a more intensive study than we have given them thus far. Many of the principles that bear on this matter are highly abstract and fairly difficult. It has been best, therefore, for us to reserve them till the later portions of this book. We are in a better position, now, to handle these difficulties, and there is a lot to be gained by coming to understand personality habits, how they are learned, and how they are used, in fairly fundamental terms.

CHAPTER 11

The Nature of Personality Habits

WHILE MR. ROPER was staying in the home of some friends, they talked to him with some concern about their six-year-old son. They were not concerned because he was having difficulty with the schoolwork on which he had just started. He had, in fact, learned to read by himself before he started to school, and his reading vocabulary was so good that he liked to sit and read the *New York Times* with his father. But, they said, they were worried because he seemed so wrapped up in such intellectual things and because there was almost a feverishness about his efforts to learn, rather than a relaxed and easy intellectual interest. "Now on the other hand," they said, "our baby—the 10-months-old—is just calm and happy and relaxed. It is our older boy who is driving us wild."

When Mr. Roper came to the breakfast table the next morning, he found the son already there. "This must be Allen," Mr. Roper said. "Yes," the mother said, "this is Allen. And, Allen, this is Mr. Roper." Allen fixed his gaze on Mr. Roper. As his first words of acknowledgment of the meeting, the boy asked Mr. Roper, "What do you know?" Mr. Roper jokingly parried by saying that he knew that $2+2=5$ and that the boy's father was named Eisenhower. Allen didn't bother to pursue these statements. He seemed less interested in what Mr. Roper knew than in what he himself knew. Soon he was giving his mother a lecture to the effect that when you want to tighten a nut you turn it clockwise and when you want to take it off you turn it counter-clockwise. A bit later he directed another question to the visitor and somewhat mispronounced his name. Both parents corrected him at once, telling him that he ought to say Mr. Roper, not Mr. Rofer.

Later he was playing with dominoes on the dining room floor, standing them in a line so that he could topple over the string of them. After he placed a dozen or so in line, one of them fell prematurely and knocked over all the rest. He complained that some unevenness in the floor had caused this, and then suddenly burst into bitter crying. When his father then came to his help, he switched off his crying with equal suddenness.

Later the same sudden starting and stopping of crying occurred in another situation.

A few months later, when Mr. Roper visited the family again, the father spoke with enthusiasm about his prospects of shifting to a better position in another university several hundred miles away. He remarked that Allen, however, was very upset at the prospect of having to move and was insisting that someone come and sit beside his bed each evening until he fell asleep. They said that if this were not done he would cry for several hours before falling to sleep.

Now, in this case, admittedly, we do not have a complete picture of the circumstances under which the boy had been living. Enough is known about him and his family to know that the parents seemed to be a very friendly and well-adjusted couple who dealt with their two children, in most matters, at least, in rather sensible ways. But in some way that had escaped their recognition, they had been building up in the older child the idea that seemed to dominate his life. He had learned, apparently, that he could get flattering attention from other persons by showing what he knew, though he must be careful as he did this because he would be corrected decisively if he made a mistake.

It is interesting that, even though both parents had talked to Mr. Roper about what seemed to them an almost pathological over-emphasis of the intellect in their boy, they had not restrained themselves from correcting him—and each one did it in turn—when he made the wholly minor mistake of substituting an *f* for a *p* in their visitor's name. In a way, they saw that they needed to help Allen get away from the idea that he had to be perfect in everything intellectual. And yet, instead of ignoring a childish mistake they did the very thing that would accentuate his feeling of need to become perfect on details. Neither the boy nor his parents could have formulated for themselves the fact that there was any such implication in this little incident. It is much simpler, often, for an outsider to see some such relationship than for a person directly involved in it.

The conceptual-motivational character of personality habits suggested by this example

In many of the earlier examples given in this book, the personality habits illustrated were habits of a much more restricted sort. We used those more trivial examples to clarify some important points. But in the present chapter, since we intend to be more precise and systematic in our treatment, the kind of example that we require must be typical of habits that are basically important in human personalities. This picture we drew of six-year-old Allen is just such material. Almost anyone would agree, "Yes, when I refer to the 'personality' of an individual, that is the sort of thing that I am speaking about." Assuming this is the case, let's try to identify the points illustrated in Allen's case.

1. To begin with, we note that Allen's learned mode of meeting life situations consists in a considerable diversity of responses that have one major quality in common. It is not that Allen had acquired an interest in reading, as such, or in how to tighten nuts and bolts. What he had learned was a more generalized habit of stressing those things in which he could show that he was smart. It was a more generalized habit of seeking recognition by displays of knowledge. Pretty definitely expressive of his basic outlook on life was the question with which he acknowledged the introduction to the visitor: "What do you know?" In school, dealing with a group of persons outside his family, he still tackled things in terms of the same basic attitude: "I can be comfortable with other persons if I show that I have unusually high ability; and, vice versa, things are not going to be right, but will be uncomfortable and unsatisfactory, if I can't do this."

Because of the diversity of situations in which Allen responded in this basically similar way, and because of the underlying similarity of his responses despite differences of specific content, we would have to say that Allen's personality habit was in a sense a concept or a conceptual habit, and not something of a limited, concrete character. The kind of perception that Allen used in different life situations was not something relatively concrete and specific to each different situation, but, on the contrary, a more abstract, pervading, generalized, or conceptual sort of perception.

Where the perceptual habit of the person seems to be of this abstract sort, and where it seems to be a really dominant feature of the individual's personality, we might do well to refer to such a perceptual habit as the *basic life construct* of the individual. In doing this we are following somewhat the terminology of George Kelly's two-volume work, *The Psychology of Personal Constructs.*[1] Other personality theorists before him have expressed much the same concept, though in different language. Thus, Alfred Adler spoke of such general modes of response as the individual's *life style* or *life plan;* Karen Horney spoke of them (at least as they appeared in maladjusted forms) as the individual's *neurotic trends;* and Harry Stack Sullivan, another very significant thinker, spoke of the individual's *self-system.*

It might seem as though the term *construct* would hardly be at home in a discussion of personality where our main terms designate processes that are warm, human, full-bodied processes. The term *construct* was coined in the philosophy of science. It embodies the idea that many scientific concepts refer, not to some directly-perceived qualities in what

[1]George Kelly, *The Psychology of Personal Constructs,* (New York, W. W. Norton & Co., Inc., 1955).

has been studied, but to inferred properties—qualities that scientists have come to know only by some more or less indirect, inferential process. However, the root meaning of the word goes back to the idea of "pile up together or set in order together." This is what Allen had done with the different experiences he had had. His life had included such incidents as meeting Mr. Roper, when both of the parents spoke up to correct him before a guest, correcting him merely for mistaking one letter in a name. Out of a multitude of experiences, some with pleasant and some with unpleasant consequences of his actions, Allen had built up a little set of hypotheses or propositions about what good things might be achieved in life and what bad things ought to be avoided, and by what means. Such products of learning are what we will speak of from now on as a person's "basic life constructs."

2. A further thing we can be sure of with reference to Allen's basic life construct is that he could not have formulated it or put it into words. He could not have verbalized the rule by which he was living. He was like a two- or three-year-old who uses such expressions as we mentioned in Chapter 1—expressions like *eated*, *goodest*, and *unfatten*—but who could not possibly put into words the rules that he proves he has learned and uses skillfully.

It is also true, as is indicated by the observations of Adler and other psychotherapists who have taken an interest in this phenomenon in personality, that we adults, too, very seldom have any good insight into our own basic life constructs. The constructs we use may be something that our associates can recognize fairly easily. But the individual himself, often partly because of the subtlety of the basic life construct and often perhaps mainly for self-defensive reasons, does not recognize what he is doing over and over again—what he did yesterday, is doing today, and will do tomorrow. Not only that, but also, if other people attempt to trace out for him the pattern of his life, he will not be able to accept what is said, even though their representations may be well-documented. This is one reason why, in this book, we are speaking of these basic life constructs as personality *habits*. We are not using the word *habit* in an altogether neutral sense (as merely a designation of products of learning, however interpreted); we want to express the idea that personality, even when it is a matter of concepts or constructs, is different in nature from what is pictured in the old rationalistic conception of human life. But we will do better to postpone the matter of a new conception of such habits till the end of the chapter and go back, further, to point out what this particular example of Allen demonstrates about the nature of basic life constructs.

3. A third fact we may observe about Allen's personality habit is that it is a concept of *how to get things by what actions*. This point should be strongly underscored. When we speak about personality as a matter

of perceptual processes and perceptual habits, these terms are only too likely to be understood by some readers as implying relatively passive, contemplative processes. When laboratory psychologists have worked on problems of perception, they have usually selected such examples as those in Chapter 6, and admittedly there is very little action-character in such perceptions. But, as we said in that chapter, those laboratory experiments were devised so that they could conveniently get at certain *special* problems of perception. For a broader understanding of perception, we certainly ought not to let our ideas about perceptual processes be limited by considerations of research expediency. And certainly, when Allen sized up—perceived—his life situations at home and at school, he was not perceiving them as something external to himself; he was perceiving life as something in which "I need to do this and this because it will bring me such and such results." His perceptual processes, or his constructs, put him under terrific pressure to *act*.

Even in the case of much more specific personality habits this same point is illustrated. Thus, one of the writers had a chance to make detailed observations on Kenny, a little boy of about 16 months of age, who had the misfortune to slip down into the bathwater on one occasion and was thoroughly frightened by this. For three months after this mishap, Kenny was willing to get into the bathtub and stay in it for his bath only if he was allowed to remain standing in the water. His parents at first tried to get him to sit down in the tub in order to show him that this was the safer way to take a bath, but when they made attempts of this sort, Kenny would start to scream and try to climb out of the tub entirely; they therefore desisted and let him handle the situation in his own way. Objectively, of course, he was following the more risky course of action. And it is interesting that at the end of about three months, his mode of response rather suddenly changed. During his bath, one evening, he seemed to forget himself and squatted down part way in the water while he pushed a toy along the bottom of the tub. The next day he did the same thing and finally sat down, without any urging, and apparently without noticing it himself. On the third day he suddenly discovered the delights of lying down in the water. For the next week he cried to get into his bath and played ecstatically in it, as if it were an entirely new and wonderful experience. His appearance almost said, "Why didn't someone tell me about this before?"

Thus it can be seen that whether we refer to minor personality habits or major ones, we might well describe a person's characteristic ways of behaving as "conditional beliefs," or "conditional constructs." Consider here that Kenny was not afraid of the bathtub as such; what he saw as fearful was *bathtubs you sit down in or lie down in.* The point illustrated by Kenny's behavior is very important for our thinking about personality habits. These habits are almost never beliefs that our environment will produce certain effects regardless of what we do to it. Instead, our personality habits are like our ideas about fire and electricity—they are beliefs that such things definitely will produce certain effects if dealt with in certain ways, but markedly other effects if dealt with in certain other ways. So, as with Kenny, Allen's main personality habit was not merely a concept, nor merely a concept that he would not have recognized; it was also what we might call a conditional construct.

4. This particular personality habit in Allen illustrates another important point about personality habits through the fact that it was a construct embodying his idea of what is good in life and worth striving for, and regarding what is bad in life and in need of being avoided if at all possible. It is as though Allen had said, "I have found that the possible experiences in life might be arranged along a line or scale or continuum, just as there is a scale of temperature that runs from very cold at one extreme to very hot at the other. I have found that the experiences in life that are awfully good are the ones where I work at things that are hard intellectually and where I can show that I am unusually smart. The more clearly and dramatically I can do this, the happier is my life. But on the other hand, if I fail in such things or have no opportunity to show my talents in this way, then I am sunk. Then things are really bad."

There are several aspects to what we are suggesting here. For one thing, all of this implies that there are no generalized ideas of happiness and unhappiness, or of good and bad, that all persons share. Each person develops his own representation of "possible good things in life" and of "possible bad things in life." He develops these representations from his own particular experiences, rather than finding them as some consequence of some inherent human nature, even though the intrinsic qualities of human life certainly help to determine what his experiences have been. But, for example, one child may have had few experiences of delight in exploring and adventuring; his conception of possible positive values may include only conceptions of rather passive pleasures such as being fed nice food and being held and cuddled by his fond but maybe not too insightful parents. Another child may also have experienced very affectionate relationships with his parents, but in situations where they showed a great deal more respect for his interest in doing things for himself and in developing his own resourcefulness; his conception of "possible good things" may consequently be mostly in terms of possible experiences of a type of social situation where other people co-operate with him as an equal. Still another child may have had many opportunities to discover the possible delights of exploring and learning—not, as in Allen's case, in order to show off what he learned—but for the sake of the intrinsic delight of climbing trees, sled riding, using carpenter's tools and constructing very simple things, collecting sea shells, building dams in streams, and even, as he gets older, engaging in complex intellectual activities. As he develops, therefore, each person comes to respond to life more and more in terms of what he has tasted of the possible satisfactions and pains that he has learned that life can bring. What he has learned may be of great value to him. On the other hand, many an individual is handicapped in his personality chiefly on the score of his never having had enough opportunities to learn about some of the possible satisfactions or positive values that life affords.

When a person thus develops a scale or continuum that defines what he regards as the best possible and worst possible experiences, he will tend to see the great task of his life as one of shifting his position as far as he can toward the good end of this imaginary continuum. It is his basic means for understanding life. But what he actually may need is a reorganization of his perception of life so that he will tend to use a different scale, instead. Thus, Allen's definition of good and bad was not bringing him much happiness or security. He had developed a scale that almost surely would eventually lead him into conflict with schoolmates who would either become jealous or laugh at him for his attempts to show off. He had developed a scale that was disturbing even to his parents, as witness their statements to Mr. Roper about their greater satisfaction in the quiet and relaxed personality of their baby.

In his book mentioned above, George Kelly has spoken of these personal constructs as *dimensional systems.* This is a good expression. Too often we tend to think of concepts as means whereby we divide things into groups, putting plants in one group and animals into another, or warm-blooded animals in one group and cold-blooded animals in another. But Kelly's term *dimensional systems* suggests, instead, this idea of a scale or continuum along which the individual might see himself as falling at any point. Our personality habits usually are of this sort, rather than of some "either this or that" character. Furthermore, Kelly's term, particularly when he elaborates it further by speaking of *bi-polar dimensional systems*, calls attention to the idea that the individual has to be understood both in terms of what he perceives as good things to be attained, and toward the other end of the continuum, as things to be avoided.

In the case of Marty in Chapter 6 we had an example of such a dimensional system. When she was at camp as a young girl, she and the other girls really had been thinking virtually in these terms when they got to talking about what was "the worst possible thing that could happen to a person." Marty had not joined in the discussion, but her thought had been that the worst possible thing would be for a person to lose part of his body. After Bill's accident, this concept was useless, because a person whom she loved had suffered such a loss, and she could not avoid what she had defined as so disastrous. Consequently she could work out a more hopeful program for her life only as she could draw her scale along some new line, so that she could come to say, "The worst thing in life is not a matter of losing an arm or even two arms. This is not necessarily disastrous. And, on the other hand, there are some other things that would be far worse than this, such as being without encouragement and a constructive outlook on life. So, henceforth I rate the success or failure of my life in new terms!"

Out of this discussion we ought not to draw the conclusion that all personality habits are such inclusive habits that we should speak of them as "basic life constructs." Personality habits range from these basic life constructs on down to personality habits of a much more specific sort. With Kenny, for instance, there was no general attitude of fearfulness analogous to his fear of sitting down in the bathtub. If he could have put the matter in words, he might have said, "Most of life is pretty good. But this business of sitting down in bathtubs—that's a special case, and there you *do* have to be careful."

The division of basic life constructs into primary and secondary strategies

Just as Allen did, so every person tends to have some basic life construct, some basic philosophy of life by which he lives for the greater part of the time. This does not rule out, however, the possibility that any person may sometimes show behavior that hardly seems to belong within the same person. How are we to reconcile such variations with the idea that each person has some over-all conception by which he lives?

We need to remember that the individual's behavior is not consistently accepted in each of life's situations. Suppose, for instance, a child is so idolized by his parents that they thrill at every demonstration of his ability and tend to teach him that he will get enthusiastic admiration by acting like a star performer. The parents respond in this way partly because, say, they have certain personality characteristics themselves (such as a basic feeling of disappointment over the way their lives have turned out and a feeling that they should have had a better chance to show what they could do). Again, they may respond as they do because their special relationship to the child makes them see his accomplishments as contributions to their own glory—"He's my boy, after all—he shows what I could have done if I had had his chance!" So the child may build up an expectation, a sort of strategy, that he always tends to use *first* in any new situation. It is as if he says, "This is the way things *basically* tend to be—this is what I usually can count on, and this is what I usually ought to try."

Actually, this particular primary strategy is not well calculated to secure from most other persons the sort of reaction it did from the parents. Other persons get bored or irritated by a boy's egocentric displays. They don't find his remarks witty, as the parents thought they were. They may grant that he knows a great deal, but they feel that talking with him is like talking with an encyclopedia—except that an encyclopedia doesn't force its attentions on the reader, whereas he does. The result is that he may be avoided by others or even ridiculed and teased, particularly at school, where other children see him as a serious contender for recognition and honors.

In such a situation, the parents may cause the child to build up a secondary or auxiliary strategy for handling such disappointments in his social relationships. They may say to him, for instance, "Don't you worry, darling, those other boys and girls are jealous just because they know they aren't nearly as bright as you. Don't pay any attention to them. Or perhaps just tell them the truth—tell them that they wouldn't be acting the way they do if they weren't jealous of what you can do. That will put them in their place even though they won't admit it." Or the child may work out some such adjustment for himself, devising the best possible solution he can for this puzzling sort of situation that does not at all conform to his primary expectations as to what he ought to meet. In one way or another, therefore, a child tends to learn both a primary basic life construct and supporting or secondary ones.

Sometimes both the primary and the secondary strategies are good, healthy ones; sometimes the primary strategy is poor, but the secondary one has good values in it; sometimes the primary one is good but the secondary one is not. With such variations possible, a great many phenomena of personality that otherwise would be very puzzling can be explained by these inconsistent factors within the person.

There are many interesting examples of primary and secondary strategies in personality analogous to those in the above case. One fortunately common strategy, a good deal sounder and more effective than the ones we have examined, is the modest and unassuming strategy of doing as good work as one can, of being conscientious and responsible, of taking real sympathy and interest in other people—which includes giving them a lot of genuine recognition—and of expecting, as the outcome of this, that life will have substantial rewards. This technique is good because it most generally elicits warm feelings from others, and then there is little need for any secondary technique. But we shall have to admit that even such generally sound strategies as this one do not always operate as anticipated. Even a person with such a primary strategy sometimes encounters persons who won't meet him on any reasonable ground, who make excessive demands or accusations, or who behave in some other difficult way. The person with the basically sound primary strategy that we have mentioned is often at a loss when he runs into such unaccustomed responses. He may have no secondary response except to develop angry feelings about those that won't play a reasonable game, or perhaps he responds in some other immature way entirely out of keeping with his usual effective strategy.

There are many persons, too, in whom the primary strategy is much less satisfactory than their secondary one. Such a person tends virtually always to get poor results from his contacts with others, and most of the time he lives in terms of these. But he may employ a secondary strategy of some better sort provided he encounters other persons who won't co-operate, as it were, with his primary strategy and who thus force him to turn to some secondary strategy instead—one that he also is familiar with, but that he does not trust as the strategy to try first in each new situation.

Not that secondary strategies are always superior to primary strategies. The best tactics of the person may be those that he tends to use as his first response in any new situation. But there are other persons—often those who have met a lot of bitter discouragements in life—who have modes of functioning they can use better than they tend to reveal at first. This is a hypothesis that seems to explain the success that has been secured by a few persons who used a rather unusual method in mental hospitals, and used it even with patients who had shown severe symptoms over a long period of time. It is hard to treat such patients patiently, even for most professionally trained workers! It is hard not to have a basically critical approach that superficially, at least, seems in keeping with the severe symptom-picture. However, some psychiatrists and attendants have insisted on treating these patients differently, with a dignity and respect that these patients don't feel even for themselves. There have been some very surprising results.

With such patients, their primary strategy is often one of provoking other people, irritating them, and overtaxing them. Other persons (including ward personnel) then tend to "give the patients what is coming to them"; and now the patients can feel justified in their bitterness and in retreating from the social world. But when a professional worker with such patients refuses to give them what they ordinarily anticipate and what, even without being aware of it, they set out to produce, and instead gives them quite insistently a very different sort of social response, then a secondary strategy that is latent in some of such patients shows itself in some more responsible and adequate behavior.

Other persons not in mental hospitals may not be quite as pathological in their primary strategies, and yet somewhat the same principle might work with them. Perhaps they are those individuals who respond to others in overly guarded and cautious terms, with the result that they make very few friendships on their own account, or even tend to build relationships with others of perhaps a competitive, or perhaps a disparaging, sort, as though they feel that defensiveness should be the primary strategy in every situation. And yet, if another person is warm and insistent enough in his friendliness or interest in them, they may relax, abandon this primary strategy, and turn instead to a secondary strategy with a really large amount of warmth and affection and noncompetitiveness about it. But such persons, if this is to happen, are dependent on meeting others who are virtual geniuses at establishing cordial and pleasant relationships. At heart they may be very interesting persons if only other people can get through their primary strategies and evoke the better set of expectations and strategies held in reserve as an auxiliary system. But such individuals are dependent on dealing with persons who refuse to pick up the wrong cues.

It is, then, evident that even though almost every person has some well-unified basic life construct, he cannot be expected always to act in the same way. His personality must be more generally understood as being based upon a life construct encompassing two or more strategies. He ordinarily acts first in terms of *a primary set of expectations* which he uses in most situations because it is so reliable, since it produces so surely the results that he counts on. But now and then (and perhaps very often) his primary strategy does not and will not yield the effects he believes that it should. In those situations he will be at a loss except as he turns to a second strategy, or even to a third one if the secondary one also clearly fails.

Personality habits—concepts, yet habits

The writers realize that it seems as though, in some respects, they are talking in contradictions. For, on the one hand, they have been urging that personality ought to be understood as a matter of the formation and use of concepts or constructs and the like. On the other hand, they keep using such expressions as *personality habits, perceptual habits, use of habits.* It may seem as though these two modes of speech are hopelessly at odds with each other. Or it may seem as though these terms are being used in senses that are entirely unrelated to the previous meanings that they have had in psychological literature.

Part of the reason for our using the term *habit* is that psychologists rather generally have come to use it in a relatively neutral sense as a broad term to designate any product of learning, regardless of whether the learning occurs in many trials or even in only one, regardless of whether the learning occurs in relatively simple ways or by complex processes, and regardless of the degree of permanence of what is learned.

However, it also is true that we are deliberately using the word *habit* with the thought that the term more or less inevitably will carry some of the popular connotation of this word—a connotation that creates a difference between *habit* and such other terms as *expectation, beliefs,* and *con-*

cepts as these latter terms *ordinarily are understood.* These latter terms ordinarily are tied up too much with our traditional rationalistic mode of thought about psychological processes. Particularly in the field of personality, we need some mode of thought and expression that will get away from the overintellectualistic traditions of everyday thought.

Let us take a simple example of the difference between a habit interpretation and a rationalistic interpretation. One of the writers, about a year ago, shifted to a new typewriter. In several respects, it has a changed keyboard. Thus the tabulator key, which gets used frequently, is beyond the upper right-hand corner of the keyboard where the margin-release key had been on the machine that he had used for the previous twelve years. He knows well enough, in an intellectual sense, that the key in the upper right-hand corner is the tabulator key, and he uses it without hesitation or error when he wants to indent for a new paragraph. But when he comes to the end of a line and needs to press the margin-release key to permit him to type a few more letters, he still, after almost a year of use of the new machine, strikes the tabulator key first, and not the margin-release key that is just below it. This fact (he hopes) does not indicate that he has reached such an advanced age that he cannot learn anything new. But it does at least mean this: To change that habit efficiently, he would have to get some practice in which his hands were actually on the keyboard and in which, furthermore, he clearly *and before the action* perceived what he was doing by reaching his finger to one key rather than the other.

Habits are not things that are changed by noting afterwards (even perhaps a second or so afterwards) that one must have made a certain response and that it did not produce the intended effect. As we mean to interpret them in this book, habits are stimulus-response mechanisms in the following special sense—habits are neural mechanisms that help external stimulation (or some equivalent of this) to evoke responses (in the sense of perceptual processes) that then in turn press for expression in overt behavior. It is risky for us to express this idea as we are doing, because the terms employed in it have been used by so many psychologists with a different meaning from that which we intend. Still it may be helpful for us to risk such misunderstanding by saying that, in a sense consistent with a perceptual interpretation, habits are S-R (stimulus-response) connections. This terminology particularly carries the implication that learned modes of response cannot be modified just by dumping into the nervous system some factual information that is inconsistent with this previously-acquired mode of functioning. Such a procedure would only build up a second habit. *If a habit is to be changed, it must be stirred into active use under such circumstances that, as an actively-operating mechanism, it can be transformed into a perceptual mechanism of a different sort.*

You will remember the incident quoted from Rufus Jones in Chapter 6 —the incident in which, as a small boy, he got out of bed in fear and trembling to reach up and try to find what the light could be that seemed to be shining in the middle of his bedroom when there was nothing there that could shine. Thereupon his long-time habit of fearing so-called "warning lights" was changed, for the reason that he was undergoing a clear new perceptual experience *in a situation where the fear-habit was actively, powerfully aroused.*

This incident is an example of the fact, as we mentioned in quoting it, that even our emotional habits sometimes can be changed in some quick and dramatic fashion. But as the concept of perceptual habits suggests, they can be changed in such a quick fashion only when certain conditions are present that would be suggested as crucial ones by a "habit" interpretation. Such habit-changes cannot occur simply on the basis of the new knowledge that a person might derive solely from a rationalistic interpretation of the situation.

Let us quote another example from the writer's typing habits as an example of some facts suggesting that a habit interpretation is more effective than a rationalistic interpretation in promoting change. On his new typewriter keyboard the key for quotation marks is off at the right-hand edge of the keyboard, whereas on his former machine it was up in the left-hand corner on the same key with the numeral 2. With a lot of use of the new typewriter, the writer has learned to strike the correct key when he wants quotation marks for usual purposes. But he also finds this: when he types a German name that involves the umlaut mark, as with the name Köhler, which requires hitting the *o*, then backspacing and hitting the quotation-mark key, he almost always has been writing *Ko*, backspacing, and then striking the @ mark over the *o*. At first he could not understand why he was doing this. But when he looked at his former machine, he saw there the quotation mark where the @ mark is placed on the new machine. Now, since the mark to produce *ö* requires a use of the same key as would be used to write quotation marks, and since he does not make mistakes in indicating quotations, you would expect that he also would be equally facile with the *ö* problem. Logically, rationalistically, intellectualistically, there should be no problem here. But there is. The stimulus situation of writing quotation marks is different from the stimulus situation of making an umlaut sign, and the change of the one habit has not changed the other.

These are some small examples. But they may help to make clear why we are using the term *habit*, although this may seem, to many psychologists, inconsistent with our effort to interpret psychological processes in perceptual terms. We are using the term with the deliberate intention of suggesting that even the complex and magnificent aspects of human life are to be understood fundamentally in the same terms as the simple typewriting matters described above.

When we look closely at other instances of learning in which muscle activity plays no such part as it does in typing, we find the same phenomena. For example, you will remember our discussion of the habits of faulty direction-orientation that people learn under some circumstances. These and other similar examples involve rather complex conceptual processes. Yet they illustrate the same point that the typing habits do—namely, that what has been learned cannot be altered merely by learning something else logically contradictory to what has been learned previously. The disoriented individual cannot keep himself from thinking a certain direction is straight north even though he sees the sun setting there. What he has learned is just as resistant to new knowledge as are certain long-practiced typing habits.

Our personality learning is of the same sort. A person can learn, after he has grown up, that it is not realistic or sensible of him to hang on to certain emotionalized attitudes he formed as a child. He may see, for instance, that it is poor strategy always to be trying to excel other persons and trying to act the part of a child who has the basic life construct that he must be the center of admiring attention from others. But even though he is aware of an elaborate theoretical set of reasons against doing this, as in the case cited earlier in this chapter, still this does not change the virtually automatic way in which he perceives the practical life situations in which he is involved.

Even though it may seem, at first thought, that we have been using a term appropriate only for the simpler aspects of human life, this is not the case. Even in very complex matters of personality we are fundamentally creatures of habits rather than of such processes as the rationalistic tradition suggests. But in matters of personality we are creatures of perceptual habits, and more narrowly still of conceptual habits, rather than creatures of habits in any sense of specific muscular movements in particular situations. The conception of personality habits that we need, therefore, is one which is drawn both from our traditional knowledge about concepts and our traditional knowledge about habits. We need a new synthesis embodying elements of both of these.

Summary

Personality habits are of all degrees of breadth. Some of them are relatively specific and are related to very particular matters, as in one example cited where a 16-month-old boy became afraid to sit down in the bathtub because he once slipped under the water. Other habits are somewhat more general in character. The personality habits of greatest significance, however, are very widely generalized habits that a person tends to use in an enormous variety of situations in his life.

Such habits are essentially concepts or constructs. In line with the terminology suggested by George Kelly, these may be spoken of as *basic life constructs.* The individual who has such habits usually cannot describe them—or, indeed, even recognize them when those who know him attempt to help him see the pattern of his behavior (the concept) that other people discern so readily. These concepts are basically *conditional beliefs*—not concepts that life situations inevitably will produce such and such results, but concepts that there are such and such ways in which life situations may be handled and that each particular way will be followed by such and such an effect. They are not concepts that classify things into several main categories; instead, they are concepts that portray possible life situations as ranging along a continuum from one end, which it is extremely desirable to attain, to the opposite end, which it is extremely important to avoid. These conceptions of what is good and what is bad, however, are not derived from any innate mechanisms in the individual—each person distills from his own experience his own representation of the desirable values that life may afford and of the possible dangers that he must avoid. The individual tries to handle life situations in such a way that he will reach or stay as near as possible the favorable end of the scale he has worked out. However, these scales or *dimensional systems* sometimes are very unsound as devices for determining what to seek and what to avoid, and the main need of a person may be to arrive at some better basis for judgments in these matters.

The basic life constructs which people acquire tend to be applied in a great diversity of situations. It is important that we distinguish between what might be called the *primary strategy* or *primary life construct* of the person and other *secondary* or *auxiliary strategies or constructs.* Sometimes a person has little occasion to deal with life except in terms of his primary life strategy, because his technique of dealing with life almost always produces the effects which he has come to expect as the most natural and dependable. This does not mean, however, that primary strategies are always sound and appropriate. Through their primary strategies, people sometimes produce unfortunate effects that actually they should avoid in their work and in their relationships with other persons. Every person at times encounters situations which fail to conform with what he generally expects as effects likely to be seen in life. Every person, therefore, needs to be understood partly in terms of his secondary strategies. These, in turn, may be either well adapted or poorly adapted, as the case may be, for handling those emergencies for which his primary strategies have proved ill adapted.

Even though such personality habits are concepts, it is appropriate also to describe them as *habits.* This term has the valuable connotation of suggesting that what has been learned cannot be altered merely by acquiring some new knowledge or habit that is logically inconsistent with those acquired previously. The term *habit* is intrinsically a neutral term covering both the good and the bad regularities of behavior. It does not carry the implication that personality habits cannot be changed. Habits may at times seem like shackles, but they may also liberate us and provide us with the means of living the fullest possible life. The term *habits* suggests that the problem of the development and changing of personality must be understood in terms that are fundamentally different from those that we tend to use as a part of the rationalistic thinking of everyday life. In the next chapter we will look more closely at the question of how personality habits are acquired.

CHAPTER 12

How Personality Habits Are Learned

MORE RESEARCH has been done on problems of learning than on any other topic in psychology. The bulk of technical writing on this subject has been enormous, and much of this writing has been involved and difficult to understand. It is a hard task, therefore, to determine what main principles from this field have outstanding importance for our understanding of personality and to give those principles a relatively nontechnical statement. Since it cannot be seriously doubted, however, that many phenomena of personality are matters of learning, any effort to meet this challenge ought to be worth while.

Some of the examples of psychological processes that we will use in this chapter will undoubtedly be much simpler than the complex phenomena of personality. They are needed to illustrate with special clarity certain principles which are basic for understanding complex personality phenomena. Our focus of interest, however, will remain on the latter, on personality in all its richness.

The general hypotheses we shall put forward are not favored by some major learning theorists. Learning, despite the vast amount of research devoted to it, is still a highly controversial field. We think, of course, that the hypotheses we defend are amply supported by the main research outcomes in the field of learning, but the reader should be warned that not all psychologists, by any means, would agree with this judgment.

Direct percept-elaboration as the simplest kind of learning

To reveal some of the most basic influences that produce learning, let us consider some research findings from Hans Wallach, who is one of the main contemporary experimentalists in the field of perception. In Wallach's experiment,[1] each subject was seated before a screen or shield. He was asked to stare at a rectangular opening in the shield and describe, from time to time, what he saw there. Behind the rectangular opening

[1]Personal communication. Related experiments have been reported in Hans Wallach, "Ueber visuell wahrgenommene Bewegungsrichtung," *Psychologische Forschung*, Vol. 20 (1935), pp. 325-380.

was a slowly moving strip of paper on which there was a zigzag line similar to the one shown in Figure 3. As the subjects stared at this paper, the reports they made at first were merely straight descriptive reports such as this: "I see a strip of paper behind the opening—one that has an angular line on it—and the paper is slowly moving in a vertical direction. I can give more details, like an estimate of the width of the line, or the sharpness of the angles, and so on, but that's all I see."

In other words, the subjects were perceiving what was actually there and what they *knew* was actually there. But as they continued to stare at the line, it changed. They no longer saw the paper as moving and no longer saw the line as a motionless mark of ink on this moving paper. Instead, a typical report ran like this: "It seems as though one end of the line is fastened at the top of the opening and is sliding back and forth, right and left, and the bottom of the line is similarly moving along the bottom edge of the opening. In between, the line is waving back and forth in somewhat the same way that I remember when we kids used

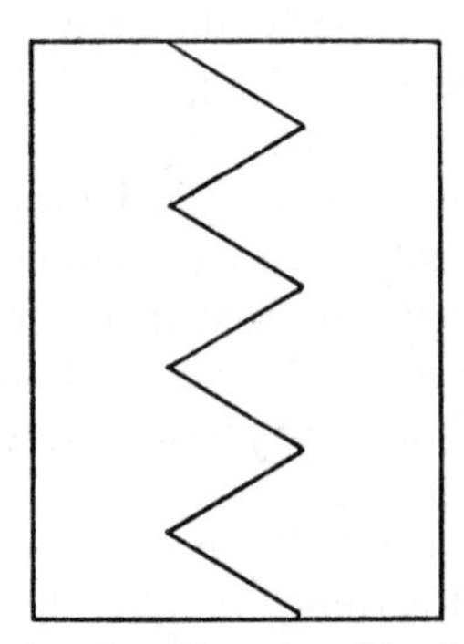

FIGURE 3. *Stimulus Situation Used by Wallach.*

to jerk a rope and sort of make waves go from one person to another. This is very strange."

The subjects knew that the apparatus still consisted of the moving band of paper with the angular line on it; but once they had started to see this wavy line, they commonly perceived it, rather than the "motionless line on a moving strip" perceived previously. But then, as they continued their staring, still another change occurred. The subjects now said that the line had become three-dimensional, rather like a spiral except for its sharp corners, and that it was actively rotating along its verical axis. After they achieved this perception, it became the characteristic perception even at the start of later testing periods, and it became difficult for them to look at the moving sheet of paper and see it in terms of the two-dimensional movement or in terms of their original very literal and reality-bound representation.

Wallach was not asking his subjects to learn anything. In fact, he himself was not thinking of the experiment as an experiment in learning at all. The subjects did not suspect that any changes would be apt to occur or that, if they occurred, they would tend to persist. But if we conceive of learning, as psychologists generally do, as "some change of mode of functioning that comes because of previous responses to stimulus situations and that tends to persist over some period of no practice," we would have to grant that learning occurred in this situation.

Let us note what we see in this example. Four points can be made: (1) Probably partly because of innate perceptual mechanisms and partly because of previous learning, each subject immediately got a first perceptual organization from the stimulus situation; (2) further exposure to the stimulus caused a second perceptual organization to appear (and actually a third organization as well); (3) the achieving of any perceptual organization apparently involved some more or less enduring modification of the nervous mechanisms of the person so that the same altered sort of perceptual organization later tended to occur when the same stimulus was met again; and (4) some perceptual organizations apparently were more stable than others and, once they occurred, tended to persist and to prevent any reverting to other perceptual organizations that originally had been easier to achieve.

Let's take another example, somewhat similar. For this second example we could cite the experiment by Volkmann mentioned in Chapter 5 (page 137), but it may serve our purposes better to take, instead, some observations reported by Heinz Werner, formerly a professor of psychology in Germany, but now for many years a main figure in perceptual psychology in America. The experiments he describes were performed with difficult pitch-discriminations.[2]

Some of these experiments involved successive presentations of pairs of tones that differed in pitch by only a few vibrations per second. Werner found that, at first, the persons who were being tested could not perceive any difference at all between two such tones. But when they were given a chance to listen to a given pair of tones over and over again, the two tones came to be heard as different from one another and, as the trials continued, this difference seemed to become more and more marked.

A particularly interesting part of the work was an experiment that Werner describes as follows:

We have extended these experiments on tonal development to include tones in a musical system which, in its physical relationships, differs from our own. The experimentally-conceived musical system was a series of tones separated by approximately equal intervals (tempered scale); the minimal step was about

[2]Heinz Werner, *Comparative Psychology of Mental Development*, 2nd ed. (Chicago, Follett Publishing Co., 1948), pp. 102-103.

a sixth of the half-tone of our normal scale. As one gradually accommodates himself to the experience of a tonal system constructed out of miniature steps, clearly defined tones, musical intervals, and melodies finally appear from the blurred tonal ground, as if by a process of crystallization.

These experiments by Werner on *micro-melodies,* as he calls them, are basically similar to the experiment by Wallach with the angular line. The only difference is that in Werner's experiment there was nothing except a rather rough, inexact perception originally, in contrast to the sharp and accurate perception with which Wallach's subjects started. But beyond this, what we see is the same four effects: that there was an original perception, that this became modified with further exposure to the stimulus situation, that the modified perceptual organizations were brought about by changes somewhere in the neural mechanisms (they were not merely transitory effects), and that certain final perceptual organizations proved to be more enduring and stable than the others that preceded them at an earlier period in the learning.

One reason for introducting these experiments is that in our everyday thought we have an unduly limited idea of the extent of learning in our lives. We tend to believe that learning occurs only when we are trying to learn. The experiments by Wallach and Werner, however, suggest that learning is a much more general phenomenon. These experiments suggest that the fundamental principle which applies to learning is the principle that whenever conditions produce some new perceptual organization, they also thereby create changed structures within the organism which will tend to facilitate the occurrence of the same perceptual organization under similar but less-adequate stimulus conditions later on.

This first means of learning, as we said at the start of the section, is one that we may speak of as direct percept-elaboration. In the experiments by Wallach and by Werner, for example, the learners did not learn to attach some further meaning to the perceptual cues that were coming to them. Instead, the learning was causing merely a change directly in the perception itself. Werner's subjects, for example, were changed in such ways that they eventually heard the micro-melodies as real melodies rather than as a series of indistinguishable tones. Their neural mechanisms were so changed that they were capable of a more precise and refined response.

Within the field of personality there is a great deal of percept-elaboration learning that we do not appreciate. The life of a mature person consists in part of many capacities that he takes for granted—the capacity, for instance, to hear music in really complex ways, the capacity to hear voices in some richer fashion, and the capacity to perceive scenery in a manner far beyond an infant's capability. A good deal of our development of mechanisms of motivation is of this sort. At birth we had merely the potentialities for development of many motives. These potentialities cannot become realities if we do not meet situations that will produce certain kinds of functioning in us. It is a type of influence which is fairly well suggested in the following statement from Alfred Adler:[3]

> . . . difficulties may arise when the normal tenderness of parents toward their children is not manifested to a proper degree. Whenever this occurs, serious consequences for the development of the child ensue. The child's attitude becomes so fixed that he cannot recognize love nor make the proper use of it, because his instincts for tenderness have never been developed.

Percept-percept relating as a second means of learning

The sort of learning that we can recognize most easily is learning in which the individual can perceive, perhaps rather easily, two separate aspects of a situation, and in which the learning comes from his seeing the relationship between these aspects. Let us give some examples first which show this learning in some of its simplest forms.

Our first story of Susan illustrates some percept-percept relating that resulted from a single experience and yet that influenced her reactions for years afterwards:

> Susan had been born in August, so that in the period when children ordinarily begin to crawl about and explore, from about the age of six months, she spent her time entirely indoors because of winter weather. Her family did not own any pets, and animals were new to her when good weather came and she began to go outdoors. She enjoyed the opportunity to explore things outdoors when summer finally gave her new freedom. Her parents had a good opportunity to note that, originally, she was devoid of fear of small crawling or flying insects. She was utterly fascinated by even a tiny ant crawling across the terrace and would follow it with her finger a few inches behind it, talking excitedly. She had the same absorbing interest in anything that crawled or flew.
>
> One day she came out on the terrace barefoot and accidentally stepped on a brown honey bee that promptly stung her. She lifted her foot with a scream and saw the bee clinging to the sole of her foot before it flew away. Very soon thereafter, any flying creature—even a housefly—aroused an intense screaming reaction. If she were outdoors and a flying bug came near, she would immediately start crying for protection.
>
> The fear of flying insects continued for years. If a housefly was in her room, she would call a parent and wouldn't play there unless the fly was killed. She collected ladybugs for a time and showed an affectionate interest in them, and in sowbugs, but didn't like to handle them directly. With flies and beelike

[3]Alfred Adler, *Understanding Human Nature* (New York, Permabooks, 1927, 1946), p. 37.

creatures, she continued to be very fearful, though she didn't scream outright as she had earlier.

When Susan was eight years old, the parents could still see definite differences between her responses to flying insects and those of the other children. During a long trip that the family took at this time, Susan played for hours with her younger brother at collecting grasshoppers and ladybugs. She "mothered" these affectionately, much in line with the interest she took in tiny dolls and animal miniatures. But when the family picnicked in a fly-infested spot, Susan became so upset that she cried and was unable to eat, even though she had said beforehand that she was very hungry. A few days later, when the family stopped in a cabin full of flying moths, all three children helped clear the cabin by catching them and putting them outdoors. Susan was careful, however, to use a paper napkin to catch them with, never touching them with her hands as the others did freely.

Susan's behavior illustrates another important point in a very clear way. It shows that the breadth or generality of the habit is determined particularly by the nature of the perceptual organization in the *learning* situation. At the time of that original learning, Susan had reached the point in her perceptual development where she could distinguish between flying insects and such things as ants, but she had no sufficient background for differentiating between bees and houseflies, for example. If she had been a beekeeper, she could have seen the further distinction between stepping on a bee in one's bare feet and opening a hive on a sunny spring day when the bees are so busy collecting honey that they hardly respond to the removal of a honeycomb. However, since Susan didn't have the background of a beekeeper and wasn't much of an entomologist, her perception of what caused her pain was merely that it was a small thing with wings. Even this represented some discrimination, however. She did not become afraid of the terrace where she had been stung, nor did she become afraid of walking about in her bare feet. The perceptual habit that she formed was a reflection, in other words, of her original perceptual organization.

While we are thinking about this example, we might use it to clear up a point that bears on the use of personality habits. This is the question of what changes are likely to be seen when the later stimulus-situation that reactivates a personality habit is different in some degree from the original stimulus-situation in which the habit was established. On this question, many psychologists have written as though *any* later changes in the situation will make it *less* effective in arousing the habit than an exact copy of the original situation would be. Their idea is that the maximal arousal of a habit will come either from the original type of situation or one very close to it, and that deviations from the original situation, in either direction, will make the learned cues less effective.

True, there are some deviations in the case of any personality habit that will make the reactivating situation less effective. Thus, though Susan was cautious with sowbugs and later with moths, she was not intensely afraid of them. But this is a matter of deviations in one direction. If the deviation were of certain other sorts, the arousal of the habit would be *more* intense than it would be with a repetition of the original situation of seeing one bee. Thus, suppose Susan had been a guest at a picnic dinner where 20 or 30 yellow jackets were circling around the table, occasionally lighting on the jelly or baked salmon or other food that appealed to them. Or suppose a child, previously frightened by a small dog that came jumping and barking at him, now sees three or four big dogs running more rapidly toward him and barking much more loudly than the small dog had done. These changes of the stimulus situation would not cause less fear just because the present situation where the habit is used is different from the stimulus situation where the habit was established. On the contrary, even though a habit is established through merely one experience, the habit nevertheless will be of such a sort that some *new* kinds of stimulus-situation will arouse an emotional response even more powerfully than would an exact duplication of the original stimulus situation.

With the sort of learning that Susan showed, we tend not to realize the contribution played by the perceptual activities of the individual. We tend to think that the learner grasps the relationship between the two parts of his situation because of the fact that "after all, they really were related." But another example will help to indicate that the percept-percept relating does not come directly from the fact that the two parts of of his situation really were related to each other, but comes because of those factors of timing and perceptual-congruity, perhaps, which cause the individual to relate things in the way that he does.

An example that shows this in a rather striking way is the following incident in the life of a man who uses a hearing aid and who, because this device brings adequate stimulation only to one ear, cannot easily tell the direction from which any sound is coming. The incident, as he describes it, was this:

I was standing at a third-floor window looking idly at the street intersection below. A flashy sports car waiting at the stop-light caught my eye. It started up with a roar as the light turned green, and I looked out curiously to watch its progress down the street.

"What a muffler!" I thought as the roar increased. "The traffic police will get him!" The car passed by with a burst of speed. As I watched it grow smaller in the distance, a curious thing happened. Instead of fading, his motor noise increased to a loud roar! I leaned far out, watching this amazing car. It disappeared far down the street—still the roar got louder!

Then I became aware, through my feet, that the floor was vibrating. The roar must be coming from the building itself! I ran out into the hall, almost upsetting an enormous load of lumber being trucked down the corridor past my office on a noisy, iron-castered wagon.

The men must have started up the corridor with the truck just as the sports car started moving. The increasing roar that I located so completely in the disappearing car was actually out in the hall, coming from the approaching truck.

At first thought, it might not appear that this was a learning situation. But it was. If the noisy truck in the hall outside had not been seen by him, this man would have been left with the strong belief that he had seen an extraordinarily noisy car. He had learned this, even though, just as with Wallach's subjects, he was not attempting to learn anything, but was merely observing the situation before him.

In fact, not only was this situation a learning situation; it also was a sort of therapeutic or relearning situation because, having noted the vibration of the floor and having gone out into the hall and perceived the cart of lumber, he achieved still another perceptual organization that destroyed the previous one and left him with a new "habit" with reference to such "roaring sounds."

This last example, let us repeat, illustrates a kind of learning where, even at the first, the person can clearly perceive each of several things separately, and where the "new perceptual organization" consists in the person's perceiving them as related to each other. In this case, for instance, partly because of his handicaps of direction-perception in hearing, and partly because the time-relations were so favorable to the new organization, the man perceived the noise and the visual characteristics of the car as both belonging to the same object. And, even though these properties did not actually belong together, this would have been his memory of the situation if he had not had the corrective influence of the later situation that led him to perceive the sound as belonging to the lumber cart instead.

A great many personality-learning situations are of this sort. Thus, consider this account by a man who actually is a very athletic specimen with a characteristically masculine set of interests on many other matters. He writes:

Mom and I always had long talks out in the kitchen after supper. I dried the dishes while she washed. We both worked leisurely. It was a time for talking over special confidences and my plans for the future—how I would get a good job someday when I grew up and have Mom come and live with me.

Al, my older brother, considered it beneath his dignity to help with dishes, and little Stevie never did anything to help if he could get away before Mom cornered him. She was overworked, and my help meant much to her, so that she was always appreciative. It was one of the few ways in which I got some of the crumbs of family praise that most often went to Al as the oldest son.

In fact, as illustrating the way that personality influences get perpetuated, this further circumstance is interesting: This man later not only was quite content to help his wife with this same chore, but was sympathetic with the wish of his own small son to help with the dishwashing too. These attempts on the part of the son, who was then only about two years old, produced a good deal of spilling of water on the floor and on his own clothes, so that the father often had a good deal of extra work afterwards to get things returned to normal. But this still was something that he could see with sympathetic eyes.

Now when he himself had been a boy, he could easily perceive the several aspects of the situation as separate things—the dishwashing activities, the comradely conversations with his mother, and the appreciative remarks that she made about his help. His perceptual habit came from the same influence that we mentioned in connection with the illusion of the car and the noise that originated off in another direction—the learning came from perceiving such separate things as belonging together.

Percept-percept relating as something that frequently is a matter of concept-formation

Many of the habits important for a person's personality are habits which may be described, as we saw in the previous chapter, as concepts or constructs. This does not mean that they have to be established by a series of learning experiences. Even in the case of Susan's fear of the bee, where there was merely one crucial learning experience, her resulting habit had a good deal of conceptual character to it. It may also be said, however, that the conceptual type of habit frequently does require a series of presentations for its development. If we are to get light on such development from the field of laboratory research, we need to turn to experiments where subjects were presented with a somewhat difficult problem which they could solve only after some series of encounters. One such study is the experiment by Rees and Israel described in Chapter 5. In that experiment, as you will remember, each subject had to work first with a set of anagrams such as *neque*, *nitra*, and *lecam*. Each of these first anagrams could be solved by one pattern of rearrangement of the letters, according to a formula that could be diagrammed as 5-4-1-2-3. The subjects had not been led to expect that there would be any generalized rule that could simplify their task. They were not treating this task as a task in learning or concept-formation, but merely as a series of little puzzles. But, as they worked on the anagrams, working in the same unsuspecting way as Wallach's subjects watching the moving strip of paper, they experienced a perceptual reorganization. Though they had not anticipated this, they came to see that there was an identical order of letters in each anagram.

As we mentioned in Chapter 5, however, a point of further interest became apparent in the case of about half of the subjects in the Rees and Israel experiment. With them, there was no conscious realization that they were learning to deal with all of the anagrams in some standard fashion. They sometimes realized that their work was getting easier as they continued, but they did not know why. But, the fact that they had learned a formula showed up when they worked on the last half of the whole set of anagrams. In this last half, each of the anagrams might have been solved in any two or more ways, just as *maste* might have been rearranged into *steam*, *teams*, *meats*, or *mates*. Those subjects who had not brought their concept-formation to a conscious state were less consistent than were those who had become conscious of a learning pattern; nevertheless, they almost always solved these *vieldeutig* anagrams in the standard 54123 fashion, when they otherwise often would have discovered other possible solutions instead, as the control subjects frequently did.

So what we see is that new perceptual organizations occur, not merely from continued or repeated exposure to some constant material, as in the experiments by Wallach and Werner, but also by repeated experiences with materials that differ in most respects, but that have some constant property running through all the diversity. Even though a person is not trying to find any constant thread, and even though he does not realize that he is learning to deal in some more generalized (or conceptual) way with the materials with which he is occupied, still the repeated exposures tend to bring about a new perceptual organization, albeit an unconscious one sometimes, that will then operate as the habitual, easily-aroused response to such materials.

The development of personality habits therefore often involves a great deal of influence from factors within the particular individual. In some marked degree the personality learning of an individual cannot be narrowly predicted from a consideration of what objective realities stimulated him.

To illustrate this point, one of the writers has often used the following classroom demonstration. He tells the students in a class that he will point to a series of things in the room and, with each item, tell whether it is an *A* or a *B*, and that their task is to learn to distinguish *A*'s from *B*'s. Then the instructor points, for example, at an upper corner of the blackboard and says it is an *A*. The rung of a chair is designated as a *B*; a board on the floor is a *B*; an exit light over the door is an *A*; and so on. Actually the rule that is being followed is that whenever there is an upward slant of the yardstick used for a pointer, the object pointed to is called an *A*, and a downward slant of the pointer makes any object a *B*. Since this slant of the pointer can be made to seem purely incidental, students tend not to notice this and tend to formulate concepts, and test them out, which are related instead to properties of the objects pointed to. But—and this is the crucial point—different students seize on different properties to embody in their concepts. Thus, from the two first objects (blackboard and chair-rung), one student hypothesizes that *A*'s are darker in color than *B*'s; another student assumes that *A*'s are more permanently fixed in position than *B*'s; and another student assumes that *A*'s are larger items than *B*'s. The ingenuity of people in devising hypotheses in such a situation is almost unlimited.

The point to be emphasized is that the same thing is true of small children, too, when they acquire their basic personality habits. Every situation through which they pass will produce effects that come, not alone from the objective features of that one situation, but also from a vast number of other complex factors which contribute to determining their total perceptual organization. Some of these factors may be chance factors of a rather small sort that will have a great influence, nevertheless, because of some special advantages of timing; still other factors will be differences of previous training.

The development of personality patterns, therefore, even though it is partly a consequence of massive external realities encountered by the individual, also comes from contributions of a very significant sort from the individual himself. Every individual's life contains a diversity of features. We might symbolize all this by letting the different favorable influences be represented by different vowels, and different sorts of unfavorable influences by different consonants. Then the realities of life for a given child during his third year might be symbolized *a h m a i a r d e e w a j m*. Out of this series of situations, two different children might both form the general impression that their life-experience during that year had been happy (that is, mainly vowels), and yet one of them would perceive the most common characteristic experiences as having been *e*'s and the other child the *a*'s. Still a third child, for causes that might be very hard to determine, would have perceived the same sequence of real events as mostly comprised of unhappy experiences (that is, consonants); and there, again, different children form such different impressions that one would almost believe that they had been exposed to quite different external realities.

Speaking practically, then, the development of personality is to a considerable extent an unpredictable thing. It follows, therefore, that if a person wants to develop a particular personality habit in himself or in some other person, he must expect that some quite different amounts of contact with appropriate objective realities will probably be needed to accomplish this effect in different cases. To establish a sense of security in different children, for instance, one and the same parents may have to try to create markedly different amounts of favorable experience in their different children. Personality development is a construct- or concept-forming activity within the individual, and concept-formation in complex matters does not follow simple rules, as if so many examples of this and so many of that would produce such and such outcomes.

Percept-percept relating as something that frequently involves trial and error and learning about consequences of actions

In some other main parts of the field of learning of personality habits, there are two other factors that should be emphasized. For one thing, the individual is trying out different kinds of responses to his environmental situation, even in cases where he does not have any conscious idea of trying to find a more satisfactory way to handle the situation. By these actions on his part, he creates effects that would not otherwise occur, and his percept-percept learning is of a kind that relates his perception of his action to his perception of the effects that occurred as consequences of his action.

To illustrate this sort of learning, one is too likely to cite examples where the learner is deliberately seeking to reach some goal and where he tries out some response deliberately and consciously to see whether it will have some advantages. Much of laboratory research on problem-solving learning in human beings has this character. But the trial-and-error learning that occurs in the field of personality often lacks deliberate "trying." Thus, you may remember the story (p. 11) of what happened when Ann returned, brimming over with excitement, from the first high school basketball game she had witnessed. It would have been fortunate if her parents had been able to welcome her enthusiasm, because she was growing up to be a person far too inhibited and far too fearful of joining the activities of her classmates. But, as she says, instead of giving her sympathy and encouragement, her parents scolded her for being so excited and said that she shouldn't have acted in such a way. As a result, partly as an outcome of this incident and of others like it, she experienced some learning that she described in this way: "I gradually learned . . . to keep my true feelings to myself with no outward display of how I felt."

Both where the consequences are painful, so that the person learns to guard against repeating some response that he tried out, and in other cases where the consequences are rewarding, the essence of trial-and-error learning is that the individual gets a perception of the relationship between two parts of the situation which for some time perhaps he perceives only as two separate things.

The goals we try to achieve by means of actions characteristic of our personalities are so complex we often do not realize that we are persistently trying some mode of response over and over again. You will remember the case from Dr. Frederick Allen mentioned at the start of Chapter 5. This girl had stubbornly fought her family for six years over questions of how much she should eat and whether she should wash and keep herself neat. Presumably she was gaining certain satisfactions by this behavior and was continuing it partly for that reason. But it probably is true, too, that her case illustrates a very general phenomenon of personality—to wit, that an individual may engage in a great deal of trial-and-error behavior, and yet continue to show what G. V. Hamilton spoke of as "persistent nonadjustive response."

In some other cases there is no doubt but that people deliberately try out new forms of response. This is sometimes effective, and part of the task in psychotherapy, as we will see in Chapter 15, is the task of supporting such efforts. Most of the trial-and-error learning of personality habits, however, must be understood as proceeding without the person's knowing he is engaged in any such process.

Common features of all learning

We have distinguished between several different kinds or means of learning in the above discussion. It would be well to point out, however, that there are certain general features that hold true of all of these several forms. All of them are cases where learning produces changes of perceptual mechanisms and changes of perceptual response, and only incidentally thereby produces changes of overt response. *The main thing that happens in learning is that our brains become capable of altered and usually more complex processes.* At any given point in the individual's life, his brain will engage in a certain process in response to certain conditions of external stimulation, internal motivation, and other factors. Thus, Werner's adult subjects could hear the micro-melodies only as a rather blurred sound at first. But with longer experience in this situation, their neural mechanisms changed, in this case in such a way as to make possible a more precise and refined response. Thereafter, these subjects were left with such changes within them that their neural machinery simply could not later on work in the way that it had worked previously. As Kurt Koffka expressed it in his *Principles of Gestalt Psychology*,[4]

Without experience, the nervous system has a certain constitution, with experience it has a different one. Consequently we can no longer expect that the same forces, the same proximal stimuli, will produce the same process in

[4] Kurt Koffka, *Principles of Gestalt Psychology* (New York, Harcourt, Brace & Co., Inc., 1935), pp. 104-105.

it. At one stroke [by this hypothesis] we get rid of all the unverifiable parts of the assimilation hypothesis, the original sensations, the added imagery, and the process of fusion . . . it does make a difference to call experience an inner condition of a process.

Frequently, of course, a person does make some muscular movements in the original learning situation and also in later situations where he uses his habit. Thus, Susan screamed and ran to her mother after her original encounter with the bee and, years later, she made movements of using paper napkins to carry moths from the cabin. Learning does frequently produce changes of overt response. But, as in this case, the changes of movement which must be attributed to learning are so enormously diverse that it would be grossly misleading to assert that learning produces some direct linkages of stimuli to movements.

It would be inappropriate, of course, to think that the nervous system of a person can do miracles, and the interpretation advanced in the present book certainly is urging that the brain operates in a more "biological" fashion, as one might put it, than the ordinary rationalistic tradition suggests. And yet, while we recognize this, we need also to recognize that the one part of the body which can be more marvelously modified in its structure and functions than any other part is the brain. This complex organ is chiefly what gives us our character as human beings. Even though we need realistically to recognize the limitations of the brain, we should not fail to appreciate the complexity and delicate accuracy of what the brain, with learning, can come to do.

Consider, for example, these few skills alone: An ordinary person can learn to distinguish hundreds, perhaps thousands, of other persons by the sound of their voices. The differences between their voices are often matters of only very slight shading, and yet the different voices come to be perceived clearly and distinctively! Or a person who is expert at such matters can readily recognize a considerable number of musicians, so that they can say that the violinist or saxophonist they are hearing must be so and so. Similarly, a forester learns to distinguish different types of fir or spruce at a glance, and the differences seem very obvious to him, whereas the novice cannot imagine how one could tell that two different trees are of different species. The person who is skilled at watching a football game can see vastly more in it than the person who is watching a game for the first time. In all such cases, the brain is capable of a vastly more complex perceptual process than can be indicated by the muscular reactions of the moment. It might take the football expert five minutes, for example, to explain what had happened on a play that he watched for three seconds, and even then he would not have been able to indicate all that he saw. We live, in other words, chiefly in terms of our perceptual processes, and the main thing that learning does is to make changes in the mechanisms for these.

Why learning does not *occur*

We have talked about some experiments in which the subjects did not attempt to learn and did not know that they were learning anything, and yet where learning occurred anyway. As we have said, such experiments indicate that learning apparently comes from whatever conditions produce some new perceptual organization as the response to a stimulus situation.

From these examples, the further conclusion might seem to be suggested that whenever there are perceptions of separate things, these perceptions will certainly unify into some new percept-percept relationship. However, the history of human culture includes innumerable occasions when people tried to find the reasons for some effect and when there were separate perceptions that they "ought" to have unified, and yet could not.

For example, throughout the Middle Ages, there was a terrible disease called St. Anthony's fire which occurred in several forms. In the form with which we are concerned, persons suffering from it had poor circulation in their arms and legs and fierce burning pains. Sometimes the arms and legs would turn black and wither away, leaving just stumps. Often the disease was fatal. Naturally there were attempts to explain its occurrence, and various elaborate hypotheses were entertained at different times. For the most part, though, it seemed as though the disease appeared from nowhere, lasted for a year or more, and then disappeared with no apparent reason—unless through the intercession of St. Anthony, as was popularly supposed.

What finally came to be realized, after centuries of difficulty, was that St. Anthony's fire had nothing to do with St. Anthony or any other supernatural influence, but occurred as a consequence of a fungus that attacked grains of rye during damp summers and changed some of the grains into blackened masses of fungus, called ergot. These damp summers were easily perceived by people. So also were the blackened grains before the rye was milled into flour and baked into bread. What we now know is that this ergot produces a chemical that acts on smooth muscles, like those in the walls of blood vessels, and makes them contract. The drug has been useful to help produce contractions of the muscles of the uterus in childbirth. People were consuming a chemical, therefore, that tended to impair the circulation of blood within their bodies and thereby produced the dreadful symptoms.

In the period of the Middle Ages there was no background of knowledge about such chemicals or about the specific parts of the body on which they acted. An understanding or perception of these matters would not have been possible then. But these perceptions were actually not needed. All that would have been necessary was that people should have associated the epidemics of St. Anthony's fire with the use of bread from rye that had been infested with this clearly visible fungus. Yet large numbers of persons suffered and died from this disease without anyone being able to learn that blackened rye grains and the symptoms of St. Anthony's fire were related to each other.

Nor do we need to go back to the Middle Ages to find such instances. Up until the end of the last century, no one perceived that mosquitoes were the means of transmitting malaria and yellow fever, and that, despite beliefs to the contrary, breathing the air from swampy places had no relation to these diseases.

These examples could be multiplied indefinitely. There are plenty of situations where mankind would have been much better off, or would be much better off now, if some new percept-percept relating could be accomplished. Learning often does *not* occur. There is really just as important a problem, therefore, in why learning does *not* occur as in the problem why it does.

This same lack of learning is seen frequently, of course, in matters of personality. Because of their personality characteristics, people often produce serious difficulties for themselves. Allen, for instance, who was described in the previous chapter, was making things hard for himself by his excessive interest in displaying how much he knew.

It is for such reasons that George Kelly interprets personality habits as he does. He suggests that personality is a matter of hypotheses or propositions on the part of the individual which are basically like the hypotheses of a scientist or of a technical worker. These hypotheses are attempts to make sense out of some very puzzling materials. Often the individual gets a first hypothesis that he ought to revise. But the reorganization proves very difficult. In fact, when a person has erroneous ideas about cause-and-effect relationships in his personal life, and consequently runs into difficulties, he is likely to intensify his efforts to use the very techniques (hypotheses) that have been producing his difficulties. The individual in such a case resembles one of the physicians of two or three hundred years ago who believed that he was benefiting his patients by the use of a bleeding cup or leeches to remove part of his blood. Having taken some blood from his patient and noting that the patient, despite this "help," was lapsing into a worse state, the physician might redouble his blood-letting. Such physicians conceivably might have perceived certain prevailing facts that would have convinced them that these methods were harmful and even sometimes fatal to their patients. But the relationships were complex and needed to be checked by something akin to statistical methods, which they did not use. Consequently, neither the physicians nor their patients learned the proper percept-percept relationships.

Such examples of nonlearning call our attention to a significant fact:

Almost all personality learning, and learning in many other fields, is not really *new learning*, but a case of *relearning*, that is, of modifying perceptual habits that have already been established. Many of the barriers to what we need to learn arise from the fact that a certain situation requires a reinterpreting, something an individual cannot discover because he is so completely unable to break away from the way he perceives things now.

Let us consider five major reasons why such reorganizations are often difficult:

1. *Some personality habits make the individual unwilling to engage in the exploratory activities that most normally precede the forming of new habits.* A research study by Solomon, Kamin, and Wynne[5] demonstrates with unusual clarity how this principle works in the case of dogs. The experimenters placed a dog in one side of a two-compartment box. The compartments were separated by a barrier-wall low enough for the dog to jump from one side to the other. The conditioning technique was to sound a buzzer and, a few seconds later, give the dog a fairly strong shock through a floor grid that could be electrified. In his struggles to get away from the shock, the dog soon learned to jump the intervening barrier into the second compartment. But there, too, after a while, the buzzer would sound, a shock would be given, and the dog would scramble back over the barrier into the first compartment. Then the whole procedure would be repeated until the animal was soon jumping back and forth with each buzz. Thus the dog acquired an emotional expectation that shock would follow shortly after the buzzer and that if he jumped quickly after the buzzer sounded, he could escape the shock, since there was always a short interval between buzzer and shock.

The avoidance habit was quickly established and proved to be remarkably persistent. In fact, the experimenters found that the dogs would apparently jump back and forth indefinitely as long as the buzzer sounded, since careful timing of the response showed they were jumping faster than ever at the end of 400 trials, when the experimenters quit in exhaustion. This persistence would be understandable if the experimenters had continued to electrify the floor grids after each buzz. Then we could picture the habit as being maintained by repeated contributions of the same factors that gave rise to it. But actually the floor was electrified on only the first ten trials and never after that.

Why such remarkable persistence? One doesn't find it under many other conditioning arrangements. For instance, had there been only one compartment, from which no escape was possible, with all other arrangements of buzzer and shock identical, the dog would have struggled

[5]R. L. Solomon, L. J. Kamin, and L. C. Wynne, "Traumatic Avoidance Learning: The Outcomes of Several Extinction Procedures with Dogs," *Journal of Abnormal and Social Psychology*, Vol. 48 (1953), pp. 291-302.

and whined when he was shocked and would soon have done the same just with the buzzer alone. But, if no shock had followed the buzzer after the tenth trial, the dog would finally have quit showing signs of expecting the shock.

It is fairly easy to see why the dogs did not accomplish some change of their habit. They never gave themselves a chance to learn that conditions had changed and that their perceptions were wrong! If the dogs had been compelled to stay within a single compartment, they would have had an opportunity to perceive that the buzzer no longer was followed by shock. But the dogs didn't hang around to find out.

In the same way, basically, many people refuse to try many things that might be of great value for them. For example, persons often live lives that are relatively barren of some of the deepest emotional satisfactions. One of their strongest needs may be for some expression of their own deepest thoughts and feelings to one or more other persons, some real psychological closeness to others, some openness and fullness of self-revelation to others. It is hard to find the right words for discussing this, because our culture does not clearly recognize it as one of the main human needs. But many persons deeply experienced in psychotherapy, such as Harry Stack Sullivan, Frieda Fromm-Reichmann, Alfred Adler, Karen Horney, and Carl Rogers have recognized this craving as one of the deepest in man's nature. The individual may have a personality where this need has been quite strongly developed. And yet he may also have learned, in his life as a child, that openness and frankness brought him criticism or ridicule or some other disagreeable social consequences. So, as with the dogs, he "learned his lesson" never to try that again. It might seem incredible that intelligent persons should be unable to recognize that they are living by such a hypothesis and that it and many other hypotheses should not be continued indefinitely without checking. But most persons never risk checking the basic life constructs by which they live. They are like the dogs, or like little Kenny who for three months was not willing to sit in the bathtub after his one bad experience of slipping down into the bathwater.

This reluctance to explore new environments and new ways of dealing with the environment is probably a chief reason why personality changes so seldom occur during adult years. We often note the relative stability of personality and tend to attribute it to some rigidifying influence of physiological factors that come with the years. But one difference between adulthood and the earlier periods of life is that drastically new experiences are met frequently in childhood and adolescence, whereas, in the adult years, fundamental changes of life situation are rather rare. Thus, at age 40, we may leave the staff of one college at which we have taught and go to a distant part of the country to teach in a new college. This may seem like a big change. But is it? We take with us our families, our furniture, our car, our books. We face the same kinds of classes, teach the same ideas, and have much the same sort of relationship with administrative and staff groups. Socially we seek out our own kind again among the new staff, and we join the same sort of church and clubs. We are almost as insulated from really new experience as if we lived in a large air-conditioned sphere that contained our family, our work, and all our social relationships, and this sphere moved as a whole across several states and deposited us gently again without disturbing our lives. By comparison, a child's first day at school might be equivalent to an adult's taking up residence in a foreign country where no one spoke his language, where his job was very different, and where he found himself without family or friends.

The stability of personality habits in maturity and old age is not inevitable. The range of potential new experience in living is extremely great. Yet, at 30 or 40, having tapped only a tiny part of these potentialities, we rarely will venture beyond a few familiar paths, thus becoming increasingly sealed off in a cocoon labeled "old people." Old age is, in an important degree, a psychological matter, a matter of unwillingness to keep exploring.

2. *A reorganization of some personality habits is difficult because of their probabilistic character.* During the first half-century of psychological experimentation on learning, experiments were usually so arranged that the subjects were rewarded on every trial on which they performed correctly. At first this seemed like the natural and obvious way to arrange an experiment. Then several different experimenters questioned this assumption. They pointed out that, in real life, we generally cannot make such confident predictions about what will happen. The clouds may look as though it will rain, but sometimes it doesn't. Experts predict winners in football games on the following weekend, but their careful predictions are often not correct. A man expects to encounter a difficult period in his business; but some orders come in that he had not anticipated, and business may be better than ever.

When these experimenters considered examples like these, they asked, "What would happen if we arranged our experiments so that the schedules of reward or punishment were not so invariable, but occurred in some way more like conditions in real life?" When they made such changes, they found that, *if they did not introduce more than a few exceptions at first,* they could introduce more and more exceptions as the training progressed, and yet produce learning just as rapidly in spite of this. This was one surprising outcome.

A greater surprise occurred when they gave their subjects further training to get them to learn *not* to respond in the way that they had previously learned. Previously they had demonstrated in their experiments with invariable rewards that the subjects, whether animals or human beings, could change their responses fairly quickly when rewards were discontinued and it became useless to continue making a response that formerly always had brought a reward. But when the learning period had included a number of unrewarded trials, even with the total number of learning trials kept the same, the "extinction training" proceeded much more slowly.

This problem has been explored most systematically and dramatically by B. F. Skinner.[6] In this work he trained animals to press a lever that delivered a pellet of food. To develop maximum "resistance to extinction," Skinner gradually increased the number of unrewarded responses after the animals had learned the basic setup. Thus, after an original period of training, an animal might be rewarded after a gap of 15 unrewarded trials, then after 4 trials, and then after further gaps of 50, 117, 23, 200, 80, 6, and 45 trials. After a training schedule of this sort, Skinner found that pigeons would peck at the lever for literally thousands of trials without getting food on any trial, and yet not even slow up their rate of work. One pigeon responded 76,000 times before it gave up.

The learning conditions that establish personality habits are mostly of this same inconsistent sort. For example, a child might *sometimes* but *not always* have been able to get what he wanted at home by throwing temper tantrums. When he begins to deal with people outside the family who are not inclined to give him any concessions in response to his complaints and demands, he finds it hard to believe that conditions have changed and that a temper tantrum will get him nowhere. Previously his tantrums had not always worked anyway. Sometimes they were successful only after long periods of seeming ineffectiveness. It is, therefore, very difficult for him to see that his experiences with playmates and teachers are not merely more of such times when you just have to keep on trying.

Some of the most heroic characteristics of human endeavor, as far as that goes, rest on this same stubbornness! A research worker does not give up merely because he has a long series of trials, none of which yields promising results. He himself has had experiences previously, and he knows of the experience of other workers, too, which teach him that splendid discoveries may come after a long period of seemingly utterly unsuccessful work. It is part of the tradition of science that scientific research is not invariably rewarded and not entirely predictable. The scientist cannot allow himself to be discouraged from making further efforts to succeed, despite long periods of defeat in his attempts to find the means of controlling polio or cancer or to find a way for helping nations to learn to live together in peace.

A very fundamental point about human life in general—and about

[6]B. F. Skinner, "The Experimental Analysis of Behavior," *American Scientist*, Vol. 45 (September, 1957), pp. 343-371.

personality habits in particular—is embodied in this rather formidable statement that we usually have learned probabilistic habits. Even pigeons and dogs and small children live in terms of statistical probabilities most of the time, and not in terms of an invariable association of one thing with something else.

3. *Relearning often is difficult because the individual has to depend mainly on reintegrative processes to indicate the true nature of the realities in his current situation.* Particularly in his relations with other adults, an individual often has relatively little direct basis for knowing what effects he is creating by his actions. A lot of adult culture is phrased in those conventional ways of behaving which are designed to avoid friction and unpleasantness. Thus—to cite a not very important example—whenever a speaker is introduced, it is the custom that some appreciative remarks should be made about how well qualified he is to address the group and how great a privilege it is to be able to hear him. Sometimes an unfortunate note may creep into these formalities. One of the authors remembers a situation years ago when a member of the faculty had had the responsibility of securing a speaker to represent his field of interest at a departmental seminar. He had not been able to secure the man he wanted and so he fell back on another speaker whom he regarded as pretty weak. In his introduction, he gave the typical warm introduction, but then misspoke himself and added, "We are particularly unfortunate, therefore, in having Dr. So and So as our speaker." Whether he realized his error as he spoke was not clear—at any rate he made no effort to retract his error, and it would have been useless for him to have attempted this anyway, because the invited speaker was a psychiatrist, and probably no psychiatrist could ever be persuaded that such a slip was a minor accident and not a reflection of the introducer's true feelings.

Sometimes, as in this case, special circumstances indicate the real situation. But for the most part, as we were saying, the speaker, despite a hearty introduction and considerable applause at the end of his talk, cannot know what these mean. These may be merely the sort of conventional behavior which men have adopted in order to avoid painful social situations. A speaker therefore has to depend mostly on his own reintegrative habits to tell him whether he has done well or not. And, if he has previously learned to distrust his own work and to steel himself to meet with disapproval, he tends to perceive the situation in these old terms.

In most of the usual instances of ordinary interpersonal contacts, in fact, we are like farmers who plant seeds of wheat in the ground. We cannot see directly that the seeds have anything in them that will produce a new crop of wheat; we have to deal with situations in terms of what we have discovered in the past. The only difference is that the farmer gets a clear-cut corroboration of his expectation year after year, but confirmation does not occur so readily in matters of personality. We mostly have to depend on reintegrative processes to judge whether, by what we have been doing, we actually have been helpful to other persons, have won their respect and affection, have added to our professional security, or have achieved something of which we have a right to be proud. There are realities in such matters, but they are subtle and below the surface of life.

Sometimes an individual may experience his life as successful when actually he has no warrant for doing so; sometimes he may experience his life in terms of disappointment or even bitter failure when these experiences do not correspond at all with objective reality. All of this makes it exceedingly difficult, often, for a person to change his personality habits. He thinks that he has confirmed, over and over again, the basic expectations that he tends to bring into his personal relationships; but, actually, the underlying realities were different from what he perceived and would have led to changes in his habits if he could have perceived them.

4. *Relearning is often difficult because the first organization that an individual achieves tends to prevent his advancing to some alternative and often better organization, even though such an alternative might have been quite possible originally.* In Chapter 5 and again in Chapter 6 we spoke about the effects produced by the ambiguous *old-woman—young-woman* picture. You will remember that a prior exposure of a simplified drawing can determine the way that people will see the composite. And their later perception of the composite will continue to be dominated by their first perception. Thus there is set in motion a well-organized process that tends to prevent perceiving any of the details except in the manner dictated by the over-all organization. With such a figure, people sometimes say: "I don't doubt that this drawing can be seen as you describe it, but I just can't see what you're talking about. I can't see how the part could be the nose that you say is the nose; I can't see how that other part could be the chin; and so on. I just can't!"

This is the same way that basic life constructs operate. An individual might listen to a detailed analysis of his own personality and be convinced that the other person is speaking expertly and without bias. The subject may hear, for example, that he apparently seeks to change every life situation into one where other people are trying to dominate him and in which he is fighting, back against the wall, for a chance to make his own decisions. He may hear a recital of detailed evidence to the effect that other people are not now, at any rate, trying to dominate him and that he *can* now work constructively on what he wants to do. He may listen attentively to a sketch of the kind of life he might live in place of his present defeated one. And yet, as psychotherapists have found over and over again, the person who has learned to see life in one way can hardly be brought to grasp what an alternative organization, with much more to recommend it than the organization that he uses, could do for him. He is like a subject looking at an ambiguous figure who is told that he will learn to see the other possible figure just by practicing seeing this other figure, but who answers, rightly enough: "Maybe what you say is true; but before I practice seeing this figure in this other way I'll have to see it that other way first, and this I can't do!"

5. *With very complex habits, even when a person establishes a new organization for handling isolated details, the organization tends to be pulled back into the older pattern when a wider situation is encountered.* At several points, previously, we have mentioned faulty geographical orientation. We have used this as an example of how impervious to

evidence our reintegrative habits can sometimes be, and of how true it is that ordinary intellectual processes may be unable to change reintegrative habits. Even the brightest of people find it hard to correct such habits, no matter how skilled in the "laws of thought." Thus, one of the authors remembers discussing this phenomenon with Professor Gilbert Ryle, of Oxford University, who is one of the keenest of modern philosophers. Professor Ryle said that he knew this phenomenon first-hand. He had spent his childhood on the south coast of England and learned from his experiences as a boy to think of the shore line as running east and west. As an adult, he said, he finds that when he visits the east coast of England or Scotland, it still seems to him that the ocean is off to the south, in keeping with his boyhood experience, even though he knows that it is not.

With such a person, we might attempt to help him reorganize his sense of directions by using a special technique. We might blindfold him and lead him through the winding corridors of a building into an unfamiliar room. There we might remove the blindfold and let him get a sense of direction within that room by examining a compass. Then we might have him leave the room and go down the halls to a place where he can look out over the sea again. All of that time he can keep the correct sense of direction. But when he sees the ocean—pfff! his new-found orientation suddenly vanishes, his old orientation-habits are operating again, and he is controlled by his habit of seeing the ocean as lying to the south. For a short time, we are possibly able to help him secure a proper sense of orientation as a response to a smaller part out of the larger context. But once he returns to the larger context again, the larger organization somehow becomes much more powerful than the other.

It is puzzling why this is true. As nearly as we can judge, it seems to be, at least in some cases, a matter of the larger scope and greater complexity of the over-all system of orientation. The orientation for the whole region has a large number of independent habits that support it, especially after one has lived in a region for some time and has oriented a great many streets and buildings and surrounding hills in terms of the faulty information that he uses. Or, in this example of the person who moves from one seacoast to another, certain major stimulus-aspects of the situation tend to dominate because they are related to such firm and long-practiced habits.

At any rate, we can see in this example that it is exceedingly difficult for the person to get a new "feel" for a region so that he can practice using this new "feel." He can learn some relatively superficial habits, such as habits of thinking "I must remember that what seems south to me is really the east." But he cannot bring into existence, within himself, a process of looking out over the North Sea and really having the "feel" of it as lying to the east.

Many of the personality habits of the individual seem to be of this very broad, comprehensive sort. They are the means whereby the person organizes and interrelates a whole series of subordinate things about his life. He has a basic feeling of guilt and inferiority, for example. This can be something that came from rather small influences in his early life—experiences that affected him as they did because he lacked proper perspective and knowledge. Once he has acquired such an over-all view, however, it is almost impossible for him to see his specific work or any of his social contacts except in terms dictated by that over-all view. He has built a broad strategy for his life that gives a place for all sorts of smaller things in terms of this over-all organization. Now, even when he can catch for the moment some specific facts that are inconsistent with his over-all view—just as the man in an unfamiliar room can use a trusted compass—he is unable to retain this same evaluation of himself when he emerges from that smaller field of thinking into the larger issues of his life again.

The element of chance in much of learning

If the above line of thinking is correct, one of its implications is that chance factors play a heavy role in much of human learning, particularly in the field of personality learning. The situations in which matters of personality play the most significant part are definitely ambiguous, that is, situations that might be perceived in a number of drastically different ways. And the factors that determine the actual perceptual organization in any given case may be rather small factors. Yet, when one organization has been formed, it tends to be favored by such sources of persistence as we have referred to earlier in this chapter.

This does not mean that personality learning does not have its causes. But it means the important causal factors are sometimes so small and so unpredictable that it is hardly possible to say what learning will occur in any specific situation, and also that factors which are really rather slight can occasionally be decisive. Sometimes one can catch these at work, as in the following instance:

A party of children and adults were taken on a saddle horse trip to a very high mountain lake. The trail was rocky and steep, winding around sharp cliffs, with awesome vistas around every breath-taking turn. The children had never before been on such a trip in such dramatic surroundings. On the way up, there was little chance to talk. The riders were spread out, and everyone was busy watching the trail and the panorama below.

When the party arrived at the lake, the children's faces were mixtures of amazement, fear, delight, uncertainty. As he dismounted, one of the adults exclaimed: "What a beautiful ride!" The various children's comments that followed were appreciative; none saw the ride as fearful.

In this case, the ride had been experienced by the children in several different ways. It had had its scary aspects, it had been interesting, it had been awesome, all at the same time. The children had experienced all of the possible reactions and had the raw materials, as it were, for developing different sorts of perception of such rides. We are not suggesting that merely because an admired adult showed his keen enjoyment of the ride, the children thereupon entirely got over their feeling of scariness about some aspects of such trips. They still needed a lot more experiences to make them thoroughly at home in such situations. But the particular circumstances that happened to surround that ride put their emphasis on the beauty and interest of the situation they had been in, rather than on some other aspects which some other adult might have encouraged them to emphasize primarily. If the adults had said, "How frightening and dangerous that was!", this could have served as an organizing seed-crystal that would have helped to develop in some of the children a lasting attitude of aversion to such high mountain rides.

The decisive influence need not have been the adult's remark, however. Many other essentially-chance factors might have had a crucial effect. With one child, the horse might have shied suddenly at some point along the way, and the sudden fear could have crystallized the perception of the whole trip. Another child might have been all aglow because he had been assigned a charming pinto horse like the ones so often seen in children's books, and this one clear feature of the whole multipotentialed experience might have set his perceptual organization going in a strongly positive direction.

It may give you a somewhat odd feeling to meet this idea that your basic personality habits may have had a high degree of determination by chance influences. This idea doesn't fit in with the concept we prefer to have—that we are the easy masters of our lives. It may make us suspicious as to whether we have developed the most desirable of possible personality adjustments. Such a suspicion is not necessarily bad. It might be fortunate if more people realized that their seemingly inescapable ways of perceiving life may not necessarily be based on objective realities at all, but may be consequences of some chance factors by which they were misled. If we are creatures in whom somewhat minor influences can arouse perceptual organizations that then endure, resisting those influences that should bring relearning, it is worth knowing this and worth considering what we might do by way of reorganizing our perspectives.

Summary

Among various ways in which we think too narrowly of what the term *learning* means is our tendency to regard learning as something that occurs only when there is a deliberate intention to learn. However, laboratory research has shown that *learning* is a term for a much greater range of phenomena than we have supposed. Experiments on sensory perceptions make it clear that learning occurs in situations where the person not only does not intend to learn, but does not anticipate that any learning might occur. In order that learning shall occur, it seems only to be necessary that conditions bring about some new perceptual organization. At times even one trial or one experience may produce a lasting change in the individual, though in other instances repeated experiences may be needed to establish a habit of any great strength and permanence.

Learning may occur, furthermore, as in the experiment with anagrams by Rees and Israel, without the person's knowing that he has learned anything.

Two types of learning are important for personality. The first of these may be called *direct percept elaboration*, in which the learning leads to the elaboration and strengthening of the mechanism for utilizing some directly present stimulation. At least some of the development of motivational habits is of this sort. The second sort of learning may be called *percept-percept relating*. In such learning the individual may have sufficiently clear perceptions of each of several aspects of his situation originally, but he has to develop a larger perceptual organization that will indicate the relationship between things at first perceived separately. Such percept-percept relating often leads to the development of concepts. Often it comes about partly by a trial-and-error process and a noting of what effects follow what ways of acting. In the latter case, though, the learner typically does not make different trials with the forethought of learning something—the trial-and-error process is simply part of his ordinary living.

Changes of muscular response of course often occur as a consequence of learning, but such changes are typically so flexible and so appropriately adapted to the particular situation in which the habit is used that we cannot properly describe the habit as a connection between the stimulus situation and muscular movements. Furthermore, even when habits are established by single experiences, they are typically what George Kelly has spoken of as *dimensional constructs*. That is, they do not reflect merely the concrete properties of that one learning situation, but are relatively abstract habits that come partly as a product of the individual's previous learning as well as of stimulation operating in the immediate learning situation. With such dimensional constructs, habits often can be aroused more powerfully by later stimulus situations that are different from the original learning situation than by some exact repetition of the cues or signals that had been "conditioned" in the original learning situation.

Because any person brings to each learning situation a host of habits from his earlier life, most learning situations are not really "new" situations where habits are being developed from the ground up. Instead, most personality learning is a matter of modification of mechanisms of response that existed previously. Our discussions of personality learning (and of other learning, too, for that matter) ought therefore to be phrased chiefly in terms of what factors permit or obstruct some *modification* of existing habits.

To a surprising degree, learning often fails to occur in situations where it might be expected to occur. The history of human culture provides many examples of this. So does the history of any individual's developing personality, even in cases where the person encounters the unfortunate consequences of his faulty personality habits and is strongly motivated to find a better way of living. Five factors are especially noteworthy obstructions to learning or relearning: (1) The individual will not try out a changed way of behavior to see what its effect might be, particularly when he has previously learned to avoid painful results by avoiding just such responses; (2) personality habits usually are *probabilistic habits*, and the individual consequently tends not to alter his habit even when he runs into a lot of evidence that otherwise would make it clear to him that his expectations are incorrect; (3) personality habits are hard to change because the individual usually has to depend on his own reintegrative processes to tell him what effects he is securing by his responses, and it is difficult to get any evidence that contradicts his usual reintegrative representation; (4) the perceptual processes established in earlier learning tend to keep the individual from perceiving life situations in new terms, even momentarily; and (5) personality habits usually get built into such complex and firmly interknit systems that even when the individual finds some means to perceive some isolated matter in new terms, his old habits overwhelm his temporary reorientation just as soon as he gets back into the context where his customary larger set of habits can operate.

Because of such influences, factors that are relatively slight in themselves, and that come from chance in some cases, may exert an enduring influence upon personality learning. People should realize that, in consequence, there may be little actual justification for those ways of looking at life that they feel are the only possible ways in which they could experience their lives.

CHAPTER 13

How Personality Habits Are Used: The Reintegrative Aspect of Personality

THE TOPIC FOR this chapter may seem like a rather odd one. "How habits are used." One might well wonder, "Why worry about that! After all, if a person has a habit that is related to a particular situation, and if this situation is encountered by the person, he will simply make use of the habit that he has. What more could there be for us to recognize?"

In our efforts to achieve understanding, however, it often proves worthwhile to look more closely at phenomena that may already seem sufficiently understood in some simple way. For example, mankind has benefited greatly because medical researchers began to study *how* people can be helped to recover from diseases instead of continuing on the assumption that they "just get better." In matters of personality, with phenomena of learning and the use of habits cropping up as they do at almost every turn, it may be definitely worth our while to get some better insight into how habits operate within the life of the individual.

Habits can sometimes create inappropriate effects

We might think first about those cases in which the use of a habit produces effects within the individual that are objectively unwarranted. In doing so, we might go back again to a type of habit that is simpler than most personality habits because it involves no strong emotional effects. This is the matter of how people get the points of the compass twisted in some particular locale and then have difficulty in really "feeling" that such and such is the north or east or whatever, even though they know in a more intellectual sense that it is. As we have said, this effect often occurs with people who come to the town of Eugene from other parts of Oregon, chiefly because the railroad and highway turn east and west in going through town, rather than continuing in their main north-south direction.

When a person uses such a faulty direction-orientation habit, one especially notable fact is that this use creates certain effects, or certain psychological realities, not directly supported by any stimuli that the person is receiving at the moment. Thus, note what happens with the person who has developed the faulty orientation so often occurring in Eugene. When he looks at the Coast Range, west of town, he has a sort of picture of Portland and Seattle as lying off beyond this row of hills. When he looks at Spencer's Butte, south of Eugene, he pictures the Pacific as lying beyond it. Actually the Pacific lies beyond the Coast Range, and beyond Spencer's Butte the highway heads down toward California. The incorrect reintegrative representations of such a person are, of course, not due chiefly to what he gets through current sensory stimulation. On the contrary, if he could see the Pacific Ocean he could hardly keep from shifting to the perception that the Pacific lies beyond the Coast Range. But it is nearly impossible for him to correct his perceptual process, at least for a long time, partly because of this very fact that his perceptual processes are creating psychological realities derived from certain of his past experiences.

Perceptual habits therefore create current effects that otherwise could not exist. The same kind of thing is true of virtually all personality processes, and this is the reason why it is important for us to try to understand how it can happen that habits so largely determine our lives. We may not give any external evidence that a particular personality habit, of a kind comparable to a twisted orientation in space, is active within us. And yet the content of our lives may be changed anyway. Consider this experience, described to one of the writers by Phyllis, a student who was highly respected by her teachers and fellow students as a generous person of high ideals. In an autobiographical analysis, this student wrote:

There is one woman in my home town whom I can hardly bear to see. Outwardly I smile and greet her, but inwardly there is the most miserable embarrassment. She is the teacher who taught me typing, and caught me erasing an error one day. She spoke to me as I deserved to be spoken to. She said, "You can't expect to get by with cheating any more than anyone else,

Phyllis. It's just as dishonorable in you as in the others." And I feel so soiled and small to *think* of it, even. I dislike seeing her, for she knows that underneath my good reputation there is a person who yields to temptation, who is not at all so good and intelligent as she likes to pretend to be. She cheats! One would think that all these years would have faded that unhappy recollection. I ought to be able to smile about it now, and to be thankful that there are few such memories to carry with me. I've seldom done a thing like that.

On later occasions when Phyllis is thinking of herself in this vein, there may be no objective realities to arouse within her the idea that this particular teacher once thought: "Yes, that's a girl who cheats!" It may actually be the case that the teacher became aware of her lack of pedagogical wisdom in so sternly correcting a highly conscientious child and that later she always saw Phyllis as a person in whom she had unusual confidence. But if this were indeed what the teacher felt, Phyllis could not see it. She responded to her typing teacher in the way that the disoriented citizen of Eugene does when he misplaces the Pacific in relation to the Coast Range.

It is quite clear that these personality habits may sometimes produce powerful emotional effects. Take another example, one involving a young college teacher known to one of the writers. This man reports that on a number of occasions when he has needed to talk with the president of the college where he was teaching the interview has been distressing to him in a way that is characteristic of almost no other social relationships. This occurred particularly on one occasion when he himself wanted the conference with the president in order to talk over with him something about his work. He called the president's secretary to ask for a conference and received a return call from the president's secretary within a few minutes saying that the president would be happy to have him come over immediately. He knew that the president was a friendly, sympathetic person and that this prompt invitation was only another indication of how cordial the man was; but, particularly because of its suddenness, the whole situation had such an effect on him that when he arrived at the president's office, he was trembling all over.

Not until he was telling another person about this experience later did he realize why he had been so disturbed by any conference with a person in authority over him. Some years before, when he had been assigned to psychological work in an Army camp, he was given the task of finding out why the program of training illiterate recruits seemed to be getting on so badly. The recruits, it was true, were passing their reading tests after several months of training at this camp. But when they went on to other camps, serious difficulties arose because it became apparent that most of these men did not have a necessary minimum of reading ability. When he checked the procedures that had been used, it seemed obvious what been happening previously. What this psychologist found was that the reading program of these recruits had consisted of direct practice on the reading test itself, and the recruits were therefore learning to memorize the material in the test, rather than learning to read. The psychologist assumed that the work should have been designed really to produce some minimum ability in reading, and that no such special coaching should be used. He worked to make the program really a literacy program, and when recruits could not attain the specified degree of ability to read, he followed the War Department orders that they should be sent back to civilian life.

The Army colonel in charge of the program, however, was dead set against letting any recruits escape Army service merely because they couldn't read or write, regardless of War Department instructions. He peremptorily summoned the psychologist to his office, made him stand stiffly at attention, and for 15 minutes or so "read him the riot act"—accusing him of incompetence and disloyalty to his commanding officers, berating him for assuming that he knew more about how to conduct the program than those who had been engaged in it for a long time previously and, finally, threatening him with a court-martial. The psychologist was intensely angry during this incident but felt completely powerless. In later years, in any situation that was at all like this in some respect—such as the conference immediately scheduled by the president of his college, he found himself acting again as though he were standing once more in front of this Army colonel.

The author remembers that when his friend spoke about the original experience, he became emotionally aroused and exclaimed with great intensity: "I'd like to meet that man in civilian life now; I'd kill him." The author doubts that this is a true prediction of what he actually would do, but the instructor in question is a powerful fellow, and even though his manner is generally gentle, the author would prefer not to be financially responsible for paying the accident insurance on that particular erstwhile Army colonel.

Habits can also create constructive effects

In discussions of personality, we perhaps tend to cite only examples such as the above—those which illustrate the point that personality habits can create difficulties and conflicts within the person, handicapping him for life. It would be extremely unfortunate, however, to give a one-sided picture of the role that habits play in our lives.

Let us go back again to the matter of direction orientation. After all, the great majority of persons within a region have correct orientation. Yet, their correct sense of direction is just as truly given by the use of habits as is the faulty orientation of other persons. Thus, when a dweller in Eugene looks at the Coast Range and has the sense, which is correct, that the Pacific Ocean lies beyond it, he does not have this correct representation because he can see the ocean there. He is experiencing the situation in terms made possible only by habits that he formed in the past and is now using.

The same holds true of those emotionally-significant processes that are a vital ingredient of healthy personality. Take the following statement by a young college student:

> As long as I can remember, our family has gone on trips to the mountains. As a result, I have a deep appreciation of the beauties of the outdoor world. Some of the strongest impressions on my mind have been made by startlingly beautiful landscapes that I have seen. Often a word or a phrase will recall them to my mind, even though I can't remember where or when I saw them. Just seeing a pretty landscape or a mountain lake makes me feel good inside. Lots of times when things go wrong I get the urge to drive up to our favorite spot in the middle of the Cascade mountains. I have so many happy memories of the place that it seems that nothing could go wrong up there.

This student is reporting on a rather limited or specific habit that she had acquired and used. But the contributions of habits, whether in hampering or in constructive ways, also show up in much more pervasive aspects of our lives. Thus, consider this description of some exceptionally fine parents and their influence:

> I suppose that the main thing I learned from my parents is that other people will respond generously and warmly to what I would call intrinsic qualities in my life, and that other people will have faith that there are such intrinsic qualities. My mother and father had a deep sense of the fineness of other human beings and a deep reverence for others even when they had obvious faults and limitations. It seemed as though they could see past the surface matters of seemingly careless or rebellious or immoral behavior and see the deeper things, underneath, that still were worthy of reverence. They didn't let us kids get away with anything that we shouldn't have, and they didn't shield us from some unhappy consequences of some of the dumb things that we did; but they seemed to have a strong confidence that we could learn from our mistakes and that we were always "meaning well."
>
> I can't remember very many of the specific incidents where this was demonstrated, but I know that the chief thing that I felt was an attitude of deep warmth and respect from them. Even sometimes when I distrusted myself it seemed that they did not waver in their confidence in me. They seemed to have a deeper and more secure trust than I had for myself, even, and gradually, from knowing that, I had a chance to learn some true respect and acceptance of myself. It isn't that they praised me for excellent work, though

they did take delight in what I did. They wanted to see me do things because I was interested in them or because they were worth doing—not because there was some possibility of surpassing others. There are a lot of things that we do in our family where we know that our performance is very amateurish—photography, woodcarving, music, and a bunch of other things. There has always been a lot of sympathy and interest in what we did in these things, and no attempt to push us into a higher level of technical excellence than we had the spontaneous interest to achieve.

The habits that a person gets from a family background like that are not just small, specific habits. They are not habits that work on rare occasions, as when someone gets a chance to go on a vacation into the mountains. They are habits that bring an unusual warmth and heartiness into the social relationships of the person and into his work. They are habits that give him the assurance that many other persons will respond to his efforts in much the same deeply appreciative and understanding way that his parents did. And yet, at any given time in the adult life of such a person, he may be having very little direct evidence that other people have such favorable attitudes toward him. For instance, he may be busy day after day in a biological laboratory, dealing with complicated laboratory apparatus for experimenting with biological preparations. And yet he works constantly with a strongly supporting mood that is in a sense the equivalent of looking at the Coast Range and saying, "Beyond there lies the Pacific"—except that, in his case, hard at work as he is, it is as though he were saying to himself: "Beyond this work lies the warm, appreciative response that many people have to it and to me. It does not matter whether I get any special recognition for it or whether I am counted an outstanding person in my field—the important thing is that I know I am doing worthwhile, useful work and that people are grateful for this even though it has its imperfections and limitations. It is a richly rewarding thing that I am permitted to do!"

In almost every aspect of human life, therefore, whether in its small details or in really major matters, the prevailing quality of our experience is determined by the habits we use. We live in terms of realities that are included within our perceptual processes only because of the past experiences that we have had. This is true with respect to matters of personality; it is also true in the rest of our lives. Whenever you look at objects around you, there are illustrations of this. When your glance falls on a book or a telephone or a chisel, you immediately perceive it in terms of its possible uses. You see some objects in your surroundings as hard, some as soft, some as easily shattered, some pliable, some movable, some fixed in place, and so on down the line. It does not matter what you look at—you experience all of these things in meaningful, significant terms because of the habits left by your prior experiences.

We could not live in terms merely of the properties of things that we sense by direct contact with them. We need to interact with objective realities in those ways that have been found appropriate and serviceable in view of our past experience. It is our great capacity for forming and using habits that potentially makes our lives infinitely richer and finer than the lives of oysters and chickens, and it also is this same capacity that sometimes introduces into human life far more anguish and terror and hatred than the lower animals give any sign of experiencing.

The concept of reintegration as an interpretation of personality habits and personality processes

As we consider the matter of how habits operate, we need to add an important term to our vocabulary in order to be able to refer to the processes of habit-use, and to designate a certain interpretation of such processes. The word we need might take the form of a noun, *reintegration*, or an adjective, *reintegrative*, as in *reintegrative habits* or *reintegrative processes*. Either word plainly suggests reassembling or reuniting or reintegrating elements that had once been together.

The term *reintegration* refers to a principle that was introduced by the Scottish philosopher Sir William Hamilton more than a century ago. It runs as follows: In the first place, in any learning situation (that is, any life situation), conditions arouse some complex brain processes (a perception of the situation or a representation of it). As a consequence of the occurrence of such a perceptual process, the brain tends to be left with an altered character related to the particular perceptual process that occurred. These changes in the brain are such as tend to make it easier for the same sort of brain activity or perceptual process to occur again. Later, when some stimulus situation recurs that is somewhat like, or is a part of, the previous one, though perhaps by itself much less suited to call out the perceptual process formerly evoked, the brain will tend to "reintegrate" the same perceptual activity that previously occurred under the conditions of more adequate stimulation.

The foregoing is a very abstract statement. Let us make it more concrete. You remember the case of the young college instructor who had been severely bawled out by the Army colonel for what the young fellow thought was careful and conscientious work with the illiterate recruits. The original situation was certainly a very complex stimulus situation and one that aroused a motivationally powerful perceptual response in the young man. He did not, of course, see this situation as one where he needed to try to learn an emotional habit. But the reintegration concept does not imply that any intent to learn is required. It suggests that learning comes merely from the original production of a complex and significant perceptual process. It suggests that any such process will tend to leave alterations in the brain and that a similar perceptual effect can be called out later by much less adequate stimulation. And this, of course, is what happened. The president who was so disturbing to him was not dressed in army uniform and did not snap "ATTENTION" at him, but there was the similar circumstance of being summoned to a conference with a superior. The former perceptual experience consequently tended to be "reintegrated" in this new setting.

The emphasis of the reintegration concept, therefore, is not on the production of overt behavior. Instead, emphasis is on the production again of a very complex brain process or perceptual process. This process may well involve some behavioral effects (just as, in the case mentioned, the college instructor was trembling), but the perceptual process is much more complex than can be indicated by the behavior of any given moment and may, in fact, be inhibited from expressing itself significantly in overt behavior. The reintegration concept, in other words, is aimed particularly at helping us understand the processes *within* the person—the *representative* processes back of overt behavior—processes that, if we can but identify them, may give us a more exact understanding of how to conceive and deal with the person in question.

Such is the general hypothesis of reintegrative effects. But we need to give detailed consideration to this concept of reintegration as an interpretation of personality habits and personality processes.

1. *Hallucinatory effects are something that should then be produced by reintegrative processes if the conditions are suitable.* One point that should be apparent from the above discussion is that when the reintegrative process is working, the resulting perceptual effects come from the operation of both the reintegrative habit and present stimulation. When we have spoken of these reintegrative processes as perceptual processes, we have used an appropriate term because the idea of perceptual processes emphasizes the frequent role, at any rate, of present stimulation.

The role of present stimulation would be underemphasized if we conceived of it solely as touching off reintegrative mechanisms carried over from the past. If this were the way that reintegrative mechanisms operated, our college instructor who had formerly been an Army psychologist would not have heard the specific questions that the college president was directing to him; he would not have seen a college president before him, but a man in a colonel's uniform; and he would have seen only a surrounding Army post. The usual result of reintegrative processes, however, is not to produce such illusory or hallucinatory effects. It is some sort of compromise or fusion between such effects as the reintegrative mechanism tends to produce and the effects of current stimulation.

Yet, it is important also to notice this: If there is some truth to the hypothesis that we have sketched with regard to reintegrative mechanisms, this further statement should hold: Reintegrative processes should sometimes produce actual hallucinations, at least in the sense of making the individual see or hear things that are not present, but that he brings into the situation simply because his reintegrative mechanisms are working vigorously and are not altered, or "corrected," by the stimuli of the moment.

It seems that this is a logical prediction from what has been said about reintegrative habits, so let us ask whether there actually are such hallucinatory effects under some conditions. Consider the following example, which happened to one of our friends:

> I was walking home for lunch when I saw our car turn in from the main highway and come toward me. It has a distinctive green-and-tan color. "How nice to get a ride home." I stepped to the curb and waved, waiting expectantly as our car approached. "Where has Barbara been to be so late getting home with the kids for lunch?" I wondered.
>
> I could see little heads bouncing around in the back seat. Sally and Paul were with her as usual. The outline of my wife's head was very distinct now; she always held it just so in driving, chin up, as if she were too little to see over the hood. Her hair and face were now plain. I smiled and stepped closer to the curb. She smiled back. I could make out her familiar expression even though the light was reflecting back from the windshield, making it hard to see. Why wasn't she stopping? Surely she saw me!
>
> Suddenly, when the car was close, I realized with a start that it was not my wife! The woman driving looked at me curiously as she passed—wondering no doubt who I was! I could see plainly that her head didn't look at all like Barbara's; yet a moment before I couldn't have been more certain! She had seemed so clearly to be smiling, but this face definitely was not smiling.
>
> As they drove on down the street two little faces stared at me out of the back window—just about the same size as our children. I stood there for some moments, taken aback by the complete reality of my having so distinctly seen my wife's face and finding so abruptly that it was not her at all.

In this instance, if the car had happened to be the right car, the man never would have known that he had not really seen the faces of his wife and children. He would have thought that he had actually received the visual stimuli for recognizing them and for seeing the smile on his wife's face. But, as it was, the circumstances forced him to recognize that even though he had been perceiving all of this as clearly coming to him from without, he had no sufficient objective basis at all for such a perception.

One of the authors had a repeated experience of the same sort. For some months there had been a bad leak around the windshield of his car. When it rained, about half a cup of cold water would get through this leak and store itself in some mysterious recess near the speedometer, and then, when the clutch was released to set the car into motion, with devilish accuracy this water would be dislodged and come down the side of his left ankle and into his shoe. This was a real experience. It happened time after time, despite all attempts to dodge that douse of water. Finally he got the leak fixed. Really fixed, and no more water ever came through. But this did not mean that at numerous later times when he started the car he did not experience the feeling of cold water cascading down into his shoe. Time after time he had to touch his sock to reassure himself that this was merely a hallucination.

You may have had similar experiences. For example, if you have been accustomed to seeing a clock with a big second hand, you may have had the experience of seeing that second hand moving if you glanced at the clock when it was stopped. You may have run indoors to answer a telephone only to hear with disbelief from others close to the phone that it had not been ringing. If you have been on long ocean journeys during which the boat pitched and tossed day after day, you will probably have had the experience, after landing, of having the hotel corridors move in somewhat the same way as the ship corridors, even though you knew full well that you were then on good *terra firma.*

Laboratory studies show that people cannot distinguish introspectively between such "psychologically-given perceptions" and perceptions based on certain sorts of objective stimulation. In one of the earliest of such studies, C. W. Perky carried out an experiment in which 27 adult subjects were asked to imagine seeing various objects such as a banana pictured on a screen in front of them.[1] Unknown to the subjects, a very faint picture of the object was sometimes projected on the same spot. Without exception the observers mistook the picture for their own imagery! They could not distinguish between times when an object was present as an actual projection and when they were imagining the object on a a blank screen.

2. *Hallucinatory effects under certain types of direct brain stimulation.* Another type of evidence throws light on the capacity of the brain to reintegrate earlier processes. The fact that it involves peculiar conditions of arousal does not make it less valuable as evidence shedding further light on these reintegrative functions. William Laurence, then science editor of the *New York Times,* wrote the following account of an address before the National Academy of Science by Dr. Wilder Penfield, Director of the Montreal Neurological Institute, and one of the world's leading authorities on brain function.[2] In this address, Dr. Penfield told about brain operations to relieve conditions producing epilepsy. In the course

[1]C. W. Perky, "An Experimental Study of Imagination," *American Journal of Psychology,* Vol. 21 (1910), pp. 422-452.

[2]*New York Times,* Nov. 24, 1957, p. E 11.

of these operations, during which the patients remained conscious, he stimulated different parts of the brain with tiny electric currents—

When a certain region of the area was stimulated by the electrode the patient would suddenly hear a long-forgotten song. "Definitely," the patient testified, "it was not as though I were imagining the tune to myself. I actually heard it. It is not one of my favorite songs, so I don't know why I heard that song." Others suddenly relived, as though these were actually happening again, long-forgotten episodes of their childhood. Stimulation of the same area, without the patient's being aware of it, always brought back the same episode, not as a memory, but as something taking place in the present, though the patient at the same time knew it was something out of the past.

"Many a patient has told me," Dr. Penfield reported, "that the experience brought back by the electrode is much more real than remembering. And yet he is still aware of the present situation. There is a doubling of consciousness and yet he knows which is the present. A patient may cry out in astonishment that he is hearing and seeing friends he knows are far away."

3. *The more usual effects of reintegrative processes.* In some ways, the experiences that we have described above seem exaggerated and peculiar. Ordinarily, we would think such things are not characteristic of our good old dependable perceptual processes. We do not see things that are not there; we do not hear things except as we are stimulated by actual sound waves; and we do not feel that things are hot or cold unless we are in contact with actual objects.

And, in truth, most reintegrative processes do not literally recreate past experiences. For example, when you hear a certain melody played on the clarinet which you have previously heard played on a violin, you do not hear the sound of the violin on the second occasion. On this second occasion you perhaps hear the music with more organization and with more enjoyment, but it is a clarinet sound that you hear, and not violin tones given to you in a hallucinatory way by reintegrative mechanisms. In ordinary living, then, we use reintegrative materials in a way that represents a creative fusion between influences from our past and sensory stimulation arising from physically present materials.

And even when hallucinatory effects are produced at first, they may be altered immediately afterward by the influence of present stimulation in a manner that we might call "perceptual correction." Thus, when you first glance at the clock that is stopped, you see the second hand as moving. But as you continue looking, you see that the second hand is motionless. Or if you are riding with someone who passes another car on a blind curve, you may reasonably and properly be afraid and expecting that another car may run head-on into yours. But if there is no oncoming car, the perceptual-correction process shapes your perception to correspond to the real situation of an empty road.

So we need to emphasize strongly that reintegrative processes are processes in which commonly there is a significant degree of determination of the present process by both external and internal factors. Even in dreams, which are the most common illustration of hallucinatory effects from reintegrative factors, there still may be some utilization of current stimulation. When someone shakes you to awaken you, you may shape your dream so that you think that you are pushing your way into a crowded subway car, but still there is *some* use of current stimulation.

On the other hand, we need also to realize that, despite this fusion with the more direct effects of current stimulation, our usual reintegrative processes—our typical reintegrative processes—do involve hallucinatory effects, in a certain sense, as a basic and maybe omnipresent factor. We do not recognize these effects as hallucinatory. We think that the process that has occurred in us has occurred solely because of external stimulation. Thus, when we look at any familiar object around us and see it in terms of properties that are not directly contacting us, we are, in an essential sense of the word, hallucinating. We are perceiving things that are not there as far as our actual stimulation is concerned. We look at a piece of ice and see it as cold, or at a steaming cup of coffee and see it as hot. When we are walking along a street and see a smooth stretch of ice, we see it as slippery and start to brace ourselves even before we step on it. We hear a friend's voice and respond to it in terms of our friend's general personality and behavior. We see a parent scolding a small child unreasonably, and we respond in terms of the humiliation and hurt that we feel it is producing in the child. We see a young girl in a new dress go past a store window and glance at the glass and then smooth or pat part of her dress, and we respond by conceiving the feeling of pride or delight we imagine she has.

In all of such cases—and they are the typical, common experiences of our life, both on small matters and on the deepest and most meaningful parts of our experience as well—the current stimulation is not giving the main part of our perceptual experience. The current stimulation sets some limits. It gives a bit of structure or framework. It compels us to perceive that we are listening to a clarinet rather than to a violin, or that we are looking at something shaped like a car instead of something shaped like a sailboat. But there is actually relatively little that is given by our current stimulation of any one moment, and that stimulation is changing so kaleidoscopically that, if we lived mainly in terms of it, our lives would be hopelessly confused. Within the framework or limits of such external-stimulation influences, therefore, most of our life is a product of reintegrative influences. It is only thus we know that one thing is to pound with, another thing is to drink, another thing is to write with, or another thing must be avoided because it would suddenly strike with poisonous fangs.

We do not recognize these processes as reintegrative because of their appropriateness, usually, to the objects or situations to which they are referred. Consequently, we do not realize that we ourselves are producing so much of our experience; we think, instead, that we have undergone a process that is entirely supported by external stimulation. We ought to realize that current stimulation and reintegrative mechanisms combine their influences to produce our ordinary life experiences, but we ought furthermore to see that most of our experience depends on the fact that we developed the reintegrative habits that we did in our own past experiences.

This is the general concept of reintegration. What we have said about it needs to be supplemented, however, by a number of more specific principles, and to these the remainder of the chapter will be devoted.

Some main principles regarding reintegrative processes

1. *The individual does not need to remember the original learning situation in order that a reintegrative process should occur.* Some of our examples have described cases where the individual had been able to remember the original experience that had established the reintegrative habit. Thus, Phyllis could recall the original situation in the typing class; the young instructor could recall the original experience with his superior in the Army. We have used examples of this sort partly because the description of the original situation has helped to explain the nature of this reintegrative phenomenon. But you may have noticed, even so, that a number of these examples were cases where the individual was not able to remember any relevant past experience at first and consequently could not understand why he was responding in the way that he was. In most cases in real life, the individual does not engage at all in any remembering or mental reviewing of his original learning situation. He merely responds to the present situation in a manner that seems appropriate to him in view of what he is experiencing—chiefly through the contribution of his reintegrative habits. When it gets dark in the room, he turns the light switch because his reintegrative processes lead to the appropriate action of turning on a light; he does not bother to remember (and probably could not remember) when he learned that light switches have this use. When a small child responds with resentment to the quiet announcement that it is time to go to bed, he does not engage in any recollecting of previous situations when going to bed was forced on him rather tactlessly and inconsiderately; he merely responds reintegratively with a type of process such as had been called out previously by more definite stimulus-situations.

This automatic mode of operation of reintegrative habits makes them much more prompt and efficient. But, because conscious recollection is rarely involved when we act out of habit, we usually do not appreciate how much of our life rests on a reintegrative basis.

2. *The extent of our reliance on reintegrative processes also tends to be hidden from us because of a phenomenon we may call "objectification."* As many of our examples have illustrated, we tend to experience situations in terms of objective qualities that seem to belong completely to the external situation. We do not realize, usually, that such properties come from our own past learning; they appear simply as "hard facts" that exist as "realities" in the situation we face—realities that we are sure any sensible person would recognize at once. Passing another car on a blind curve is something that we see as dangerous because it is an actual risk; yet, similarly, if a person is superstitious, he believes that it is really ominous to break a mirror or to have a black cat cross his path. In some cases the qualities given by objectification are legitimate, in some cases not. In either event, however, the individual thinks he is reacting to something in the object.

You see such differences when persons with different backgrounds encounter the same external situation. Thus several persons in a car might drive past a horse livery in Colorado. One person will say that the horses are beautiful. He wants to stop the car to look at them and suggests taking time out for a ride. It is no accident that the fine lines of the horses would typically be appreciated by the person who grew up around horses in childhood and who had found horseback riding pleasant, while his traveling companion, who had never touched a horse, would look upon the horses only as rather bored animals switching off flies with their tails. The unenthusiastic companion may have his turn when they drive up to an alpine meadow ringed with sharp firs and clean-washed rocks. He wants to get out to drink in the beauty of the scene. He simply can't go on, he says, until he has walked over to an inviting rock at the edge of the meadow and sat on it and drunk his fill of this wondrous scene. He urges that they take a cabin for the night right there, watch the sunset, and get up at 5 A.M. to feel the freshness of the early morning. While his hypothetical companion who responded so strongly to the horses would be likely also to have had childhood experiences of a kind that would incline him to agree with his friend who loves alpine meadows, many another acquaintance who grew up in a New York apartment might simply shiver, call attention to the mosquitoes, and wonder how such a desolate-looking spot could excite anyone. "Let's get back down to civilization before we stop for the night," he will say as he hurriedly consults his map to find out the distance to the nearest town.

Objectification—or responding to situations in terms of what we *suppose* to be their real qualities—tends to lessen our insight into ourselves, our own personalities, and those of other persons as well. It hides from us the degree to which reintegrative habits determine our lives. It tends to keep us from being able to realize how much difference there might be between the experiences of different persons in the same objective situation. It is part of the reason why we hang on to the old rationalistic idea that psychological processes are naturally reflections of the objective realities affecting us.

3. *Another reason why the extent of reintegrative processes is hidden from us is that many reintegrative processes are unconscious.* Repeatedly, throughout the preceding chapters, we have stressed the point that modern psychological research recognizes psychological processes as not necessarily conscious processes. We have pointed out that this idea goes farther even than psychoanalytic theory has recognized, and that repressed processes are only one among many types of unconscious processes. We hardly need any extensive repetition of this point here. But, since we have been using such expressions as "how the individual perceives or experiences the situation," and since many psychologists still stick to the old tradition that words like *perceive* and *experience* are designations solely of conscious processes, we do need to echo what we said earlier on this score.

Take a simple example. You must surely have had the experience of picking up an empty bucket which you thought beforehand was full of water. Ordinarily, in such a case, you would not have been consciously expecting how much resistance you would get from the bucket and how much force you would need to use to lift it. And if the bucket actually had been full, you would have thought that your muscular response was a reaction to the pull of the handle on your hand. It would not have dawned upon you that your reaction really came before the lifting rather than after it. What betrays the fact that you were reacting reintegratively is the surprising effect that hits you when the bucket is empty—the bucket seems almost to fly up from the ground. It is from effects like this—effects on behavior, or effects on mood or the like—that we can infer reintegrative effects of which you were totally unaware.

The realm of reintegrative processes, then, is much greater than we might have imagined merely from introspective evidence. These processes are really the continuing, perpetually-present content of our lives.

4. *The adequacy of a reintegrative process often depends partly on the adequacy of the stimulus-situation.* Many of our examples have illustrated the point that reintegrative processes often occur even though there is very little to set them off. However, we need to realize that there is no all-or-nothing character to the reintegrative arousal. Instead, the degree of such arousal depends upon the similarity between the arousing situation and the previous learning situation.

This shows up particularly when considerable time has elapsed between the establishment of the original habits and the stimulus-situation—and there has been a good deal of forgetting or overlaying of the early habits by later ones. Thus, Rufus Jones gives the following account of his boyhood:[3]

. . . I was dreadfully afraid of the dark. I thought it was "inhabited." It seemed to me as though some kind of "beings" were in it. Nobody ever told me anything about this—it all came from my own imagination. The cellar where we kept our year's stock of apples and all our winter vegetables was terribly dark. When I went for apples I always carried a lamp, but there was a compartment of the cellar unfortunately near the apple-bin which was partitioned off and absolutely dark. I always felt that "something" might come out of there any minute and "get me." I leaned away from it and was always braced ready to run to safety if anything happened. I never went down to the cellar without talking in a loud voice, or singing, and I indicated by my conversation that I had strong helpers above stairs. But when I reached the top of the stairs on my return to light and civilization, I always felt as though I had had an "escape" from pretty certain danger.

A few years ago I had a strange confirmation of how deep-seated these early fears must have been. I went into that old dark compartment of the cellar, when I was on a visit to the early home, to look for something. All of a sudden, I found my body trembling like an aspen leaf. My mind was calm and unafraid but a subterranean memory had for an instant swept in on me and possessed my body with a fear which my mind did not in the least share!

In the decades after his childhood experiences, Rufus Jones had long since overcome—*in general*—his fear of the dark. He could go into other dark places without having any fears aroused. But when he returned to the identical situation where he had so frequently experienced childhood fear, the full reintegrative effect flooded over him. And, contrary to what he says, it of course was not solely his "body" that was disturbed, because the body has no means of trembling in such a situation except as reintegrative processes produce this effect in the muscles.

A similar effect was seen in a person who is well known to the authors. His account was this:

As the train rattled along, getting further toward my old home town, I tried to imagine how Mother and Father would look, and what I would say to them. Seven years away was a long time, and I felt anxious, as well as happy, at the prospect of being home once more.

I tried to think of what they would say and how I would reply, but none of my childhood language would come to my mind. For 17 years I had spoken

[3]Rufus M. Jones, *Finding the Trail of Life* (New York, The Macmillan Co., 1926), pp. 33-34.

Welsh with them every day. I had learned it as a child before I learned English, but now it seemed completely gone!

How should I say, "How are you?" or "I'm glad to be home!" I racked my memory. It all felt as if it were surely there, like a name one knows perfectly well but can't recall at the moment. But during the seven years of my absence I had rarely thought of home, and hadn't spoken Welsh during that time. I recalled several years ago that I tried to talk to a girl who knew a little Welsh and that I was unable to recall more than a few sentences.

Finally, the word for "cow" came to mind—of all things!—and the words of a nursery song, but no more. I finally fell asleep and when I awoke we were at the station.

Mother, Dad, and my older brother were there and rushed to greet me. Suddenly, I found myself talking excited Welsh to Mother, almost as easily as if I had never been away. I had to slip in an occasional English word and hesitate here and there, but I understood instantly all that I heard and was able to converse fluently.

The reintegrative process, in other words, must be pictured as an extensive brain process that can occur more easily and powerfully when there is external stimulation that provides support of this process at a whole series of points, rather than at merely a few.

Further grounds for confidence in this principle are seen in the greater effectiveness of extensive stimulation in the case of persons who have suffered serious brain injuries. Such was evidenced by the famous *Case Lanuti* described by Hanfmann, Rickers-Ovsiankina, and Goldstein.[4] When this subject was presented with such common objects as a comb, a key, or a pencil, he could not say what they were. But when he was placed before a mirror and then given the comb, his face cleared immediately, he used the comb appropriately on his own hair, and said what it was. Given the key when he was facing a door, he immediately tried to use it properly and was able to name it. In some ways it might seem paradoxical to say that because of his limited brain capacity, he was less able to use restricted visual stimulation than more extensive visual stimulation. But his greater ease in the complex stimulation seems less paradoxical when we go back to the principle that reintegrative processes depend both on reintegrative mechanisms and on current stimulation. When it is realized that reintegrative mechanisms were established by relatively complex stimulation, rather than by combs or keys presented against a bare background, we can see that the more complete the reproduction of the previous learning situations, the more ample is the reintegrative effect that occurs.

The reintegrative concept, therefore, is not a "rationalistic" concept.

[4]E. Hanfmann, M. Rickers-Ovsiankina, and K. Goldstein, "Case Lanuti: Extreme Concretization of Behavior Due to Damage of the Brain Cortex," *Psychological Monographs* Vol. 57. (1944).

It is a concept that fits in with the modern tendencies in psychology to think of psychological process in physiological terms. It is a concept that puts emphasis on the idea that our personality processes are matters of the functioning of nervous tissue.

5. *Reintegrative processes may be facilitated by the prior arousal of a motivational state that favors them.* One of the authors remembers a dog's behavior which gives a clear example of the arousal of a motivational state in such a way as to cause certain reintegrative processes to take place. This dog, whose name was Dumbo, was playing with a small cocker spaniel that was very lively and friendly. The dogs romped together for some time, jumping at each other and racing around. A German shepherd dog in the next yard, aroused by all this sociability, came to the fence and barked. Dumbo left the cocker spaniel and went to the fence to engage with the other dog in a performance which they had worked up into a fine ritual—snarling and growling at each other in a way that was entirely safe, since neither of them could get through to the other one. But then, having worked himself up over this, Dumbo finally turned away and moved back toward the middle of his own yard. The cocker spaniel jumped playfully at him in the same way that he had done before this interruption. But now Dumbo turned fiercely on him, knocking him down and standing stiff-leggedly over him for several minutes, teeth bared. When allowed to get up, the small dog beat a hasty retreat.

This is a phenomenon that has been extensively described in psychoanalytical discussions of motivation under the term *displacement.* It is worth relating to our present discussion of the use of habits, however, because we ought to realize that the emotional response that is displaced does not transfer to just *any* other object or situation at all. Dumbo did not turn to attacking the trees around him. The emotion gets displaced only to some object or situation that tends of itself to arouse some reintegrative process, but that would not then operate powerfully in this way except for the reinforcing influence of the reintegrative process already aroused by some other part of the whole situation.

6. *Even though many reintegrative processes are modified by perceptual corrections, the reintegrations that constitute most personality processes cannot usually get such perceptual correction.* When we spoke earlier about the hallucinatory effects that reintegration can produce, we mentioned that some of these effects are quickly eliminated by perceptual corrections. Only momentarily do we see motion in the second hand of the clock that is stopped—our reintegrative process dominates for a split second, but when the current stimulation continues, it corrects our first reaction. We may expect to hear a friend speak with his customary voice, but he has a bad cold, and we hear him not in terms of what we expect reintegratively but more nearly in terms of the current reality.

These are cases, however, where our reintegrative mechanisms cause us to anticipate some clearly tangible effects. In almost all personality processes, on the other hand, the "realities" that we anticipate reintegratively are such indefinite or concealed or future matters that there is no possibility of clear-cut evidence as to whether our representations are actually correct. Even when our personality processes are very powerful ones, they rest usually on only very slight cues. The individual has almost no opportunity to see that his reintegrative processes are in error.

For example, how tragically common it still is—because our methods of sex education are so inadequate—that an adolescent gets the idea that any expression of sexual drive through masturbation is disgraceful, and that it is bound to have some harmful effects on his physical development, his intellectual and emotional life, and his later capacity for full enjoyment of normal sexual relations in marriage. Most young persons have no means of knowing that a considerable amount of masturbation occurs in almost all boys and young men whose ordinary sexual activity is postponed, and also in a large, though perhaps somewhat smaller, proportion of adolescent girls. They have no means of knowing that the physiological effects of masturbation are not different from those of regular sexual relations and that there are no necessary ill effects such as they have supposed. Any one individual, having only his own life to judge from, cannot possibly by himself obtain clear evidence about such a question, and he may therefore continue to believe what modern physiological and psychological knowledge shows to be quite incorrect.

A majority of reintegrative processes involved in personality are similar to such faulty interpretations of the consequences of autoerotic activity. The realities they represent are so subtle, so remote, or based on such precarious evidence that it is very hard to get the means to produce a new sort of experience when they are incorrect.

7. *Reintegrative mechanisms, in some cases, can operate even when the individual has trustworthy indications of the incorrectness of his perceptions.* You will remember the discussion, in the preceding chapter, of those persons who happen to build up a faulty direction-orientation in a particular city or region and who later have it brought to their attention that the directions are actually different from what they supposed. As we said, people find it remarkably difficult to change their original reintegrative habits in such cases. One may even learn to indicate the correct directions in a rational, intellectualistic sort of way. But the sight of the sun setting in the west does not suffice to make that direction seem like the west to such a person—it may still seem like the north or the east or whatever.

If this principle applied solely in matters of direction-orientation, it would not be significant enough to mention in this book. But, generally, personality processes seem to be like this example. It has therefore been particularly important for us to seek to understand how intelligent people can receive so much clear-cut evidence and yet not be able to change their basic outlook on something. The task of perceptual correction is not always an easy one!

8. *Reintegrative processes are often by-products of the general concepts an individual possesses, rather than consequences of relatively concrete experiences.* Many of the examples we have used have been instances in which a person's reintegrative habit is a fairly specific product of a particular situation. It is important for us to realize, however, that reintegrative habits may be either concrete or abstract and that reintegrative processes often involve a utilization of very generalized concepts about the self or about other matters. As an illustration, consider the following example reported by a college girl whom we will call Carol:

> I was sitting in the lounge watching a televised version of the fairy tale of Rumpelstiltskin. It was early in the evening. I had been trying to get started on a term paper that I had been putting off and was procrastinating a bit with some of the girls on my hall who were killing time watching the program. It was well done, and we were all enjoying it as thoroughly as if we had been six-year-olds. There were many appreciative comments from the group gathered round. For the moment I had forgotten my waiting paper and was absorbed in the drama of the poor miller's daughter.
>
> Part way through I found that my mood was changing. The story lost its charm, and I began to feel so pained that it was hard to watch the program. The other girls still were enjoying it, but I finally had to leave, unable to bear it longer. The plight of the miller's daughter who was left to spin a roomful of straw into gold, on pain of death if she failed, suddenly seemed excruciating. I felt ridiculous. I told myself it was only a fairy story, but I had to go out of the room and stay out.
>
> The command to spin straw into gold kept ringing in my ears as I walked. "Spin straw into gold" indeed! Then, suddenly, I knew. It was my old feelings about my own worthlessness that had come up, feelings I had struggled with for years. They particularly came to a head when I had to write papers. My own worthless thoughts were "straw."

The habit touched off by this TV program was no limited, specific habit. Carol's convictions about the worthlessness of her own efforts were pervasive, generalized attitudes that showed up in many particular areas of her life, not simply in her efforts to write term papers. She had been a subject in an extensive personality study, and it is known that she felt the same, for instance, about her general social relationships. The particular TV situation that touched off her feelings of distress had never been associated with these feelings of hopeless inability before. So reintegration is not a principle that applies exclusively to concrete or exclusively to abstract products of learning. What is reintegrated is what has been experienced in one or more original learning situations. If what had happened originally was an abstract grasping of the situation, it is that abstract understanding which gets reintegrated later. There is nothing in the reintegration notion that restricts it merely to concrete reintegrative traces.

Another instance which clearly indicates this broader influence of reintegrative habits is the case of the young college instructor who found himself so upset when he had face-to-face conferences with the president of his university. It might seem as if his powerful reintegrative process could be understood solely in terms of the single, very vivid, original experience in which he was unfairly denounced by his superior officer in the Army. But that explanation would be too simple, for, in the first place, we also would have to dig around to find what factors made the original experience so intense. And, second, we would need to ask whether larger or more generalized habits were involved that continued to contribute to the operation of the reintegrative habit derived from that particular situation.

It turns out that, from early boyhood, this young man had become imbued with a basic conviction that it is worth while to do careful, high-quality work and that such work can be counted on to win recognition from one's superiors. He had followed this principle in his relations with his parents and teachers and had built the main pattern of his personality around this basic reintegrative habit. But, when the Army colonel severely reprimanded him for his work with the illiterate soldiers, he was making it evident to the young man that superiors are not always fair and that there is no such sure and simple basis for security as he had learned to assume. Consequently, the Army colonel was doing far more than inflicting a painful experience on the young lieutenant. He was proving that superiors can be unsympathetic and biased. He was making it clear that one cannot confidently anticipate whether one will receive hearty approbation or the severest kind of condemnation for work done in the most careful fashion possible. Therefore, as the young lieutenant continued his life, he was not worried particularly because he thought he might be asked to assume some heavy responsibilities or undertake some difficult tasks. He had often proved to himself that he could handle such things. But because of his generalized personality pattern, it still was important to him to win the sympathetic approval of his superiors by careful and effective work. He was not one of those persons who work more for self-approval than for approval of others. Consequently it was a real threat to him to feel that his college president, with whom he was to have the conference, might follow the line that the colonel exemplified, rather than act in the good old dependable way that his parents and others had acted previously.

When we talk about reintegrative habits, therefore, we are not talking solely about minor personality habits. We have cited some examples where the habits were rather specific. These examples may have helped us to clarify many of the principles concerning reintegrative processes, and we have used them liberally with this intention. The principles of reintegration are not limited, however, to isolated or specific habits; they also apply to the broadest characteristics of our lives. We have been dealing in this chapter with a matter that is of the utmost importance for anyone who wants to have an understanding of the deepest and most significant aspects of human personality.

Summary

Almost all personality processes depend at least to some extent on habits formed in earlier situations. And usually they depend very heavily on such habits. It is these earlier-formed habits that permit the individual to experience his present situation in ways that would not be possible otherwise. The fact is that, in any given situation, the individual has normally only a slight direct contact with what we think of as the situation's present reality. Most of his experiencing has to be by means of *reintegration*, a type of process first described and entitled by the Scottish philosopher, Sir William Hamilton, about a century ago. From the stimulation that is received in a given situation, the individual engages in a perceptual process that is partly a consequence of the particular features of the present situation and very much more significantly a *REintegration* of perceptions such as he had previously experienced in earlier situations where the stimulation was perhaps more adequate or extensive than in the present.

The cues to which the person is responding at a given instant may not actually be associated with such other realities as the individual thus reintegratively represents. Consequently the use of personality habits can lead the individual to experience situations in a way that, while completely convincing to the individual himself, is nevertheless grossly unjustifiable. On the other hand, however, it is also true that our wisest and soundest experiences of objective reality depend equally on such reintegrative processes. Our direct contacts at any given instant with *what is* are always so inadequate that we would succeed in grasping only the most meager features of those situations in which personality plays a part if our experience had to be constructed entirely from direct contacts.

Such reintegrative processes ought then to produce hallucinatory effects under some situations. The individual should experience some processes as direct sensory perceptions that are not such, but have been made possible only through past experiences. Observations in everyday life and in laboratory situations indicate that such effects are common. Direct electrical stimulation of certain spots of the human brain also arouses vivid hallucinatory memories. Usually a person cannot recognize that his reintegrative processes are producing effects not directly supported by current stimulation; the reintegrative effects are commonly so appropriate to the situation (or at least so little subject to any check at the moment) that he does not realize he is injecting many features into the situation by virtue of his reintegrative habits rather than through directly experiencing what really confronts him.

A number of main propositions apply to such reintegrative processes: (1) The individual of course does not need to recognize that the present situation has any relation to previous learning situations; reintegrative processes are not dependent on the individual's knowing that he is reintegrating. (2) The extent of reintegrative effects is hidden from the individual by the way that he *objectifies* what he experiences. (3) Even though reintegrative processes may provide the basis for overt reactions of the person, they may themselves be unconscious. (4) The vividness or adequacy of a reintegrative process depends partly on the concreteness and fullness of the stimulation from the present situation. The more the present situation reproduces cues that have been experienced as crucial in some original learning situation, the more powerfully will the reintegrative process be aroused. (5) Reintegrative processes tend to be faciliatated also by prior arousal of motivational processes harmonious with the reintegration in question. (6) Even though reintegrative processes are often subject to some degree of *perceptual correction*, the reintegrative experiences involved in personality processes typically concern realities that the individual cannot recognize in his present situation except through reintegrative means. It is much more difficult for the individual to discover whether his reintegrative processes are correct when he is representing what is important from the standpoint of his personality than in cases where he reintegratively is representing the simple physical properties of a stimulus situation. (7) In some cases, the reintegrative processes can continue to operate even though the individual recognizes that there is convincing evidence of the incorrectness or inappropriateness of his experience of the situation. (8) Reintegrative processes do not concern merely those past experiences where there had been some relatively concrete experience. The individual reintegrates highly generalized reactions as well, and these highly generalized reactions often help to support the way the individual experiences particular situations.

CHAPTER 14

Unity, Disunity, and Conflict

A NUMBER OF years ago, in the region around the University of Oregon, there occurred what the local citizens euphemistically refer to as a silver thaw. Sleet froze on the branches of trees and caused so many heavy branches to fall across the transmission lines that the electric power of the town was cut off for about three days. During that period, it was remarkable how much difficulty people showed in adapting their thinking to the fact that electricity was not available. It is not merely that they would repeatedly flick various electric light switches, expecting the lights to turn on. The more remarkable fact was that often, even within the limits of a single sentence, a person would refer to the fact that there was no electricity and yet also propose the use of some electrical device. Thus, one member of the psychology department said, "There is no use going to the library, because it would be too dark for reading; but I can get in a good afternoon's work with the calculator." He was thinking of the electric calculator, but it was not till he turned on the switch that he realized the inconsistency of his different notions. Another person said, "At least there's one thing we can do even though we can't read—

we can always listen to the radio." One of the present writers, aiming to cut a piece of plywood to cover an attic ventilating-opening so as to conserve heat, since the electric blower on the furnace was not working, tried to cut the board on his electric saw. Another time, when the family was sitting around the fireplace, cooking food on the open fire there, since the electric stove was useless, the writer's wife suggested, "This is sort of like a picnic—why not turn on the Christmas tree lights and make it a real occasion!"

The same lack of unity appears in other matters. The writer remembers, for instance, a graduate student whose research was related to a prior experiment by Dr. L. Cole. When this student referred to Dr. Cole, he used the feminine "she" and "her." The writer stopped him and asked, "Why do you say *she?* Who do you think that Dr. Cole is?" The student replied he had felt unsure on this matter, but that the only L. Cole he knew of was Luella Cole, and that he assumed the experiment had been hers, even though it did not seem to be along the line of her interests in education and in adolescent psychology. "No," the writer explained, "it is Lawrence Cole, at Oberlin College—quite a different person." Then he took down from his shelves a copy of the introductory psychology textbook by Cole, explained its viewpoint, and gave some further details about Lawrence Cole's work. The student expressed satisfaction at having this confusion cleared up. And yet, all through the rest of the year, and even on the oral exam on his thesis at the conclusion of the work, whenever L. Cole was referred to by him, it was always "she" and "her." Whenever he was stopped and questioned about this, he could remember immediately who L. Cole actually was. But this did not mean that his original reintegrative habit was eliminated or was unable to operate merely because he also had acquired this new knowledge about L. Cole.

These are merely examples of ordinary psychological activity, rather than examples of personality processes, because they do not involve emotionally significant processes. But in matters that more clearly have to do with personality functioning, the same lack of unity often can be detected. Thus, you will remember the experience that Rufus Jones had, as described on page 350, when he went back to his childhood home and down into the dark cellar that had been an object of so much fear on his part when he was a small child. He had long since corrected his childish idea that the dark might be inhabited by mysterious and dangerous beings of some odd sort; and yet, as he says, he suddenly found his body shaking like a leaf. The maturity of his personality in general did not prevent his retaining and, on that occasion, using an emotional habit that was quite inconsistent with his adult personality. One of the writers remembers a similar example. A friend of his, a psychologist, had agreed to take him to a Jewish New Year's service. This friend had been brought up in an orthodox Jewish family. He still respected deeply the ethical teachings of his childhood religious training but had come to view most of the special Jewish observances and theology as possessing only historical and symbolic significance. In many ways he might have been described as definitely antireligious. Yet as the two approached the synagogue where the service was to be held, the friend handed over to the writer the prayer book that he had borrowed for the occasion, asking him if he would carry it for the several remaining blocks. "I know it's silly," he explained—with real embarrassment—"but, you see, this is a holy day and a person is not supposed to do any work on a day like this. The prayer book should be in the pew where we will sit—not even carried from home. And while I do not respect such a rule any more, I simply cannot carry this book." Here was an emotional reaction that occurred far from his home town and where no one in the congregation would be likely to recognize him.

Both Rufus Jones and this psychologist were able to recognize that they were doing something inconsistent with their own main body of habits. In some other cases, however, the person does not realize, at least until afterward, that he has used such an inappropriate means of response. He has simply carried over into the present something he learned in the past, a response that was natural at the time of learning in view of his knowledge and experience at that time. Just as we said in the chapter on reintegrative processes, he may not tend to use this habit in many other situations that are distant in character from the original learning situation, but situations that are closer to the original one still may tend to call out a response which the individual would prefer to outgrow. Thus, despite a person's general maturity, he still may employ some definitely immature habits on occasion. These continuing immaturities in our adult personality sometimes become especially apparent when we are with our parents, who act as powerful reintegrative supports for childhood attributes, as in this husband's account of his wife's behavior:

Patty becomes unbearable when we visit her mother's house. The moment she enters the door she wilts on the couch and stays there for most of the visit.

Her mother falls into the whole act just as automatically as Patty. She urges Patty to sit, cautions her not to exert herself, asks if she's comfortable, and insists that she doesn't get up. She treats Patty like a small child who is sick in bed.

When we visit anywhere else, Patty is so conscientious about helping with meals and dishes and the extra work that having guests entails.

The first baby born to a couple tends, in the same way, to reintegrate our remaining childish, even infantile, reactions, as in this man's report of a sibling-like jealousy on the occasion when his first child was born:

I remember our first baby vividly. I glowed in a fatherly way when I passed around cigars. But when we were driving home from the hospital I noticed a different feeling. There was Jean beside me, holding the baby, and they were coming home at last. It was wonderful! At the same time everything felt unreal and vaguely uncomfortable.

When I watched Jean nursing the baby at home, a distinct memory came back from my own childhood. It was a picture of my mother sitting in a rocker nursing my baby brother. I must have been about four. I snuggled up close to her, and half-ashamedly, asked if I could nurse too. She laughed and poked fun at so old a child wanting to nurse.

It was some time before I realized clearly that I was jealous of the baby. Jean was so wrapped up in him. We had been so close until then; now she didn't even seem to find time for a distant kiss. It wasn't actually that she was neglectful of me, and I could see intellectually that the situation in our home was actually what I would have anticipated and would have wanted, because it gave me a lot of satisfaction to see that Jean was so naturally a mother as well as a wife. But even at that, I must confess, it was hard on me for some time!

Often these inconsistent reintegrative effects produce behavior inconsistent with our real needs. The following is a good example of this:

A scattering of people were seated at a U-shaped table for a luncheon meeting of a club. People came in and chose seats here and there, with the room gradually filling up. A guest speaker was seated at the head of the table and on his right was an officer of the club.

Mr. Jones came in. Like the others, he paused momentarily at the door, surveying the seating situation. He looked toward the guest speaker, who was turned partly away just then, talking to another person. His survey continued on around the room. Finally, he sat down abruptly at a vacant seat nearby.

Later, Mr. Jones gave the following account of his actions: "I went to the lunch today. Sam Rhodes was our guest speaker. My wife likes Mrs. Rhodes. I met both the Rhodes briefly when they went by the house last week and felt very friendly toward them. I was thinking, as I went into the luncheon meeting, that this would be an opportunity to see more of Sam and show the friendly interest I felt for him.

"When I saw Sam at the head of the table with our club president, I looked at the empty chair beside him and thought, "Well, this is good. I can go right up and sit with him." But when I tried to move toward the head table I felt frozen inside. The compelling thought flashed through my mind that "The seats near the guest speaker are for the officers of the organization, it wouldn't be right for *you* to go up there." I sat down quickly near someone I didn't even know. A sense of inner dissatisfaction kept returning between pauses in my lunch-time chat with my unknown neighbor.

"The incident kept returning to mind for several days, along with a feeling of self-annoyance that wouldn't go away. Finally I looked squarely at the situation. I could see, then, that I was annoyed at myself for not having sat with Sam in the way I really wanted. My excuse for not doing so seemed to me quite ridiculous, now that the occasion was past. Actually I *was* on the staff of the organization and it was more than right that I should have gone up and sat with the guest speaker, especially since I knew Sam, and he was among strangers. I could have made him feel at home. As it turned out, no one sat next to him at all.

"Why had I invented such a flimsy excuse? I realized that I felt two ways about the Rhodes. I wanted to know them, especially since my wife liked them, but I also wanted to avoid them. They came from a New England family, the kind that spend their summers at Cape Cod. I have never been able to get over a conviction that people like that won't like me.

"I realized how my old familiar feeling that people from such families as Sam's wouldn't like me was at work here again. This was a bad habit of mine with which I was unhappily all too well acquainted, but it had caught me unawares once more."

Many everyday instances are like this. After the tension of the situation has passed, we can, if we are interested, often see through our own actions in a transparent way. At the moment that anxiety grips us ("Then I felt frozen inside"), some diverting thought becomes more persuasive and more compelling than the other course of action, and we adopt it. Later, freed from the immediacy of the threat, we can see that the rejected line of action was in fact the right one, and the one we fundamentally wanted to follow.

In still other cases, even after the pressure of the particular situation is past, the individual cannot locate the reason for his unusual mood or impulse. All he may know is that he has experienced some effect, perhaps expressed only in some dream, that came "from nowhere" and yet that had a surprising power in his psychological processes.

The tendency of psychoanalytic workers, in interpreting such instances, it to place very heavy emphasis on the inconsistent response which thus appears "from nowhere." The psychoanalysts tend to say that such unusual responses show the real personality of the individual to a fuller extent than do his more ordinary modes of functioning. On the contrary, however, if such inconsistent responses are merely infrequent ones, the more accurate and realistic way for the individual to regard such responses would be for him to admit that his full repertoire of habits or of reintegrative mechanisms apparently includes a small minority of habits, ones that get activated in certain situations, that are surprisingly discrepant with the reintegrative processes usually governing his life. Furthermore, even if a person finds that he is seriously maladjusted in major portions of his life, this should not blind his eyes to the fact that, along with the faulty modes of response he perhaps recognizes so easily and finds so painful to himself, there may be other personality habits that give him a lot of resources for more successful and happy means of life. Even though these better means of response may be logically inconsistent with some main modes of functioning he cannot doubt he possesses, he need not conclude that the only psychological realities within himself are the hampering emotional habits he sees operating in such distressingly persistent fashion.

Theoretical reasons for expecting inconsistencies in the functioning of personality

There are a good many factors, of course, that do tend to produce a high degree of unity or consistency in our lives. For one thing, our environments often operate very persistently on us in ways to produce some harmony in our different reactions. Thus, when the electricity was off at the time mentioned above, the environment continued to disappoint people who neglected this fact. Though the person expected to use an electric calculator in a room that he could not brighten up by turning the light switch, the calculator refused to work anyway. If the electricity had stayed off long enough, people finally would have been bludgeoned into recognizing, in almost every respect where they had habits of using electrical devices, that these were out of commission.

Even just within our psychological processes themselves there are a number of influences that tend to produce some consistency. We saw examples of this with the simple perceptual figures we examined in Chapter 6. As we noted there (p. 183), when one part of a reversible figure is reorganized in the perception of the individual, all of the other parts change simultaneously in harmony with the shift. Thus, with drawing *E* in Figure 2, if a person sees one of the stairs as if he were looking at it from above, he will see all of the rest of the stairs in the same way for the time being. With the "old-woman young-woman" figure on page 147, if we know what a person points to as the nose, we know what he will designate as the eyelash and the chin. We could cite many other examples and point to a number of general influences which work in the same way because there actually are a good many factors that tend to produce some high degree of unity within human life.

However, certain other factors tend to produce *inconsistent* habits within the same person and tend even to permit inconsistent responses to occur at the same moment within a given person. One main source of such inconsistency is the fact that a person is made so he will carry over from one example to another what he has learned. He does not need to treat each new example as though he possessed no relevant past knowledge about it. The other main source of inconsistency is that the individual is able to learn to respond in different ways to different members of the same general class of things. In other words, we have the two main phenomena within us of stimulus generalization and of differentiation. Sometimes each of these is a help; sometimes it gets us into trouble. Thus, there are advantages in the fact that after a child has learned to use the word *doggie* with reference to one dog and has learned to expect certain behavior from it, he will transfer these habits to other dogs of other colors, shapes, and sizes. But there are disadvantages in the fact that the small child says *doggie* when he sees sheep. He needs to alter his habits so that he can make some finer differentiations, treating each of these groups of animals in terms of its own particular characteristics.

Another factor producing inconsistencies is that after an individual has formed some new habit, there are advantages in his tending to develop it into a widely-spread-out system which can be touched off by rather slight cues, thereby not requiring some elaborate process of thought regarding the situation. Thus, if a child's parent is very strict and tends to give sharp punishment for any failures to do what the parent expects, the child will tend to act around home in a consistent manner even though the parent is not within sight and even though the situation is one where, on the playground, he might tend to act in some noisy, boisterous way. The child, on the other hand, who has a lot of confidence in the affection and genuine sympathy of his parents will tend to respond with appropriate emotional reactions in all sorts of situations, even though these would not produce any warm and secure feeling in another child. To be efficient, a person's habits have to operate fairly automatically and with very little immediate "justification," as one might say.

If we were logically-perfect machines, one might imagine that we would have all of our knowledge arranged in abstract categories, and whenever we got some new knowledge that required a change of our response to some item in a category, we would make the necessary readjustments in all of the items where this new information would logically apply. Thus, to cite again our example about faulty direction-orientation, if a person sees that the sun is setting over some hills that he thought were due north, and if he subsequently recognizes that those hills lie off to the west, he ought (if he were a logically perfect machine) to alter his thinking about the direction not only of those hills, but also of everything else in the town that he has been perceiving in the 90°-off fashion. But, at least on many matters, it seems that we simply are not such logically-organized creatures, but rather creatures who operate by neural mechanisms whose properties are better suggested by some of the ordinary connotations of the term *habit*. This term seems reasonably to apply even to those learned modes of response that are so complicated and involved there can be no question but that they are complex concepts.

Using these capacities for learning different things in different situations, the person often builds up new habits which are different from older ones that he learned before. Thus, though Rufus Jones as a child always felt called on to whistle or to talk in a loud voice when he went down into the vegetable cellar, he learned habits of confidence in other dark situations as he grew older. But this did not mean that these habits of confidence then carried over into the dark-cellar situation to which, logically, they ought also to have applied. Or when the friend of the writer had grown older and had learned to think in new ways about the training he had received in old Jewish customs when he was a child, this did not of itself mean that he thereby had altered his entire system of habits acquired in childhood. In matters of personality, too, therefore, we can see that a person can learn that L. Cole means Lawrence Cole, and yet still retain habits that cause him inconsistently to speak of L. Cole as "she" and "her."

The really serious disunities in personality, however, are those created by certain faulty ways of living

The most serious problems of disunity in personality, however, are not such problems as we have been considering, even though these may sometimes be distinctly troublesome. The more important disunities are those that arise because the individual has learned to live by some hypotheses or constructs which produce side effects that intensify his problems.

Thus, suppose that an individual has developed the habit, amounting to the chief trait of his personality, of putting his main reliance on a policy of appeasing others—of being submissive, obliging, and dependent. A person might come to adopt this mode of living through fear of being unable to deal with life except as he is under the protection of other persons toward whom he feels as he once felt, perhaps, with reference to his parents.

In carrying out this role of extreme compliance and submissiveness, the individual is certain to have to forfeit his rights to express his own interests and needs. He tries to do things he is not spontaneously motivated to do; he abandons things he does not want to abandon. Consequently, as Karen Horney has pointed out in her very insightful analysis of this style of adjustment, the person creates situations for himself that inevitably make him bitter and resentful.[1] Once this happens, the tendency is to redouble his efforts to carry out his basic strategy of sweetness and

[1]Karen Horney's discussions of this personality pattern and of the two following patterns are given in her book, *Our Inner Conflicts* (New York, W. W. Norton & Company, Inc., 1945), Chs. 3-5, and in her book, *Neurosis and Human Growth* (W. W. Norton & Company, Inc., 1950), Chs. 8-13.

obliging submission. In such a person, consequently, there is likely to occur a vicious spiraling of effects, with his pattern of adjustment *intensifying* his emotional problems rather than gradually bringing solutions for them. He has a problem of disunity and conflict, not merely because he had learned some inconsistent things during the earlier part of his life, but because of the fact that his present main mode of adjustment forces him into situations which would tend, almost in any person, to produce much more resentment and bitterness than is the average lot in life.

Furthermore, one other characteristic of maladjusted persons, Horney has found, is that, driven by fear, they tend not to make the differentiations they should but deal with other people in too uniform or stereotyped a fashion. Thus, consider a type of personality such as Horney described that is very close to the above, but in whom the emphasis is on the matter of winning affection from other people. A well-adjusted person might also place a lot of value on affectionate relations with other people, but he would not be bothered if he did not win affection from everybody. In fact, he would expect many people to have interests and standards different from his own, and realize that they would pay little attention to him. When the maladjusted person sets himself to win affection, however, adopting this as his main pattern in life, he feels sufficiently driven by fear that he cannot stand the deprivation of having to wait until he finds persons with whom he would have a solid foundation of common interests. He seeks affection from those who are almost bound to disappoint him and grow impatient with him. Consequently, his affectionate relationships, rather than leading to deep satisfactions, often lead to irritating, anxiety-producing situations that he ought never to have gotten himself into.

Another faulty pattern of life, also outlined by Horney, is that of the person who, because personal relationships often have been so unpleasant for him, has adopted the strategy of isolating himself from other persons. This may involve actual physical separation from others, but it does not necessarily mean isolation in a simple sense—the person may actually be a great "joiner" and spend a lot of time with other persons. But he does not give other persons a chance to know his inner thoughts and wishes and emotions; nor does he let himself depend on other persons for anything more than a superficial kind of companionship. He is afraid of close emotional relations with others and tries to avoid doing anything that would bring deep commitments to other persons.

When an individual lives in this way, it is inevitable that other persons will find him less interesting than he could be with greater spontaneity and freedom of self-expression. They cannot get the true flavor of his life. They cannot deepen their experience of life through spending time with him, because he insists on maintaining a great distance from others, much as though he feared that if other people did get to know him well, they would despise him for what they discovered. Hence, his pattern of life tends to produce a loneliness and general emotional hunger that he can hardly admit. He has some conflicts that come, not merely because of what he carries over from childhood, but because he creates some adverse situations in his adult years by his pattern of actions then.

Another pattern of personality described by Horney is that seen in the individual who, again because of fear of rejection and attack by other persons, has adopted a strategy of trying to dominate them, control them, or exploit them to his own advantage, or who has adopted, perhaps, a pattern of surpassing other people and humiliating them. Such a person may even consciously adopt the philosophy that life is a bitter struggle, and that the law of human life is the law of the jungle—"eat or be eaten." In consequence, he may not be at all disturbed by feelings of hostility and resentment within himself such as would arouse anxiety in the submissive sort of person; he may even take pride and feel a sense of security in the fact that he plays a belligerent role in life. But, Horney has found, the individual who adopts this role will usually have misjudged himself in part. He will have failed to recognize some parts of his own nature that make him long for more friendly relations with other persons, or even that make him wish, now and then, for a chance to be dependent on other persons. He underestimates the degree to which he desires, not merely security and status, but also affection. In addition, his strategy is based on misjudgments of the personalities of other people. What he is likely to find is that his attempts to intimidate or surpass other persons, rather than making them submissive, arouse such hostile responses to him that his situation becomes more precarious than ever.

Where there are emotional conflicts in maladjusted persons, therefore, this is not a consequence merely of incongruous habits carried over from earlier periods of life. It is a consequence, rather, of what amounts almost to a vicious circle or vicious spiral within the life of the individual himself. Because he is afraid of encountering certain dangers, he adopts a certain technique, only to find that the technique makes his situation seem still more threatening, which in turn intensifies his pressure to use this trusted technique in a more intensified and more disastrous way than ever.

Unity, disunity, and conflict within well-adjusted persons

Sometimes we tend to imagine that unusually well-adjusted persons would be at least almost completely free from disunities and conflicts. But this is a hypothetical picture—not what comes from actual empirical studies of well-adjusted individuals.

For one thing, it must be recognized that the individual, because of the very fact that he is more discerning and well adjusted than most other persons, may have objectives that he will be unable to reach. There were many fine persons in Nazi Germany, for instance, who were shocked by the developments they saw within their own country and who did everything they could to resist Hitler's movement. But it was inevitable that they would go down in defeat. Even knowing this beforehand, most of them would have preferred to resist anyway. But there was no escape for them from conflicts and bitter disappointment.

The conflicts that are seen in healthy personalities, however, are conflicts for the most part that involve processes the person is not afraid to face and, as far as possible, do something about. Such a person may come to see that he has to lay a cherished objective aside because it is beyond his best efforts. But he does this without deceiving himself and shows no tendency to repress the wish that, had circumstances permitted, he might have achieved his desire.

In addition, however, it is also probably safe to say that there are no personalities so healthy that they do not involve some inconsistencies, some repressed processes, and some conflicts which, if they gained the upper hand and became dominant within him, might make him a seriously maladjusted person. This conclusion is suggested particularly by the research of A. S. Maslow, who attempted to locate and study a small number of exceptionally well-adjusted and effective personalities.[2] Even though, in general, he found their lives characteristically marked by comfortable relations with reality, by more complete acceptance of self, and by much more spontaneity in thought and impulse, Maslow said of them: "They too are equipped with silly, wasteful or thoughtless habits. They can be boring, stubborn, irritating. . . . These people are *not* free of guilt, anxiety, sadness, self-castigation, internal strife and conflict."

Almost any person, for example, would say that we ought to attribute an unusually successful personality to Dr. Albert Schweitzer, who has made such a role for himself in the modern world not only through his medical work in Africa, but also through his work as a philosopher and as an organist. One would think that a person with the seemingly boundless energy and stamina that Schweitzer has displayed and who has shown so much love for the different phases of his work, would have found life a deeply satisfying experience. And yet, near the conclusion of an autobiographical account that he wrote in 1931, Schweitzer stated:[3]

Only at quite rare moments have I felt really glad to be alive. I could not but feel with a sympathy full of regret all the pain that I saw around me,

[2]A. H. Maslow, "Self-actualizing People: a Study of Psychological Health," in Werner Wolff, ed., *Values and Personality* (New York, Grune & Stratton, 1950), pp. 11-34 (the following quotation is on pp. 30-31).

[3]Albert Schweitzer, *Out of My Life and Thought* (New York, Henry Holt & Company, Inc., 1932), pp. 279-280.

not only that of men but that of the whole creation. From this community of suffering I have never tried to withdraw myself. It seemed to me a matter of course that we should all take our share of the burden of pain which lies upon the world.

Schweitzer was probably not aware that the rarity of his moments of feeling "glad to be alive" was any expression of personality habits within himself; his view apparently was, instead, that he was facing the objective realities of suffering and death with unaverted eyes, whereas most men turn away from such things. But one might become doubtful about this if he compared Schweitzer's experience with that of Wilfred Grenfell, who similarly was a missionary and physician, but along the coast of Labrador. Grenfell equally assumed that he should take his share of the burden of easing the pain of the world. But, if he had been asked if he had had Schweitzer's experience of life, it seems he might have expressed himself in some such way as this:

> There are pain and suffering in the world, of course. There is death. It means a lot to me to try to reduce this pain and suffering as much as possible and to fight those things that would bring death prematurely. But these things are concomitants of life and not the main part of human experience, in general. These fisherfolk that I deal with do not mainly find life a sorrowful experience. They are not a glum people. There is beauty and wonder and colorfulness in these stretches of ocean, in the snow-covered hills and mountains of this wild coast, and in the lives of the people themselves. It is a joy to be engaged in medical work in a setting like this.

In talking about conflicts and disunities in healthy personalities, however, perhaps we ought to go back to some more fundamental consideration of what constitutes healthy personalities. It is hard to say much about this because healthy personality may take such diverse forms in different persons. Furthermore, there is a temptation to speak of good personality in negative terms, most often describing what it is not. This is the case, for instance, in the interpretation by William C. Schutz.[4] He has given more thought than most other psychologists to the task of trying to define healthy patterns of personality; but still it is true that he tends to speak of them in negative terms. For example, in discussing the extent of a person's demands for being included with others in group situations, Schutz describes the well-adjusted person as one who enjoys a certain moderate amount of participation with others, but who is comfortable with groups or in circumstances that make it more natural for him to be

[4]William C. Schutz, *FIRO: A Three-Dimensional Theory of Interpersonal Behavior* (New York, Rinehart & Co., 1958), pp. 27-31.

alone. On the matter of affectionate relations with others he is neither "overpersonal," acting as though he needed to win the affection of everybody, nor "underpersonal," acting as though the affection of others meant almost nothing to him—he values, instead, his affectionate relations with some other persons and yet can be quite comfortable when he sees that some other persons are indifferent to him. On the matter of control—that is, on the matter of whether he can accept decisions and direction by others in some situations and also play a responsible role in making decisions and serving as a leader—the well-adjusted person, Schutz says, can be comfortable in either situation, as the occasion demands.

Statements of this kind impel us to search further. You might say that we need a concept of some common feature running through this diversity. If the person sometimes seeks situations where he will be away from others and sometimes seeks participation with others, what more general goal does he seek? Is the well-adjusted individual a person with a fortunate lack of unity within himself in his interpersonal relationships?

It seems as though we can recognize some unified features in such seeming diversity of behavior. For, much as Schutz says, the behavior of the well-adjusted person must be understood as having certain profound convictions back of it. Schutz speaks of these convictions as "unconscious" beliefs—an apt term if understood in the sense of beliefs that have widespread roots rather than being merely relatively intellectual convictions:[5]

> Unconsciously, he feels that he is a worthwhile, significant person and that life is worth living. . . . Unconsciously, he feels that he is a lovable person who is lovable even to people who know him well. . . . Unconsciously, he feels that he is a capable, responsible person and therefore that he does not need to shrink from responsibility or to try constantly to prove how competent he really is.

Let us add a bit to this. Because the person does have this strong confidence in himself, he does not need to try to handle life situations in any one rigid way. Instead, he is relatively free to handle different specific situations and personal relationships in different ways. But as he does so, he is likely to be guided by certain consistent objectives which will be evident in most of his choices. To wit: the well-adjusted person does have two basic objectives that we might recognize: first, the objective of having as deep an *appreciative experiencing* of life situations as possible; second, the objective of making *constructive contributions* that will be as valuable as he can make them.

If we want a better image of what is meant by the first of these two objectives—that of appreciative experiencing—we can hardly do better

[5] *Ibid.*, pp. 27-31.

than to watch the activity of a small child. If he has not run into a good many frightening and discouraging experiences, an emphasis on appreciative experiencing will appear as a main characteristic of his life.

Take a baby of 10 or 11 months of age, for instance. When he is given some large cardboard cartons to play with, he will spend considerable time pushing them around, climbing into them, tearing them, and doing whatever else he can with them. When he gets a bit older and can walk through the region around his house, he will be fascinated by the great wealth of things around him. He does not complain that the world is a bare and meager place. When he sees the rain he wants to go out in it; he wants to splash through puddles; he wants to watch leaves floating down the streams along the curbs; he wants to peer down through the gratings over the sewer entrances and see where the water goes. In fact, one of the most appealing things about a small child is that he has such a capacity for sensitive, imaginative experiencing of the situations he meets.

But we ought not to speak entirely as though the small child naturally has a capacity for keen delight and as though what happens as the child matures is merely whether or not he "loses" what he possessed to start with. In many respects, the small child does not yet possess the capacity to respond sensitively and richly to a large number of things which can mean a great deal to him later. The question in the individual's development, instead, is which direction his development will take—toward a deepening of his capacity for experiencing the possibilities of the world or toward a dulling and stultification of his interest in life. This question really involves the ultimate values in human life. As Walter Bowie suggests in his book, *On Being Alive,* unless a person does develop and use these capacities for deep and rich experiencing of life, he is not fundamentally alive in the most real sense of this word.

The second primary objective of good personalities—that of making constructive contributions to the world—is not really absent either from the life of the small infant. He does not contribute, of course, in the sense of preparing meals or sweeping floors. But in the sense of contributing greatly to the enjoyment of other persons, just through helping them get some better sense of the possible wonder and interest of life, he is contributing something that almost any parent responds to as invaluable. It is worth mentioning this, because people often forget that, from adults too, really one of the most important contributions is the contribution of providing a personality and social situation that will help others to experience life as appealing and significant. Perhaps even the main contributions of an individual with a healthy personality are ones he does not realize he is making.

The individual does need, however, as he gets older, to focus some considerable effort on achieving worthwhile objective goals. After all, each person lives in a real world, one that is affected by the behavior of himself and others, and one that powerfully will affect him and other persons in return. It is not sufficient, therefore, that he enjoys a neat house, good meals, a pleasant town, a good school system, or living in a nation that has some traditions of democracy and fair dealing—it is important that he act in ways that will foster the objective realities that mean a lot to him. A person is not a disembodied spirit floating in space. A good personality, therefore, can hardly be conceived except partly in terms of constructive contributions and objective goals. Even when an individual sees that his contributions are modest in comparison with those of others, he respects those contributions anyway if he sees that they are working in the proper direction and if they are as great as he can make them. Perhaps he is a person whose training and abilities are so limited that all he can do is to go around on a campus or in a park and pick up the paper that other people have scattered carelessly, but he still can feel with pride, "This place is beautiful partly because of what I do!"

The healthy personality is bound to run into difficulties, conflicts, and disappointments when he sets himself to experience the world in a deep and significant way and when he sets himself to make as great a contribution as he can. But the sort of unity that we seek in life is not the sort that would be purchased at the cost of avoiding difficulties. As G. E. C. Catlin has expressed it in his stimulating book, *Preface to Action*,[6]

> However powerful and great a civilization man builds, with health and good for all, there will never be a time when those who are full, who have forgotten humility, poetry, and understanding of sorrow, will be preferable, as human beings, to those who seek a more difficult perfection.

Summary

People are not made so that they inevitably show complete unity or consistency in their responses. Even in the same instant, almost, they can have ideas and tendencies that are incongruous. Different parts of the past experience of the individual can have taught him different habits that are inconsistent with each other. Generally the person will not realize he is making a response at odds with one he would make in some other logically-equivalent situation. At other times the person may realize he is guilty of logically-inconsistent responses; yet perhaps the best that he can hope to do, at least for the time being, is to achieve some attitude of acceptance of this fact that he does possess different reintegrative mechanisms.

The most serious disunities, however, are not those that come from

[6]G. E. C. Catlin, *Preface to Action* (New York, The Macmillan Co., 1934), p. 308.

these inconsistencies carried over from different parts of the individual's past history. They are conflicts that arise in the present because the present pattern of living tends to generate effects, either directly within the individual or indirectly through his environment—effects that are threatening or depriving to him. This is a matter that Karen Horney, particularly, has clarified in her discussion of several main patterns of faulty personality. Thus, the person who has tried to gain security by always being deferent to the wishes and commands of others will often tend to develop hostile and resentful tendencies because he accepts excessive demands on himself and makes excessive sacrifices of his own interests. As he senses these resentful responses within himself, however, he tends to feel even more insecure or threatened and therefore tends to intensify the very response that produces these threatening emotional processes. What he tends to repress, therefore, and what tends to operate as unconscious emotional tendencies, is something that comes more from his present adjustment than from his previous history. The same vicious-circle effect appears in those persons who try to handle their insecurities by dominating or surpassing others or by isolating themselves from them.

There is no one sort of well-adjusted personality. All, however, appear to be characterized by a considerable degree of aliveness to the world and a deeply appreciative experiencing of things—they are organized to make worthwhile, constructive contributions to the world. Such features in their lives do not protect them from all conflicts and inconsistencies—they may even bring conflicts that a less vital personality would have escaped. But, in many respects, these features of their lives tend to bring a unity that is in striking contrast to the inner conflicts seen in less well-adjusted persons.

CHAPTER 15

The Changing of Personality

IT IS THE rare person, nowadays, who has perfect teeth. In this modern scientific age, this should not be the case. We ought to be able to get and use sufficient knowledge of the influences affecting the health of teeth so that there would be no need for dental repairs. But this happy day is not here yet. In the same way, it would be beneficial to develop and put to use an understanding of personality which would be sufficiently exact to minimize the need for special efforts at changing personalities. If, however, we ask what actually is the situation at present, rather than what hypothetically might be the case, we would probably decide that the different degrees of personality adjustment are scattered out in much the same way as different levels of intelligence. That is, just as it is true that there are relatively few persons with very high IQ's, so also would it be true that there are relatively few persons with unusually healthy and successful personalities. And further, just as it is true that most persons have a moderate level of intellectual capacity, so it is true that most persons have personalities that are mixtures of assets and liabilities, with some satisfactions in life and yet with a good many distressing aspects in their lives too. And just as it is true that only a relatively small part of the population is seriously defective in intelligence, so also is it true that it is a relatively small portion of the population whose personalities are so seriously maladjusted that they find life a terribly harrowing and bitter experience. But, *most* persons are not up in the part of the distribution where the results of personality development have been really good.

There is a great deal of room, therefore, for efforts to change or improve personality characteristics. In fact, there is hardly anyone to whom this is not a legitimate topic of interest. As Maslow's studies have indicated, even the persons at the top of the distribution have some appreciable number of personality handicaps, too. Furthermore, even on those scores where his personality is strong, a person with a good personality might well take the same sort of view as would be taken by a person who has an unusually good singing voice even before he takes any training in music. His asset gives him something that is worth developing, rather than something that he should neglect merely because he already has some advantages as compared with other people.

In the large majority of persons, however, there are handicaps or difficulties that are fairly important and that justify some serious efforts at personality changing. It is true enough that often, when we learn about some difficulty that a person experiences and learn what conditions have produced it, we are tempted to exclaim that "a thing like that should never have happened. No one, child or adult, should ever have to face a problem like that!" But to say this does not help at all. Things *have* happened that way, they *have* left handicaps or shortcomings, and what is called for is some specific effort to clear up the difficulty.

For example, here is part of the record of one small boy's experience:

Christopher started nursery school at age three and a half. He had had considerable play experience away from home with neighborhood children and was eager to go. The first four weeks passed happily enough. It looked as though Christopher had successfully made the transition from home to school. Then he began to ask his parents to stay with him at school and each morning increasingly resisted the idea of going, frequently at breakfast crying over the prospect before him.

The parents were familiar with such temporary setbacks from their experiences with their older children and treated the matter lightly. But Christopher became increasingly upset, insisting that he would go only if a parent were with him (he had till then been walking alone, since the school was very close to his home). When he was accompanied, however, he clung tearfully to the parent, refusing to part. He was left crying with a teacher several times. Finally, however, he began to scream in such a disturbing way on being left that it was clear to the parents that this was no minor setback.

Christopher was allowed to stay at home for a few days, but this intensified his fear. In an effort to help, a friendly teacher invited him to her house for lunch, and he spent a happy afternoon with her. But his terror of school remained so strong that he had to be withdrawn.

During the latter stages of the difficulties, the parents were able to discover the source of Christopher's fears when he began to say tearfully that "Bill will hit me if I go to school." Since he had given other excuses earlier, this was treated lightly until it came to be repeated insistently whenever he was questioned about his fears.

Upon investigation it was found that Bill was indeed the problem. Bill was a five-year-old at the school who had been an extreme problem child for several years. Bill, it seemed, very much enjoyed hitting other children in a sadistic way, especially smaller boys. He did not simply hit in the course of ordinary childish fights over toys but sought out boys playing alone and attacked them without warning. He had discovered that Christopher was particularly sensitive to aggressive attacks and picked on him especially. The teachers were unable to prevent his stealthy assaults, and Christopher was understandably terrified at the continual threat of being attacked without warning whenever he was absorbed in play.

Bill was finally removed from the school, but Christopher would have nothing to do with returning and stayed at home for half a year. He not only refused every suggestion of going to another school; he also began to be afraid of going to play in the homes of his friends, and even this usually much-enjoyed activity had to be discontinued.

Later in the chapter we will return to this story, relating there what the parents did to break up this unfortunate personality habit in their little boy. For the time being, though, let us merely note that this example illustrates one type of personality difficulty that develops from "conditions that should not have existed." This is the sort of personality problem in which some negative motive operates to such a strong degree that it markedly handicaps day-to-day living.

A second kind of difficulty is seen in a person who has never developed enough strong positive motives. He is like the young woman we mentioned in the Chapter 9 discussion of emotional poverty—the one who had read glowing accounts of outdoor life, but who never had built up the motivational mechanisms which would permit her to enjoy it, and who consequently was having an extremely miserable time of it while on a camping trip in Colorado. This may be a difficult matter to remedy, but it is not uncommon in our culture. Our vision has been too much restricted to the more tangible aspects of the development of children, and frequently we have not helped them to acquire the strong positive driving forces that they need for a full life.

A third type of difficulty occurs in those cases where positive motives have developed, but of a sort that is inappropriate or handicapping. Such was the case with a student counseled by one of the writers. This student had had a long-standing history of overt homosexual behavior. He had grown up on a ranch where all of the six or seven children in the family were boys. Partly because of the loneliness of her life, his mother had longed to have a daughter. This boy was unusually pretty as a baby and responded willingly to the mother's encouragement when, later, he started to help her in the house rather than work on the farm. She gave him a lot more attention than he could have won in any boy's role. The father was a hard-driving sort, seldom inclined to hand out appreciation. An older schoolmate initiated the boy into homosexual activities when he was about 12 or 13; later he was dishonorably discharged from the Navy because of homosexual behavior, and even after he had accomplished a first marriage that had seemed to his friends, from the outside, almost ideal, it disintegrated because of discontent that came from this same problem.

In the counseling interviews, the young man said he felt bitterly cheated that he had not been a girl. He was sure, he said, that he could handle a wife's type of responsibilities much better than most girls he knew, and ordinary domestic activities appealed to him much more than any work he was expected to do as a man. Even sexually he could feel little satisfaction in his marriage. A woman's figure did not seem beautiful or appealing to him. From the standpoint of pure aesthetics, he said, he doubted if one could find anything more grotesque. While with other men in a flying unit during the war, he obtained his deepest satisfaction from having some of the fellows take a protective, possessive attitude toward him. It was not merely a matter of sexual satisfactions of a direct sort; what he craved more was a general pattern of life with certain positive emotional values that were not easy to secure in a man's inevitable lot in life.

There is a fourth main group of difficulties that call for efforts at personality change. These are instances where the primary or secondary strategies of the person (such as we were discussing in Chapter 11 (pp. 298-301) tend to produce trouble. Sometimes, as in the first case that follows, the difficulties are ones that the person anticipates. What he does not realize is that he himself creates them.

The wife of a faculty member of a college complained to a friend about the indifference and unfriendliness of the other wives on campus. Much of their attitude, it was clear, resulted from her own actions. Thus, at a social gathering given in honor of the new couple when they first arrived on the campus, the wife managed to say, within the first few minutes of conversation, that the new town was a poor place compared to the one from which they had come. Furthermore, she announced within the hearing of some of the women that she enjoyed the company of men, but didn't much like women!

At another time the couple was invited to dinner at the home of an already-established faculty member. The wife failed to reply to the invitation, making it necessary for the hostess to call her on the day of the event. The hostess had heard from the husband of the new couple that they were free to come that particular evening, and she had therefore gone ahead and arranged a dinner party with a group of guests whom she felt the newcomers might be particularly interested in knowing as potential friends. But when the hostess called the new wife, the latter begged off. She was "tired," she said. The dinner party was held without the guest of honor.

In some cases where the person uses a faulty strategy he actually thinks that he is creating a good effect on others, though his technique may be as bad as it is in the following instance.

Two staff members in a university met in the hall during a morning coffee break. One of them (Al) waved a letter casually in front of the second, who had just recently joined the staff.

"Look, an offer at nine or ten thousand a year, and me getting only seven thousand! They keep coming in all the time. Why in the world do I stay here?"

"They must think you're pretty good to offer that!" grunted the second, trying to see the waving letter, which Al carefully kept away.

A long pause ensued. Both lit cigarettes. Finally Al pulled another letter from his pocket with a $100 check in it.

"They sent it to me just for nothing," he remarked in an offhand way. "Just for a lousy article I wrote. I just dashed it off."

A longer silence ensued. Finally the second staff member started to discuss some interesting current research work that a third member of the staff was doing. Immediately Al cut in with an account of similar work he had done years before.

"Didn't even bother to publish it," he finished off.

Silence. The second member returned to his office. A few moments later Al appeared with a large stack of reprints of articles he had published, and presented them to the other man.

"Just some stuff I've done," he said, leaving the unrequested and probably unwanted reprints on the other man's desk.

To sum up these points thus far, we might say that personality difficulties may come because of negative motives such as fears and feelings of guilt, or because of positive motives that we ought not to have developed or do not know how to serve, or because of faulty tactics that we tend to use to evade what is distressing or to secure what seems worth our efforts. Sometimes the difficulty lies on one of these points, sometimes on another.

Or there may be some advantages in boiling down what we have said in this chapter into a briefer statement. Assuming our discussion in earlier chapters has been correct, all of these things which have been mentioned —fears, cravings for acceptance, strategies or defenses, and so on—are perceptual habits and processes. Still more narrowly, they are *conceptual* habits and processes. Hence, in a general way, the problems of changing personality are problems of changing the way an individual conceives different life situations. We shall not always want to speak so generally when we characterize personality change—sometimes we will want to speak specifically about the need for reducing some particular negative motive, or about developing some positive motive, or about the need to help an individual acquire more skill in dealing with some particular type of life situation. But, in all these cases, it is also true that there are common elements, and sometimes we will want to remind ourselves of the generic principle underlying each one of them by speaking in terms of this more general problem of changing basic concepts of whatever sort they may be.

How personality difficulties are revealed in the life of the individual

Often the individual with a personality difficulty does not realize, of course, that he has any problem. He may not have been getting much satisfaction out of life, but his experience may be like that of many very nearsighted children. They have never seen trees or hills except as vague blotches of color. But of course they have never realized that anybody else sees them in a more interesting and better way, and they are amazed when they get spectacles and find what other children have been able to see all along. In the same way, many persons suffer because of a disproportionate anxiety or an unwarranted sense of guilt or hostility in their lives, and yet they have no comparative basis from which they might conclude that they are handicapped.

In some other cases, the person knows that something is wrong, and seriously wrong, but he mistakes the origins of his symptoms. He is like the little boy who had seen the picture about cannibals before he went to bed. What he complained about, when he burst out into the living room time after time, was not that he was afraid of cannibals, but that he was thirsty, his blankets were coming off, and so on. A patient who illustrates this principle clearly is described by Gerhard Adler:[1]

> She was a handsome German woman who looked considerably younger than her forty years, the mother of two obviously gifted and attractive children who gave her life its meaning and content. Her husband had died a few years previously. To find out the causes of her anxiety and depression, I had asked her to tell me the story of her life, with special reference to her marriage. Everything appeared to have been in order and, according to her account, she had lived on the happiest and most harmonious terms with her husband, who had been a very distinguished doctor and scientist. She herself, before and immediately after the outbreak of the first World War, had been a medical student, and it was at the university that she had got to know her future husband. From all she told me, and indeed from all I could gather in other ways, her husband had been not only an eminent scientist, but also a most devoted and kindly human being, and she had in addition every reason

[1] Gerhard Adler, *Studies in Analytical Psychology* (New York, W. W. Norton & Co., Inc., 1948), pp. 158-159.

to be proud of her two children. Moreover, her financial circumstances were assured, so that the only external cause to account for her depression was, apparently, the loss of her husband about five years previously. Oddly enough, however, she always strenuously denied this very obvious suggestion. She admitted willingly that she had suffered deeply and was still suffering from his loss, but she was absolutely convinced that this was not the cause of her neurosis, more especially as she now remembered that even during her marriage she had suffered from similar, apparently causeless and quite inexplicable, attacks.

As in the earlier case of Christopher, we shall postpone, for the moment, the discussion of the sources of this difficulty and its mode of correction. It is very important, however, to realize that the disguising of personality problems, as in this case, is very common and of the greatest importance. It becomes the rule, almost without exception, in psychotic patients. This is shown, for example, in a patient who is described by Anton Boisen in his book, *Exploration of the Inner World.* This patient, it happens, was a woman known to one of the present writers. For a long time before her stay in a mental hospital, this woman had been troubled by underlying frustrations and resentments. For decades she had struggled to preserve her marriage with a morose, suspicious man who ought really to have been hospitalized for paranoia, and who actually did have to be committed for a time. She had not been free emotionally to face the fact that she had made an impossible marriage, just as her friends had predicted when she first announced her engagement. Instead, she had kept on trying desperately to preserve the marriage, even though it meant that she and her husband had to live apart from other people and that life held almost no emotional satisfactions for her. During the psychosis that finally developed, however, she was not bothered by straightforward feelings of hostility and of guilt over the fact that she was disappointed in her husband. Instead, her thoughts kept dwelling on what she believed were facts—that she had caused the inflation in Sweden, that she had burned down the cathedral in the town she grew up in, that all the patients arriving at the hospital were ill because of things she had done, and that she had killed different neighbors in the community where she had formerly lived. Her feelings of guilt were so strong that she would not eat and had to be tube-fed for months. During that time, she thought that she had died and kept wondering why they insisted on feeding a corpse. She eventually recovered, apparently partly because of some kindly attention that was shown her and partly through some spontaneous working out of her problems with time. But during this psychotic period, her symptoms kept her from realizing the real source of her difficulties, her disastrous marriage.

Still another important form in which personality difficulties express themselves is through psychosomatic symptoms. Thus, the man described in Chapter 3 who was bothered by his lack of frankness and honesty with his wife had consulted a series of physicians and psychotherapists, *not* about his interpersonal relationships, but about his stomach troubles. Still other persons betray emotional troubles through such apparently physical symptoms as unnecessary fatigue, functionally-caused high blood pressure, migraine headaches, certain forms of asthma, and excessive sleepiness or insomnia. Such persons may not realize that they have any problems except these conditions, which (as they see them) are physical ills. Even on medical examination, such emotionally-produced disturbances are often difficult to distinguish from ills that come about from primarily physical causes.

In other individuals, the difficulty may show up in a person's work or in his interpersonal relationships. We cited instances of this at the end of the preceding section when we described a faculty wife and a faculty member who were so badly out of step in their relationships with other persons.

There are many reasons, therefore, why there may be a need for attempting to change the personality processes of an individual. This may not be an easy thing to do, and it may be hard for the person himself to see that there is any need for it. But the need for working out some better solution for what is at the bottom of a personality problem is so common and so vital that we ought to find some place for introducing this problem in a book of this sort, even though we have not intended to write a book that is primarily oriented toward this problem.

Without further ado, therefore, let us turn to the question of what methods are available for us in any deliberate attempts to bring about changes of personality in a worthwhile direction.

Changing personality through changing the objective life situation

There are two senses in which personality can change. In the most usual sense of the phrase, when we talk about personality change, we are speaking about *the changing of personality habits.* We are talking about such instances as, for example, the individual who alters his previous habit of being afraid to speak up in class or who revises his previous habit of expecting that he must always subordinate his wishes to the wishes of other persons or, on the contrary, who changes his habit of feeling that everybody else ought to subordinate their wishes to his own. In these instances, we are talking about habit changes that help the individual to function in a changed way in some situation that previously produced an undesirable sort of response.

The second sense in which we might speak about the changing of personality concerns *the changing of personality processes because of some change in the objective stimulus situation* to which an individual is subjected. In this type of change, the person's habits remain virtually unmodified. Here is an example. In a certain family, the younger of two boys, about a year and a half old, sprained his hip. In consequence he received a lot of attention and had to be carried around a good deal. One morning the older boy, seven years old, awoke with a severe pain in *his* hip and side. He couldn't get out of bed and could hardly bear to have anybody touch him where he felt the pain. The father stayed at home from work, and the parents decided, after a while, that they ought to call the doctor. He said it would be hard for him to come, but asked if they could bring the child to his office. They wrapped the boy in a blanket and carried him to the car and up to the physician's office. The doctor greeted the boy cheerfully, commented that he was looking pretty well, took his temperature and found it normal, was attentive to him, pushed with his finger to see if there was pain indicative of appendicitis and didn't get protests from the boy. So, the physician asked him, "I need to look at you some more—can you jump up on the table here?" The boy did so with alacrity, to the amazement of the father, and easily pulled himself out of his pajama top when asked to remove it. After a bit of further examination, the doctor signaled to the father to come into the adjoining room. What he said was: "There's nothing wrong with the boy, of course. But don't be hard on him. The only trouble is that you've been paying so much attention to the baby that you've been forgetting about this boy and taking him for granted. These pains that he's had today are real ones, but there's no reason for them to continue if you and your wife will just be careful to divide your attention more and see that he doesn't get left out as much as perhaps he has been." Sure enough, when they carefully took him home and were attentive to him through the rest of the day, his activity was back to normal by evening, and there were no further problems of that sort.

Later, when the younger boy got to be about eight years old, this same doctor gave them some more advice: "You'll need to remember," he cautioned them, "that even though he's as big as most 12-year-olds, he's still a very small boy in a lot of other ways. He doesn't have any more experience and independence than an 8-year-old. So, don't ask too much of him." With this boy too, as with their older one, they found that, when they eased the standards he was supposed to meet, he responded a lot more happily and normally than he had under the social pressure that they had put on him previously.

Then there is the case of George, who entered high school at the age of 12. It was a small high school where most of the boys took some active part in athletics. George was too young and too small to compete on equal terms, although he tried valiantly in every sport. He was an exceptional student; on the Otis Group Test his IQ was 142.

About the middle of the first semester, it became evident that George's failures in athletics were bothering him. His success in other activities did not satisfy him. He was always present in the gymnasium during basketball practice, and he developed an unusual knack for analyzing plays. The coach conceived the idea of making George the team manager. The effect on George's behavior amazed everyone. He not only performed his duties as manager devotedly, but he also became nearly as proficient as the coach at taping injuries and in administering first aid. His general school performance showed great improvement. Whereas previously he had appeared bored with class work and had accomplished far less than he was capable of, he now became the outstanding student in school. It was the manager's letter that was awarded to him at the end of the season, however, that was obviously his most valued possession.

With adults, too, marked benefits can often result from changing the situation a person is up against, even when there is no fundamental alteration in his personality habits. An interesting example of this appears in a case study made by one of the writers as a part of a research project where the subjects were soldiers suffering from stomach ulcers. This soldier—Richard Brooke, we'll call him—had experienced a long series of alternations in his health. Study showed that the times when he had been under most strain, however, were not those when he was at the front and sometimes in constant fighting. He had expressed a preference for regular military service, but the commanding officer learned of his pre-Army experience as a short-order cook and consequently assigned him work as a cook. Richard did not object to this assignment at first, when he was working under an older sergeant whose personal characteristics are suggested by his battalion nickname, "Mother McCracken." As a boy, Richard had actually had a lot of experience helping his mother with household work and had learned to enjoy keeping things neat and clean in the way his mother liked to do. He therefore got more pleasure from his cooking duties than he had anticipated, and because he did his job so well he was made a sergeant and given a crew of his own. His new responsibility coincided with the completion of training in regular quarters where there had been ample facilities, where the hours were regular and there was good food to serve, and where the kitchen could be kept as tidy as Mom's at home. The unit was then constantly on the move, and Richard had to contend not only with his new and unfamiliar role in command of men, but with all the confusion, mess, dirt, and disorder inherent in field cooking under temporary and rapidly changing situations.

As Richard put the matter when interviewed at the hospital to which he was returned from Europe:

I wasn't as much at ease when I had my own shift. When I was under McCracken, I wasn't responsible, and I didn't have to worry. But I had my own shift as chief cook all through maneuvers. The food was hard to get; but, if I didn't feed the men well, they griped. I wanted to get everything done right, and I really didn't have much help. Lots of times we had night firemen who were supposed to keep the fires burning, and I would worry all night that they would let the fires go out. Sometimes they did, and I had to run like hell to get it all done. When I had all that worry, my appetite would fall off, my stomach would feel weak, and I wouldn't eat.

This is the whole story of Richard Brooke's experience in the army in a nutshell. His gastric symptoms were almost like barometer readings. They did not increase or decrease, however, in accordance with how hard he was working or how much danger he was in. The situations that were tough on him were those which required him to take responsibility for commanding other men—which he was not temperamentally qualified to do—and which made it necessary for him to work under messy, disorderly conditions and with inadequate food supplies and which made it impossible for him to escape the griping and complaining of his "customers."

Many other cases that illustrate this same principle—that personality is affected by change in the objective stimulus-situation—are presented in vivid detail in *Emotional Maturity* by Leon Saul, a book based mainly on his experience as an Army psychiatrist. Saul's Army cases led him to develop his concept of "specific emotional vulnerabilities." The soldiers he describes provide evidence too, of course, that the fatigue and danger and terrible inhumanity of war are factors creating emotional strains in a great proportion of the men who show that they are in trouble. But many of Saul's cases also show conclusively that the stress-situation from which it was sometimes most important to rescue a man was not the sort of situation that created maximum tension in his fellows, but rather some situation that significantly singled him out as vulnerable because of his past experience and present personality habits.

When psychiatrists and psychologists have written about how we may deal with personality problems, they have often tended to belittle the common-sense means that we have been describing and illustrating. And it must be admitted that there are important limitations to the efficacy of this method which depends on changing a person's objective situation. The personality habits of a person may be such that he can respond happily and successfully only under very special conditions, conditions so difficult to produce that it is impracticable to expect them to occur. He may be a person who feels happy, for instance, when he is receiving the admiring attentions of other people; but unfortunately he may do very little that is likely to evoke such attention, and much, on the other hand, that tends to arouse disapproval and rejection. It may be, therefore, that the only effective way for him to escape from his usual reactions of disappointment and resentment is to change some one or more of his personality habits. Similarly, if the individual habitually demands impossible achievements or moral perfection of himself, it may be out of the question for him actually to achieve what he would need in order to function contentedly and happily.

However, though this is true, we ought not to neglect the fact that the person, as a going concern, an actually functioning dynamic system of forces, is a product both of his habits and of the objective stimulus situation that is affecting him. As we said in Chapter 4, when talking about anthropological observations, one of the principles that we need to incorporate more thoroughly into our thinking is the *field concept*—the concept that the emotional processes which show up in a person's life can never be explained solely by the enduring personality habits of the individual, but must be considered also as a consequence of the stimulus situations or reintegrative supports that he encounters. This is an idea that we have assimilated only very imperfectly, as yet, into our understanding of human beings. Our thinking tends to be like that of people in earlier days about such a question as the source of weight of a stone. As we have said previously, people used to believe it was obvious that the weight of a stone came from its intrinsic qualities, and that a particular stone, therefore, would weigh the same no matter where that stone was weighed or with what type of scales. Now, however, even a fourth-grader is apt to be able to discourse about the fact that the stone would weigh less on the moon and that, out in a space ship in interplanetary space, the stone might float easily within the space ship and have no weight at all.

The field concept does not need to change our thinking about the weight of stones on this earth because all stones on the surface of the earth are in practically the same constant environment, regardless of whether they are at the North Pole or the equator or wherever. But the environmental settings in which personality habits operate are by no means constant, and profoundly different effects can be called out in the same person by different environmental situations.

Therefore, when we are thinking about ourselves or about other persons, it may be very important to ask in what ways the objective life situation might be changed so as to locate us where we can function more effectively and comfortably. For example, when a person is being considered for promotion to a supervisory or managerial position in an industrial concern, it is important to ask whether this new setting will be one that is actually suited to his personality characteristics. Perhaps he has been getting along very well and happily at some work where he has not been required to make decisions, but this does not necessarily indicate that he will be happy in a work situation where he will be on his own. Each person has somewhat different personality habits. This means that if he is to live in the best possible manner, he may very possibly need a special sort of objective life situation to touch off the habits in him that are of most value. One man's meat, the old saying goes, is another man's poison.

There are important and significant changes of personality, therefore, that can be produced merely by the device of changing the objective life-situation of the individual. In the case of some individuals, this is where effort ought to focus if a change in the personality life of the person is to be sought. But in other cases, as we have said, it may be completely unfeasible to set up the sort of stimulus-situation that the individual's personality habits demand for their satisfactory fulfillment.

Personality may be altered through changes in an individual's concepts of his real self

Thus far in this chapter we have spoken about only one means of personality changing. This is the sort of case where, if there are any changes of personality habits, these are minor, and where the change is mainly a change in conditions that determine how the personality habits of the individual will be used. We need now to turn to the other type of change where the major habits of the person are altered in such a way that he becomes capable of functioning productively under unchanged objective conditions.

Within this second kind of personality changing, we need to make a further division, even though, admittedly, the two subclasses shade into each other. Both of them are cases of changes in personality habits. But there is a difference—the first subtype of habit-changing includes those instances where the individual is primarily changing what might be described as his concept of what constitutes his "real self."[2] The second subtype of habit-changing is composed of cases where the individual alters some of the personality habits which make up that "real self."

We cannot be sure that the terms we have used in making this distinction are as good as might be found. In any case, they require elaboration. For one thing, it must be made clear that, when we speak of an individual's "real self," we are not adopting exactly the same concept that Karen Horney designated by the same term. The *real self*, as Horney used the term, refers only to constructive and healthy tendencies within the person. We have in mind something broader than that. Thus, in the case of Christopher, who was afraid of going to nursery school because

[2]This process of getting a better conception of the real self often involves the person's coming to realize that he has had a faulty concept, in the past, about his real self. This faulty concept typically has a flattering character to it, a quality that Karen Horney has sought to suggest by speaking of it as the person's "idealized image." Particularly in her final book, *Neurosis and Human Growth*, in 1950, Horney gave a very stimulating discussion of this whole matter.

he had so often been suddenly attacked by a bigger boy there, his fear would be part of Christopher's real self, as we use the term, and if Christopher had been able to put his problem into words, he might well have said, "Part of my real self is a fear that when I play with other children, I'll get clobbered." What he needed to change, therefore, was not his concept that he was afraid of big boys, but the personality habit of fear.

What makes these terms elusive in their meanings, though, is that the person's *concept* of what constitutes his *real self* is also a personality habit. But, it is a habit of a special sort. It may be true, perhaps, that such a concept is a kind of habit more easily changed than some of the "real-self habits." Or perhaps it may be that the influences required for concept change are somewhat different from those required for changes in "real-self habits." Much of our knowledge about the changing of personality habits could be clarified if we would make this distinction. Let us, therefore, grant this tentative distinction and see where we can get with it.

When a person makes changes in his way of thinking about his real self, this may sometimes constitute, just in itself, a significant and helpful change in his personality as a whole. In some other cases, however, his change of concept becomes an influence for the better through the fact that it gives him a means of making changes in his life in other respects. For example, the person may come to realize he possesses some strong positive motives that are among his important assets, but which he has not hitherto been using. Or, through having achieved a better concept of his real self, he may have arrived at a point from which he can proceed more effectively to try to change parts of the real self. Or, even if he cannot change some part of his real self that he recognizes as a handicap, he may still have reached a better position from which to try to control the troublesome part of himself (as when an alcoholic learns that he apparently cannot take *any* alcoholic drink in *any* amount without touching off a good, substantial binge).

Changes in concepts of the real self do not, therefore, always produce significant effects merely of themselves, but they may constitute steppingstones to a better adjustment only because they lead to changes in a person's life situation, or some other indirect effect. Nevertheless, the attempt to get a better concept of the real self often seems to be the most strategic objective at which to aim in one's efforts to effect changes in personality. But we have been talking in abstract terms too long, and it is now time for us to consider some concrete examples and then to try to identify some of the chief means whereby such concept changes occur.

Earlier in the chapter we quoted the case of a woman who had come to Gerhard Adler for psychotherapy after suffering from recurrent spells of depression. The objective circumstances of her life seemed very favorable, except for the fact that she had been left a widow five years before. When Adler suggested to her that the loss of her husband was a possible cause of her depressions, she denied this and pointed out that she had suffered from similar depressions before her husband died.

In the course of therapy, what became apparent was that the patient's symptoms of personality maladjustment were primarily a consequence of some strong positive interests that she was failing to recognize—or, indeed, that she had been trying to deny or forget—and that what she needed to do was to provide some real means of expression for these in her life. The particular type of therapy that Gerhard Adler was using originated with Carl Jung (Gerhard Adler is not to be confused with Alfred Adler, whose approach differs to a considerable extent from that of Jung). Jungian therapy puts much emphasis on the study of a patient's dreams as a means of helping him to get better insight into his personality. A therapist of a different school might have used some other means to help this woman reach the same goal, which was to arrive at a better conception of her real self. But in a way very characteristic of Jung's methods, the progress achieved with this particular patient came through dream analysis. Two dreams in particular were singled out by Gerhard Adler as most helpful in achieving the new insight. The interested reader who would like to go deeper into Jungian thought will do well to look up and reflect upon the full description of this case and, for that matter, others in Adler's book. We will quote here merely a part of the account:[3]

> The second dream was as follows: "I was in a large, beautiful ante-room, built in the classical style. Although there was a good deal of open space between the pillars, there was no view, as the view was entirely blocked by hanging rugs. The space between the two middle pillars was filled in by a beautiful soft blue-grey kangaroo skin. I knew that it was from between these two pillars that the sources of the Nile should gush out, and I was longing to see them burst forth. I attempted to drag away the skin but it was so firmly attached that this was impossible. It was only in my mind's eye that I could see the waters flow."
>
> . . . when she told me the dream [Adler continues his report], the obvious thing to do was to enquire further about the striking kangaroo skin. At first she could tell me nothing about it. But at last it suddenly occurred to her that she had seen this very kangaroo skin twenty years before in the house of her mother-in-law. Once the ice was broken she told me, with considerable emotion, the following story:
>
> Shortly before the outbreak of war in 1914 a young English doctor was working at the university where she was studying medicine. The two became very friendly, and eventually fell deeply in love with each other. They were just about to become engaged when war broke out, and the abrupt departure

[3]*Op cit.*, pp. 158-164.

of her English friend put an end to all these beautiful plans. Meanwhile she had, during her student days and concurrently with her attachment to the young Englishman, formed a friendship with her future husband, who held an appointment at the same hospital. He fell in love with her and made her an offer of marriage. Although she liked him well enough, she had at first refused his offer, as she intended to marry the Englishman, but in the difficult situation in which she found herself, she agreed, not without considerable inner conflict, to become engaged to the German. Her inner resistance finally became so strong that she decided, in spite of all her liking and sympathy for her fiancé, to break her engagement. With this purpose in view, she took the train to another town where her fiancé happened to be staying with his mother. As she entered the house of her future mother-in-law, the first thing she saw was an enormous kangaroo skin, which had a peculiar connection with her fiancé. In his scientific capacity, he had been commissioned by the directors of a large Zoological Garden to carry out post-mortems on their deceased animals. In this way the kangaroo skin had come into his possession, and he gave it to his mother.

What happened on this visit was that my patient was so overwhelmed by the affectionate greetings of her mother-in-law and by pity for her fiancé that she felt unable to carry out her original intention of breaking off her engagement, and succeeded only in binding herself to him even more closely, with the result that she very soon married him.

In the course of her harmonious and, on the whole, very happy married life, she had managed to repress all this, and consequently she also managed to forget completely the existence of the kangaroo skin. . . . This story provided an opportunity for getting at the meaning of the dream. . . . Just as the kangaroo skin had dammed back the accumulated waters of the Nile, and prevented their flow along their natural channels, so my patient's marriage had put a stop to the development of her own personal life and individual abilities. She had obviously made a heroic attempt to suppress her dimly-felt knowledge of having made a mistake, by subordinating herself entirely to the interests and personality of her kindly and gifted husband, at the cost however of completely losing her own line of life. . . .

To confine the meaning of the dream to a mistaken decision made twenty years ago would, however, be altogether too one-sided and would completely fail to do justice to its compensatory and constructive character. No doubt this mistaken decision had hampered my patient's inner development very considerably, but it must not be forgotten that, in spite of this, her marriage had been very happy and had consequently provided her with sufficient positive values to compensate for its more doubtful aspects. . . .

Gerhard Adler continues with a type of comment very characteristic of Jung's approach:

Dreams function with supreme economy; if a dream reproduces a situation belonging to the remote past it is because of its bearing on the present. . . . If the recognition of past mistakes is to be valuable, in other words productive, it must contain a hint as to how the error can be rectified and so conduce to a better life in the future. This is the constructive and synthetic aspect of a dream in contradistinction to its reductive and analytical aspect. This constructive aspect is immediately seen if the mistake, as revealed in the dream, is understood to refer not only to one isolated instance in the past but is considered typical and symptomatic of the patient's whole attitude to life. The dream disclosed a difficult situation in which my patient had acted against her "better judgment" and allowed herself to be fatally influenced and led by the wishes and needs of others instead of pursuing the path which she herself instinctively knew to be the right one. She had submitted passively to the influence of others instead of actively shaping her own life. In other words, she had adopted a typically one-sided feminine attitude. . . . the dream reveals her typical attitude to life. . . .

Further analysis made it clearer and clearer that the neurotic symptoms had been due to the neglect and retardation of her individual development. From a dependent and undecided person the patient turned into an active and independent woman who could shape her life according to her needs. Thus for instance she built up a new career for herself, based on her former medical training, in which she found an adequate and satisfactory outlet for her energies. Moreover, new and unexpected human relationships opened up for her which corresponded to her nature and furthered her spiritual development. To her it appeared as if she lived in a changed world; but it was really in herself that the change had taken place.

Some of the general remarks that Gerhard Adler makes on this case should be added.[4] They are comments very expressive of the thinking about personality for which Carl Jung is responsible.

The neurosis consists precisely in this damming up, this estrangement from the real self. . . . One could define the feeling of fear which crops up in every neurosis as an instinctive feeling of being separated from one's own essential needs; or a feeling of discrepancy between actual life and life as it should be lived. The tragic element . . . is that . . . this feeling of being separated from the main stream of life only intensifies the tendency toward self-protection, resulting in an increased withdrawal from life. . . .

The positive counterpart of anxiety or dread, however, is longing. . . . Longing is also a feeling of something lacking but in the opposite sense, inasmuch as longing drives a man to try to obtain that which he lacks. . . . In the last resort, the task of an analysis is to liberate this positive force . . . from the

[4] *Ibid.*, pp. 169-172.

negative toils of fear; for, however strange this may appear, both are but different manifestations of the same psychic energy. . . .

Considered from this point of view, a neurosis represents the last convulsive effort of the psyche to reach a positive solution, inasmuch as it gives a man no peace and drives him into such a state of unrest and dissatisfaction that at last his need to escape from the bonds of fear becomes stronger than all the negative forces. That is why the psychotherapist often finds that some of the potentially most valuable human beings come to him for help, because their neurosis, with all its fear and anguish, nevertheless acts as a spur driving them to overcome the obstacle which is alienating them from their real being . . . in the last resort, the element of fear in a neurosis is due to the very split which prevents a man from realizing his true personality, and this breach can be healed only by his adopting a new orientation toward life.

If you will think back to some of the therapeutic cases described in Chapter 3, you will recognize that key features of some of those were such changes of the individual's concept of his real self. Thus, you will remember the account by Arthur Shedlin (pp. 80-83) of a man about 50 years old who had suffered from a long history of psychosomatic difficulties, and who was confronted with the question of whether he should finally tell his wife frankly the truth about his ancestry and religious background. He was afraid she would be so hurt by his prior lack of confidence in her that it might wreck his marriage. But it was as though he came to see: "This is simply not the way that I want to live, continuing to be secretive about this matter. So, even if there is some serious risk, I must take this step. To do so will be more consistent with what I really am, as a person."

In coming to this conclusion, he was not primarily building all at once a new personality habit of openness and honesty in his interpersonal reactions. The fact is that if he had not possessed such a habit previously, his deception of his wife would not have bothered him so deeply. Primarily what he was changing was his concept of his real self, as we have defined this term above. When he seized upon this new concept, he was helped to act in a different way than before, thus creating something new in his marriage. And the happy outcome, presumably mainly by virtue of this, was that the psychosomatic difficulties that had persisted so stubbornly cleared up.

In the case of Austin Wood (pp. 76-78), the change of the patient's concept of his real self was a change which permitted him to see that, all the time, he had really felt love for his father as well as the resentment which was all he had previously been able to recognize. In the cases reported by Franz Alexander and George Humphrey (pp. 74-76), on the other hand, the improvements that came from therapy hinged particularly on the patients' dawning realization that they had felt intense hatred toward the brothers who had helped them, perhaps somewhat patronizingly, and whom they had not known that they viewed with any such emotion, or at least had not so admitted to themselves.

All of these are cases where technical psychotherapy was the means that brought about the achievement of a transformed concept of the real self. Most of our knowledge thus far about personality change has come from the work of psychotherapists, and we do not yet know to what extent changes in the concept of one's self may also spring from day-to-day experiences. It does appear, however, that ordinary people, going about their everyday life, sometimes experience some considerable changing of their concepts as to what is most real about themselves. For a well-rounded knowledge of how personality may be purposefully changed, we need much more information about changes which occur without benefit of therapy. At the time of choosing an occupation, for example, the individual often realizes that, however firmly he had earlier sized up his interests and motivation in a particular way, something has since happened to direct his motivation toward a markedly different sort of career.

The course of one such change of direction in the life of a student named Alfred was studied in some detail by one of the writers and his students in a research project on personality. Alfred was a young man who came from an unusually favorable family situation. He had had plenty of opportunity to share activities with his father, such as building their house and working up a small business providing the services of a tractor they purchased. Alfred had developed a strong interest in music, also, and, partly through the social contacts involved in music camps and school bands, had always gotten along splendidly with his age-mates. In spite of his good social skills and his high academic ability, however, he had run into a lot of difficulty when he reached college. In high school he had been one of the best students in his class in math and physics; but when he enrolled in an engineering course in college, his grades dropped so low that he was in danger of flunking out. In his non-engineering courses his grades were much better. These apparently appealed much more to him and brought him more satisfaction, although he did not realize this for quite a while, because he had entered college with the preconceived idea that engineering was the natural field for him. He knew that his father approved of this choice and that, on the other hand, his father had frequently talked disparagingly about the humanistic studies and social sciences toward which Alfred's interests seemed to turn in college. His father, incidentally, was a university professor in one of the natural sciences.

The study of Alfred's personality showed a long record of painful conflict. For more than a year he had been painfully unhappy over the poor work he was doing in his chosen field, yet he was unable to see that his real interests lay elsewhere and that his troubles might originate in his trying to force himself to do what basically he did not want to do. Eventually he came to the conclusion that his hesitation over changing his field was because he did not want to risk the disapproval of his father and cause him disappointment, but that it might be well for him to change his field nevertheless. Actually, after he made his choice, his father did not prove unsympathetic. Alfred's academic record in his new field proved eminently satisfactory, and Alfred found that his father had been much more interested in seeing his son succeed academically than in seeing his son enter any particular field.

Alfred's difficulties could have been avoided, probably, if he had had a more correct understanding of his father's personality and attitudes, but it was not any new insight into these that permitted him to make the significant change in his vocational objectives. The change came primarily because he achieved a new concept of his own real self and, as a result, decided to alter his course of study even though he thought (incorrectly) that doing so might provoke his father's opposition. This change was made—it is significant to note—without any recommendation by an outsider and without the benefit of any therapeutic interpretations. It is quite possible, nevertheless, that his experiences as a subject in the aforementioned research study (which involved such procedures as relating his past history at length and describing his current feelings) may have helped him clarify his self-concept in a way he could not otherwise have done. Even though there was no "feedback" to him along the line of suggestive questions such as "Don't you think that maybe such and such may be an element in your problem?" it still may be true that the conditions involved in making the study inevitably had some of the same character that psychotherapy might have had.

Even if this be true, however, it leads in turn to this conclusion: In the everyday life-relations of parents with children, teachers with students, and friends with friends, there are certain relatively simple procedures that could profitably be taken over from psychotherapy into ordinary interpersonal relations. This does not mean that contacts in everyday life should get involved with any attempts at dream interpretation—far from it—or with any attempts by one person to tell any other what his real nature appears to be. In fact, if laymen really knew how psychotherapists operate, they would discover that the great difference between most psychotherapists and most laymen is that psychotherapists are vastly more willing to *listen* than the rest of us usually are in everyday life, and particularly more willing to listen without at the same time feeling called upon to make evaluative comments such as: "I think you're right there," "That was a courageous thing to do," "Obviously, what is needed is. . . ."

The psychotherapist, in great degree, is the person who, out of his technical study and experience, has developed an increased confidence that people can work out more accurate concepts of their real selves if they are given a chance to speak freely to a person who is interested in them, feels a basic respect for them, and does not feel that he is called on to advise or exhort. Some methods of psychotherapy, admittedly, also act on the premise that suggestions are allowable and indeed should be made at *some* points to the person who is being helped. Other systems of psychotherapy, as we said in Chapter 3, proceed on the principle that no such guiding is required, even in cases that seem extreme. At least this much may be put down, however: A *major* factor in all main types of psychotherapy is the sort of factor that was more or less inevitable in the research study of Alfred—namely, merely a careful, painstaking, respectful, interested listening to the story and opinions of another person and an abstaining from efforts to "make him over" or to mold him into some other kind of person that the listener would think more desirable.

This is a type of approach that all of us might well bring much more extensively into our everyday interpersonal relationships. It is a way of responding to people that recognizes what some of the main influences are that permit people to go forward toward a more penetrating understanding of their own real selves.

Why changes in the concept of one's real self are difficult to achieve

When individuals need to get a more accurate understanding of their own real selves, there are two main sources of difficulty that stand in the way. One type of difficulty is intellectual, just as it is in trying to get a new conception of *any* complex matter. It is the same sort of difficulty that made architects blind, for a long time, to what they should be doing. Year after year, the design of houses and schools continued to follow one or another of the old stereotyped patterns that we now recognize as failing to realize so many of the interesting possibilities both of function and of beauty. Architects were giving a great deal of thought to matters of design, but it was exceedingly difficult for them, even just from a purely intellectual standpoint, to free themselves from the conventions sufficiently to see the possibilities in their materials in a new way. Similarly, a person accustomed to a life organized after one fashion finds it hard to see, even just in an intellectual sense, that there are other ways in which his characteristics and potentialities might be organized. And, of course, we are all the while trying to get on with the business of living; our continuing practical responsibilities tend to keep our thinking in the old ruts.

A second type of difficulty is also a major one. In addition to intellectual difficulties, the emotional responses of the person are very likely to set up obstacles that keep him from thinking differently—and freshly—about himself. For one thing, and we may as well face this fact, most persons are unwilling to recognize the implications of some of their experience because they hate to admit to others that they are wrong and that they need to change! One of the writers, when a boy, developed the idea that he did not like pears for dessert. His parents kept insisting that he try some. He did so at intervals, on their insistence. In a sort of halfway fashion, he could see that he liked them; but still he maintained that he didn't like them, and he could hardly face the fact, even within himself, that he had judged pears too hastily and that really he was missing something. The same sort of discomfort bobs up to obstruct the thinking of any child or adult who faces the question of whether his familiar picture of his real self is sufficiently accurate for the needs of his life.

A new concept of his real self may confront the individual, too, with some emotional processes or tendencies that he has learned to fear. Thus a child may have adopted, as his basic life construct, the idea that he must always subordinate his wishes obediently to the behests and wishes of other persons. Through this policy perhaps he has won much affection from his parents and a firm sense of security. It is not surprising, therefore, that he is unable to see, both then and as he gets older, any other way in which he might live. With this basic pattern of living, he would also have learned to fear any self-assertive or resentful emotional processes in himself, because these would tend to jeopardize the pattern of response on which he pins his faith. Whenever he becomes aware of such aggressive or self-assertive responses thrusting themselves forward, his habit will be to feel the same fear of rejection and helplessness that such tendencies had touched off in him as a child. As a result, when he struggles to see whether there are now resentments within himself that he is not acknowledging, or whether he has some wishes of his own that are legitimate even if others are critical of them, any steps he may take toward recognizing such aspects of his real self tend to be obstructed by his even stronger fears.

Significantly, therefore, new concepts about one's real self are almost certain to demand of the person some new kind of behavior that threatens to be uncomfortable, or embarrassing, even humiliating, and inevitably in some respects frustrating.

The older Freudian work revealed that psychotherapeutic patients commonly feared both their sexual motives and their destructive, aggressive tendencies. Later the Freudians came to see that people were afraid also to admit their own fears and anxieties. This development in the understanding of personality was an important one, but it was a one-sided development, after the usual fashion of work in a new field, as we noted in the introduction to Chapter 11. The Freudians were seeing only the more tangible sources of conflicts.

As psychotherapy has developed, many of its professionals have come to believe that the most difficult motives for persons to face are likely to be of a more subtle character. Thus, Frieda Fromm-Reichmann, who has carried forward the thinking of Harry Stack Sullivan, has expressed the idea that the most significant fear to which patients are prone is a "fear of realizing and expressing their own friendliness and therefore of accepting friendliness from others . . ."[5] Further elaborating this point, she says:

> In my experience the wish for closeness and tenderness with the beloved parent and the envious resentment about the authoritative power of the hated one, both without recognizable sexual roots, constitute a more frequent finding in childhood histories of healthy, neurotic, and psychotic people than do their sexual Oedipal entanglements with the parents of their childhood. . . . People of this western culture do not seem to find it too difficult to talk about sexual attachments, falling in love, etc., but . . . many of us are reluctant, if not afraid, to speak about the friendly, tender, asexually loving aspects of our interpersonal relationships.

This statement is not to be taken, of course, as meaning that individuals with personality maladjustments have no difficulties with repressed sexual and hostile tendencies. But partly because of the striking contributions of Freudian theory, it has become widely recognized in our culture that strong sexual and aggressive tendencies may cause conflicts in behavior; in consequence, as Fromm-Reichmann says, people are much more able to face some measure of these tendencies in themselves. (On the other hand, this does not mean that they can always face the full strength exerted by these tendencies in their particular lives; and people who feel that they have faced the truth about the motives which the Freudians stress still receive some rude jolts on this score in the course of psychotherapeutic work.) However, Fromm-Reichmann is probably correct in asserting that the most serious single source of disturbance is unsatisfied hunger for close personal relationships. In fact, the evidence from psychotherapy regarding persons in whom the sex motive seems extremely powerful is that this excessive strength is primarily a disguised expression of various emotional needs, including the craving for closeness and intimacy in a psychological sense, rather than the sheer physiological sex drive that, to the person himself, it seems to be.

Why should a person be afraid to face the fact that he craves to express his feeling of friendliness toward other people? Why should he hesitate to recognize that he longs for some really open and spontaneous expression of his deepest self in interpersonal relations? It would seem at first that this is just what our culture recognizes and encourages and that the individual would never have reason to hide such a motive from himself. These fears seem strange. But when we look closer, we may observe how strongly our culture also encourages conformity and uniformity.

[5]Frieda Fromm-Reichmann, *Principles of Intensive Psychotherapy* (Chicago, University of Chicago Press, 1950), pp. 84, 99.

We simply have not learned to respect individual differences in our culture. Perhaps we do so less today than when the country was young and pioneering was honored. Today we seem in danger of forgetting that a social system can be secure and more enjoyable—even more secure, perhaps, than ours is—when society makes generous room for individual differences in great variety, much more than we now either permit or enjoy.

Whatever the origins of this attitude may be, however, the net effect is clear. The individual who is struggling to get a better concept of his real self is not wrestling with a problem that is difficult merely on intellectual grounds. He is struggling with a problem that is difficult also because there are emotional barriers that tend to prevent him from considering facts and drawing generalizations. Just as in Alfred's case, he may be finding it difficult to follow some clear path of thought because its consequences threaten to be painful.

How such changes in one's self-concept may be accomplished

As we have said, important changes in the concepts of the real self often come through the help of skilled counselors and therapists, even when that help is obtained only by virtue of the basically "accepting" attitude of the therapist, through his willingness to listen carefully and sympathetically, and through his willingness to avoid trying to mold the other person.

Most human beings, however, never get to the point where they see a therapist professionally. It is important to ask, therefore, whether there are means that people can use on their own responsibility in an effort to get sounder and more insightful concepts of their own real selves. In short, how can any one of us, by himself, come a bit nearer to the goal of the Socratic injunction: "Know thyself"? Four methods may be recommended:

1. *The individual can sometimes make progress toward a more insightful self-concept if he tries to understand more completely and honestly the introspective knowledge he already possesses about himself.* The task of a person in this matter, it should be remembered, is a task of concept formation, and progress in concept formation often requires one to go back and re-examine the data from which he is drawing some conclusion. Thus, a person might say to himself: "I *think* my attitudes and motives and interests can be summarized as such and such; but this may not be correct. Let me go back and consider, one by one, the concrete experiences I can recall from which my conclusions have been drawn, watching carefully for any failures to find support for what I have been thinking are my real characteristics."

This is a type of approach that has been used particularly by one school of psychologists, the phenomenologists, better known in Europe than in America. If a phenomenologist wanted to help an individual identify his own motives, he would not ask him such a question as: "What was your feeling toward your mother?" From any such general question he would expect to get a pretty stereotyped response, perhaps a culturally determined one expressing the convention of affection for one's mother, and he would know that it *might* be quite incorrect. Instead, he would ask the person: "Tell me, one after the other, all the incidents that you can think of that involved your mother, and tell me as concretely as you can, in each case, what were your feelings and thoughts in that incident."

Out of such a review as this, the person might find that his already-formed picture of his own responses was on the whole an accurate reflection of his "data," or he might be surprised to see how different a concept was actually demanded about his real self. This is one method, and its potentialities are very great.

2. *The individual generally will need not merely to consider what his own conscious experiences have been in the past, but also to examine with fresh eyes his own overt behavior as well.* As we have said at many points, it seems quite possible for persons to acquire and keep using personality habits that they do not know they have. Consequently there needs to be some self-examination that goes beyond an examination merely of subjective experience. As an expression of this point, here is a quotation from a book by Rudolf Dreikurs, a man whose writings express primarily the ideas of Alfred Adler:[6]

> Ideas, wishes and emotions [by which Dreikurs means merely *conscious* ideas, wishes, and emotions] throw far less light on the personality than actions. . . . feelings and above all wishes very often contradict what is actually done. Actions are the only safe guide for understanding the personality, which so often turns toward fictive goals. We must make up our minds to regard everything else as mere embroidery. In fact, all wishes and feelings that contradict actions are misleading.
>
> Power to appreciate the significance of actions . . . is most valuable in connection with self-education. Particularly in our own lives we find that apparent contradictions in our thoughts, emotions and wishes occupy the foreground of our consciousness, so that we forget to judge our actions. The reason why self-knowledge is so difficult to acquire is that for the sake of maintaining an ethical personality we try to hide any of our impulses which are hostile to society from ourselves. Further, true self-knowledge would bring us disconcerting revelations. Our own fictive goals would be disclosed.

[6]Rudolf Dreikurs, *Fundamentals of Adlerian Psychology* (New York, Greenberg, Publisher, Inc., 1950), pp. 58-59, 112.

We should see that they were mistaken goals and they would have to be given up.

[The person's resistance to recognizing the implications of his actions] . . . is always an expression of fear—fear of having to recognize his own responsibility, of having to make a decision, of having to give up safeguards.

3. *Sometimes gains can come through the person's using, on his own responsibility, a sort of free-association procedure that is encouraged, either explicitly or implicitly, in a number of different forms of psychotherapy.* This procedure calls for a type of thinking that does not try to proceed in any orderly and directed way toward a predetermined goal. Rather it seeks to let the thinking move in as unrestrained a fashion as possible.

Particularly important in this free-association procedure is to let the thinking move with complete freedom, even when what it turns up may produce emotional effects of a rather disturbing sort. Ordinarily we try to head off such processes. We may find that we feel discouraged or bitter or fearful, and if we think such processes lack a realistic foundation, then we try to change our emotional response into something "more appropriate." To learn more about his "real self," however, the person ought to do the opposite of this. When he finds himself in the grip of a mood that he feels or judges to be unreasonable, he ought to take this opportunity to push the process deliberately and see where it leads him.

One of the writers remembers an occasion when a young woman—a student of his—used this procedure to advantage, although it must be admitted that she also got some small amount of help from the outside. She came to ask for some counseling because, she said, she was having the feeling, from time to time, that what she was doing was not really being done by herself. She seemed to herself to be up near the ceiling in the corner of the room, watching herself in action. She said she felt she ought to talk with someone about this. But on the other hand, she asked, "Isn't there some way that I might work on this by myself? I'd rather do it that way if possible." So, I suggested to her that she follow the procedure we have just described. Several days later the girl returned. She had tried what had been suggested. What she found was that, when she pushed these feelings of things being unreal, she started wishing that other girls would make love to her in direct physical ways. "That was disturbing to you?" she was asked. "Yes," she replied, "maybe some people laugh at matters of homosexuality, but I don't look at it that way." Some questions were put to her about her attitude toward men and the idea of marriage. Her general manner was pleasant and feminine, but she replied definitely that she did not plan to marry, but intended instead to have an independent career as a designer (which, of course, is a relatively feminine occupational choice, at that). She spoke of her childhood as having been marred by a lot of conflict with her father, whom she thought of as very strict and arbitrary. Finally I hazarded a guess: "Well, would this be true, that you wouldn't mind being married if you didn't have to have a husband?" She laughed and then assented to the suggestion. The matter was put to her more strongly: "Men, after all, are rather uncouth and unpleasant, aren't they?" "Oh," she objected, "I don't think that's true of all of them, and one only has to marry one person." "Yes, but you can't tell for sure what any particular man is like, and the chances are bad, aren't they?" "Well, maybe it wouldn't *have* to be. . . ."

With virtually no more help than that, she worked through to a realization that the attitude she had taken toward "career vs. marriage" was not expressive of her real self. With no more than this, a problem that at first looked rather serious proved not to be really deep in character at all. For her it was a baffling and threatening problem, however, as long as she tried to head off these moods rather than explore them.

4. *When a person gets a new concept about his real self, it will usually be the case that, however valuable this concept may be, the individual will need to engage in patiently practicing with it, perhaps for a long time.* In a sense, as said on pp. 386-387, this changing of one's ideas about the real self is still a matter of changing personality habits. And although once in a while habits can be changed in a twinkling and a person may show almost no tendency to revert to his former mode of response, habit-change is not something that can usually be expected to occur easily and without tendencies to slip back into the former mode of functioning.

To some extent, therefore, even the changing of personality in this first way of gaining insight into the nature of one's true self must also be understood in terms of principles related to actual changing of personality habits which are part of that real self.

Changing of personality habits that are part of the real self

Thus far, what we have said about changing personality habits has actually been concerned almost solely with changing a person's *concepts* about his *other* personality habits. For example, by rethinking her attitudes toward men and marriage, the student mentioned above got rid of her feeling that she was not really doing things herself, but watching herself do them. Now, however, we need to turn to the problem of how to change such other habits. It may be a case in which some negative motive of an unwarranted and hampering sort has developed, such as Christopher's fear of play situations that involved other children. It may be an instance of the inadequate development of positive interests. It could involve an individual's concept of how he should deal with certain situations in order to avoid serious danger or how he is to reach some positive goals of great importance to him.

We can be sure of one thing—there is no one simple assertion that we or anyone can make as to whether such changing of personality habits will be easy or difficult, fast or slow. The mere fact that personality habits involve emotional factors does not guarantee that the change will occur either faster or slower than the changing of other habits in which emotional factors are absent, or almost absent. Thus, you may recall the incident (p. 162) when Rufus Jones quickly changed his fear of mysterious "warning lights" when he pulled the chair to the center of his room, reached up to see what the "light" might be, and found that someone had hung an ear of corn up to dry and that the moonlight was shining on it. An example like this shows that fears sometimes can be removed suddenly.

On the other hand, we all know that some fears are removed, if at all, very slowly. Take the rest of the story of Christopher's fear of nursery school as an instance. After he had become more and more disturbed at the thought of going to school, his parents allowed him to stay away from school for a half year. During that time he had no further unhappy experiences with other children, but, instead of "forgetting" his fear, he became more and more reluctant to get involved in play situations with other children, and it was then that the parents decided they ought to make an attempt to help him get over his fears. Accordingly, after some months, the parents began taking Christopher to visit another nearby nursery school playground during after-school hours, but without telling him that the playground was a "school," since even the word was enough to evoke tears.

At this different school, Christopher very much enjoyed playing on all the outdoor equipment. One day he was taken there before school opened, and presently children began to appear on their way to the morning session. After some hesitation, he joined them, since basically he always had liked to play. He was taken away before school actually began, still without hearing the playground identified as belonging to a "school." After several such short visits, Christopher had made a number of friends among the children and teachers and became eager to return.

When the director of the school had gotten well acquainted with him, Christopher was taken through the room, and it was explained to him that this "playground" was, in fact, a school. This did not seem to perturb him too much as long as there was no suggestion that he was to be left there. He did shopwork, and the director let him paint, both of which he especially liked.

Finally, when the director felt that Christopher was strongly drawn to the other children and the activities they were engaged in, Christopher was asked whether he wanted to go to school there. This immediately produced tears, but he was left, screaming loudly, in the arms of the director. She reported that he quieted in a few minutes after the parent disappeared and thereafter played happily. This tearful scene was repeated on several mornings, after which Christopher announced, at home, that he wasn't going to cry any more. And, in fact, he didn't. In a short time he became and continued to be a happy member of his class group. When the following fall came around, even though the school was moved to new quarters, Christopher went into it alone and showed every sign that his fears had vanished for good.

In Christopher's case the procedure of merely separating him from the situation that aroused his strong fear seemed to contribute nothing toward the elimination or changing of his habit. Yet, throughout that time, Christopher had no experience of other children attacking him in the sudden unprovoked ways that he had encountered at the hands of one boy in his first nursery school. Even in the original situation, of course, he was not being continually attacked. Christopher's relearning task therefore resembled that of one of Skinner's pigeons. The pigeon had learned that food-rewards were available only after widely-spaced pecks on the lever; he consequently tended not to desist from lever-tapping even after the rewards were discontinued entirely. Christopher's habit of being afraid did not disappear until after his parents made attempts to attack the problem in a more direct and positive fashion, bringing the boy into the same sort of situation where he previously had had such unhappy experiences and slowly building new positive habits that might in the end prove stronger than his fear, as indeed they did.

We are faced with a complex problem when we ask what factors might be used in this way in an intelligent effort to change some unsatisfactory personality habit. However, a number of principles do seem to be suggested by the experimental and clinical studies of habit-change. We will confine our discussion of these to six points of outstanding importance:

1. *Old personality habits as a rule can rarely be disposed of by forgetting, erasing, or simple inhibiting. They can rarely be eliminated by any merely negative type of approach. Instead, they can be eliminated only as they are transformed in some fashion into another habit of a more constructive and satisfactory sort.* Much of our past cannot be altered. We did certain things, and the effects of our actions are, with some degree of firmness, registered in our brain. Often our memories of regrettable episodes, or of our shortcomings, are only too fully and painfully clear. If, as children, we were cruel to younger brothers or sisters, or if we felt guilt about masturbation, or if we simply recognized that we were awfully homely, we cannot expect to eliminate these memories—they are simply there, and are, perhaps, lumps that weigh on our emotional lives.

But take Phyllis's experience with the typing teacher (pp. 336-337) who scolded her for erasing mistakes and told her that "this was just as much cheating as anything else ever could be." This disparagement is something that Phyllis apparently could never forget, and it probably spilled over into her other personal relationships too. The mere fact, however, that this incident was an unalterable fact in Phyllis's past history did not mean that she would forever have to think, whenever she saw her typing teacher, "There is someone who knows that, inside, I am not what I pretend to be." Whether she continued to make this particular response would be a matter of how she interpreted things. What Phyllis could reasonably expect to do, as she gained in maturity of understanding, would be to change the habits that remained as a residue from that old experience—not by erasing the memory of the event, but by coming to see the action of her former teacher in a different light. This might mean that, whenever she saw her typing teacher, she still would think again of the old incident, but now in a new sense, perhaps like this: "There is the teacher who in a curious way helped me to know, more deeply than I otherwise would, how important it is to be considerate and sympathetic in reproving other people, and how important it is to correct others in a way that preserves their self-respect rather than tears it down." Or maybe something like this: "There is the teacher who has opened my eyes to the importance of getting teachers for our school system who will be constructive rather than destructive influences in their pupils' lives." Or maybe: "There is a woman who reminds me that persons who make mistakes very often do so from basically praiseworthy motives, if one can only look deep enough. The lesson that she taught me was painful, and it took me a long time to see that I ought to view life in a manner different from hers; but she has helped me to learn one of life's most important lessons, after all."

We do not know whether Phyllis actually ever achieved such a reconstruction. Here, however, is the story of an important change of personality habit of a broader scope. The statement is by a college professor, born in this country:

My parents grew up in Poland. For my first sixteen years we lived among groups of Polish and other foreign origins. Mom and Dad spoke Polish at home, and that was all we children spoke there. Our holidays, customs, even our food, were Polish.

As a child I remember long evenings of sitting on the stairs listening in on Polish parties at which the main interest always centered on stories of the old country, where life was pictured in heroic, sentimental terms. During childhood our greatest wish was to visit this wonderful land some day.

We Poles looked upon the occasional American family in the community with the greatest disdain, since they were usually dirty, thriftless, and immoral compared to ourselves. We did not realize, then, that these were lower-class Americans.

As I grew older, I became increasingly aware of the outside world. At first its very existence puzzled me. It seemed unreal, even vaguely threatening. During high school we went by bus to a distant, entirely American town. It was during this period that our attitudes toward being Poles began to change. Polish life began to look more and more negative, until finally we thought of our Polishness as a stigma. We were nothing but "hunkies," as the high school gang said.

In junior and senior high school it became my burning passion to get rid of my Polishness. College provided the opportunity. I chose a school that was thousands of miles from home, in a region where there were no Poles. I did not return for years.

Some years later I made my first acquaintance with sociology and anthropology. I read about cultural differences and especially about ethnic groups. One author described the effects of such ethnic group membership upon second generation children, and I began to see myself in the light of a new understanding of society.

My shame of being Polish changed to a feeling of growing pride at finding myself a person who had had the valuable experience of living and knowing two different cultures, something that was rare even among the most educated people whom I admired. At the same time there was a great welling up of affection and sentiment for my parents and a strong desire to visit them. I saw my own striving to escape "Polishness" in the perspective of a wider conception of culture, and the negative qualities of my family origins vanished.

Thereafter I visited home regularly and found myself enjoying speaking Polish, and even preferred to use it, even though my parents themselves had largly shifted to using English in the meanwhile. I realized how much Mom and Dad meant to me and felt horrified at having stayed away from home so many years.

When we think again about Rufus Jones and the "light," we can see that this same sort of incorporation of the old memory into a new organization is illustrated there, too, and probably helps to account for the speed of his habit-change. For, Jones did not have merely a rather ambiguous situation of seeing a "warning light" which then was not followed by some disaster. Instead, he had the almost ludicrous experience of reaching, greatly frightened, toward a "warning light" and having his fingers close on a dried ear of corn. This habit-incorporation effect is what several psychologists have had in mind, among them particularly Prescott Lecky, in his little book on *Self-Consistency*,[7] and Richard Wendt, in his experimental studies of learning. In both of these it is made to appear likely that old habits can never be simply erased or un-

[7]Prescott Lecky, *Self-Consistency: A Theory of Personality*, 2d ed. (New York, Island Press, 1951), pp. v, 275.

learned; they must be destroyed through incorporation of old "facts" into some new and more powerful habit structure.

2. *The form that the new, constructive habit needs to take will often involve a more careful discrimination as to exactly what conditions bring what results, with the end in view that this discrimination will reveal a technique for getting results of the sort that the individual desires.* For example, there is a person whose emotional reactions to other persons are unfavorable because, as a child, he had many really tough experiences that taught him the risks of close emotional relations with other people—people perhaps who were too dominating or too smothering in their attentions, people who constantly misjudged his motives and put interpretations on his actions that tended to destroy his self-respect. Such a person is like Susan with bees. Susan had been stung by only one bee, but it was an unforgettable experience, and no one could have convinced her that bees are harmless creatures. Such clear, unforgettable knowledge cannot be bluntly repudiated by the person.

Frieda Fromm-Reichmann describes the case of a woman in her late thirties who came for psychotherapy at the point where she had just terminated the fourth of a series of unhappy love affairs. The therapist suspected that there had been disastrous family relationships somewhere in the woman's past because she showed such odd fluctuations of response to him.[8]

Her attitude toward the therapist was characterized by a marked degree of deference, hero-worship, and overacceptance of, if not submissiveness in the presence of, his authority. This attitude alternated with an equally marked display of a great sense of superiority.

Very early in life this woman had developed a great sensitivity to the marital problems of her parents. She had learned to protect and to take sides with father against mother and vice versa. That is, she had assumed, as it were, the parental role of both. Of course, at the same time there was an intensive longing simply to play the role of a young child, denied her because of her parents' marital difficulties. So she was torn between her longing to be a child, acceptant of authority and capable of admiring the adults, and her actual role of being a superior parental figure in the family group.

Both attitudes repeated themselves in the two facets of her relationships with her lovers. Unable to establish relationships on a basis of mutual equality, she knew only how to play the superior parental figure upon whose protection her parents had called or that of the submissive child who was ready to admire authority in the role for which she longed and which had been denied her in her childhood. As a result, she consistently became entangled with people whose personalities, background, or age group were such that they elicited the patient's living out one of these two alternatives, yet blocked

[8]Fromm-Reichmann, *op. cit.*, pp. 104-105.

her from establishing a mature, mutual relationship on her present age level. Because of this she had also modeled her relationship with the psychiatrist along the same psychopathological prototype.

Now, it is easy to see that it would be obviously impossible for this woman to repudiate her knowledge that there can be adults who are immature and who want to be treated like dependent children. She could hardly deny, once she had come face to face with this fact, that she herself had longed to play the same kind of dependent role—perhaps partly because she wished that she could be like her parents. But, to change the habit-residues from her childhood, it would not be necessary for her to repudiate what she had learned. Not necessary and, for that matter, not possible. The only thing she possibly could have done would be to formulate things like this: "Yes, there actually are persons like that, and often marriages and love affairs are tragically unhappy because the partners in them have not grown up. But this doesn't mean that every person is like that, any more than it is true that every flying insect can sting like a bee. My task is one of learning to distinguish different sorts of persons, of learning how to conceive different sorts of interpersonal relationships that can exist, and then of learning how to deal with others so that I may develop the kind of relationship with them that can be more solidly and enduringly satisfying."

Such learning of positive tasks may be difficult, but not in the way that it is difficult to try to deal in a negative way with mischief-making memories or habits from the past. To try to forget the past is like the task that Leo Tolstoy remembers his older brother used to give to him when they were small children. There was a beautiful fairy palace in the woods, Tolstoy's brother said, and he would guide his younger brother to it if the brother would accomplish the simple task of standing in a corner for 10 minutes and not thinking of a white bear. Leo Tolstoy tells that he tried this over and over. But the harder he tried, the more the white bear stayed with him. The person with personality problems is very likely to be trying to do something similar. "If only such and such had not happened!" or "If only I could forget about such and such!" If only that white bear would leave me alone! But some residues from such happenings are more or less unalterable parts of one's real self. There can be no erasing them. The thing one regrets must be transformed, molded into a place as part of some deeper, more sympathetic, more humane understanding of life.

3. *Old personality habits may be dealt with partly by arranging for new influences to be working while the old habits are in a state of active arousal.* At this point we are moving from methods that have unmistakably proved their worth to a group of methods that are newer and which, though they clearly have value in certain instances, must be worked out

further before we shall know their precise value and the limits of their applicability.

From experiments on learning in animals, Kenneth Spence[9] has suggested that if learning is to occur, actions and their consequences must be much closer to each other in time than had been imagined before and that, in fact, perhaps no learning can occur if there is some delay between a response and the registration of the effects of that response. Even with human beings, the occurrence of long delays of effect seem not to permit learning of an association. This is one reason, apparently, why is it difficult for people to break the habit of chewing on their fingernails. When they try to get rid of this habit simply by not permitting themselves to do it, they may go for weeks without once chewing their nails. Then, when such a person comes out from a tough exam, he looks down and sees that his finger nails are chewed back, and he knows he has been up to it again. Regret and shame don't break the habits, and in the next stressful situation he will be right back to it again.

It seems like a worthwhile hypothesis, at least in some situations, to say that the action and consequences must be brought very close together, as Spence has proposed. Suppose a person regularly mispronounces some word in a characteristic way when he is talking along without thinking, though he can give the correct pronunciation at once when challenged. "Did I really say *similiar?*" he asks. "Why, my dad has been correcting me on that ever since I was 10 years old!" Why is it, we wonder, that all of his training in the correct habit had merely built up a second and rather artificial habit alongside of the first, rather than changing the original one?

What seems to be particularly relevant here is a theory that Knight Dunlap developed[10] as a consequence of his effort to correct a persistent typing error. He had the habit of typing *the* as *hte*. "I'm a psychologist interested in learning," he said, "and I should be able to alter this bothersome habit." He therefore set himself to practice the correct response and wrote out page after page of the word *the*. But when he went back to his regular typing at regular speed, there came the *hte*'s. Thereupon some bit of inspiration led him to ask himself, "What would happen if, instead, I practiced making over and over again the response that I want *not* to make and if, all the time that I'm practicing it, I keep feeling my annoyance and dissatisfaction, not as a process that comes *after* the response, but as an active process occurring simultaneously with what I am doing?"

Dunlap tried this and found, as has been substantiated in subsequent

[9]Kenneth Spence, "The Role of Secondary Reinforcement in Delayed Reward Learning," *Psychological Review*, Vol. 54 (January, 1947), pp. 1-8.

[10]Knight Dunlap, "A Revision of the Fundamental Law of Habit Formation," *Science*, Vol. 67 (1928), pp. 360-362.

studies, that this method of "negative practice," as he called it, is indeed an unusually effective method of changing old habits.

It seems, therefore, that we can infer something like this: the brain apparently does not work in the simple way that the old armchair (rationalistic) theory suggested. To change habits, it is not sufficient just to build new associations into the brain. Instead, one has to arouse the old habit to active functioning in order that the new processes of the brain can make functional contacts with it and make changes in it. But if the undesirable old habit is sleeping over in some corner of the brain when the fine new practice is taking place, it *may* still lurk there, ready to operate in its characteristic old way in the sort of stimulus-situation to which it is most intimately related. That is, it may still operate in spontaneous real-life situations, even though it does not operate any more when the person, checking himself, responds deliberately and in a highly self-conscious fashion.

Parents who read accounts of play therapy with children are sometimes shocked at the extremes of behavior permitted in such therapy. They may worry about the after-effects of the therapist's acting in an acceptant way even when the child smashes porcelain doll figures with a hammer, smears clay messily about the room, or expresses the meanest feelings toward a sibling or parent. Parents wonder if the child won't be made a little hellion by such freedom from restraint.

But such extreme permissiveness has its point. If an overinhibited child has a deeply ingrained fear that he will be criticized and punished for spontaneity in an emotional response, he will respond with such fear in the situation in the play-therapy room, particularly when he sees that unquestionably he is doing things that previously brought punishment or criticism from his parents. But now there is the possibility that his habits of overfearfulness can be changed partly because, *as he now acts in objectionable ways,* the therapist gives him no assurance that his actions are safe, and he does them with intense fear. What makes some changing of personality possible is the fact that he is using his habit of fear, but finding conclusively that his expectation of being punished is incorrect, and finding this *at the same time* that he is responding so fearfully.

4. *Changes of personality habits probably come sometimes from a creative instability that is inherent in very complex systems like personality.* To some extent there may be reorganizations of personality habits through the influence of chance factors such as inevitably occur in complex systems through what might be called their "creative instability," if we might accept a term that E. C. Tolman once proposed. This instability is important in any system (even an inanimate one) that can be made to work on the basis of very slight stimulation and that works by dynamic organizations, thus tending to make shifts of an overall kind. Such chance influences do not always produce more favorable

patterns of response, but even so they do provide a wider range of processes for the person to choose from.

The case of Marty (Chapter 6) illustrates such a possible chance factor. Perhaps you remember how unshakable her first guilty outlook had been during the period when she was preoccupied with why the accident had happened and how she might have prevented it. Then, one morning as she was waiting for the coffee to drip, she happened to look out of the window, and there she saw the spring rain and the swelling buds. Her thoughts wandered to one of the pleasures of her childhood when she made candy on rainy days, and this led to memories of a crocheted throw her mother had made for her and to her recalling how she took care of her calf when it had gotten caught in the cold rain. Suddenly her whole attitude toward Bill shifted remarkably. She had "found" him.

To be sure, this change may have been inevitable, in time. But, why do such changes come at all? Perhaps "inevitable in time" means that one will eventually hit the mark given the fact of the myriad chance influences continually bombarding us.

5. *Changes in the habits of personality sometimes come from "satiation effects."* Back in Chapter 6 we spoke about surprising reorganizations that occur when simple figures of some sorts are perceived, even when the person viewing these figures does not suspect that any reorganization might occur. This phenomenon raises the question as to whether or not personality mechanisms sometimes change in an analogous way. If this is the case, however, it is important to note that the perceptual figures do not reverse unless we look at them in a sustained way. We rarely give equally sustained attention to the same stimulus-object under the conditions of ordinary life.

But important emotional processes do tend to be long-sustained. Marty's every waking hour was filled with a sense of her tragedy. Even in her sleep she heard the ring of the phone telling her of the accident. Perhaps such long-sustained processes tend inevitably to be self-satiating, as are simpler perceptual processes, and their continuance gradually builds up some kind of physiological obstruction to their own further existence, an obstruction that has to be dissipated before the full emotional state can be resumed. These effects of satiation could work to weaken temporarily the dominant emotional process sufficiently to give other blocked-out habits a chance to take over.

Perhaps what is involved in the effectiveness of some therapeutic procedures is that they lead to a sustained focusing on emotional problems that in everyday life would be pushed aside too quickly. A person may feel "I'm hopelessly defective and inadequate," but in everyday life he tries to "snap out of it," to think of things that would prove this was not the case. But in therapy the person with such discouraged thoughts thoroughly lets himself go during the interview hour. He feels overwhelmed by his conviction of his worthlessness and feels he cannot possibly go on—and yet, out of such things, there often comes change.

As we said in Chapter 3, the nondirective therapists developed the concept that the counselor's job is particularly the task of capturing the emotional essence of what the patient is saying and, whenever it seems timely to do so, reflecting this back to him. Doing this seems almost like a custom-made technique for inducing satiation. The person's chief emotional preoccupation is bound to come out if he feels secure enough to speak, and everything tends to make him continue his preoccupation.

For example, in the "Marjorie Winkler" case[11] counseled by Virginia Axline, one of Carl Roger's group, an 18-year-old girl spent only one hour with the counselor. Even in this short time the good atmosphere that the skilled counselor was able to establish led almost immediately to the appearance of Marjorie's central problem, her hatred for her mother, a mother who had recently arbitrarily sent Marjorie to a plastic surgeon to have her face "redone." The outcome of the operation had been good from the standpoint of improved appearance. But when Marjorie returned to college, she said, "For no reason at all I cry. I just feel like crying and never stop crying. I don't know why." For virtually the whole hour, then, Marjorie lashed at her mother in a furious outpouring.

Here are a few typical sentences:

> My mother was the ruling force in the house. I hated her. She never said a kind word to me. It was always orders. "Get supper ready early tonight." "Do the washing after you get home from school." . . . She didn't care how I looked then.

This flow of hatred kept up without interruption for most of the hour, as with the comments,

> I just wished she would die. I wished she would never get home again. I wished that so strongly that I got sick. For years I have carried that wish in my heart. I couldn't get rid of it. It came between me and everything. *(Pause)* No, don't say anything yet. It has been with me so long. For years. But you see—it's just occurred to me, really right now, that I'm big enough to live and let live. I was really putting off facing a decision by hoping that something would happen to her. But it's up to me. *(Pause)* I really pity her.

Marjorie ended the hour by saying, much as she did when she started the interview, that she could see no reason why she should discuss any of her problems with a counselor, and that since she had now carried out the promise to her physician that she would come for at least one in-

[11]W. U. Snyder, ed., *Casebook of Non-Directive Counseling* (Boston, Houghton Mifflin Co., 1947), pp. 313-319.

terview, she would not be back. However, a follow-up inquiry showed that this simple hour of therapy had made a profound difference in Marjorie's life, making it possible for her to get a new perception of herself in relation to her mother and to other people generally. It seems altogether probable that what helped to produce this reorganization was the same kind of sustained, intense focusing on a first perception that occurred in Wallach's experiment where his subjects were watching the moving belt of paper with its zigzag line and where once they had learned to see this line as a three-dimensional spiraling, this way of perceiving tended to stick.

6. *The changing of basic life constructs may require a slow, difficult building up of new and complex concepts that can be achieved only with great intellectual effort.* To many psychotherapists, it seems almost axiomatic that personality habits cannot be changed by any intellectual type of activity. Yet we want to end this discussion of how personality may be changed by suggesting that this is probably precisely what is required in the case of some of the most difficult and important changes in human beings that can ever occur.

Let us go back for one more time to the example we have used over and over again, of habits of faulty orientation in geographical space. We have seen that they can arise sometimes from apparently rather trivial influences and yet be terrifically persistent, even in the face of the most clear-cut intellectual awareness of their incorrectness.

How may such an inaccurate orientation habit be corrected? It seems clear that the needed reorientation cannot come merely by trying to hang on to particular, specific ideas such as "the sun sets over there, as I have often seen, and so that must be the west." This type of approach will not improve orientations. What will improve them, then?

From admittedly rather limited work on this problem, it seems that these faulty orientations can be changed if the individual will make the effort required to build up an *elaborate* new conception to replace the one he had—or that had him!—previously. One of the present writers developed such a faulty orientation in the region where he lived as a boy, near Pittsburgh. He can hardly understand how he could have held to his mistaken orientation because during several years of his boyhood, he slept on a porch where the morning sun shone directly on him each morning, though all the time he *felt* that the direction where the sun rose was the north. He remembers the incident which he believes started the faulty orientation. This occurred when he was a pupil in the third grade in Braddock and the teacher told the children to stand and face in the direction of North Braddock. "That is north, children," she said, "and so this is east off at your right hand." But for some obscure reason known only to those who traveled the early roads of that region, North Braddock is not really north of Braddock, and this teacher was creating in one pupil, at least, a habit that did not square with the points of the compass.

Having conceived a theoretical interest in the problem, the writer, when adult, tried to see whether he could at last get this region properly turned around. What he found was that it proved to be a long, slow, complicated task, though not an impossible one. He had to begin the job from a few facts he felt confident of. He knew that he could see the North Star off in one direction and that the sun rose and set at certain other points. Then what he had to do was say, "Since these things are true, it would then follow that, if I went on down this road and over this hill, and on in such and such direction, I would come to the Lincoln Highway, or to the Turnpike, that would take me to Philadelphia. And, since the North Star is where it is, if I went down this other road and then turned right on the road that it enters, I would be going north on this other road. And, off in this other direction would lie Washington, D. C., and Virginia; off here would lie . . . ." This work was elusive, because, whenever he attempted to revisualize long-familiar landmarks, his old orientation habits would tend to swing into action and pull his perception back to the roughly 75°-off misorientation that he had always lived with. Thus, even while saying to himself, "This familiar hill, then, would be off to the west," he would find that he was perceiving it (in a more basic nonverbal sense) with his old incorrect system of habits.

Those old habits, after all, had been tied to thousands of particular stimulus-situations in that region. Indeed, what makes such a system efficient is that the individual does not have to think back to his main point of reference from which he originally got his north-south bearings; he possesses a multitude of perceptual-orientation habits, derived from the original source, that are now ready to operate from local, specific cues. Consequently, when he tries to look at part of such a region, or think about part of such a region in a new way, he is fighting against a host of older habits that have a tendency to shove out the new orientation-process and replace it with the older and more elaborately-based system. What the author found was that to change these directional habits, he had to go back, time after time, to some starting point where he could get an orientation he knew was correct, and then work further and further out from that on successive tries, gradually building up an elaborate conceptual system that could compete with the old one.

In the same way, the most fundamental changes that can be made in personality are changes of very inclusive conceptual systems, the basic life constructs of the person, we have called them. These may have originated in minor occurrences or from the effects of the more persisting major influences in childhood. But, once these life constructs got started, the person will have worked out a way of seeing life, in a vast series of situations, in terms of certain premises or basic concepts which he has accepted as his frame of reference. Working from such a guiding line, he will have established a multitude of more specific reintegrative habits linked to a great array of situations that now directly call out his most general and all-inclusive mode of response.

Suppose, for example, that a person learned as a child that successful interactions with other persons depended on his "showing off" as a way of proving how smart, how cute, or how talented he was, ahead of all competitors. As an adult, he may be able to see, in abstract terms, that this is a wretched basis for life, and that "the North Star, actually, is off in this other direction." He may be able to see that a sound society cannot possibly be based on such universal competitive striving. He may be able to see that each individual needs to learn to take pride in making constructive contributions in whatever measure corresponds to the reasonable best of his ability, even though he is aware all the while that many others are able to make more impressive contributions. He may be able to grasp this abstract point in a very clear way. But he may not be able to stick to it beyond the abstract level when it comes to his own concrete perceptions of many life situations.

Therefore, even though it may seem inappropriate to think of personality changes as coming by elaborate intellectual processes, it seems that the same complex type of thought would be required for this purpose as was required with regard to correcting directional orientations. The individual has to get some premise to start from that he knows would be more sound than the premise he previously used. Then he has to try to work out from that. He has to say, "If it is true that I ought to strive merely to make constructive contributions and to give appreciation to others for their contributions, and if it is true that my present associates do not have the reasons for interest in my accomplishments that my parents had, then it follows that, in such and such situations, the way that I ought to experience things would be. . . ."

This is difficult, complicated work. But if a person is willing to pay the price of sustained hard work and of going back, after innumerable failures, to try again to work out the concrete implications of the best and truest perceptions he has achieved, it may be that this is another means whereby really significant changes of personality may be made.

We get discouraged, often, when we contemplate changing our personality. We imagine that we ought to be able to make major changes by passing some New Year's resolutions and deciding, in an abstract way, to put them into operation on some particular day. We will make one grand effort of will, and then we will have to do nothing more about them. But we really know this can't be done. Hence the discouragement. We know, of course, that we could not possibly use this method to change, say, our handwriting—to make it more legible—or to improve our use of the English language in a way that would, all at once, stick.

And yet when it comes to personality habits, where the problems of change are much more difficult, we expect miracles to happen. If we can stop expecting miracles, and if we can find and utilize techniques that are actually suited to the problem, perhaps desirable changes in personality can be achieved much more frequently.

Summary

A need for modifying personality for the better often exists. Many different difficulties occur in different persons, such as too many or too strong negative motives, insufficient positive motives, inappropriate positive motives, and poor understanding of the nature of the situation one must cope with and of what might be done to improve it. Such troubles as these may show up directly in the subjective experience of people, but more frequently they are at least partly disguised and hidden from the person himself and are likely to manifest themselves in discontent, psychosomatic symptoms, or just generally unsatisfactory effects on a person's work and his interpersonal relations as well.

Some efforts to change personality ought to be directed solely at providing an improved objective life situation to help the person to use his habits differently so as to bring more satisfactory effects. Both with children and with adults, this often ought to be the chief aim. Personality does not function in a vacuum, but as the field concept teaches us, its characteristics are those of "the individual in such and such a context." Frequently it is more feasible to change the functioning of the personality of an individual by changing the context than by changing his enduring habits.

The poorly adjusted individual is, however, frequently one in whom some change of personality habits is required to make it possible for him to respond in a new way to an objective situation that will remain pretty much as it was. The first of two main types of such change involves no alteration in that great body of personality habits that might be described as the *real self* of the individual. Instead an attempt is made to change only a special portion of his personality habits that we might describe as the individual's *concepts about his real self*. A change of concepts about one's real self may exert an influence in such a way as to cause the individual to change his objective life situation to one that is better suited to his deeper interests; it may help him to see certain habits that need to be changed, or at least held in check. In any case, the crucial point where change is needed is to be found in the concepts about the real self. Much of therapy is directed toward inducing such changes in these concepts. This sometimes requires interpreting dreams and giving technical suggestions to an individual, though perhaps the person is often helped more in arriving at accurate and honest concepts merely because he has found a listener who is deeply interested in him and who makes it his practice to abstain from efforts to mold him. The technique of "listening," in this sense, might well be much more commonly adopted in our everyday interpersonal relationships.

Achieving new concepts about the real self is difficult partly for intellectual reasons, partly also because it costs something emotionally. People almost without exception hate to admit that they have been wrong on major matters. Arriving at new insights confronts us with the fact that our real selves include motives that in some way threaten us. People do not fear only those motives that are socially disapproved. A main trend of contemporary psychotherapeutic thought stresses the idea that the individual is most likely to have concealed from himself how intense is his hunger for close personal relationships with other people.

There are several methods that can be used with profit by the person who seeks a better knowledge of his own real self. These include: (1) going back carefully in his own introspective knowledge to the raw data from which he has developed his concepts about his real self; (2) examining his own behavior, as contrasted with his introspective knowledge, in an effort to see just exactly what it may indicate; (3) adopting the procedure of deliberately letting his thinking and feelings proceed without restraint, just to see what will turn up, even though he may have a tendency to reject his thoughts and feelings as "unjustified" and "unreasonable"; (4) working patiently with new concepts of the real self to learn what they involve.

Personality habits on the primary level may also need to be changed. Even though these may be habits that touch off strong emotional reactions, they can sometimes be changed quickly; in other cases extreme slowness and difficulty must be expected. Some of the main points that apply to such changes are: (1) faulty personality habits cannot usually be forgotten or eliminated in a negative way by simply banning them; what usually is necessary is that the individual must incorporate what he has previously experienced into some new habit making a more constructive use of his past; (2) such new habits often require developing new skill in differentiating between situations with apparently similar but actually different properties and in dealing with old situations in a new and more successful fashion; (3) old habits need to be brought into active functional contact with processes that might transform them, somewhat after the fashion of Dunlap's negative-practice method; (4) habit-changing can sometimes be traced to the *creative instability* inherent in complex systems; (5) habit-change sometimes arises out of satiation effects produced by vigorous and sustained activation of an old habit; (6) changing old habits may require a slow, difficult building up of complex new concepts by a complicated intellectual process—a process of working out the implications of new key insights into the opportunities and possibilities of the individual's life.

CHAPTER 16

The Possibilities Ahead

OVER AND OVER again, in the long history of mankind, it must have seemed that human life was up against utterly insuperable difficulties. Furthermore, it must have seemed as though these difficulties existed, not because people were putting out too little effort or because they did not have sufficient knowledge about their world, but because the world itself was inherently poor.

Thus, during most of the half-million or so years that man has existed, the problem of finding sufficient food was often more than man could solve. Other creatures, in comparison, must have seemed abundantly provided for. But the experience of ancient man must frequently have been one of insufficient food or outright starvation. With his poor hunting tools he was unable to capture many of the animals that he would have liked to use for food; he was unable to live on the grass that was adapted for rabbits and deer; and berries, nuts, and seeds were too seasonal in character and often too rare.

Perhaps ancient man was not given to philosophizing, but still there must have been many occasions when he dimly thought: "Woe is me that I am placed in a world where so few things are adapted to my needs!"

It is amazing how long it took for man to realize that his world had greater possibilities in it than he originally thought. Not until about ten thousand years ago did he come to know that when seeds fall to the ground, they can sprout, produce a similar plant, and later yield a greatly multiplied supply of the same sort of seed. It took that long—some hundreds of thousands of years—before man realized that he could deliberately produce more plants of the sort that he wished to see. Ever since then, he has been increasing his knowledge of the potential food-producing capacities of the earth. He has learned to watch for rare mutations of plants, such as those that have produced vastly better apples and pears than the pulpy, sour, and almost useless original specimens. He has learned how to fertilize. He has learned how to fight insect pests—sometimes by turning one insect against another. He has learned to cross-pollinize in order to produce new sorts of fruits and vegetables that probably never would have existed under natural conditions. And, in consequence, he has had abundant means to learn that the world is not really the meager place it must have seemed in ancient times, but that it has almost unlimited resources to be unlocked with increased understanding and with long, patient development.

As the problem of food supply came to be solved, however, this progress helped to accentuate another difficulty. For, as cities developed and travel and transportation brought humanity closer together, there came to be terrible problems of disease. Throughout the Middle Ages in Europe, for example, the plagues of cholera, typhus, diphtheria, tuberculosis, malaria, smallpox, and others were really terrible scourges. They seemed to come from nowhere. There seemed to be no means of preventing them. There seemed to be nothing that could be used for cures. Once again, it would have been understandable if man had said, "Woe is me that I am placed in a world where there are so many sources of suffering and death, and where there are no means by which I can protect myself against these ills!"

But here too, as we know now, the trouble did not come because the world inherently was so ill-adapted to man's needs. We know, for example, that there never was any reason why beriberi should have existed in the rice-eating areas where it was rampant—except for the fact that, because of their lack of knowledge of what was involved, the people in those areas were polishing the brown husks (containing the anti-beriberi factor) off the grains of rice and were throwing these polishings away. We know now that the mold that grows on cantaloupes is not a pure nuisance, but has been the means of opening out whole new horizons in the field of antibiotics. We know that goiter, endemic to some regions, was not inevitable, but could be prevented in very simple ways by the addition of small amounts of iodine to the diet. Consequently, as with man's food supply, we know that people need not have taken any view that the world simply could not provide the resources for fighting disease. We know they should have said, instead, that their difficulties came only because they had not learned to understand and use the enormously diverse and wonderful resources that actually existed in the world around them.

The story of chemistry and chemical engineering would illustrate the same point. What an incredibly different picture we now have with regard to the chemical materials and chemical possibilities of the earth as compared with the picture that ancient man must have had! Each of the natural sciences would illustrate the same point.

Yet, in our own day, we are tending to take a fatalistic and despondent or complaining attitude toward the world on a new score. True, we say, we have found the means of producing a great amount of food. True, we have found the means of preventing or curing many diseases and of minimizing physical suffering in human life. True, we have learned techniques of research by which we can wrest from nature the answers to many problems that utterly baffled our ancestors. And yet, we tend to say, "Woe is man because his own nature is so hostile, so greedy, so cruel, so lacking in decency, love, and understanding of others. Woe is man because the inherent limitations of his own nature permit him no escape from crime, racial hatred, mental disease, neurosis, overpopulation, and the slaughter of hideous wars. Ugliness, waste, and senseless strife—how can there be anything but despair if one looks realistically at the world in which we are placed?"

There are real problems here, of course. It would be childish to blind our eyes to them. We need to realize, in all soberness, that the factors that can destroy modern society may accomplish this end before the work of gaining and using a better understanding of human nature can proceed far enough. We know that different cultures in the past failed to solve their major problems and came to an end. We need to realize that our culture can do the same and that unless it develops some better means of dealing with international relations than to rely on our present precarious juggling of military threats, culture probably will destroy itself. We need to realize, even, that there is nothing to guarantee there will be any mankind in another twenty or fifty or hundred years.

Yet, while we need to grant all this, we need to see too that if we do not turn seriously enough to the task of trying to understand the sources of our greatest dangers, we will be disregarding the lessons we ought to have learned from the other problems with which mankind has been sorely burdened in earlier ages. For, when we say that human nature is such a woefully poor material and that there are no possibilities, really, of dealing with this material in such a way that it could achieve what we would like to see, the chances are that we are wrong. The chances are that a sufficient investment of research and development with regard to human life would reveal the same things that have been revealed on these other matters. The chances are that we would find human nature to be a vastly more complex and wonderful thing than we have been able yet to demonstrate. If such proves not to be the case, it will be the exception that stands in opposition to everything we have learned in every other field.

Without giving such matters really careful thought, we tend to assume that were some broadened and more valuable knowledge about human nature possible, we already would have explored this matter, seeing that we have such fine mastery over the tools of research in so many other materials. But when we make this assumption, we do not realize how primitive our knowledge may remain in some areas while it develops in really splendid forms in other parts of life. We fail to realize that some matters are difficult to understand and yet could readily yield to research if a great deal of effort were devoted to the problem of trying to find some solution to those problems. We need to realize that some problems can be difficult because either the causes or the effects that are important are intangible—as was the case with the dietary-deficiency diseases that were so widespread in the world in earlier times. We need to realize that some problems are unusually difficult because the causes and effects are so separated in time—time-separation prevented people from attributing malaria to the bites of mosquitoes, even though they always had known that mosquitoes produced the swelling that came immediately after mosquito bites. And we need to realize, as so many sciences have demonstrated, that new understandings sometimes call for subtle and yet profound reorganizations of our whole conception of things.

These things are difficult. But we have the benefit, in this present day, of a wealth of experience in other aspects of life where the world originally seemed altogether lacking in resources and yet turned out merely to be waiting for careful, patient, and imaginative work. There is every reason, therefore, why we ought to take the gamble—no, why we will be criminally negligent if we do not take the gamble—of making some enormous investments in trying to get a deeper and fresher understanding of human life in all of its aspects.

In this book we have tried to sketch some of the new concepts that we think are already suggested by the research that has been done. Particularly we have proposed these points: (1) We have proposed that the personality processes within an individual cannot be understood by assuming that they necessarily will reflect the objective realities and logically impressive demonstrations with which he is presented. People have to be understood in terms of organized processes, psychologically. (2) We have proposed that our thinking about human life must seek to recognize some relatively subtle and intangible factors that we are only beginning to appreciate. We are proposing, for example, that we need much more adequate ideas about the various techniques or strategies by which people attempt to handle problems in their lives and attempt to handle their relationships with other persons. (3) We have proposed that the driving forces of human nature must be understood in terms of motives that are not primarily rooted in tissue needs, but that are matters of perceptual processes at the same time that they are matters of motives. And we have proposed that these perceptual-motivational processes often are quite subtle in character, rather than being the motives that we have found it easy to recognize in our everyday thought thus far.

It may seem as though such propositions are not markedly different from the outlook in everyday life that we have spoken of as the rationalistic tradition. And yet there are fundamental differences, even though they may be subtle ones. They are differences, furthermore, that reach far beyond merely the implications of all of this for individual lives such as we have stressed through these chapters. In the international relations of modern countries, there could be an entirely new note if our thinking about other countries could shift from an outdated faith that we can understand either ourselves or other peoples merely in terms of what we think are the objective facts, or in terms of relatively tangible motives, and if we could offer, instead, some more penetrating understanding of what human life and thought and aspiration really are like.

Suggestions for Further Reading

For many of you who have read this book, it might be helpful to have a list of those books and articles which the present authors regard as particularly worth recommending to you, either because they explain more fully certain points covered in the preceding pages, or because they provide excellent illustrative material or give careful summaries of research methods and findings, or because they present some mode of interpretation different from that which we have advanced on many issues.

In order that this collection of titles will be easier to use, the entries have been grouped in two ways. First, they are grouped under an outline of different types of content. Secondly, a system of asterisks has been used to indicate three different levels of technical difficulty, since there are marked differences in difficulty in this collection of references. One asterisk preceding a reference designates a relatively nontechnical or popularly written discussion; two asterisks mark the references of moderate difficulty; and three asterisks indicate the references that would be difficult for the person with limited technical background. We believe that all of these references have value for technically trained readers. However, the relative novice in the field of personality would find little satisfaction or profit in most of the more difficult books.

At the end of this list, we make a few suggestions on how these references might most fruitfully be used.

REFERENCES PROVIDING MATERIAL FROM GENERAL EXPERIMENTAL PSYCHOLOGY AND FROM ANIMAL PSYCHOLOGY

* Hediger, H., *Studies of the Psychology and Behavior of Captive Animals in Zoos and Circuses* (London, Butterworths Scientific Publications, 1955).

** Köhler, Wolfgang, *Gestalt Psychology*, 2nd ed. (New York, Liveright Publishing Corp., 1947).

** Leeper, Robert, "Cognitive Processes," in S. S. Stevens, ed., *Handbook of Experimental Psychology* (New York, John Wiley & Sons, Inc., 1951).

* Lorenz, Konrad, *King Solomon's Ring* (New York, Thomas Y. Crowell Company, 1952).

*** MacKay, Donald M., "Towards an Information-Flow Model of Human Behaviour," *British Journal of Psychology*, Vol. 47, (1956), pp. 30-43.

*** Oldfield, R. C., "Memory Mechanisms and the Theory of Schemata," *British Journal of Psychology*, Vol. 45, (1954), 14-23.

* Scott, John P., *Animal Behavior* (Chicago, University of Chicago Press, 1958).

** Tolman, E. C., "Cognitive Maps in Animals and Men," *Psychological Review*, Vol. 55, (1948), pp. 189-208.

** Woodworth, R. S., "Situation-and-Goal Set," *American Journal of Psychology*, Vol. 50, (1937), pp. 130-140.

GENERAL DISCUSSIONS OF PERSONALITY

** Combs, A. W., and Snygg, D., *Individual Behavior*, 2nd ed. (New York, Harper and Brothers, 1959).

** Diamond, Solomon, *Personality and Temperament* (New York, Harper and Brothers, 1957).

*** Guilford, J. P., *Personality* (New York, McGraw-Hill Book Co., 1959).

*** Hall, Calvin S., and Lindzey, G., *Theories of Personality* (New York, John Wiley & Sons, Inc., 1957).

* Leeper, Robert, "Current Trends in Theories of Personality," in Wayne Dennis and others, *Current Trends in Psychological Theory* (Pittsburgh, University of Pittsburgh Press, 1951).

** Monroe, Ruth L., *Schools of Psychoanalytic Thought* (New York, The Dryden Press, Inc., 1955).

*** Murphy, Gardner, *Personality* (New York, Harper and Brothers, 1947).

** White, Robert W., *The Abnormal Personality* (New York, The Ronald Press Company, 1948).

* ———, *Lives in Progress* (New York, The Ronald Press Company, 1952).

PERSONALITY DEVELOPMENT IN CHILDREN

* Baruch, Dorothy, *New Ways in Discipline* (New York, McGraw-Hill Book Co., 1949).

** Erikson, Erik H., *Childhood and Society* (New York, W. W. Norton & Company, Inc., 1950).

*** Macfarlane, Jean W., Allen, Lucile, and Honzik, Marjorie P. *A Developmental Study of the Behavior Problems of Normal Children between 21 Months and 14 Years* (Berkeley, Calif., University of California Press, 1954).

* Read, Katherine, *The Nursery School* (Philadelphia, W. B. Saunders Co., 1955).

** Sears, R. R., Maccoby, Eleanor E., and Levin, H., *Patterns of Child Rearing* (Evanston, Ill., Row, Peterson & Company, 1957).
* Spock, Benjamin, *Baby and Child Care* (New York, Pocket Books, Inc., 1957).
** Tanner, J. M., and Inhelder, B., eds., *Discussions on Child Development*, Vol. I (London, Tavistock Publications, Ltd., 1956).

PLAY THERAPY WITH CHILDREN—CASE MATERIAL AND METHODS

** Allen, Frederick H., *Psychotherapy with Children* (New York, W. W. Norton & Company, Inc., 1942).
* Axline, Virginia, *Play Therapy* (Boston, Houghton Mifflin Co., 1947).
** Rogerson, C. H., *Play Therapy in Childhood* (London, Oxford University Press, 1939).

PRESENTATIONS OF DIFFERENT MAIN SYSTEMATIC THEORIES OF PERSONALITY

Alfred Adler's Theory

* Adler, Alfred, *Understanding Human Nature* (New York, Greenberg: Publisher, 1927).
* ———, *Social Interest* (London, Faber & Faber, Ltd., 1938).
** Ansbacher, H. L., and Rowena, R., eds., *The Individual Psychology of Alfred Adler* (New York, Basic Books, 1956).
* Bottome, Phyllis, *Alfred Adler: a Biography* (New York, G. P. Putnam's Sons, 1939).
* Dreikurs, R., *The Challenge of Marriage* (New York, Duell, Sloan & Pearce, Inc., 1946).
* ———, *The Challenge of Parenthood* (New York, Duell, Sloan & Pearce, Inc., 1948).
* Orgler, Hedda, *Alfred Adler: the Man and His Work* (Ashington, Rochford, Essex, England, C. W. Daniel Co., 1947).
** Way, Lewis, *Adler's Place in Psychology* (New York, The Macmillan Co., 1950).

Karen Horney's Theory

* Horney, Karen, *The Neurotic Personality of Our Time* (W. W. Norton & Company, Inc., 1937).
** ———, *New Ways in Psychoanalysis* (New York, W. W. Norton & Company, Inc., 1939).
** ———, *Our Inner Conflicts* (New York, W. W. Norton & Company, Inc., 1945).

** ———, *Neurosis and Human Growth* (New York, W. W. Norton & Company, Inc., 1950).

SIGMUND FREUD'S THEORY

** Freud, Sigmund, *Civilization and Its Discontents* (London, The Hogarth Press, 1930).

* Fromm, Erich, *Sigmund Freud's Mission: an Analysis of His Personality and Influence* (New York, Harper and Brothers, 1959).

* Hall, Calvin S., *A Primer of Freudian Psychology* (Cleveland, The World Publishing Company, 1954).

** Jones, Ernest, *The Life and Work of Sigmund Freud* (New York, Basic Books, Vol. I, 1953, Vol. II, 1955, Vol. III, 1957).

* Sachs, Hanns, *Freud: Master and Friend* (Cambridge, Mass., Harvard University Press, 1944).

** White, Robert W., "Review of Sidney Hook, ed., *Psychoanalysis, Scientific Method and Philosophy* and Philip Rieff, *Freud: the Mind of the Moralist*," *Scientific American*, Vol. 201, (1959), pp. 267-276.

CARL JUNG'S THEORY

** Adler, Gerhard, *Studies in Analytical Psychology* (New York, W. W. Norton & Company, Inc., 1948).

GEORGE KELLY'S THEORY

*** Kelly, George, *The Psychology of Personal Constructs* (New York, W. W. Norton & Company, Inc., 1955).

OTTO RANK'S THEORY

** Karpf, Fay B., *The Psychology and Psychotherapy of Otto Rank* (New York, Philosophical Library, Inc., 1953).

CARL ROGER'S THEORY

* Rogers, Carl R., "Significant Aspects of Client-Centered Therapy," *American Psychologist*, Vol. 1, (1946), pp. 415-422.

** ———, *Client-Centered Therapy* (Boston, Houghton Mifflin Co., 1953).

* ———, "A Process Conception of Psychotherapy," *American Psychologist*, Vol. 13, (1958), pp. 142-149.

HARRY STACK SULLIVAN'S THEORY

*** Fromm-Reichman, Frieda, *Principles of Intensive Psychotherapy* (Chicago, University of Chicago Press, 1950).

** Hill, Lewis B., *Psychotherapeutic Intervention in Schizophrenia* (Chicago, University of Chicago Press, 1955).

** Mullahy, Patrick, ed., *The Contributions of Harry Stack Sullivan* (New York, Hermitage House, 1952).

** Sullivan, H. S., *The Interpersonal Theory of Psychiatry* (New York, W. W. Norton & Company, Inc., 1953).

THE STIMULUS-RESPONSE THEORY OF PERSONALITY

** Cameron, Norman, and Magaret, Ann, *Behavior Pathology* (Boston, Houghton Mifflin Co., 1951).

** Dollard, J., and Miller, N. E., *Personality and Psychotherapy* (New York, McGraw-Hill Book Co., 1950).

* Guthrie, E. R., *The Psychology of Human Conflict* (New York, Harper and Brothers, 1938).

** Rotter, Julian B., *Social Learning and Clinical Psychology* (Englewood Cliffs, N. J., Prentice-Hall, Inc., 1954).

** Shaffer, L. F., and Shoben, E. J., *Psychology of Adjustment*, 2nd ed. (Boston, Houghton Mifflin Co., 1956).

** Wolpe, Joseph, *Psychotherapy by Reciprocal Inhibition* (Palo Alto, Calif., Stanford University Press, 1958).

In commenting on the above list, let us follow roughly the groupings of the outline we have used. Among the books stressing more general psychological phenomena, we would recommend to "beginners" especially the three books dealing with psychological phenomena in animals. Of these the most captivating reading is Lorenz's book, but Hediger and Scott are excellent, too. For a very brief presentation of basic psychological principles, we would give the top prize to Woodworth's 1937 article. It ought to be much more widely known. Very clear and of basic value is Köhler's book, *Gestalt Psychology*.

The books that we have listed as giving general discussions of personality might seem the most logical starting material for persons new to the field. Generally, however, the books in this grouping would be read more profitably after books dealing more concretely with more limited subject-matter. Out of this group of general books, for the majority of readers, Solomon Diamond's *Personality and Temperament* would be our first recommendation or Robert White's *The Abnormal Personality* for those who want a discussion of the pathology of personality.

One of the best means of introduction to the literature on personality is biographical discussions of several main leaders and their work. Thus there is great value in the books by Phyllis Bottome and Hedda Orgler on Alfred Adler and in the little book by Hanns Sachs on Sigmund Freud. Ernest Jones' three-volume work on Freud is strenuous reading if one includes the chapters summarizing Freud's writings, but if one takes merely the more purely biographical parts, this book ought to be marked as a one-asterisk book and a very worthwhile one, too. Fromm's little volume is a very valuable commentary on it.

Another good means of introduction to the field of personality is those books particularly rich in case material. We particularly suggest Robert White's

Lives in Progress, Virginia Axline's *Play Therapy*, Frederick Allen's *Psychotherapy with Children* (skipping the first two chapters, probably, and much of the theoretical interlarding of the cases), and C. H. Rogerson's Play *Therapy in Childhood.* Another excellent book of this sort, but not included in the list because it did not fit well under any category, is Leon Saul's *Emotional Maturity* (Philadelphia, J. B. Lippincott Co., 1947).

The other references that discuss personality in children are of quite diverse sorts. Katherine Read's book is outstanding among books that describe nursery-school work, which has been important as a source both of new ideas and of new techniques for dealing with small children. Erikson's volume is outstanding as a somewhat modified psychoanalytic study of anthropological material on children. Spock's book is the widely used and valuable popular guide to practical problems of child care. The book edited by Tanner and Inhelder is a verbatim account of a conference where some very capable experts from different fields of psychology and anthropology talked back and forth very informally about their ideas and observations relevant to childhood. It particularly gives an interesting picture of thinkers at work.

The books that have been listed as bearing on the various main theories of personality have been selected with a double purpose—not merely to explain the different theories listed, but also to give valuable discussions of the considerable array of questions about personality indicated in the titles of these books.

The most detailed and systematic account of Adler's theory is that in the Ansbachers' book, or perhaps in the book by Way; but neither of these would be as profitable as one of the simpler and briefer books for persons beginning to read about this point of view.

Of Karen Horney's books, her *New Ways in Psychoanalysis* is by all odds the most systematic. Each chapter explains a main aspect of the regular psychoanalytic theory, the reasons it holds that place in psychoanalytic thought, the reasons she challenges it, and the concepts that she would urge in its place. The organization of her last book, *Neurosis and Human Growth,* is much harder for the reader to follow, but it is valuable for those who want to get the benefits of her rich observations of clinical problems.

It is difficult to select from the huge number of books on Freudian theory. Calvin Hall's is good as a simple introduction. Freud's *Civilization and Its Discontents* is not only very readable, but unusually valuable both because it reflects the later developments in Freud's thinking and because it presents his views on the implications of his concepts for broader social problems. The best comprehensive survey is Ernest Jones' work. The review by Robert White in the Scientific American impresses us as one of the most profoundly wise general comments on Freudian thought that we have seen.

The reference that we have suggested on Carl Jung's theory is relatively understandable partly because Gerhard Adler, though regarding himself as a fully devoted Jungian, has added a sizeable amount of his own mode of thought and speech which makes it easier for non-Jungians to use this book than Jung's own writings. The same sort of thing is probably true of Fay B. Karpf's book on Otto Rank, whose work led on to that of Frederick Allen and Carl Rogers. Sullivan, though of major influence in current American psychiatry, wrote relatively little himself, but his theory has been reflected in a number of other books such as those that we list, though the book by Hill perhaps ought to be described as intermediate between Sullivan's thought and regular psychoanalytic thought. The book edited by Mullahy has outstanding value both for its comments about Sullivan's work and for its carefully chosen quotations from Sullivan.

As examples of an approach to personality that is rather fundamentally different from that developed in the present book, we have listed six books under the heading of "Stimulus-Response Theory of Personality." Shaffer and Shoben's book might well have been listed with the group of books giving general discussions of personality. It is the outstanding general discussion of personality from a primarily S-R approach. The books by Julian Rotter and by Cameron and Magaret are less committed to S-R thought than the others listed and represent attempts to utilize that basic mode of thought in somewhat modified ways.

As our final suggestion, let us recommend the monthly publication, *Contemporary Psychology: A Journal of Reviews.* It has proved itself an excellent source of critical reviews on current books in all fields of psychology, including personality, and it will prove itself invaluable for those who want to keep in touch with forthcoming volumes.

INDEX